Communications
in Computer and Information Science 248

Goran D. Putnik
Maria Manuela Cruz-Cunha (Eds.)

Virtual and Networked Organizations, Emergent Technologies, and Tools

First International Conference, ViNOrg 2011
Ofir, Portugal, July 6-8, 2011
Revised Selected Papers

 Springer

Volume Editors

Goran D. Putnik
University of Minho
Department of Production and Systems Engineering
Campus de Azurem
4800-058 Guimarães, Portugal
E-mail: putnikgd@dps.uminho.pt

Maria Manuela Cruz-Cunha
Polytechnic Institute of Cávado e Ave
School of Technology
Campus do IPCA - Lugar do Aldăo
4750-810 Vila Frescainha S. Martinho BCL, Portugal
E-mail: mcunha@ipca.pt

ISSN 1865-0929　　　　　　　　　　e-ISSN 1865-0937
ISBN 978-3-642-31799-6　　　　　　e-ISBN 978-3-642-31800-9
DOI 10.1007/978-3-642-31800-9
Springer Heidelberg Dordrecht London New York

Library of Congress Control Number: Applied for

CR Subject Classification (1998): I.2, H.4, H.3, H.5, C.2, D.2

Typesetting: Camera-ready by author, data conversion by Scientific Publishing Services, Chennai, India

Printed on acid-free paper

Springer is part of Springer Science+Business Media (www.springer.com)

Preface

This book of proceedings presents the selected papers from the International Conference on Virtual and Networked Organizations Emergent Technologies and Tools, ViNOrg 2011. The International Conference on Virtual and Networked Organizations Emergent Technologies and Tools embraces the rapidly emerging field of information technologies and systems developments to support new organizational models such as networked and virtual organizations.

With the objective of contributing to the development, implementation and promotion of advanced emergent IC technologies to be used in future virtual and networked organizations, through the discussion and sharing of knowledge as well as experiences and scientific and technical results, 50 academics, scientists and professionals from all over the world were joined in this event, held in Ofir, Portugal, during July 6–8, 2011, and organized by the by 2100 Projects Association – Scientific Association for Promotion of Technology and Management for Organizational and Social Transformative Change.

The main topics of ViNOrg 2011 covered ubiquitous computing and organizations, cloud computing and architectures, grid computing, human – computer interfaces, serious games, data mining, Web services, cognitive systems, social networks and other emergent IT/IS approaches in various function domains, such as decision support systems, planning, design, control, negotiation, marketing, management and many others, in the context of virtual and networked enterprises and organizations.

Over 60 manuscripts were submitted, of which 35 were selected for oral presentation and inclusion in the conference proceedings. Due to the high quality of the selected papers, this book of proceedings represents a significant contribution to the literature in virtual and networked organizations.

We are grateful to all the authors for their contributions to this conference as well as to the Program Committee members for their valuable collaboration.

We hope this book meets your expectations.

Goran D. Putnik
Maria Manuela Cruz-Cunha

Table of Contents

Cloud-Based Contextually Aware Adaptive Systems for Enterprise Transformation

Gabrielle Peko, Ching-Shen Dong, Max Erik Rohde, and David Sundaram

Department of Information Systems and Operations Management, University of Auckland,
Auckland 1142, New Zealand
{g.peko,j.dong,m.rohde,d.sundaram}@auckland.ac.nz

Abstract. More than ever before, enterprises nowadays are faced with an environment characterised by asynchronicity, complexity, and uncertainty. We see three major shortcomings of many current approaches of enabling enterprises to adapt under these conditions: the proposed processes and systems often do not deal with the whole context surrounding the enterprise; enterprises still follow rather deliberate approaches when dealing with strategy and its execution; and decisions are limited in terms of their reach and range. Cloud computing has particular characteristics that address these shortcomings. In this paper we propose Cloud-based contextually aware adaptive lifecycle models, frameworks, and architectures that enable networked and virtual enterprises to learn, adapt and be transformed.

Keywords: Cloud, context, adaptive, services, enterprise transformation.

1 Introduction

It is a common thread in many streams of research, such as ERP implementation, that information technology is not a silver bullet. Many factors besides the technology must be considered in order to achieve positive enterprise transformation. However, one common theme still persists in the literature; information technology is often seen as a central enabler of enterprise change such as in traditional IT-centric projects. In this article we want to argue for redefining the perspective on what adaptive IT can and cannot do and suggest the notion of IT as mediator of enterprise change rather than an enabler. This next generation of adaptive IT uses business context as a driving force for technology-mediated enterprise change.

We first investigate the notion of enterprises as multi-dimensional, complex, networked and open systems. Given this we reflect on the traditional perspectives of seeing technology as the central enabler of enterprise change. We contrast this with recent literature that emphasises the importance of linking the deliberate approach with the emergent approach in order to achieve an adaptive enterprise. Based on this discussion we propose perceiving technology as a multi-dimensional mediator of context-driven change. To demonstrate this notion we propose a framework and architecture of a Cloud-based context-aware adaptive system for enterprise transformation. We conclude with a call for a wider perspective on adaptive systems for networked enterprises.

G.D. Putnik and M.M. Cruz-Cunha (Eds.): ViNOrg 2011, CCIS 248, pp. 1–11, 2012.
© Springer-Verlag Berlin Heidelberg 2012

The modern world is characterised by, asynchronicity, complexity and uncertainty. Enterprises that want to compete in the dynamic markets of today need to be able to respond rapidly to the ever-increasing rate of change. They have to deal with this complexity, uncertainty and rapid change at both the macro and the micro levels of their internal and external environments [8]. Enterprises are far flung in terms of space and time. Enterprises need to be able to reach anyone, anywhere, anytime and be able to conduct simple to sophisticated transactions in automated to semi-automated manners. Some of the changes that are currently taking place are consumers' growing demand for new, innovative products and services that are price competitive. Customers are less loyal to products, they want greater choice. Consequently, there is an increasing pressure on enterprises to constantly innovate. Yet, there is a global shortage of business talent. In addition, investors demand superior returns on their investment and they are more active and flexible in the way they invest.   Added to these factors are the relentless stream of mergers and acquisitions that change the enterprise's environment. The volatility of the business environment creates uncertainty that necessitates change in terms of the way business is conducted [4], [8]. This means there is a corresponding change in business models along with the business processes and computing requirements that support those models [2]. Customers demand that their orders are fulfilled promptly so business processes need to be created and executed more quickly resulting in demand spikes for resources and sophisticated services.

To address these problems, issues, and requirements we propose and discuss Cloud-based contextually aware lifecycle models, frameworks, and architectures that enable networked and virtual enterprises to learn, adapt and be transformed. This paper primarily consists of two parts. The first part explores the concept of an adaptive enterprise and the issues associated with enterprise adaptation. The second part proposes conceptual models and frameworks that attempt to address these issues especially in context of networked and virtual enterprises.   Finally, system architectures to realise the proposed frameworks and support our model of enterprise adaptation are introduced.

2   Enterprises as Adaptive Systems in Context

Weick [21] understands enterprises as systems processing ambiguous and difficult to interpret information [14] by reducing equivocality. Ultimately, the reduction of equivocality is meant to enable the enterprise to adapt in a mindful manner. According to Levinthal and Rerup [13], an enterprise adapting in a mindful manner is able to recombine and alter its existing practices according to unpredictable changes in the environment. In order to understand the process by which enterprises adapt we refer to Haeckel's [10] "Adaptive Loop", which describes how enterprises adapt to changes in the environment. The system must first sense a change. This sensing is in terms of 'seeing' or 'hearing'. In the next step of the cycle, the sensed information must be interpreted in terms of understanding its meaning for the system. For instance, is what is sensed a threat or an opportunity? Based on this information a decision is taken as to the best response to what is happening in the environment.

Finally, the system acts based on what has been decided. The first two steps can be grouped under the phase of "sensing", while deciding and acting can be grouped under the phase "responding".

A key element that is not explicit in the adaptive loop is context; internal and external. Benbya et al. [3] have provided a finer distinction that differentiates a "technical context" that considers the design, usability and effectiveness of systems; a "managerial context" that considers questions of leadership in knowledge management initiatives and the alignment with the firm's strategy; and a "business context" that reflects commitment to knowledge management, the influence of the enterprise culture, and issues of trust. These three contexts intersect and influence each other. While Benbya et al.'s orientation is predominantly internal; Scott-Morton [19] explicitly considers the external context and suggests that an enterprise bathes in the external socio-economic and technological contexts. We suggest that the Adaptive Loop explicitly considers the various enterprise contexts in terms of sensing, interpreting, deciding, and acting.

A number of authors have used Jazz music improvisation as a metaphor for the adaptive management of enterprises [15, 18]. Applying the jazz metaphor to the management of enterprises, the jazz group's process of improvisation is analogous to a source of constant emergent change. While the scaffold that the soloist uses determined by the lead music sheet is analogous to deliberate change. The metaphor of jazz improvisation can be used to illustrate the management of emergent change.

Scheer [18] argues that for enterprises to be adaptive they need to balance flexibility with stability. He suggests that low levels of connectivity and high levels of control (no improvisation) prevent flexibility and creative behaviours. The presence of rigid enterprise structures and rules and the lack of communication and interaction mean the work processes are set and people isolated. Therefore, management of the enterprise is deliberate and the enterprise is unable to react in a timely manner to contextual changes. Scheer goes on to suggest that enterprises with traditional top down hierarchical management structures have high levels of intensity of control and low connectivity. These enterprises are inflexible and only succeed in a stable environment. They follow a deliberate approach while there are enterprises at the bleeding edge. These enterprises are very reactive, connectivity between parties and the external environment is very high. They are constantly sensing the environment and trying to respond to change. However, these kinds of highly reactive volatile enterprises, such as many high tech start-up companies, have low levels of intensity of control [18]. Neither of these extreme positions is good [6], [18]. One is characterised by deliberation, control and stability and the other position is characterised by chaos, flexibility and possibly innovation and even anarchy. However, Scheer [18] suggests that the best place is to be on the edge of chaos where enterprise's balance flexibility and stability.

The adaptive approach is when enterprises have deliberate approaches that support stable evolutionary growth and also flexible, emergent approaches that support more opportunistic growth. Therefore, it can be argued that it is not a choice for an enterprise between deliberate or emergent but that they should adopt a deliberate and emergent approach, namely an adaptive approach. Moreover, it is not a choice between being stable or flexible it is about being stable and flexible. We suggest that an enterprise develops the ability to be deliberate and emergent, stable and flexible and hence be an adaptive enterprise.

3   Cloud-Based Contextually-Aware Adaptive Enterprises

Cloud computing, in the broadest sense, is a utility type model that consists of clouds of commoditized computing services that are delivered, consumed and charged on an as-need, as-used basis [2]. The cloud can be any of the following: private, public, community and hybrid Cloud systems. A private Cloud is controlled by the enterprise and is used to integrate internal systems and public Clouds. A public Cloud is the commoditised services provided by vendors whereas a community Cloud is restricted to several enterprises with similar requirements that motivate a shared infrastructure. Lastly, a hybrid Cloud consists of many internal and/or external providers [17] [25].

3.1   Cloud-Based Enterprise Adaptation Strategy Model

Based on the previous discussion we define the adaptive approach as a combination of deliberate approaches that support stable, evolutionary growth and emergent approaches that support more opportunistic, organic growth. Enterprises should interweave the deliberate and the emergent aspects of each subsystem of Scott-Morton's MIT90s framework [19] to form a cohesive adaptive whole. One way to achieving this is to leverage the power of the Cloud computing paradigm [20]. It makes sense for enterprises to leverage the flexibility and cost advantages offered by Cloud computing to augment and enhance their adaptive behaviours and ultimately transform the enterprise [7].

An adaptive business strategy that is cloud enabled can be developed and implemented through the migration of services from the cloud. These services can provide competitive advantage to the enterprise, which reside in private clouds, or provide the necessary routines for the enterprise to survive in its current environment, namely competitive necessities [20]. An adaptive strategy that embraces the Cloud computing model significantly enhances an enterprise's ability to continually adapt to the environment by the constant creation of innovative services that provide competitive differentiation for sustainable business growth [16]. However, competitive differentiation in today's rapidly changing environment does not last long. Inevitably, innovative services are replicated by the competition and therefore cease to offer a competitive advantage. When this happens these services are converted to commoditized services and may be relocated to the cloud.

The development of an enterprise's innovative services, and their subsequent commoditisation, follows an adaptation strategy that starts with the creation of new services which mature overtime (Fig. 1). Initially, services are created in response to the implementation of emergent, enabling activities. These services are combined to form composite business processes that perform particular tasks within the enterprise. As executable services they are further developed through composition to build higher level, cross-enterprise, innovative services and business processes [17, 3] that provide competitive advantage.

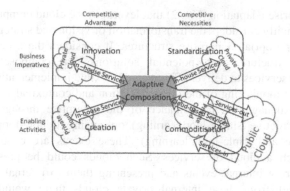

Fig. 1. Cloud-based enterprise adaptation strategy model

As these innovative services and processes mature over time they lose their ability to differentiate for competitive advantage. At this point, when they cease to be innovative, they are standardised. Standardisation involves the rationalisation of process variety and variability to further reduce costs and diminish risks [16]. Once standardised, the services and processes mature further to become commodity services that are made available in the cloud. [11]. Essentially, an adaptive enterprise will leverage services and processes available in private, public, community, and/or hybrid clouds to compose services and business processes that support the implementation of an adaptive strategy for sustained competitive advantage and business growth.

3.2   Cloud-Based Contextually Aware Enterprise Adaptation Lifecycle Model

Many models for enterprise adaptation have been suggested but most of these models are either management oriented or technology oriented. Bhattacharya et al.'s [5] framework and Kumaran et al. [12] transformational approach are some of the few models for enterprise adaptation that interweave managerial concerns with technological responses in an integrated and holistic fashion. Bhattacharya et al.'s [5] framework differentiates four different models on different levels of abstraction. The strategy level model is at the highest level of abstraction, where business objectives are specified. These objectives drive the operational models. These models describe the structure of enterprise routines. In order to support enterprise routines with information technology, solution composition models are designed that combine necessary information technology functionality and the operational models. Solution composition models can be seen as an intermediate layer between business and information technology; rather than having to deal with implementation specifics, "solution architects" can operate on a more abstract level that simplifies the matching of business requirements to IT. This is sometimes referred to as "programming in the large" [9]. IT implementation models are closer to the implementation of the software and are platform specific.

A synthesis of the above concepts and frameworks with respect to learning, context, adaptation, and strategy-driven processes and systems leads us to propose a model for enterprise adaptation (Fig. 2) that leverages the cloud computing paradigm. This model explicitly considers the transformation of vision and strategy into business processes and appropriate enterprise structures. It considers the translation of these processes and structures into potential solutions that compose and integrate components and services to deliver effective and flexible implementations.

Execution and monitoring of the implementation and contextual events enables us to pro-actively manage the performance of the enterprise through three distinct mechanisms; corrective (single-loop learning), optimising (double-loop learning), and aligning (double and triple-loop learning). These events are captured and made available through a cloud of services. Such clouds could be present within the enterprise capturing internal events and presenting them to internal and/or external consumers. Apart from these internal private clouds there would be numerous external public, community, and brokered clouds that would be capturing and presenting events to the adaptive enterprise. Cloud computing technologies provide new and better options for enterprises to respond and adapt to their rapidly changing environments.

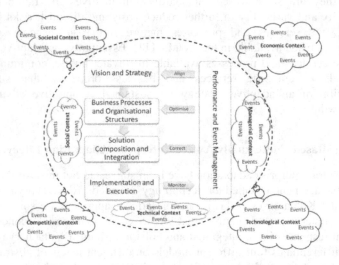

Fig. 2. Cloud-based contextually aware enterprise adaptation lifecycle model

4   Cloud-Based Contextually Aware Adaptive Systems Framework

Commonly, technology is understood as an enabler to solve problems. For example, machines and software have been used to significantly increase efficiencies of many enterprise processes. In a predictable environment the traditional approach of define strategy, design processes and implement software solutions is an appropriate response. However, in a rapidly changing environment enterprises are under fierce pressure to adapt to the environmental change. New paradigms of management for adaptation (and innovation) depend heavily upon technology. Open innovation (and adaptation) is difficult to implement without technological mechanism to access the knowledge of the various stakeholders. We suggest that technology should not be seen only as a means to achieve ends determined by a higher conceptual level but also as an integration, coordination and collaboration mechanism to facilitate change.

To illustrate this perspective of technology as an integrator, coordinator and collaborator to drive change and to support our model of enterprise adaptation, we propose a cloud-based contextually aware adaptive systems conceptual framework (Fig. 3). In this framework technology is understood as a central mediator between the different kinds of context and events (internal and external). The events collected through private and public cloud systems drive the change. The whole learning and changing process or process of enterprise adaptation as described above is mediated by cloud service technology. These cloud service technologies work as mediators between the context and the enterprise subsystems. The mediation should, on the one hand, help to channel events for the decision maker. On the other hand, technology should help to transport the decision maker's decisions back to the context. For instance, if a change of strategy is decided upon this change must be reflected in the operational plans and communicated to decision makers.

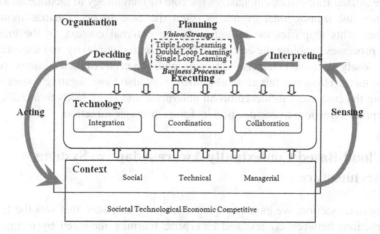

Fig. 3. A framework for Cloud-based contextually aware adaptive systems

The proposed framework illustrates that events, originating from the event cloud, can be of different natures as they might originate from different contexts (Fig. 2). Real-time events are the type of events traditionally emphasised in discussions of event-driven architectures. These predominately allow capturing events from the managerial and competitive context. Transactional events are events occurring in the predictable course of a business process. Our framework emphasises the importance of capturing unpredictable competitive, social, managerial and technological events through cloud-based services. We see these events as primarily driving an enterprise's ability to learn and adapt to novel circumstances. This can be, for instance, the dissatisfaction of an employee with the way he has to conduct his work. There must be channels in which he can articulate his concerns and which directly influence decisional processes including the meta-decisional processes of strategy that influence enterprise reorientation. Capturing these events is an important aspect of controlling emergent developments in formalised channels, as discussed above, and ultimately integrating the deliberate approach with the emergent approach.

The framework distinguishes three central learning processes informed by Argyris and Schön's notion of single loop learning and double loop learning [1]. Single loop learning occurs when processes are improved on an operational level. This learning process is driven by events deriving from the external context and is technology-mediated. The events arrive at the social, technical and managerial subsystems and filtered by technology. Based on these events, the changes that the decision makers decide on are made a reality using technological means. Double loop learning occurs when the controlling subsystem reacts to events, leading to a change of business processes or enterprise structures or both. Triple loop learning occurs when the meta-level subsystem of the enterprise reacts to events by changing the enterprises strategic direction. Besides single loop learning, which in some instances can be controlled by automated systems, the learning processes that enable the enterprise to evolve and adapt require a decision maker or a collective of decision makers to take a decision.

Above all, the framework emphasizes the role of technology to mediate all kinds of events, not just transactional events as often the case in performance monitoring approaches. This amplifies the influence of the external context on the enterprise learning processes enabling the enterprise to cope with complexity and uncertainty. It helps to closely align the enterprise's strategy with the needs of their business partners and consumers. However, this close alignment may also have negative consequences. Increasing the customers influence on an enterprise's strategy leads to a reduction in the enterprise's freedom to decide upon its future strategic direction.

5   Cloud-Based Contextually Aware Adaptive Systems Architecture

In the previous section, we have provided a simple framework that sets the focus on the interactions between context and enterprise learning mediated by technological mechanisms. Cloud services consist of software, atomic, platform and infrastructure services [19]. Cloud services can either be consumed directly or are adaptively combined with other services/systems to provide agile changes required by the enterprise. In this section, we design a Cloud-based contextually aware architecture (Fig. 4) to realise the proposed framework. In the architecture Cloud computing is used to support enterprise adaptation. The different kinds of events that drive learning in the framework require different kinds of cloud systems to be processed. Transactional events are traditionally handled well by ERP systems or service oriented architectures (SOA) whereas real-time events can be processed using Event Driven Architecture (EDA) systems.

Based on the internal and/or external events sensed from the cloud systems, the decision makers interpret the implications of the events. Then they design responses using service integration, orchestration, choreograph and improvisation within the enterprise or across enterprise boundaries to achieve different levels of adaptability and agility for enterprises. The changes can be at the business process, policy or strategy levels to support integration, coordination and collaboration within the enterprise and across organisational boundaries. The combination of Cloud computing and the contextually aware event driven architecture provides enhanced flexibility, agility and ultimately adaptability in comparison to more traditional system architectures.

Cloud computing can be implemented for inter-organisational business integration (virtual enterprise for employees) and intra-organisational collaboration (virtual enterprise for networked business partners and allies). Our argument is to use both approaches for innovative enterprises. Existing technologies can be used to implement cloud based context aware systems for virtual organisations. At the context sensing layer, Web 2.0, EDA, CRM and social networking technologies can be applied to detect events from various sources in the clouds. While at the interpreting level, BPM, rules based systems, databases and business intelligence etc. technologies can be used to analyse the activities and contexts.   Data mining and decision making technologies can be employed for strategic planning and selecting at the planning and deciding layer. At the acting level, ERP and BPM technologies can be utilised for performing and monitoring the operations responding to the events detected. At the organizational structuring layer, grid, cluster, Web services, SOA, virtualisation, software agents, enterprise portal and middleware technologies can be exploited to integrate various clouds and enterprise information applications in a traditional system landscape.

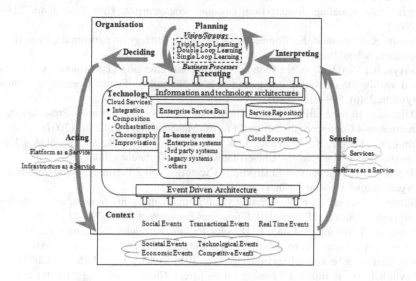

Fig. 4. An architecture for Cloud-based contextually aware adaptive systems

6   Conclusion

Truly adaptive systems are not merely technological systems. They need to be strategy driven, learning oriented, process oriented, and service oriented to be truly adaptive. Consideration should also be given to the rapidly evolving managerial, technological, social, economic, and competitive contexts. To support these ideas we have proposed a) learning oriented enterprise adaptation models b) Cloud-based enterprise adaptation strategy and lifecycle and c) Cloud-based contextually aware framework and architecture. We posit this is one possible way for enterprises to adapt in a changing world of complexity and uncertainty.

References

1. Argyris, C., Schön, D.: Organizational Learning: A Theory of Action Perspective. Addison-Wesley (1978)
2. Armbrust, M., Fox, A., et al.: Above the clouds: A Berkeley view of cloud computing. EECS Department, University of California, Berkeley, Tech. Rep. UCB/EECS, p. 28 (2009)
3. Benbya, H., Passiante, G., Belbaly, N.: Corporate portal: a tool for knowledge management synchronization. International Journal of Information Management 24, 201–220 (2004)
4. Betts, B., Heinrich, C.: Adapt or Die: Transforming Your Supply Chain into an Adaptive Business Network. Wiley (2003)
5. Bhattacharya, K., Caswell, N.S., Kumaran, S., Nigam, A., Wu, F.Y.: Artifact-centered operational modeling: lessons from customer engagements. IBM Syst. J. 46, 703–721 (2007)
6. Brown, S., Eisenhardt, K.: Competing on the Edge: Strategy as Structured Chaos. Harvard Business School Press (1998)
7. Buyya, R., Yeo, C.S., et al.: Cloud computing and emerging IT platforms: Vision, hype, and reality for delivering computing as the 5th utility. Future Generation Computer Systems 25(6), 599–616 (2009)
8. Dale, S.: Holistic BPM: From Theory to Reality. In: Keynote Presentation, 5th International Conference on Business Process Management, BPM 2007 (2007)
9. Emig, C., Langer, K., Krutz, K., Link, S., Momm, C., Abeck, S.: The SOA's Layers. Cooperation & Management. Universität Karlsruhe, Karlsruhe (2006)
10. Haeckel, S.: Adaptive Enterprise: Creating and Leading Sense-And-Respond Organizations. Harvard Business School Press (1999)
11. Huang, J., Newell, S., et al.: Creating value from a commodity process: a case study of a call center. Journal of Enterprise Information Management 20(4), 396–413 (2007)
12. Kumaran, S., Bishop, P., Chao, T., Dhoolia, P., Jain, P., Jaluka, R., Ludwig, H., Moyer, A., Nigam, A.: Using a model-driven transformational approach and service-oriented architecture for service delivery management. IBM Systems Journal 46, 513 (2007)
13. Levinthal, D., Rerup, C.: Crossing an Apparent Chasm: Bridging Mindful and Less-Mindful Perspectives on Organizational Learning. Organization Science 17, 502–513 (2006)
14. March, J., Olsen, J.: The Uncertainty of the Past: Organizational Learning Under Ambiguity. European Journal of Political Research 3, 147–171 (1975)

15. Meyer, A., Frost, P., Weick, K.: The Organization Science Jazz Festival: Improvisation as a Metaphor for Organizing Overture. Organization Science 9, 540–542 (1998)
16. Moore, G.A.: Living on the fault line. Harper Business (2003)
17. Oracle, SAP ERP in the Cloud (2011),
    http://www.oracle.com/us/solutions/sap/database/sap-erp-cloud-352626.pdf (retrieved)
18. Peltz, C.: Web services orchestration and choreography. Computer, 46–52 (2003)
19. Peng, B., Cui, B., Li, X.: Implementation issues of a cloud computing platform. Data Engineering, 59 (2009)
20. SAP, Cloud Computing and SAP Where We Are and Where We're Going (2010),
    http://specialfeatures.sapinsideronline.com/archive/spi_2010_3b_SAP.pdf (retrieved)
21. Scheer, A.W.: Jazz-Improvisation and Management. ARIS Expert Paper (2007)
22. Scott-Morton, M.: The Corporation of the 1990s: Information Technology and Organizational Transformation. Oxford University Press, USA (1991)
23. Walters, D.: Operations strategy. Palgrave Macmillan, Basingstoke (2002)
24. Weick, K.: The social psychology of organizing. Addison-Wesley Pub. Co. (1979)
25. West, D.M.: Saving money through cloud computing. Governance Studies at Brookings. Studies, B.I.G (2010)

Toward a Centrality Index for Computing Grids

Paulo Mourao

Department of Economics, School of Economics and Management, University of Minho,
Gualtar, 4700 Braga, Portugal
paulom@eeg.uminho.pt

Abstract. The computing grid has emerged as an attractive field in Computer Science. However, little attention has focused on the centrality of each computing grid. In this article, we suggest a Centrality Index based on the economist and geographer Walter Christaller's Central Place Theory. With a Centrality
Index, each grid can be evaluated in terms of function concentration and user distribution.

Keywords: Computing Grids, Central Places Theory, Indexes.

1   Introduction

Grid computing is explosive, as Ian Foster [1] states. This "explosion" is the result of an intense interest in grid computing by academicians, scientists, and citizens. Grid computing fosters computation and the distribution of empirical results or of software programs in a way that was previously unknown (or, at least, much slower).

Currently, there is increasing interest in grid architecture. The way in which a grid is "built" can make all the difference. If the main purpose of a grid is to provide "coordinated resource sharing and problem solving in dynamic, multi-institutional virtual organizations" (Foster and Tuecke [2]), then it matters how users are connected, how CPUs are interlinked and how data are processed.

At a 'coffee lounge' experience, I asked a group of friends (with different professional skills and academic courses) to tell me which of the following images (Figure 1 a to f) do not belong to the group of "computing grids" figures.

For most of them, even for the Computer Scientists, it was not an easy task because Images b, d, and f did not belong to the group of "computing grids" but rather to the group of "urban grids" developed by Walter Christaller ([3], [4]).

The sets of grids have many similarities, as we are going to argue further. The richness of studying computing grids embodying the suggestions of good urban distributions of people, places and services can empower research on grid computing.

In this article, we focus on the first-step – a discussion of the centrality index for each grid. With an index of this kind, it is possible to recognize different architectures of grid computing and to identify the main objectives of each grid. Grid users should know more about the grids in which they are working.

G.D. Putnik and M.M. Cruz-Cunha (Eds.): ViNOrg 2011, CCIS 248, pp. 12–17, 2012.
© Springer-Verlag Berlin Heidelberg 2012

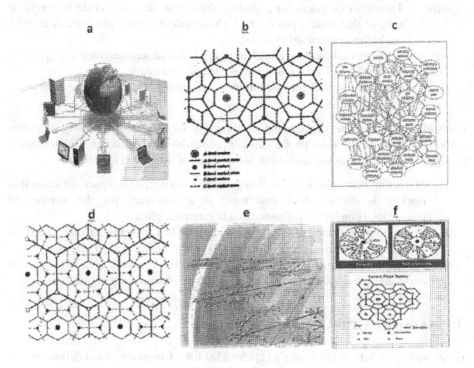

Fig. 1. Types of Grids

Section 2 introduces Christaller's urban grid discussion. Section 3 notes how this discussion is linked to computing grids. Section 4 suggests the main steps for constructing a centrality index for each grid. Section 5 provides the conclusions.

2 The Urban Grid of Walter Christaller

Walter Christaller was one of the first authors to develop a theory to analyze the different dimensions, distributions and number of places in a human-occupied space.

To develop his theory, Christaller [3] used the following set of assumptions:

i) The population is evenly distributed;
ii) All natural resources are evenly distributed;
iii) The area is flat without any geological barriers;
iv) Services are located in central places;
v) Services are demanded by all those living in the region around a central place;
vi) All consumers maintain the same purchasing power;
vii) Services are ranked according to the frequency of their demands (more frequently demanded services are ranked the highest;

viii)   The rank of services for a given central place depends on the hierarchical rank of that central place (the highest ranked central place tends to offer the highest ranked set of services);

ix)   A higher ranked place can also supply lower ranked services;

x)   No provider of goods or services can earn excessive profits;

xi)   Only one type of transportation exists, and it is equally accessible in all directions.

Christaller [3] tested his claims empirically using the frequency/intensity of phone calls. Using his database on phone calls, he observed that the urban grid follows a hexagonal shape. This hexagonal shape is the result of three principles:

1)   Marketing Principle (k=3): In this principle, the economic space (or economic market) is divided such that there is a minimum for the number of places/points under the influence of a higher rank place.

2)   Transportation Principle (k=4): According to this principle, a place must be served by a rectilinear route that also serves two higher ranked places.

3)   Administrative Principle (k=7): In this case, the evolving area of a place is completely inside the area of the place with an immediately higher rank.

3   Foster's Grid Checklist

Here, we largely follow Ian Foster's [1] checklist for a Computing Grid definition. According to this author, a Computing Grid "is a system that:

1)   *Coordinates resources that are not subject to centralized control [...];*

2)   *Uses standard, open, general-purpose protocols and interfaces [...];*

3)   *[Allows] to deliver nontrivial qualities of service [...]."*

It is easy to compare this short list to the set of assumptions that Christaller used to develop his model. Point 1 in Foster's list ("coordination of resources") relates to Christaller's assumptions x) and xi) – ('distribution of profits'). Point 2 in Foster's list ("grid freedom") relates to Christaller's assumptions i), ii), iii), v) and vi) - ("urban sellers elasticity"). Point 3 in Foster's list ("specialized supply of services") relates to Christaller's remaining assumptions ('specialized supply of urban services').

4   Toward a k-Index to Characterize a Computational Grid

The main purpose of this article is to suggest a k-index to characterize a Computational Grid. We labeled it a 'k-index' because we are referencing the k-indexes that Christaller [3] used to identify the predominant principles on the place distribution of a space.

To construct this index, we must identify our 'places' in a computational grid and our 'services' in that grid.

Our most simplified suggestion is as follows:

- each CPU represents a "place" in this analysis;
- each function developed by a CPU represents a "service" provided by that CPU;
- demand is determined by the set of connected users;
- data flow represents "traffic".

Therefore, the centrality rank[1] of each CPU is a positive function of the following:

- "market size" (number of users),
- "managed traffic" (processed data),
- "services" (computational functions)
- "lower ranked places" (subordinated CPUs).

Using the centrality rank and combining all of the centrality ranks in a grid, we obtain the dominant k-index.

The k-index may be one of the following:

-if k=3[2,] then we state that the dominant principle in that computational grid is the Marketing Principle. When the Marketing Principle dominates, the economic agents opt for efficient mechanisms, sell the goods they produce at marginal cost and avoid excessive profits. In a computational grid context, if the Marketing Principle dominates, then its users are especially concerned with efficiently distributing functions for the different processors to allow the most complex processes to be assigned to the most powerful CPUs. Two examples of computing grids following the Marketing Principle are the "Distributed ASCI Supercomputer (DAS-3) system" (http://www.cs.vu.nl/ das3/overview.shtml) and the "TeraGrid" (https://www.teragrid.org/web/about/ teragrid-partner-information).

-if k=4[3,] then the dominant principle in the grid is the Transportation Principle. When this principle dominates in urban grids, the economic agents are trying to minimize transportation costs. In a grid context, the dominance of this principle means that grid users try to accelerate data flow inside the grid and minimize "distance costs" among the computers. An example of a computing grid clearly preferring the Transportation Principle is the "Data Grid Project" (http://eu-datagrid.web.cern. ch/eu-datagrid/Project-Structure/Project_Structure.htm).

-if k=7[4], then the dominant principle is the Administrative Principle. In an urban grid, the dominance of this principle means that lower ranked places are completely subservient (mainly in the administrative dimensions) to higher ranked place. For instance, this scenario occurs when a municipality depends directly on district capital for a given function (e.g., Civil Security). In a computational grid, the set of functions

---

[1] For an extensive list of centrality ranks, see Short et al. [5], Beaverstock, Taylor and Smith [6], or Shin and Timberlake [7].

[2] Each high-order place has 1/3 of each satellite place; thus, $K = 1 + 6 \times 1/3 = 3$.

[3] Areas in the central place hierarchy are four times more significant than areas in the next lowest order place.

[4] Areas in the central place hierarchy are seven times more significant than the area in the next lowest order place.

of a CPU depends entirely on a higher ranked CPU. For example, this setup might occur for dependent users/workers in a corporation grid.

An Index like ours is useful for Virtual organizations. Within Virtual organizations, individuals and/or institutions share resources. Our index can be useful for Virtual organizations because it will clarify the structure of the Virtual Organization, it will identify the individuals which will concentrate resources or which will use more often certain functions (Foster and Tuecke [2]).

5   Final Remarks toward Centrality Indexes for Computing Grids

Indexes suggest relative positions in a list. A centrality index (like ours) suggests how computing grids should use autonomous CPUs or how these grids should use hierarchical CPUs. This measure is useful for recognizing the concentration of functions inside a grid. This is extremely relevant for Virtual Organizations, characterized by the dynamism of the members sharing resources.

In addition, an index such as the one discussed here also provides information about how the grid architecture is built. If the grid follows Marketing Principles, then the main CPUs share some functions with less powerful computers and divide the market area with them. If the grid follows the Transportation Principle, then each CPU tries to be linked to minimally two more powerful CPUs. If the Administrative Principle holds, then each CPU depends entirely on a more powerful CPU.

Clarifying the finality of each grid's architecture and studying its centrality level will help grid architects/designers to better distribute users, resources and functions; grid computations can be optimized using urban grids that consider regional economics.

Acknowledgments. The author is indebted to Luís Miranda (EEng/U Minho) for useful comments on this thematic.

References

1. Foster, I.: What is the grid? A Three Point Checklist. Mimeo. Argonne National Laboratory and University of Chicago (2002),
   http://dlib.cs.odu.edu/WhatIsTheGrid.pdf
2. Foster, I., Kesselman, C., Tuecke, S.: The anatomy of the Grid. International Journal of High Performance Computing Applications 15(3) (2000), doi:10.1177/109434200101500302
3. Christaller, W.: Die zentralen Orte in Suddeutschland. Gustav Fischer, Jena (1933); Translated (in part), by Charlisle W. Baskin, as Central Places in Southern Germany. Prentice Hall (1966)
4. Christaller, W.: How I discovered the Theory of Central Places: A Report about the Origin of Central Places. In: English, P.W., Mayfield, R.C. (eds.) Man Space and Environment, pp. 601–610. Oxford Univ. Press (1972)
5. Short, J., Kim, Y., Kuus, M., Wells, H.: The Dirty Little Secret of World Cities Research: Data Problems in Comparative Analysis. International Journal of Urban and Regional Research 20, 697–717 (1996)

6. Beaverstock, J.V., Taylor, P., Smith, R.G.: A Roster of World Cities. Cities 16, 445–458 (1999)
7. Shin, K.-H., Timberlake, M.: World Cities in Asia: Cliques, Centrality and Connectedness. Urban Studies 37, 2257–2285 (2000)

Sources of Images (Figure 1):

a)

http://www.comp.ua.ac.be/?q=desktop-grids [consulted on 9th December 2010]

b)

http://www.yck2.edu.hk/onlinestudy/form6/ychui02.pdf   [consulted   on   9th December 2010]

c)

http://www.uiowa.edu/~mihpclab/facilityMICG.html [consulted on 9th December 2010]

d)

http://www.uwec.edu/bfoust/155/G155_RS3/RETAILING%20AND%20SERVIC ES%20PART%203.PDF [consulted on 9th December 2010]

e)

http://programmingmore.blogspot.com/2010/10/grid-computing-in-java-english-version.html [consulted on 9th December 2010]

f)

http://www.csiss.org/classics/content/67 [consulted on 9th December 2010]

Towards Agent-Based Models
for Synthetic Social Network Generation

Enrico Franchi

Dipartimento di Ingegneria dell'Informazione, Università degli Studi di Parma
Parco Area delle Scienze 181/A, 43124 Parma, Italy
efranchi@ce.unipr.it

Abstract. Agent-based modeling is a powerful tool to perform simulations over heterogeneous autonomous entities and, consequently, it can be used to analyze intrinsically emergent phenomena such as social networks. In the present work we present a meta-model that takes into account features of existing network models and describe an agent-based generation system built around such a meta-model. Our system is meant to provide a framework to ease the transition between analytic network models and newer agent-based models, where the nodes are autonomous, pro-active and potentially learning agents.

Keywords: Social Network Models, Agent-based modeling, Multi-agent Systems, Complex Network Analysis.

1 Introduction

Considering the ever-growing phenomenon of social networking sites, social scientists have the unprecedented possibility to access massive data sets to study the structure of large-scale social networks and the social network formation processes.

However, developing analytic models that account for such diverse and sparse data sets is a daunting task. On the other hand, agent-based modeling can use such data with little pre-processing, essentially building the models bottom-up, from the micro-level data to the macro-level social processes of interest.

Another possibility with agent-based modeling is to describe the behavior at agent level, using the expertise of social scientists to describe human actions and compare the global trends obtained from running the multi-agent system with those inferred from the real data. Moreover, agent-based models suited to yield realistic social networks are needed because such networks are the ideal test-bed for algorithms and protocols coming from research on social networking and P2P systems.

This paper is organized as follows: in the next section we introduce agent-based simulation in some detail. In Section 3 we present some analytic network generation models and extract a meta-model, which is then analyzed from an agent-oriented point of view in Section 4. In Section 5 and Section 6 we present the design and the engineering process of an agent-based generation system built around the ideas presented in Section 4. Finally, in Section 7 we draw some conclusions and sketch some possible lines of future work.

G.D. Putnik and M.M. Cruz-Cunha (Eds.): ViNOrg 2011, CCIS 248, pp. 18–27, 2012.

2   Agent-Based Simulations for Social Sciences

Although there is no single definition of "agent" [1-3] all definitions agree that an agent is essentially a special software component that: (*i*) has autonomy; (*ii*) provides an interoperable interface to an arbitrary system or (*iii*) behaves like a human agent, working for some clients in pursuit of its own agenda. In particular, an agent (*i*) is autonomous, because it operates without the direct intervention of humans or others and has control over its actions and internal state; (*ii*) is reactive, because it perceives its environment, and responds in a timely fashion to changes that occur in the environment; (*iii*) is pro-active, because it does not simply act in response to its environment and it is able to exhibit goal-directed behavior by taking the initiative.

The same features (i.e., autonomy, reactiveness, pro-activeness) that are necessary to build adaptive, evolving and complex software systems, can also be used to model adaptive, evolving and complex real-world phenomena. Agent-based modeling and simulation (ABMS) is the modeling paradigm that uses agents to simulate such systems. The approach has successfully been used in sociology [4, 5] and many other different scientific disciplines.

ABMS is especially convenient when the system to be analyzed is complex in terms of: (*i*) the number and diversity of the entities which compose the system; (*ii*) the number of interdependencies among such entities; and (*iii*) the level of autonomy they have. Moreover, ABMS provides a descriptive and almost operative point of view on the system and captures emergent properties, i.e., properties of complex systems that arise from of a multiplicity of relatively simple interactions.

Because of these properties, ABMS is a powerful tool to analyze social networks, considering that a social network is intrinsically emergent, since it is a complex structure made of the interactions of the single nodes. Moreover, the explicit description of the single actions at the individual level allows an easier framework than directly working with the global processes at the system level [6].

The massive availability of data at the micro-level is another important factor for the popularity of ABMS, since such data is easily used to describe the micro-behavior of the agents and the whole system computes the macro-behaviors [7]. This aspect is going to become extremely important in social sciences because of the widespread adoption of online social networking systems, which provide the kind of micro-level data needed to perform simulations.

Eventually, the analysis of agent-based models allows relaxing many unrealistic assumptions made in analytic models in order to be tractable (e.g., studying the models only near to the equilibrium or at some limit, or considering the entities as completely homogeneous). This is a huge advantage itself, but combined with the descriptive nature of ABMS leads to models which are: (*i*) easier to understand by domain experts; (*ii*) easier to create; and (*iii*) easier to modify.

Epstein [8] has an even more radical point of view on agent-based simulation and modeling: agent-based computation permits a distinctive approach to social science for which the term *generative* is suitable. This is in contrast to both "inductive" and "deductive" sciences.

One of the perceived drawbacks of ABMS is that the usual ambiguity on what an agent is becomes an ambiguity on the expressive power of the modeling units and, in turn, of the whole model [9]. Essentially, ABMS agents vary greatly in the degree of "intelligence" and "autonomy" they have.

3   Analysis of Selected Models

In [10] we reviewed several network generation models to find the most suited ones for general-purpose synthetic social network generation. Although we identified a couple of promising models, the Biased Preferential Attachment (BPA) [11] and the Transitive Linking (TL) [12] models, we also noticed an interesting pattern common to most models. In the rest of this section we briefly introduce the BPA and TL models, along with apparently very different classic and widely known models, the Watts-Strogatz (WS) [13] and the Barábasi-Albert (BA) [14] ones. Then we will single out the general structure shared by all the models. For further details on the mathematical properties of the models we refer to the respective original papers and to [10], where we also reported observations on the interdependencies of some widely used metrics.

One of the more important early models in modern social network theory is the Watts-Strogatz model [13]; it was created to be as simple as possible and yet generate networks with both very high clustering coefficient and short *average shortest path*, since both features were present in the social networks the authors considered.

The model starts with a closed linear structure where each node is connected with k neighbors and then the local connections are rewired to remote nodes with probability p, a parameter governing the transition from the very regular lattice model ($p=0$, no rewiring) to a Poisson random graph model ($p=1$, all links random). The model itself is not suitable for realistic social network generation as the starting lattice structure is a very restrictive assumption from the sociological point of view. Moreover Kleinberg proved that the networks generated by this model are usually not navigable [15], a property which real social network often have [16].

Another important model is the Barabási-Albert model (BA) described in [14]. The model was originally conceived mostly to investigate biological and technological networks. The BA model starts with n_0 nodes and no edges. At each step a new node with m random links is added. The m links are directed towards nodes with probability proportional to their degree.

The Transitive Linking model [12] stems from observation of the real world. In every step of the process two things occur: (*i*) a random node is chosen and two of its neighbors are linked (this is the transitive linking, in short TL); (*ii*) a node is chosen with probability p and removed from the network with its edges and replaced with another node with one random edge. If the node chosen in (*i*) does not have two edges, then the node is linked to a random node. The parameter p dictates how frequently nodes are removed from the social network and is assumed to be much smaller than 1.

The BPA [11] model was created to reproduce the actual formation process of some social networks. The authors had snapshots of a couple of online social networks and the networks they generated assumed (during the generation process) values of parameters describing the network similar to those of the real networks.

In the BPA model, the set of nodes V is partitioned in three sets: P (passive nodes), I (inviter nodes) and L (linker nodes). At each new step (i) a new node is added to the network and is assigned to one of the three sets according to a distribution of probability p; (ii) a number $\varepsilon > 0$ of edges are added to the network. D_β is a probability distribution such that for each node u:

$$D_u^\beta \propto \begin{cases} (\beta+1)\cdot(k_u+1) & u \in L \\ k_u+1 & u \in I \\ 0 & u \in P \end{cases} \tag{1}$$

The ε edges are added according the following rule: for each edge (u, v), u is chosen with distribution D^0 and (i) if $u \in I$, v is a new node and is assigned to P; (ii) if $u \in L$, v is chosen according to D^γ, where γ is an input parameter.

In the BA, TL and BPA models, the generation algorithm is already presented in a step-wise way. However, it is easy to interpret the rewiring procedure that occurs on each node as a single step of the global rewiring process. Using this point of view, we notice how at each step some nodes are created, destroyed or some actions are performed upon them. However, each model differs in the criteria used to choose the nodes: (i) on which to perform actions; (ii) to be destroyed and (iii) whether new nodes should be created.

4   Towards Agent-Based Models

In the previous section, we reviewed some models to generate synthetic social networks and sketched a general pattern common to most models. Essentially, we identified a single decision point, which is the choice of the nodes on which we operate during each step that are passive entities in the process. In this section we present how to make the transition from nodes as passive entities of the generation process to nodes as main actors of the process itself.

We do *destroy, create* and *perform actions on the nodes*. This has two essential implications: (i) the nodes are essentially uniform and (ii) all the decisions are made according to probability distributions. When we want to account for different node behavior, like in the BPA model, we need introduce different sets of nodes and use set membership to distinguish among the nodes; however, this approach becomes infeasible when the number of the different behaviors increases or is possibly bounded only by the number of nodes.

While it is possible to derive remarkable conclusions from mathematical models and while they have the important property of being simple and hopefully amenable of analytic study, it is not clear to what point it is possible to understand human behaviors and relationships using only probabilistic models. If, instead of considering the nodes as passive entities, we consider the nodes as agents in a multi-agent system, it is possible to develop models with richer decision processes, as the nodes are empowered with the possibility to choose their connections using the desired level of "intelligence".

Once the nodes are the agents, we do not *perform actions on them* anymore. Rather, we *ask* them to perform actions, or, in other words, the simulation *activates* the node. Instead of adding an edge to the network using some probability distribution, an agent sends a link proposal to another agent, which can also refuse the connection, if the model accounts for that possibility.

An example on how the link creation/destruction is expressed considering the nodes as agents comes from the WS model. In the original formulation of the model, for every node, we rewire each link with probability p. In the agent-based formulation, each agent, when activated, rewires each of its connections with probability p. The probability is still present, because it is part of the model, however the node is active in the rewiring process. Moreover, in principle, variations of the WS model could be developed where the rewiring process is not governed by probability, but by other criteria, e.g., similarity between agents.

In BPA, the different cases in the original algorithm depend on the set membership of the chosen node; the concept is translated in difference in behavior of the different agents. When activated: (i) a passive agent (which represent a node in P) simply refuses to act; (ii) an inviter agent (a node in I) "invites a new agent", that is to say, it asks the simulation engine to create a new agent; (iii) a linker tries to link to an existing node in the network with preference to "popular" agents. Probability can be replaced with different decision strategies and agents can also change behavior during the simulation.

The authors of the TL model use the term "people" rather than nodes; moreover, the choice of words expresses the active nature of the participants. In fact, the model is directly presented in terms of the phenomenon they are trying to mimic (i.e., people getting to know other people or introducing friends); essentially the nodes are already presented as agents. However, another important difference is that the agents are removed from the network because they "die". Such a forced termination is unusual in regular MASs, but is acceptable and common when dealing with ABMSs.

The idea here is that at each step an agent is activated and, depending on the number of connections it has, it either: (i) introduces two friends one to another; or (ii) it introduces itself to another random node. At each step a node is chosen and with probability p it is removed and replaced with new agent with one random link. More accurate models could be easily devised: after defining the concept of similarity between agents, the introduced agents may refuse to connect if they are not "similar" enough, and the broker agent should introduce "similar" friends one another.

Essentially, we are proposing a meta-model where at each step in the simulation: (i) some nodes are activated; (ii) some nodes are destroyed (iii); and some nodes are created. Each of these three groups may be empty for a particular step or even for all steps. For example, in the WS model nodes are never created. When a node is activated, it decides what actions to perform; most of the times, the actions consist in linking to another node according to a predetermined criterion. In the next section, we will show how to transform this meta-model in a concrete multi-agent design.

5   Design of an Agent-Based Social Network Generation System

In this section we present an agent-based design for the abstract meta-model we introduced at the end of the last section. The meta-model can be instantiated as an actual generation model providing the specifications of: (*i*) the selection process of the groups of nodes to create, activate or destroy; (*ii*) the behavior of the nodes themselves. The system provides the framework to run the simulations, providing only the two specifications mentioned early. Communication between the agents of the systems is made through message passing. The agents have their own thread of control and explicitly receive and send messages when they consider it appropriate. The general structure of the system is presented in Fig. 1.

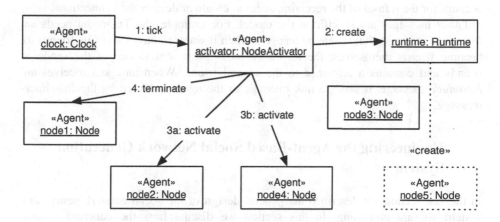

Fig. 1. Interaction diagram of the main agents in the Social Network Generation System

Since the models are essentially discrete event simulations, we introduced a clock, which essentially sends *Tick* messages to interested agents, so that ages in the simulations are clearly divided. When the simulation ends, the clock sends an *EOW* message informing the agents that they should start the cleanup process.

A specific agent performs the selection of the nodes to activate and we refer to that agent as the activator. In fact, the selection of the nodes to activate is only one of its tasks, as it is also responsible to select the agents to be destroyed and to feed those to be created with the initialization parameters. The specification of the activator tasks is done providing: (*i*) a node selector object to select the nodes to activate; (*ii*) a node selector object to select the nodes to destroy; and (*iii*) a node factory object to determine the class and the parameters of the nodes to be created.

When the activator has selected the nodes to be activated, it sends them an *Activate* message. When a node agent receives an *Activate* message, it decides the following course of actions. Whichever actions they are, when completed, the node agent acknowledges the activator that it has finished. This way the activator knows when all the actions of a given simulation step are terminated.

As: (*i*) some models may require the agents to terminate before the end of the simulation and (*ii*) the system should be shut down when the simulation ends, we have introduced two different termination messages: (*i*) the *ModelTerminate* message is sent by the activator when a node has been selected for removal and (*ii*) the *SystemTerminate* message is sent by the system to inform the agents that the simulation ended and they have to terminate. The *SystemTerminated* is sent when the activator receives the *EOW* message.

As we anticipated at the beginning of the section, providing also the behavior of the agents (the behavior of every single agent, in principle) the meta-model is fully specified. Usually, the reception of an *Activate* message triggers further actions from the agent. The more frequent action is to select another agent and send it a message to: (*i*) create a link towards the node; (*ii*) destroy a link with the agent. Some models account for the refusal of the receiving agent to create or destroy the connections.

Other messages are specific to the model. For example, the TL model needs an *Introduce* message, that is sent by an agent when it wants to have two of its friends to become friends themselves: the *Introduce* message is sent to one of the sender's friends and contains a reference to the second friend. When an agent receives an *Introduce* message, it sends a link message to the agent specified by the *Introduce* message.

6   Engineering the Agent-Based Social Network Generation System

In the last section we described the general design of the social network generation system we are proposing. In this section we discuss how the concrete system implementing the design has been engineered.

Many frameworks and tools for agent-based simulation exist. Among these, the most used are RePast [17], Swarm [18], NetLogo [19] and Mason [20]. For our system we decided to use none of them for two reasons: (*i*) we plan to support both discrete events simulations and continuous simulations and (*ii*) we want to provide a domain specific language especially tailored to write social network generation simulations. Both these goals are described in detail in Section 7. All the tools we mentioned above are excellent, but they only support discrete event simulation. Moreover, we are only interested in social network generation, thus we do not face many complexities that arise in generic ABMS (e.g., specifying the environment).

Our system uses the *Heterogeneous Distributed System* (HDS) [21, 22] software framework as middleware. This software framework allows the realization of systems based on two types of software entities: actors and servers, which can be distributed on a (heterogeneous) network of computational nodes (from now called runtime nodes). Actors have their own thread of execution and perform tasks interacting, if necessary, with other software entities through synchronous and asynchronous messages. Servers perform tasks on request of other actors. HDS is implemented using the Java language and takes advantage of preexistent Java software libraries and solutions for managing concurrency and distribution.

HDS provides two different ways for the deployment of actors and servers that allow either: (*i*) to assign a thread to each actor and server; or (*ii*) to share a thread among a set of actors and servers. Therefore, we could implement node agents on the top of HDS actors and have them share a single thread, thus making it possible to scale the simulation upwards in the number of nodes without exhausting operating system resources.

One essential difference between HDS and other agent-based simulation-modeling tools is that, essentially, HDS is not specifically an agent-based simulation-modeling tool. HDS is a full middleware to build distributed and agent based systems: consequently, the interactions between the agents occur exclusively through message passing. This is especially interesting, since the object of the simulation is people, which interact through explicit communication.

In our current design, we explicitly introduced a clock to perform a discrete event simulation. However, the clock is above the HDS level and is essentially not part of the simulation engine. Although all the generators we have created up to now explicitly instantiate the clock, this is not mandatory. It is possible to use "more autonomous" agents, which do not need triggers to act and instead act according to their own schedule.

Another feature of HDS we use extensively is the possibility to add composition filters [23] at runtime. In HDS each agent has a list of input and output composition filters; when a message is sent or received, it goes through the output list or the input list, respectively. Each filter can: (*i*) define constraints on the reception/sending of the message; (*ii*) manipulate the message; and (*iii*) log or replicate the message to another agent.

We used the replication feature to create a spy agent, which receives all the messages, which are relevant to keep an updated view of the network (link or node formation or removal). The complete network is memorized as a JUNG graph [24]. Consequently implementing the node agents' behavior and the node activator behavior is completely separated from writing and plugging-in code to perform runtime network analysis or to perform any other action on the network itself (e.g., visualize it or save it on file). At the present moment, both concerns are solved writing Java code. In principle, any language available on the JVM can be used to implement the agents' behavior.

7   Conclusions and Future Work

In this paper, we have first reviewed some archetypal network generation models from which we have extracted a meta-model common to all the models. Given the meta-model, we detailed both the general design and the actual realization of our agent-based system, which allows creating specific models by specifying only a few classes. We have also mentioned many possible areas for improvement, which we are going to detail further in this section.

This work can be considered as a step towards the development of true agent-based models for general-purpose synthetic social network generation. A further step could be the introduction of more discrete network generation models, where decisions use some degree of intelligence. These models could be based on the description of actions people perform in the real world and could use standard techniques in MASs, such as game theory or learning. Such new models need a thorough study of their network analytic properties.

One of the reasons we are interested in increasing the number of models, is that this should give us a better understanding of what a node is expected to do. This should lead to the definition of a domain specific language to ease the social scientist in writing his own models without having to write Java code.

An interesting subsequent step could be to move towards continuous generation models or at least to remove the necessity for an *Activate* message. However, while there is nothing inherently wrong in the discrete event model, informing all the agents that an event occurred represents an efficiency problem as soon as the size of the network increases, since the number of messages sent at the same time would be one for each node agent, in contrast with the current models, where few nodes are activated after each event.

Consequently, we strongly feel the need to move towards continuous models. In [9], the authors point out that: "agents nowadays constitute a convenient model for representing autonomous entities, but they are not themselves autonomous in the resulting implementation of these models". Essentially, the agents in simulations (including our own) have almost no decisional autonomy, are not pro-active and have no learning. Consequently, we believe that models with gradually increasing presence of such features are extremely interesting. Although it is possible that such properties are not really required to generate synthetic realistic social networks, attempts should be made to introduce autonomy, pro-activeness and learning in the node agents.

Acknowledgments. Stimulating discussions with Prof. A. Poggi are gratefully acknowledged.

References

1. Genesereth, M.R., Ketchpel, S.P.: Software agents. Communications of the ACM 37(7), 48–53 (1994)
2. Russell, S., Norvig, P.: Artificial Intelligence: A Modern Approach, 3rd edn. Prentice Hall, Upper Saddle River (2009)
3. Wooldridge, M., Jennings, N.R.: Intelligent agents: Theory and practice. The Knowledge Engineering Review 10(02), 115–152 (1995)
4. Axtell, R.L., Epstein, J.M., Dean, J.S., Gumerman, G.J., Swedlund, A.C., Harburger, J., Chakravarty, S., Hammond, R., Parker, J., Parker, M.: Population growth and collapse in a multiagent model of the Kayenta Anasazi in Long House Valley. Proceedings of the National Academy of Sciences of the United States of America 99(suppl. 3), 7275–7279 (2002)
5. Gilbert, N., Terna, P.: How to build and use agent-based models in social science. Mind & Society 1(1), 57–72 (2000)

6. Bonabeau, E.: Agent-based modeling: Methods and techniques for simulating human systems. Proceedings of the National Academy of Sciences of the United States of America 99(suppl. 3), 7280–7287 (2002)
7. Macal, C., North, M.: Agent-based modeling and simulation: Desktop ABMS. In: WSC 2007: Proceedings of the 39th Conference on Winter Simulation: 40 years! The best is yet to come, pp. 95–106. IEEE Press, Washington D.C (2007)
8. Epstein, J.M.: Agent-based computational models and generative social science. Complexity 4(5), 41–60 (1999)
9. Drogoul, A., Vanbergue, D., Meurisse, T.: Multi-Agent Based Simulation: Where are the Agents? In: Sichman, J.S., Bousquet, F., Davidsson, P. (eds.) MABS 2002. LNCS (LNAI), vol. 2581, pp. 1–15. Springer, Heidelberg (2003)
10. Bergenti, F., Franchi, E., Poggi, A.: Selected Models for Agent-based Simulation of Social Networks. In: 3rd Symposium on Social Networks and Multiagent Systems (SNAMAS 2011), pp. 27–32. Society for the Study of Artificial Intelligence and the Simulation of Behaviour, York (2011)
11. Kumar, R., Novak, J., Tomkins, A.: Structure and evolution of online social networks. In: Proceedings of the 12th ACM SIGKDD International Conference on Knowledge Discovery and Data Mining, KDD 2006. ACM Press, Philadelphia (2006)
12. Davidsen, J., Ebel, H., Bornholdt, S.: Emergence of a Small World from Local Interactions: Modeling Acquaintance Networks. Physical Review Letters 88(12), 1–4 (2002)
13. Watts, D.J., Strogatz, S.: Collective dynamics of "small-world" networks. Nature 393(6684), 440–442 (1998)
14. Barabási, A.L., Albert, R.: Emergence of Scaling in Random Networks. Science 286(5439), 509–512 (1999)
15. Kleinberg, J.: The small-world phenomenon: an algorithm perspective. In: Proceedings of the 32nd ACM Symposium on Theory of Computing, pp. 163–170. ACM Press, Portland (2000)
16. Watts, D.J., Dodds, P.S., Newman, M.E.J.: Identity and search in social networks. Science 296(5571), 1302–1305 (2002)
17. North, M.J., Howe, T.R., Collier, N.T., Vos, J.R.: A Declarative Model Assembly Infrastructure for Verification and Validation. In: Advancing Social Simulation: The First World Congress, pp. 129–140. Springer, Japan (2007)
18. Minar, N., Burkhart, R., Langton, C., Askenazi, M.: The Swarm simulation system: a toolkit for building multi-agent simulations. Working Paper 96-06-042, Santa Fe Institute, Santa Fe (1996)
19. Tisue, S., Wilensky, U.: NetLogo: A simple environment for modeling complexity. In: International Conference on Complex Systems, Boston, pp. 16–21 (2004)
20. Luke, S., Cioffi-Revilla, C., Panait, L., Sullivan, K., Balan, G.: MASON: A Multiagent Simulation Environment. Simulation 81(7), 517–527 (2005)
21. Bergenti, F., Franchi, E., Poggi, A.: Using HDS for realizing Multiagent Applications. In: Proceedings of the Third International Workshop on LAnguages, Methodologies and Development Tools for Multi-Agent Systems (LADS 2010), Lyon, France (2010)
22. Poggi, A.: HDS: a software framework for the realization of pervasive applications. WSEAS Transactions on Computers 9(10), 1149–1159 (2010)
23. Bergmans, L., Aksit, M.: Composing crosscutting concerns using composition filters. Communications of the ACM 44(10), 51–57 (2001)
24. The JUNG Java Universal Network/Graph Framework,
    http://jung.sourceforge.net/

MMORPG – Towards a Sustainable Livelihood Model for Africa and Beyond

Andre Mostert[1] and Russell H. Kaschula[2]

[1] Royal Docks Business School, University of East London
University Way, E16 2 RD London, United Kingdom
`moster@uel.ac.uk`
[2] School of Languages, Rhodes University, P O Box 94, Grahamstown, South Africa
`r.kaschula@ru.ac.za`

Abstract. The burgeoning worlds of massively multiplayer online role-playing games (MMORPG) coupled with increasing access to the internet is opening a new paradigmatic window for a number of disciplines. Many of these have been slow to take up the challenges associated with this emergent framework, due, in no small measure, to the perception that work and play are mutually exclusive. The dominance of this dichotomy contributed to the slow uptake of the potential for these virtual worlds to be harnessed in the fields of education and employment. This reticence was due in no small measure to the technophobia that tends to characterise the adoption of new technologies within fields that have customarily eschewed an embrace. Buying implies selling; with the existing predominantly real economic exchanges being between the players and the suppliers of the game/world/platform/universe; however this is evolving with more and more people earning some income from their engagement with a MMORPG. This paper aims to explore the leading options for earning real income in virtual world with the view to developing a model for generating a sustainable livelihood for low skilled and unskilled workers in developing countries as they develop their ICT skills base and establish an on-line presence with concomitant opening of wider non-geographically constrain variables.

Keywords: Virtual worlds, employment, technology, role-playing, sustainable livelihoods.

1 Introduction

That the electronic gaming industry is a significant element of the global economy is evidenced by the fact that in 2005, with a market size in the region of $US 29 billion, it was almost $US 7 billion larger than the movie industry (1). Complementing this are the increasing levels of expenditure in various 'games', for example, recently in Entropia a virtual world space station sold for $US 330,000 (2) while a piece of real estate in the same universe sold for $US 6 million (3). While 'the most successful online games rank amongst the world's most valuable media properties, with the most famous of all – *World of Warcraft* – generating over $1 billion a year in revenues from over twelve million subscribers' (Chatfiled 2010: 30). With this level

G.D. Putnik and M.M. Cruz-Cunha (Eds.): ViNOrg 2011, CCIS 248, pp. 28–39, 2012.
© Springer-Verlag Berlin Heidelberg 2012

of impact it is imperative that more attention is given to the opportunities emanating from this sector, more especially in terms of how marginalised communities and those in poverty can also benefit. This imperative is driven by some of the unique characteristics associated with the electronic gaming industry when juxtaposed against the movie industry; most important is the lack of geographical limitations, and considerably less barriers to labour market absorption issues.

Massively multiplayer online role-playing games (MMORPG) have grown extensively in popularity since they first emerged on the internet in 1996, with the first recorded 'believed to....(have been) Meridian 59' (4), however, the genre's manifestation was secured when Ultima Online become popular(op cit). There is common consensus that the MMORPGs evolved out of Multi-User Dungeons (MUDs), with the first developed by Roy Trubshaw and Richard Bartle which ran on a PDP-10[1] (5). Everquest which Sony rereleased in 1999 and was the leading MMORPG before the introduction in 2004 of World of Warcraft (WoW), which heralded the modern age for MMORPG, 'in WoW's 'first 24 hours sold over 240 000 copies......................any given time has an average of 500 000 users are online' (5). The realms, worlds, platforms, universes (real and fantasy) are now myriad with games, quests, adventures for almost all conceivable historical, present day and fantasy experiences, with the associated mix of free, fee, subscription based and/or software purchase with free or fee based use.

Notwithstanding this wide range of MMORPGs, there is limited scope for earning a viable living through the player's avatar[2], but it is possible to earn a basic income. However the term basic here is extremely relative. 'Almost half the world – over three billion people – live on less than $2.50 a day' (6), when this figure is juxtaposed against the income that some 'players'[3] are earning in certain realms/universes[4] it is clear that the viability of establishing models for marginalised communities to enjoy some form of income is possible. Obviously the problems of access to the Internet will continue to create challenges, but it is the contention of the authors that there is an anachronistic approach to the problem of technology and poverty, namely that access to the Internet and computer skills will enhance the life opportunities for the developing communities across the world. These are a necessary but insufficient condition for establishing a sustainable livelihood structure. MMORPG offer a viable model for creating a source of some income while 'players' develop their skills base and offer a viable route to other wider opportunities. 'The best sign that someone's qualified to run an internet start-up may not be an MBA, but level 70 guild leader status' (Chatfield 2008: 1).

One of the problems associated with analysis of the employment or work potential is the 'cultural premise that work and play are an inherent dichotomy' (Lee 2006: 68),

---

[1] A mainframe developed by Digital Equipment Corporation it formed the basis of ARPANET (now the Internet) (WR3).

[2] An avatar is the player alter ego or representation of themselves in the realm or platform; this can invariably take many different forms.

[3] The term player is used in this paper in inverted commas as an acknowledgement that not all are there for entertainment purposes only.

[4] The terms realm or universe will be used as a generic for the environment of the MMORPGs.

this tension has to be viewed within an environment where it is hard to reach an income in any realm that mirrors the basic minimum wage rate a hour, £5.73 (UK) and $6.55 (USA), these wage rates are huge when comparing an 8 hour day to what the average player could earn in all realms. However, a rate of $0.10 an hour in a universe would translate into $0.80[5] which represents almost a quarter the survival income people in poverty in developing economies need . The moral debates associated with low skilled and reparative jobs will abound, however, it is imperative that these arguments are seen within a context of limited alternative opportunities for earning some income plus the associated flexibility associated with these realms i.e. 24/7, wide choices, etc[6].

2   Making a Living in MMORPGs

As realms and universes continue to grow and expand more and more players will be asking the inevitable question, 'can I make a living from my game or hobby?' the short answer is depending on your basic income requirements. The opportunity cost in most developed countries is high, every hour spend in a realm could, with exceptions be generating the minimum wage in another low skilled employment[7]. However, similar opportunity costs do not operate in most, if not all developing countries. Consequently, the nature of a living from realms will be best assessed in terms of wider economic conditions that the 'player' finds themselves.

That the potential exists to make some form of a living is clear and receiving more and more attention, Forbes Magazine 'still toiling away as an elementary school teacher or a firefighter? Turns out you could probably be making more money as a troll or a night elf playing World of Warcraft' (WR4). Others have gone further and stated '{v}irtual worlds may also be the future of ecommerce, and perhaps of the internet itself' (Castronova 2002: 4), whichever sentiment that is accepted and adopted it is clear that the potential for the realms as being part of the solution for creating sustainable livelihoods needs to be explored in some depth.

3   Developing Real World Skills in MMORPGs

Many will argue the gaming element associated with realms and universes represent this as a strictly leisure based past time, and it would be disingenuous to attempt to dismiss this argument, due to the fact that most gaming activity is undertaken in an informal setting with little consideration for capturing the skills that are developed as a 'player' enhances their status. However, against this view is the concept of 'Serious Games' which is a term associated with the use of computer and videogames for purposes other than simple entertainment. That skills can, and are, developed by

---

[5] This figure is very low when players are using more advanced characters.

[6] This paper will not explore this debate at this stage; however, it is acknowledge that mundane repetitive and unfulfilling activities are associated with some playing in certain realms.

[7] This assumes that the impact of the present recession is not to detrimental to employment opportunities at low skill levels.

'players' is clear, from developing the basic ability to interface with ICT through to high level negotiations and strategy skills, a 'player' may run an ambit of situations that required deft abilities.

The challenge that presents is how to capture and formalise these skills to make them transferable to real world contexts, their transferability is unquestionable, in the Prospect interview with Mogwai[8], he states 'in WoW I've developed confidence; a lack of fear about entering difficult situations; I've enhanced my presentation skills and debating. Then there are the more subtle things; judging people's intentions from conversations, learning to tell people what they want to hear.' Mogwai continue and acknowledges that 'I am certainly more manipulative, more Machiavellian. I love being in charge of a group of people, leading them to succeed in a task' (Chatfield 2008:1).

Motives for playing in any realm will be various and range from Mogwai's need for Machiavellian expression through pleasure and entertainment to the desire to find alternative sources of income. Whatever the motives, the innate potential for engagement in realms serving a number of educational and economic outcomes is reasonably clear. The challenge facing researchers and practitioners is how to capture the skills, develop the economic opportunities in environments where the opportunity costs are almost zero.

4   MMORPGs as Economic Opportunity

Harnessing the potential of realms and universes to earn some level of income has historically been limited to highly experienced 'players' and/or entrepreneurs; this has contributed to the scope of realms as tools for sustainable livelihoods being viewed as unrealistic. It is our contention that this is erroneous and a consequence of misperceptions associated with the potential of these realms.

Forbes (3) identifies 10 characters, careers or professions in the virtual world which show potential for earning income, each requires differing levels, abilities and skills but they represent opportunities which are not limited necessarily by demographics and real life mobility, the only significant barrier to enter, especially in the case of free games, is access to suitable hardware and bandwidth[9]. These barriers should not be taken lightly as they continue to be the most significant problem for the harnessing of the innate potential of ICT for developing countries, however, the access issue is high on the agenda of most governments; access issues will be addressed as these are easier in the end that the problem of endemic poverty and lack of economic opportunity.

The ten virtual professions or careers identified by Forbes:

- **Gold Farmer**
- **Power Leveler**

---

[8] Mogwai is a guild leader in WoW and wields the Twin Blades of Azzinoth, he was recently offered $8000 for his account.

[9] The bandwidth issue presents the biggest contemporary challenge for many countries and often cited as a potential problem by stakeholders.

- **Merchant**
- **Sell your character** (*Character dealer*[10])
- **Designer**
- **Prostitute** (*sex worker*)
- **Beggar**
- **Architect**
- **Gambler**
- **Landlord**

Each carries different requirements, skills and abilities and the potential for earning an income will be dependent on variables such as time spent 'playing', speed of machines and bandwidth. The rest of the paper will address each of these virtual professions (referred to as the Forbes List) against their viability as vehicles for the creation of sustainable livelihoods.

Addressing the Forbes List it is possible to categorise them wider[11], namely those that are predominately time based and require relatively low skills base, Low- Skilled Character (LSC); then there are those that will require time and social skills, Social-Skilled Character (SSC); others are more reliant on luck and a mixture of skill and time, Luck-Based Characters (LBC) and finally, characters that require High Skills (HSC). This categorisation maybe viewed as artificial but, for the purposes of developing a livelihood model, allows for an analysis of suitable strategies and activities to establish the viability beyond a theoretical analysis and a priori sentiments.

For the sake of simplicity, for each of these categories three characteristics will be developed,; obvious there will be extensive overlaps, however, this model will allow the development of entry and exist routes (in terms of the skills they develop) for potential inexperienced 'players'. It is important to note that all characters will require differing investments of time to reach the relevant level; with it being more or less proportional to the level i.e. LSC opportunities will require less investment of time by the 'player' than opening HSC opportunities.

4.1   Low- Skilled Character (LSC)

- Repetitive actions
- Fighting, dancing, sweating, etc for low rewards
- Limited real life skills development

In terms of the Forbes List the best example of this would be a 'Gold Farmer' where ' Players concentrate on fighting monsters that drop lots of money or carry valuable weapons, and spend hour after hour fighting and collecting' (3). This 'loot' is then resold through various channels for real currency, customarily via the Internet sites; 'E-Bay' or www.ige.com.   Commercial gold farmers are presently predominately located in Asia, where 'companies pay employees to work eight hour or longer shifts

---

[10] Authors addition in *italics*.

[11] Later papers will aim to apply the Job Characteristic Models to these and other professions.

in game, and then sell their accumulated wealth to players in Europe or America' (3). Other games have similar activities that require the 'players' to engage in a mind-numbing activity to generate some in-world currency, in Entropia 'players' are required to 'sweat', ' Getting started in Entropia Universe without depositing is very hard...... {d}uring this period, I spent a lot of my time gathering vibrant sweat and the PED[12]'(7); in Second Life 'players' can usually find dancing opportunities to earn Linden Dollars (L$)[13], however, most affluent 'players' recognise that the easiest way to secure L$ is to purchase them with real currency. Some examples of LSC jobs in Second Life are inter alia, security guard, dancers, etc.

4.2 Social-Skilled Character (SSC)

- Mixture of repetitive and other actions
- Sex Worker, Designer, Landlord, Retail Assistant, etc.
- Numerous real life skills development

Unsurprisingly, sex workers have 'made quick inroads into virtual life' (3), where it is possible provided the 'player' is willing to accept payment using the realms currency, however, it should be noted that not all universes would support such activities, with the leading area for sex workers being red light districts in Second Life. 'For example, "Khannea" took her first client on her very first day in Second Life, and since then has been busy working many days per week, several hours per day. She dresses her avatar in provocative clothing, and simulates sexual activity using a variety of animated actions and pre-recorded sounds' (3). Obviously, being a sex worker in a virtual world is unlikely to be a model that many agencies would encourage; although it must be recognised as one of the most seamless and effective opportunities for generating in realm funds. Khannea earns in the region of L$750 for half an hour which translates into $US3, this may seem very lucrative but needs to be evaluated in the light of availability of clients.

Less contentious and consequently less lucrative are roles such as Designer, Landlord[14], Retail Assistant, etc. These all offer opportunities to earn income, the nature and level of which will vary from realm to universe, but could offer suitable alternatives for those who find LSC too mundane. Landlords tend to be players who have been 'in world' for an extended period of time and are able to sell land to new 'players', ' Second Life land baron "Anshe Chung" reportedly owns property worth about $250,000.' (3).

---

[12] PED = Project Entropia Dollars.

[13] Linden Dollars (L$) is the currency used in Second Life, it has a floating exchange rate with the $US.

[14] Landlords would also include some HSC characteristics in terms of the skill of land purchase and overseeing construction. However, they have been listed here due to the overriding social nature of their position.

4.3   Luck-Based Characters (LBC)

- Repetitive actions
- Gambler, general manufacturer, etc.
- Few real life skills developed

In its infancy when the internet became increasingly more accessible to the general public, the two entertainment growth areas were pornography and gambling, with the former far outstripping the latter. So it is not surprising that these areas are also popular in virtual worlds, being a gambler carries with it the standard risk and rewards associated with real life or other gaming sites. Electing to engage as a gambler would require an investment in both time and money and will very little guaranteed return and does not represent a viable route to earning a basic return.

General manufacturers are included here, as opposed to specialists in the HSC categorisation, in recognition that some realms have a high element of luck associated with any production activity. For example in Entropia, an avatar can elect to be a grafter or tailor or similar, through combination of resources and depending on their skill levels they can produce products for resale. However, in this case the output quality is random and is conditional on the random generators in the universe which is tantamount to gambling.

4.4   High-Skills Character (HSC)

- Varied and sophisticated actions
- Architect, merchant, pharmaceutical manufacturer, guild leader, etc
- Extensive real life skills developed

In the case of a manufacturer there is wider scope, however, it is very mundane and potentially mind numbing. However, it does require a certain level of skill, 'pharmaceutical manufacturers {Star Wars Galaxies} create their products by combining raw resources. These resources, such as chemicals or minerals, must be located using geological surveying tools and harvested using installations brought from other players skilled in industrial architecture (Lee 2008: 2). Lee continues and acknowledges that resource gathering requires extensive travelling across the Galaxy, hence time consuming, and constant maintenance, hence involving cost. 'Typically, pharmaceutical manufacturers relay on dedicated on dedicated resource brokers' (Lee 2008: 2). Unlike other realms the qualities associated with the final output are dependent on the quality of the inputs, so an astute manufacturer will be able to earn income provided they are able to 'decide which products make the most advantage of the resources available to them and must also take into account the demand of the market' (Lee 2006: 2).

Operating as an Architect, Designer or Merchant would create different opportunities in different realms or universes, carried with the obvious implicit skills that would be found in similar real world pursuits. However, the level of opportunity would vary. In some cases the activity would be almost identical to those associated with similar real world activities, for example, opening an architect's firm in Second

Life would require the avatar to engage in standard client seeking activities, despite the fact that the building will predominately if not totally located in Second Life.

Perhaps the most generally lucrative would be the building up to the status of Guild Leader with the associated benefits and opportunities for generating income. apart from the obvious time investment. Mogwai acknowledges his status as 'e-famous' having recently been 'offered $8000 for his Warcraft account, a sum he only briefly considered accepting. Given that he has clocked up over 4500 hours of play'... (Chatfield 2008: 1). While the economics would not make it viable to sell a character in this context when the opportunity costs are assessed, in an environment where the alternatives to playing World of Warcraft all day are unemployment, the attractiveness and potential returns to social investment become worthy of investigation.

This analysis has addressed some of the common and well publicised opportunities. This has by no means been an exhaustive exercise but rather aims to bring the debate into a serious focus as a possible model for poverty alleviation. Present logic regarding the digital divide is that people should have access to a computer and the Internet, as a necessary and sufficient condition for opening a path to opportunity and a suitable livelihood. This evidenced by the support for the One Laptop per Child project (OLPC):

'A small machine with a big mission. The XO is a potent learning tool designed and built especially for children in developing countries, living in some of the most remote environments. It's about the size of a small textbook. I t has built-in wireless and a unique screen that is readable under direct sunlight for children who go to school outdoors. It's extremely durable, brilliantly functional, energy-efficient, and fun.' (8)

While the project is a significant advance on previous solutions, the statement implies a number of issues that are integral to the existence and perpetuation of the digital divide, viz: teacher training, software, etc.

That projects such as OLPC are central to the solution is a given, however, it is imperative that there are a raft of support activities, from training facilitators and teachers through effective context driven software to significant online based opportunities to earn income.

5   Towards a Model for Generating a Basic Livelihood Online

Developing a character in a realm or universe that can generate a reasonable return for a 'player' is contingent on a plethora of factors; however the three key variables would be:

- Time available and alternative economic opportunities
- Financial resources
- ICT skills and access

This list could be expanded to include factors such as; which realm is selected, how much support the character receives, social skills and many other variables associated with the selected career or profession. However, for the development of a model, the generics associated with these three selected variables offers a context for creating a suitable model for assessment and evaluation.

Applying these variables to most developing societies will deliver the following contexts:

Time and Economic Opportunity – the most heavily consumed resource associated with online realms and universes are time, with many 'players' spending an average of 20 hours a week (Lee 2006). These figures are predominately generated from 'players' located in developed countries with their associated infrastructures and alternative economic opportunities. Unemployment rates in developed countries range between 4% - 12% (9), this has started to rise and can be expected to continue rising for the next few years as the 'credit crunch' impacts wider, this is against an unemployment figure for non-industrialised countries of 30%. These figures do not always offer a clear picture regarding the labour market absorption rates, and those that have removed themselves from the labour market due to search fatigue and other local factors. Notwithstanding a critical element for assessing the viability of online realms as an alternative economic activity is to weigh up what employment opportunities exist. When 'almost half the world — over three billion people — live on less than $2.50 a day' (6) it is fairly obvious that any activities that can generate some income will be welcomed.

Consequently a necessary condition for the development of a model based on virtual realms must be that no suitable alternative employment opportunity exists. In conditions where there are idle economically active human resources, with the desire to engage in some form of income generation, the first condition can be said to have been met.

There is of course an important caveat if that basic condition is met, namely, that there are no guarantees that the engagement with the selected realms will generate income. This makes it imperative that structures are developed to capture skills that are developed through engagement within the realm, for use elsewhere. This is a very important secondary consideration under the time variable, insofar as the 'players' must see some concrete returns from their time in realm. Therefore, selection of realms must be both driven by potential finance gain for the players and the garnering of transferable skills[15].

Financial Resources – Some would argue that it is artificial to make a distinction between time and financial resources in this analysis, offering the aphorism 'time is money'. Without doubt time is money, however that is only true in environments where the time applied in activity A forgoes that which could have been earned in activity B. In terms of these criteria the distinction is made, as above, where the time allocation has no viable economic alternative[16].

Most realms or universes require some financial investment to promote character advancement; some exceptions have been mentioned above i.e. dancing – in Second Life, sweating – Entropia, begging – most others, etc. The models vary from those

---

[15] This is a matter for further research in terms of qualifications and realms/universes. This will form the focus of a future paper.

[16] It is important to acknowledge that in some contexts the alternative activity is one that engages the person in survivalist activities, which is presently beyond the scope of the discussion. However, the aim of the mode is to develop a structure where survivalist activities can be pursued in terms of a basic income.

that require an upfront payment, through those that are free to download with monthly subscriptions to free games and those that require you to buy in -world currency.

Obviously, in terms of income potential, the more 'players' are able to outlay the more likely their avatar is to advance through the levels with the concomitant opening of in-world opportunities and situations for securing more mechanised, loot[17] and other useful items or skills. Moreover, the gaining of in-world knowledge is also proportional to both investment in time and money.

In terms of developing a model for creating a basic livelihood it is acceptable to assume that 'players' will have no financial resources to invest in their avatars, therefore, they will either have to be given power levelled[18] characters and/or allocate their time to the more mundane initial phases of avatar development. This point to the fact that perhaps the distinction in the economic contexts in question between time and financial resources is spurious, however, it must be acknowledged that since the target audience, marginalised communities, will only be able to bring time, the financial resources will be have to secured through conventional agency-based funding structures.

ICT Skills and Access – integral to the debate are the problems associated with ICT access and the skills profile of the potential 'players', the former is the focus of many governments, agencies and NGOs across most of the world, the latter is in this context less important. An unskilled online 'player' may strike many as an oxymoron, however, many realms start avatars off as 'babies' in terms of ability to move and make progress. In fact most have an orientation phase, island or tutorial etc which has to be 'passed' before any advance into the real world. Thus creating a natural learning phase, which with minimal effort can be captured within many ICT basic qualification frameworks, promoting wider skills acquisition and offering an early exit for those that fee they are not suited to this model.

More problematic are hardware and access issues that continue to plague developing countries, with broadband and infrastructure being at the forefront of the digital divide. That these present a justification for abandoning the possibility of harnessing these worlds. The ICT infrastructure problems will in all likelihood not persist for too much longer, and it would be negligent of researchers not to explore and test the viability of these realms, so that once the infrastructure is in place, models of this or a similar nature can be mobilised.

6   Conclusion

The economic potential associated with virtual worlds, realms or universes is growing as more and more people build their avatars and immerse themselves in a mix of fantasy, entertainment and opportunity. Leading companies are increasingly having presence in Second Life, for example IBM not only 'using it as a location for

---

[17] Loot is the generic term used for items gained through hunting, found, etc.

[18] Power levelling involves creating an avatar and up-skilling as fast as possible with the view to resell to other existing or future players.

meetings, training and recruitment, but the company is also eying revenue opportunities that could have it vying with Second Life design firms to bring real world business into the virtual realms' (11). Apple held a launch for its iPhone in Second Life (12). These are two examples among countless others.   Clearly the economic potential is being recognised and attempts being made to harness the associated opportunities.

Friedman stated in 'The Earth is Flat' (Freidman 2005), to reflect that the conventional hierarchies that have characterised the earth are disappearing; in a realm all avatars are equal in terms of the human presence behind them. The 21 year old unemployed illiterate rural herd boy with access to a computer playing in World of Warcraft, at whichever level, is in all intense and purposes equal to the New York banker playing at the same level.

It is this equality that points to these realms offering a suitable agar plate for addressing some of the contemporary issues associated with creating viable economic opportunities in areas that do not lend themselves to convention economic development paradigms.

References

1. Castronova, E.: Virtualworlds: A first-hand account of market and society on the cyberian frontier. CESifo Working paper no 618. Center for Economic Studies &IfoInsititute for Economic Research, Munich (2002)
2. Chatfiel, T.: Fun Inc. Why Games are the 21st Century's Most Serious Business. Random House, London (2010)
3. Chatfield, T.: Rage Against the Machines. Prospect, 147 (2008)
4. Friedman, T.L.: The World is Flat. Farrar, Strauss and Girox, New York (2005)
5. Lee, N.: The Labour of Fun – How Video Games Blur the Boundaries of Work and Play. Games and Culture 1(1), 68–71 (2006)
6. Philips, J.R.: Business Management Education – Electronic Games and Gamers as Managers. In: Current Developments in Technology-Assisted Education. FORMATEX, Badajoz (2006)

Web References (WR)

1. http://www.dfcint.com/news/prsept262006.html
2. http://www.futurecrimes.com/virtual-world-crime/world-record-set-for-sale-of-a-virtual-item/
3. http://www.stuff.co.nz/technology/digital-living/4873553/Virtual-real-estate-selling-for-millions
4. http://games.uk.msn.com/gaming/photos/photos.aspx?cp-documentid=156540573&page=4
5. http://iml.jou.ufl.edu/projects/Spring05/Hill/mmorpg.html
6. http://www.forbes.com/2006/08/07/virtual-world-jobs_cx_de_0807virtualjobs.html

7. http://www.columbia.edu/acis/history/pdp10.html
8. http://archive.gamespy.com/amdmmog/week1/
9. http://www.globalissues.org/article/26/poverty-facts-and-stats
10. http://www.kabalyero.com/2007/05/17/struggling-in-entropia/
11. http://laptop.org/en/laptop/
12. https://www.cia.gov/library/publications/the-world-factbook/geos/xx.html#Econ
13. http://laborsta.ilo.org/cgi-bin/brokerv8.exe
14. http://secondlife.reuters.com/stories/2006/10/24/ibm-eyes-move-into-second-life-v-business/
15. http://www.capgemini.com/ctoblog/2007/07/iphone_launched_in_second_life.php

Model of a Game for Improving Integrated Decisions in Production Management

José de Souza Rodrigues[1], Débora Scardine da Silva Pistori[1], Kátia Lívia Zambon[1], Ariane Scarelli[1], Rui M. Lima[2], and José Dinis-Carvalho[2]

[1] Faculty of Engineering of Bauru – UNESP, Av. Luiz Edmundo Carrijo Coube, 14-01, 17033-360-Bauru-SP, Brazil
[2] Dep. of Production and Systems, School of Engineering of University of Minho, Campus of Azurém, 4800-058 Guimarães, Portugal
{Jsrod,katia}@feb.unesp.br, debora@nlphd.com.br, ariane.scarelli@gmail.com, {rml,dinis}@dps.uminho.pt

Abstract. This paper presents the results obtained with a business game whose model represents the decision making process related to two moments at an industrial company. The first refers to the project of the industrial plant, and the second to its management. The game model was conceived so the player's first decision would establish capacity and other parameters such as quantities of each product to produce, marketing expenses, research and development, quality, advertising, salaries, if purchases will be made in installments or in cash, if there will be credit sales and how many installments will be allowed and the number of workers in the assembly area. An experiment was conducted with employees of a Brazilian company. Data obtained indicate that the players have lack of contents, especially in finances. Although these results cannot be generalized, they confirm prior results with undergraduate and graduate students and they indicate the need for reinforcement in this undergraduate area.

Keywords: Serious Games, Production Management, Integrated Decisions.

1 Introduction

The movement known as reengineering, despite the criticism it has received, made many companies strive to more precisely define their business areas and keep their administrative structures lean. However, the expansion of technology within them is generating another wave, characterized by a growing number of companies that acquire organizational knowledge through the acquisition of systems from the technology area. This is particularly visible in the strategies adopted by manufacturers and ERP developers and specialist systems applied to industry problems. They present their systems as products that incorporate the best managerial practices in the market and the best business models. Acquisition of the product implies the absorption of a current managerial knowledge base that incorporates the best market practices.

Large suppliers of ERP such as SAP and Oracle have thousands of best practices rules incorporated into their systems [1]. These companies spend large amounts of

G.D. Putnik and M.M. Cruz-Cunha (Eds.): ViNOrg 2011, CCIS 248, pp. 40–51, 2012.

money identifying and describing best industry practices with the objective of incorporating them into their systems. In order to take advantage of resources offered by the companies' systems, their clients need to use much of their energy redesigning their business models and incorporating new techniques, strategies, processes, actions and methodologies.

The incorporation of best practices occurs from the correction and alignment of the organization's practices with business management systems [2], [3] and [4]. Since the technology is a support for work processes where people are involved, the people become part of the equation for change. They must adjust to new procedures and ways of thinking and have a minimal understanding of how their tasks and responsibilities affect the organization and other people.

Since the administrative structure is organized around functions, an environment is created where people tend to specialize excessively in their tasks without understanding how the organization, as a whole, is affected by them. Thus, the creation of learning opportunities from a systemic perspective is of utmost importance for the conditions in effect at modern organizations. And this was one of the proposals when the Virtual Market company game was created, to become a facilitator of learning in a systemic logic in which diverse contents can be exercised and learned in the same environment.

This paper seeks to explore the use of the business game database for identifying user level of knowledge in specific contents. The data used in the study were obtained from an experiment conducted with the Virtual Market game at a drug distributor. The exercise aimed at putting the participants in the function of managers so they could exercise diverse managerial skills and thus put themselves in the position of their actual superiors. Furthermore, it also aimed to broaden understanding of how several processes were integrated in a same system, the company.

2   Method

The research was conducted as an experiment, registering a game with the name of the company whose employees participated in the experiment. Three moves were made based on the time made available by the company for training, and an extra move was made to reduce system operation errors. This preparatory phase enables considering observed errors to later be considered a lack of content knowledge. For the company, the objective of this experiment was to develop a systemic view of the company's managerial process in its collaborators and how these affect and are affected by it. The objective of the researchers was to analyze player content knowledge based on their decisions and the pertinence of using this system as an object of learning and evaluation of content control with people in the Job Market, expanding the scope of prior research made by undergraduate and graduate students. The game was registered to be played by teams (up to 4 people per team), where 22 teams were formed, distributed into two groups of 10 and 12 teams, respectively. The model presented was adopted as a strategy to play the game (Fig. 1), and onsite observation. After the game finished, data were analyzed.

3   The Virtual Market Business Game

Management can be understood as the process of organizing, directing, controlling and planning organizations [5]. Another approach found dismembers the direction in command and coordination, while keeping the rest [6]. It can also be analyzed using the functions, and not the processes, as a reference. In this case, it can be classified in marketing, production/operations and finance [7]. In the first case, the focus is the organization itself and the administration as science, whereas in the second, the focus in how the organization acts. Thus, the modeling of a company or organization should consider the organizational functions and/or administrative processes.

The administrative process involves the managerial effort of identifying and driving the organization to achieve its objectives. The "organizing" process refers to the formalization of the administrative structure, that is, the definition of functions, hierarchical relations, responsibilities, authority and rationality of the physical space [5] and [6]. However, all of the "organization" systems' parameters cannot be clearly and precisely defined without confronting available and demanded resources, internal and external conditions , the environment in which the system is immersed and the competitors it will have [8] , [9], [10] and [11].

The analysis and fixation of these parameters comprises what can be called an organization project founded on a business concept and their explanation in a given format comprises what is called a business plan [12]. This is the central point for formulating the Virtual Market company game. It permits the decision making process related to management of an industry to be tested from the moment the company is being configured [13].

Although it is necessary to define the capacity based on market data and available financial resources, in the Virtual Market game, evaluation of this process is not part of the game itself. The game ranking supposedly reflects the quality of decisions made by the players since company performance is an indicator of its quality as a competitor. Given the number and complexity of variables to be analyzed and defined during the business formulation process, a series of abilities and skills, models, techniques, concepts and philosophies can be exercised or used.

The model of the game presents two very distinct moments. The first consists of the definition of the company investment and indebtedness level. In order to make this decision, the player must define the capacity to be installed, and therefore, he needs to evaluate the quantities that can be sold of the four products he will produce and sell. The second consists of managing the production plant and the company.

Plant management consists of evaluating and deciding on capacity and defining production volumes based on the results from the previous move. Company management, in turn, consists of setting prices, fixing investment volumes in each modality, allocating company financial resources, reading and interpreting available data on the market and competition and adjusting pertinent parameters.

In order to make the first decision in the game, it is not necessary to formulate a business plan, however, the players who dedicate time to making a business plan will have greater chances for success, because the model of the game follows the logic of hierarchical planning of production [14], [15], [16] and [17], simulates a push productive environment where all of the competitors compete in the same market and produce four products [18].

The hierarchical planning model for production presupposes a certain order in the decision process, from the definition of a business plan to the management of production operations. Since those companies that best manage their operations are the ones that tend to obtain "greater added value", because they improve their long term competitiveness and profitability [14], we can assume that a game that presents the conditions for exercising at least part of the activities projected in the hierarchical model and in the decision / administrative process can contribute towards improving the understanding of the managerial process and the alignment of an organization's labor force.

3.1   Use of Business Games

Company games fit in the category called serious games, so defined because their educational objectives are more important than their entertainment objectives [19] and [20]. The first games with an educational purpose originate in war games and were created in 3,000 BC in China, for simulation of the Wei-Hai war, and in India, with Chaturanga [21]. Modern games stem from developing a game for the Prussian Army in the 19th Century [22], and in 1957 there was the first demonstration of a war game with educational purposes for executives in North America [23] and in 1958, RAND Corporation and Charles Roberts developed a board war game in an independent manner [24].

Company games fit in the category called serious games, so defined because their educational objectives are more important than their entertainment objectives [19] and [20]. The first games with an educational purpose originate in war games and were created in 3,000 BC in China, for simulation of the Wei-Hai war, and in India, with Chaturanga [21]. Modern games stem from developing a game for the Prussian Army in the 19th Century [22], and in 1957 there was the first demonstration of a war game with educational purposes for executives in North America [23] and in 1958, RAND Corporation and Charles Roberts developed a board war game in an independent manner [24].

3.2   Model Characteristics

Company management consists of the decision making process that aims at achieving the goals and objectives defined for it [25]. Since the game reflects a new investment, it implies "designing" the company and defining its objectives. Later, when implementation of the business has finished, the management effort consists of aligning results with the objectives established in the design phase. So the manager must make decisions with the objective of correcting deviations, identify and take advantage of new opportunities and those not perceived initially. It is thus expected for the trainee to use the model shown in Fig. 1 to define the best way to use the financial resources available when structuring his company. For such, he should define priority niches, prices, quantities, company indebtedness, inventory policy, product sales policy and policy for purchasing raw materials and inputs (term / cash), investments in research and development, quality, advertising, contribution margin, investment return goals, economic feasibility studies, among other variables of a strategic nature.

Fig. 1 shows a general model integrating the business model and planning and production control. Using it as a basis, the player's actions shall include a definition of the risk assumed, use of the expected cash flow model, investment analysis, rough calculation of capacity use, preliminary studies of demand (niches and their characteristics, market size, prices, margins, etc.), decisions on volumes to be produced for products, use of forecasting methods, etc. [26].

Since the game was designed to simulate months as plays and permits making as many as wanted, the long term can be simulated and in this case, planning capacity becomes an important decision variable, especially if the game is parameterized to maintain fixed capacity in certain time intervals.

In the long term, the objective is not to define the exact quantities to produce, or to detail the products, but rather to form an overall view of future capacity needs. It is about analyzing whether new investments will be necessary, and if they are, begin studies with the objective of facilitating the decision making process about making them or not. For example, factory expansion and modernization, installation of new factory units, product diversification and innovation of existing ones fit here.

In the mid-term, RCCP (Rough Cut Capacity Planning) aims at analyzing capacity occupation, if there will be peaks and bottlenecks that can be solved with re-managing, overtime, hiring or using outsourced capacity. The master production plan that will guide short term decisions emerges from there.

Actions geared towards supplying materials and inputs are found in the short term, as are allocation and detailing of capacity use. It is a more detailed planning of the operation on the shop floor. After conclusion, we go to the very short time, when what was planned begins to be executed (Shop Floor Control).

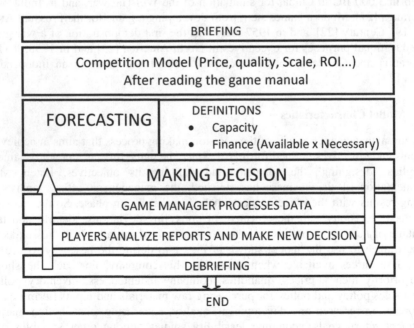

Fig. 1. General Player model in the Virtual Market Game

Last minute changes (client requests, non-availability of manufacturing resources, changes in demand and the supply chain) and unforeseen problems (equipment breakdowns, strikes, supply failures) can demand emergency adaptations in this planning [26]. The decision to make corrections is made considering the possibility of redoing planning and its cost.

In the Virtual Market game the general model the player should follow includes briefing [27], [28], [29] and [30], debriefing [31] and [32], definition of the business model, sales and operations and the production master plan, as shown in Fig. 1. Production times shown in the game manual include processing time, set up, waiting and movement.

After reading the game manual and participating in the briefing and debriefing sessions, the players formulate their strategies and record their decisions in an appropriate place, the decision sheet, on which the following fields should be filled in: quantity to produce, price, investment in marketing, advertising, research and development (R&D) for each product, worker salaries, quantity of each equipment used to process products (seven different types of equipment), number of workers in the assembly sector, loan (request and payment), number of installments for purchases (0 to 9 installments), percentage of term sales (0-100%) and number of installments in which term sales may be paid (0-9 installments).

Player decisions are processed and the first operation carried out by the system consists of comparing the quantities to produce decision with capacity. If the production order demands production capacity greater than what is available, the system corrects the capacities in a linear manner. This is a point that permits using the database to evaluate the player's level of knowledge regarding specific contents.

The system was designed this way to permit the player to make incoherent decisions. The assumption was that limiting player actions in this matter may not contribute towards testing his ability to project capacity and release orders for production. In order to test each player's potential, the game model uses diverse functions to generate product demand, as shown generically by equation (1).

$$D_{ij,P_k} = F(P,M,R\&D,Q,A,S) \tag{1}$$

where

P=Price; M=marketing investment; R&D = R&D investment;

Q=quality investiment; A=Advertsing investment; S=mean of salary paid;

i=enterprise i; j=round j; P_k =product k

Calculated demand for each company is compared to the production decision, after the adjustment made by the system, as described above. If calculated demand is greater than the quantities produced plus prior stock and deducting back orders from the previous move, the company will have a shortage of product to sell, otherwise, it will have stock. At the end of each move the players will receive 7 reports to use to make their next decision. They are: cash, quick report, ranking, inventory, decision sheet, indicators and income statement. Only the ranking and indicators reports are highlighted here, because the others follow the standardization of the Brazilian accounting area, in general lines, and similar can be found in literature. Ranking organizes the companies in terms of the move's gross profits and accumulated profit, whereas the indicators report shows several indexes for the decision maker to have an idea of how the competitors and the Market behaved with the last move, as can be seen in Table 1, which shows a report extracted from a game with 9 teams.

Table 1. Indicators Report

Team Investment				
Item	Product 1	Product 2	Product 3	Product 4
Quality	550,000.00	520,000.00	510,000.00	500,000.00
Advertising	680,000.00	650,000.00	640,000.00	630,000.00
Marketing	700,000.00	690,000.00	680,000.00	670,000.00
R&D	570,000.00	550,000.00	530,000.00	510,000.00
Maximum and Minimum in the period				
Item	Product 1	Product 2	Product 3	Product 4
Quality (max)	550,000.00	520,000.00	510,000.00	517,000.00
Quality (min)	3,000.00	3,000.00	3,000.00	3,000.00
Advertising (max)	680,000.00	650,000.00	640,000.00	630,000.00
Advertising (min)	4,000.00	4,000.00	4,000.00	3,500.00
Marketing (max)	700,000.00	690,000.00	680,000.00	670,000.00
Marketing (min)	4,000.00	4,000.00	4,000.00	4,000.00
R&D (max)	570,000.00	550,000.00	530,000.00	556,000.00
R&D (min)	3,000.00	3,000.00	3,000.00	3,000.00
Market Share				
	Revenues	Quantity	Indebtedness	Profitability
Team	1,187	1,058	1,918	2,889
Best Indicator	1,187	1,365	1,918	2,995
Market Data				
Item	Product 1	Product 2	Product 3	Product 4
Market Tt	71,838	48,834	12,051	10,926
Sales Max	10,254	7,449	2,213	2,697
Losses Max	11,656	9,568	2,631	2,263
Price Max	6,400.00	7,100.00	8,300.00	15,000.00
Price Min	1,250.00	1,950.00	2,300.00	8,560.00
Stock Tt	9,182	7,567	3,451	3,643

4   Findings

One of the points exercised in the game and that can be analyzed is financial decision consistency. This study opted to classify decisions as a result of potential to make the company need to take out a loan. For such, decisions related to purchasing, sales and investment were initially analyzed in an integrated manner. The combined decisions with major probability of generate cash shortages, considering that the decision maker does not have complete control of cash flow management concepts, it would be a decision in which the managed company purchases by cash, sells on terms and invests part of the money. At the other extreme would be the decision of buy on terms, sell in cash and not invest. This would be an extremely conservative decision and it would tend to make the company have opportunity costs, however, for the objective defined herein, this will not be analyzed. The table below shows the list of possibilities from making a decision obeying the hierarchy of less probability of generating cash shortages to the greatest probability (Table 2).

Table 2. Hierarchy of decisions in relation to the probability of not having cash shortages

Acronym	Decision	Hierarchy
CP_VA_NAP	Bought a term, sold cash and did not invest	1
CP_VA_AP	Bought a term, sold cash and invested	2
CP_VP_NAP	Bought a term, sold term and did not invest	3
CP_VP_AP	Bought a term, sold term and invested	4
CV_VA_NAP	Bought by cash, sold a term and did not invest	5
CV_VA_AP	Bought by cash, sold in cash and invested	6
CV_VP_NAP	Bought by cash, sold a term and did not invest	7
CV_VP_AP	Bought by cash, sold a term and invested	8

This proposal was elaborated considering that the group that participated in the training was not uniform in terms of technical formation and occupied function. The objective of the activity was to provide conditions for company collaborators to understand the managerial process from an integrated perspective, enabling them to put themselves in the manager's position when making decision as well as in the collaborators position when affected by the same decision. Therefore, each participant's control of content was variable and it was expected that there would be a reasonable incidence of inconsistencies in decision making. That is the motive that guided this analysis.

In a group of people with control of content from finance, the criterion of decision consistency could be used in terms of risks assumed as a result of existing parameters at the moment the decision is made. In this case, all individual who made the decision to buy term, sell term and invest should be analyzed, because that decision would demand a reasonable degree of technical knowledge of project cash flow and the capacity to assume risk.

Using the aforementioned criteria, potential for generating a cash shortage, the data shown in Table 3 were obtained.

Analyzing the results, we notice that as new moves are made, the number of decisions that strengthen the company's cash position increase, that is, the probability for cash shortages is reduced. This is an indicator that some progress is being made (learning) in relation to the company's cash flow management essentials. On one hand, it shows the game's potential to contribute to a teaching-learning process, and on the other, it shows that this sort of analysis is pertinent, collaborating towards

Table 3. Decision on purchasing, selling and investing in the moves

Strategy	Round 1	Round 2	Round 3
CP_VA_NAP		1	
CP_VA_AP			1
CP_VP_NAP	8	5	5
CP_VP_AP	2	6	6
CV_VA_NAP	6	5	4
CV_VA_AP	3	3	3
CV_VP_NAP	2	2	2
CV_VP_AP	1		1
Total	22	22	22

enriching and accelerating user learning, because it is possible to automate this procedure. If this analysis is complemented with decisions on requesting loans and the occurrence of emergency loans in the move (the decision made led to a cash shortage).

In order to refine the above analysis, the Table 4 was constructed. It shows the decisions made by the players in relation to loans. Decision makers are free to choose to loan or not loan. If the decision that he took generates cash shortage, the game calculates the amount of money necessary and registers it as emergency credit. So, the occurrence of emergency credit is a consequence of other decisions made by them. Therefore, emergency credit may be understood as a consequence of errors or risks assumed. The first case results from cash flow projection failures in the period, whereas the second results from a risk consciously assumed by the player, that is, he assumes the risk of cash shortage if his overall strategy in the move fails, and thus, it is not a cash flow planning error.

Comparing tables 3 and 4, we see that the companies that adopted the strategies with the greatest probability of generating cash shortages were the ones that had to resort to emergency credit, which is more onerous because of the higher interest rates. On the other hand, a tendency can be observed among the companies to increase cash protection, due to the incidence of requested loans. Although it is not possible to

Table 4. Loan and occurrence of emergency credit

Strategy	Emergency Credit			Loan		
	Round 1	Round 2	Round 3	Round 1	Round 2	Round 3
CP_VA_NAP		0			1	
CP_VA_AP			0			0
CP_VP_NAP	0	0	0	5	4	5
CP_VP_AP	0	2	0	2	4	3
CV_VA_NAP	0	0	0	1	2	3
CV_VA_AP	0	0	0	0	2	1
CV_VP_NAP	1	2	0	1	2	0
CV_VP_AP	1		1	0		1

affirm there was a complete control of the company financial planning theme, it can be said there was improvement in understanding of the theme and that more moves and appropriate support could significantly improve control of area content.

5 Conclusion

In accordance with the objectives of this paper, it can be said that the use of this game in particular is able to point out learning gaps in users, making it possible to elaborate complementary strategies to eliminate them, in combination with the game or not. Although several experiments have been carried out with this game in diverse situations (undergraduates, graduates, public universities, private universities, different countries), it would be necessary to further broaden the sample so the data become significant and permit a generalization of conclusions obtained through this experiment. However, prior evidence revealed [33], [34], [35], [36], [37], [38] that the companies' financial management is an area in need of greater attention by managers in relation to their collaborators. This experiment, in particular, made it possible to observe how much actions that provide a systemic view to collaborators can contribute towards facilitating the managerial process, because during the exercise there were several manifestations in the sense of "now I am beginning to understand my superiors' decisions and the reason why they were made in a certain way." This indicates the need to make the managerial process more significant for the diverse collaborators, and to provide more precision in the execution of tasks and functions with diverse training activities. Finally, it is worth underscoring that the game, with technological support, can provide integrated learning, in the sense of presenting demands for various kinds of knowledge within the same exercise (plan the company and manage it) and in the sense of uniting fun with technical and conceptual learning.

References

1. Bradford, M.: Modern ERP: Select, Implement & Use Today's Advanced Business Systems, 2nd edn., p. 248. Lulu.com, Raleigh (2010)
2. Soffer, P., Golany, B., Dori, D.: Aligning an ERP system with enterprise requirements: An object-process based approach. Computers in Industry 56, 639–662 (2005)
3. Mabert, V., Soni, A., Venkataramanan, M.: Enterprise resource planning: managing the implementation process. European Journal of Operational Research 146(2), 30–314 (2003)
4. Umble, E.J., Haft, R.R., Umble, M.M.: Enterprise resource planning: Implementation procedures and critical success factors. European Journal of Operational Research 146, 241–257 (2003)
5. Appleby, R.C.: Modern Business Administration, 6th edn., p. 512. Pearson Educational Limited, Harlow (1994)
6. Robbins, S.P., Decenzo, D.A., Coulter, M.: Fundamentals of management, 7th edn., p. 480. Prentice Hall (2010)
7. Stevenson, W.J.: Production/Operations Management, 6th edn., p. 896. McGraw-Hill, Irwin (1999)
8. Porter, M.E.: Competitive Strategy: Techniques for Analyzing Industries and Competitors, 1st edn., p. 397. Free Press (1998)

9. Kaplan, R.S., Norton, D.P.: The Balanced Scorecard: Translating Strategy into Action, 1st edn., p. 322. Harvard Business Press (1996)
10. Kaplan, R.S., Norton, D.P.: Strategy Maps: Converting Intangible Assets into Tangible Outcomes, 1st edn., p. 454. Harvard Business Press (2004)
11. Kaplan, R.S., Norton, D.P.: Alignment: Using the Balanced Scorecard to Create Corporate Synergies, p. 302. Harvard Business Press (2006)
12. Pinson, L.: Anatomy of a Business Plan: The Step-by-Step Guide to Building a Business and Securing Your Company's Future, 7th edn., p. 352 (2008); Out Of Your Mind ...And Into The Mark
13. Rodrigues, J.S., Crepaldi, A.F., Zambon, K.L.: Virtual Market – jogos de empresas no ensino de engenharia. In: GCETE 2005: Proceedings of Global Congress on Engineering and Technology Education (2005)
14. Gaither, N., Frazier, G.: Operations Management, 9th edn., p. 811. Thomson Learning (2002)
15. Danreid, R., Sanders, N.R.: Operations Management: an integrated approach, p. 671. John Wiley & Sons, Hoboken (2007)
16. Starr, M.: Foundations of Production and Operations Management, p. 653. Thomson Higher Education, Mason (2007)
17. Collier, D.A., Evans, J.R.: Operations Management: goods, services and value chains, 2nd edn., p. 830. Thomson Higher Education, Mason (2007)
18. Rodrigues, J.S.: Game Manual, p. 24. UNESP (2011)
19. Iuppa, Nborst, M.: End-To-End Game Development: Creating Independent Serious Games And Simulations From Start to Finish, Elsevier Science (2009)
20. Michael, D., Chen, S.: Serious Games: Games That Educate, Train, and Inform. In: Defining Independent Games, Serious Games, and Simulations, 001 edn., ch. 2, pp. 9–16, 352. Course Technology PTR (2005)
21. Keys, J.B., Wolfe, J.: The role of Management Games and Simulation for Education and Research. Journal of Management (1990)
22. Tanabe, M.: Jogos de empresas. Dissertação (Mestrado em Administração) – Departamento de Administração da FEA/USP. Universidade de São Paulo, São Paulo (1977)
23. Burch, J., John, G.: Business Games and Simulation Techniques. Management Accounting 51(6), 49–52 (1969)
24. Smith, R.: Technology Disruption in the Simulation Industry. Journal of Defense Modeling & Simulation: Applications, Methodology, Technology 3(1), 3–10 (2006)
25. Chiavenato, I.: Administração: teoria, processo e prática, 3ª edn., p. 417. Makron Books, São Paulo (2000)
26. Correa, H.L., Gianesi, I.G.N., Caon, M.: Planejamento, Programação e Controle da Produção MRP II/ERP. São Paulo, Atlas, p. 452 (2000)
27. Fritzsche, D.J.: The Role of Simulation Games: Supplement or Central Delivery Vehicle? Journal of Experiential Learning and Simulation 2, 205–211 (1981)
28. Warrick, D.D.: Leadership Styles and Their Consequences. Journal of Experiential Learning and Simulation 3-4, 155–172 (1981)
29. Jennings, D.: Strategic management: an evaluation of the use of three learning methods. Developments in Business Simulation & Experiential Learning 27, 20–25 (2000)
30. Green, J.C., Mcquaid, B., Snow, S.: Use of External Interventions in a Computer Based Simulation. Developments in Business Simulation and Experiential Learning 29, 73–78 (2002)

31. Mcafee, R.B.: Using a case as the basis for a modified debate. Insights into Experiential Pedagogy 6, 11–12 (1979)
32. Boud, D., Keogh, R., Walker, D.: Refletion: tourning experience into learning. Nichols Publishing Company, New York (2005)
33. Rodrigues, J.S.: Ensino de gestão da capacidade e da empresa com o apoio do jogo Virtual Market no curso de Mestrado Integrado em Engenharia Industrial e Gestão da UMINHO/Azurém e no Programa de Pós-Graduação em Engenharia de Produção da FEB/Bauru/UNESP, tese de livre docência, UNESP (2010)
34. Rodrigues, J.S., Nagano, I.L., Zambon, K., Scarelli, A.: Desenvolvimento de um Jogo de Empresas para apoiar o Processo de Ensino-Aprendizagem de Empreendedorismo. In: Proceedings of Second Ibero-American Symposium on Project Approaches in Engineering Education Creating Meaningful Learning – PAEE, pp. 73–78 (2010)
35. Nagano, I.L.: Uso do Jogo de Empresas Bom Burguer no processo ensino – aprendizagem com ênfase em Empreendedorismo em alunos do Ensino Médio. Tese para a qualificação ao Mestrado, material impresso, UNESP (2011)
36. Scarelli, A.: Mediação do processo ensino-aprendizagem com o jogo de empresas Virtual Market: uma pesquisa de opinião. Dissertação (Mestrado em Engenharia de Produção), Universidade Estadual Paulista (UNESP), Bauru (2009)
37. Pistori, D.S.S.: Análise do uso do jogo Virtual Market como mediador do processo de aprendizagem de gestão empresarial, tese de dissertação de mestrado, UNESP (2010)
38. Zuccari, P.: O uso do jogo de empresa Virtual Market como apoio ao processo ensino-aprendizagem em instituições de ensino superior de bauru e região, tese de dissertação de mestrado, UNESP (2010)

A Serious Game for Supporting Training in Risk Management through Project-Based Learning

Túlio Acácio Bandeira Galvão[1], Francisco Milton Mendes Neto[1,2],
Mara Franklin Bonates[1,2], and Marcos Tullyo Campos[1,2]

[1] Technological Center of Software Engineering, Rural Federal University of the Semi-Arid,
Mossoró - RN, Brazil
[2] Postgraduate Program in Computer Science, Rural Federal University of the Semi-Arid,
Mossoró - RN, Brazil
{tuliogalvao,miltonmendes,marabonates,
marcostully}@ufersa.edu.br

Abstract. The increasing demand for Software Engineering professionals, in particular Project Managers, and the popularization of the Web platform as a catalyst of human relations nowadays has made this platform interesting to be used for training this type of professional. In consonance to that, we have observed the dissemination of the use of games as an attractive instrument in the process of teaching and learning. However the project of a web-based instructional game that fulfills all pedagogical and technical requirements for training a project manager is not a trivial task. There is a gap between the theoretical concepts that are normally learned in traditional courses and the practical aspects required by the real tasks. In an attempt to contributes to that problem, this paper proposes the use of a persistent browser-based game intended for Risk Management as a component support in qualifying process of new professionals of Project Management. The game provides to the player some experience in a real context of Project Management, where new challenges are frequently posed to the enterprises.

Keywords: Game-Based Training, Intelligent Agents, Persistent Browser-Based Games, Project-Based Learning, Project Management, Risk Management, Serious Games, Software Engineering.

1 Introduction

The importance and the real needs of the adoption of methods and principles of the Project Management [1] in organizations are currently widely discussed and accepted. In such organizations, the main role of the Project Manager is the task of conducting a project to its successful conclusion. However, that is not what usually happens in software projects [2].

In an attempt to explain the high number of projects that fail due to reasons related to bad management, some studies have discussed a possible relationship between the lack of certain abilities by managers and the traditional teaching methods. This is one

G.D. Putnik and M.M. Cruz-Cunha (Eds.): ViNOrg 2011, CCIS 248, pp. 52–61, 2012.
© Springer-Verlag Berlin Heidelberg 2012

of the consequences of acquiring knowledge without an experience in some real project or complementary educational approaches, such as games and simulations.

In order to provide a solution for this deficiency, in this paper we propose a tool to provide a new way of learning that is not only attractive, but efficient and collaborative as well. This paper proposes the eRiskGame tool, which is a Persistent Browser-Based Game for educational purposes. The game is about the tasks that a Project Manager must perform in an organization. Its focus will be on Risk Management, more specifically in the Planning, Control and Monitoring (budget, time schedule and software quality).

This serious game uses Project-Based Learning – PBL [3] to bring the player a way to acquire knowledge on project management, particularly in the risk control involved in this process. To that end intelligent software agents were employed in monitoring and controlling of the environment, which is in constant change and affects the professionals, the organization and its customers.

This paper is divided into eight sections. Section 2 presents an overview of risk management. Section 3 describes the use of PBL in software engineering. Section 4 presents the concept of persistent browser-based games. Section 5 presents the application of intelligent agents in computer games. Section 6 discusses related works. Section 7 describes the agent-based approach proposed in this paper and the role of each agent. The last section presents our final considerations.

2   Risk Management

Risk management is increasingly seen as one of the main jobs of project managers. It involves anticipating risks that might affect the project schedule or the quality of the software being developed and taking measures to avoid or mitigate the impacts arising from those risks [4], [5] apud [6]. So we can understand risk as an unwanted event that has negative consequences [7].

In a software project, various risks may exist and are best understood if we divide them in three categories [6]: *Project risks*, which affect the project schedule or resources; *Product risks*, which affect the quality or performance of the software being developed; *Business risks*, which affect the software developing or procuring organization. Therefore we can identify the implications of a particular risk in the projects and plan how to deal with these risks should they occur.

Project managers are subject to uncertainties related to the difficulty of defining requirements, time and resources estimating or even to organizational or customer needs changes. To avoid that these risks jeopardize the project, the manager must anticipate them, understand their impact and take appropriate action. This process consists of four steps [6]: i) Risk Identification, in which possible project, product and business risks are identified; ii) Risk Analysis, in which the likelihood and consequences of these risks are assessed; iii) Risk Planning, in which plans to address the risk by avoiding it or minimizing its effects on the project are drawn up; and iv) Risk Monitoring, in which the risk is constantly assessed and plans for risk mitigation are revised as more information about the risk becomes available.

Risks can have different impacts and occurrence probabilities, therefore different strategies must be followed to manage them. A preventive strategy requires that measures to reduce the likelihood of a certain risk to affect the project are taken. However, many risks cannot be avoided. A minimization strategy implies taking measures previously to soften the impact of risk if it occurs. A contingency plan must also exist to deal with the problem if it cannot be avoided.

3   PBL Applied to Software Engineering

Project-Based Learning (PBL) was proposed by [3] as a mean to conduct the education where the personal and collective skills are devised through the development of learning capabilities which allow short term reasoning. This theory presupposes that a project centered on tasks where the pressures of short term prevail, the participants must be in balance between action and reflection, in order to build the competence of the learning capacity [8].

The traditional approach in the Software Engineering teaching is based on a reading model. However, this model brings a big problem for students, mainly due to the little involvement with the theme. Students play a passive role in the educational process, differently of the role of Software Engineer which must be alert to what occurs in the projects which he or she coordinates and make decisions that will be the foundation for their successful conclusion.

The PBL can be understood as an education technique, where situations of an actual context are modeled on a fictitious project in which the students must commit-to-finish it, and thus build knowledge regarding that experience.

Integrating the PBL in the learning of Software Engineering makes it possible to provide the student with a practical experience that cannot be obtained in activities performed in a laboratory [9]. In the traditional approach, the problems are normally adapted and simplified in such a way that they do not appear to be relevant or are linked to solutions already pre-manufactured, which prevent reasoning and gathering of the students' ideas to deal with problems of this nature. In addition, some issues, like process models, appear to be so theoretical that do not show the students how this will be used in practice.

4   Persistent Browser-Based Games

In this context, we can define a Persistent Browser-Based Game (PBBG) as an electronic game that can be played and accessed by a Web browser and presents a shared persistent virtual environment, where the events continue to occur even in the absence of user. The user may recover his session later and continue in the game [10].

In a heterogeneous audience, with specific requirements of time and resources, the characteristics offered by PBBGs may be the key-point in the success of a learning tool. Since it provides people with separate provisions to interact, compete or exchange experience using the same tool. PBBGs can also run on mobile devices, most of these with limited capacity. This is possible because most part of browser games do not count on complex graphs or sounds, which normally are compensated with one ludic aspect, thus maintaining their attractiveness.

Due to the frenetic emergence of new multimedia titles, in many styles, qualities and themes, it has been avoided in this work cite examples. However, we can indicate [11] as a wide and detailed list of the main browser games currently available.

5 Intelligent Agents in Computer Games

To improve the effectiveness, or even the autonomy of computational tools, some techniques of Artificial Intelligence (AI) have been employed in various areas. Due to some of their abilities, such as: behavior guided by goals, reactivity, reasoning, adaptability, learning, communication and cooperation, Intelligent Agents have gained space and become very popular in computer games.

There are several types of agents, but each one is elaborated in accordance with the environment in which they shall be inserted and the functionalities which they should provide. An autonomous agent set which agents cooperate among themselves aiming to solve a problem that is beyond the capacity of a single agent is considered a Multiagent System (MAS) [12].

Intelligent Agents may be used in games with many purposes, not only in the representation of opponents or partners, but also in the representation of the environment itself, since the virtual environments try to represent in the real environments the most accurately possible way. These environments are subject to the most diverse circumstances, like climate changing or disasters, among other things that can influence the game progress.

6 Related Works

Several initiatives in the Software Engineering area have been carried out, and we may cite a few, such as TIM: The Incredible Manager [13], a single-player simulation game with focus on Planning and Control (budget, time schedule and quality) developed on the Java platform. Dealing with budgets and schedules is done similarly to the eRiskGame, but in TIM there are tasks that the player must assign to each developer and determine the limit time for completing the task, the number of inspections, among others, to finally submit this specification to a possible acceptance. In the eRiskGame this process doesn't occur: the project plan has already been fully defined and it is up the player to conduct the project as well as possible to completion.

In [14] a simulation model that uses the games paradigm is presented. In that work, agents are used to represent the developers and each agent has a different behavior pattern, assembled from observed statistics about PSP (Personal Software Process). The user assembles the team and, unlike the eRiskGame, the users themselves specify the data of developer's performance and productivity.

The game developing takes place by following a XP process. Due to this, its context focuses strongly in stories described on cards. Already in the eRiskGame the used process follows a waterfall model. Some points of the two works are quite similar, such as the game progress showing the number of code lines produced, the found errors, the time spent at each phase, among others. The presentation of these data to the user is done only in textual form in the first work while in the eRiskGame graphics and other artifacts are used to improve the user's control over their projects.

We can also mention the SimSE [15], whose focus is the software project management, including the phases of analysis, design, construction and tests; it is also developed on the Java platform. Another example is the SESAM [16], which approaches the development software process focused on quality assurance.

7   eRiskGame

This session brings to the reader the serious game developed according to the themes presented here, in addition to the module developed for the teachers, where these evaluate the attitudes taken by players in accordance with the game progression.

7.1   Scenario and Storyline Game

The eRiskGame was created to simulate an experience in managing software projects, where the player can get ready to control the expenses, to comply with the targets and deadlines laid down, in addition to accompany the team work productivity. In view of that, as a real company, the work will be subject to changes in the administration of the organization, requiring changes by customers and other risks which may prevent the success of their projects.

The game's storyline consists of a Software House that goes through changes and is seeking new project managers. At the start, the player is involved in this context, which it is presented in the tutorial form. The ludic aspect tries to captivate the player, to unwittingly submit concepts and leaving him or her free to reach them when the player considers it necessary to transpose any challenge imposed by the game. Besides the tutorial, an additional material about Risk Management, with integrated questionnaires is made available to the trainee. The questionnaire results may increase the final player's score.

Once inserted in the scenario, the player can start new projects, which have budgets, deadlines and targets, varying in acceptable intervals. Each project is divided into phases which in turn are divided into weeks and days.

Players can monitor the result of their actions by means of numbers and graphics (Figure 1), which gives them better prospects of success in their decision making.

In the eRiskGame, the planning of the teams and, consequently, budget is highly important. For this, the user may contract the most varied professionals and fire them at the time the user may deem advisable. To this end, the game brings a Professional list, with detailed profiles, to analyze their characteristics and determine which of them better fits the needs of the project at the time. Each professional has characteristics such as Teamwork, Leadership, Concentration, Technical Vision, Abstract Vision, Motivation, Hourly Cost, Productivity in Code, among others. These characteristics will influence the performance in the team project. It is up to the player dealing with different profiles so that he or she can maximize the results.

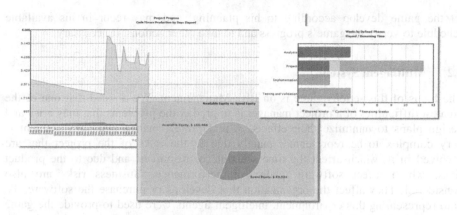

Fig. 1. Monitoring Graphs

Due to the fact that the game is multiplayer, hiring or firing professionals require that the player remain attentive to other factors besides the professional characteristics. The list which includes the available professionals for recruitment, called market, is the same for all in the game. Thus the player should be cautious with the deadlines, because a professional that he or she intends to hire just for a specific phase may not be available anymore in that period. This same concern should also be watched over when firing, since in the game, the newly recruited professionals have a smaller productivity curve. That may hinder an exchange of these professionals in the final stages of a project phase.

The amount of available professionals on the market is controlled by the game in order to supply only the needs of ongoing projects. There is no excess of professionals, but it could have a shortage in certain moments.

To confer greater dynamics to the game, the professionals' attributes (Vigor, Motivation, etc) are not static. Over the days, professionals get tired, lose the motivation or even get distracted, affecting their productivity. To deal with this, the player can make new acquisitions, through which he or she can invest and revitalize the staff.

A new project, once started, brings fairly detailed planning done to the whole project and also for each stage: budget, time in weeks, artifacts and codes to be produced, among other details. Thereafter, the player's mission is to meet these targets and deadlines in the best possible way. However, it is given the option to negotiate the deadlines or budget. This fact entails a decrease in the project's final score.

Each project concluded, successful or not, gives the player a certain score, calculated in accordance with the fulfillment in a timely manner of each phase, financial balance or loss, production targets and quality affected. These points generate some rankings in which the player can measure his performance compared to other players.

The eRiskGame has its own time. The days elapse without the player's intervention and they progress differently from real time to prevent that the projects prolong for months or even years. This way, the player can prepare his strategy and let the game develop according to his planning, and may recur in his available schedule to verify the game's progress and to take other actions, if necessary.

7.2   Multiagent System

The focus of this serious game is on Risk Management. We noticed that one of the greatest difficulties of a project manager is to predict the problems that may arise and design plans to minimize their effects. A real project management environment is very complex to be represented, mainly due to the risks of the project that are involved in it, which affect the time schedule or resources, and due to the product risks, which affect software quality or performance. Business risks are also considered. They affect the organization that develops or purchase the software. To help representing this environment, intelligent agents were used to provide the game with some of these risks in different stages and different conditions for each project.

Due to the diversity of problems, many agents had to be implemented, being each one of them in charge of monitoring several game aspects to act in their respective risks. However, agents are sociable and when one acts, providing some adverse situation; the others are informed, increasing or decreasing the risk of occurrence of other mishap. For instance, when a professional quits, the agent in charge for "rumors" may influence the other ones concentration.

Some different AI techniques were used to provide intelligence to the agents, being the Fuzzy Logic the most used. One of the applications that use this logic is the agent responsible for examining a professional's health conditions and keeps them off temporarily by medical leave. This is a simple reactive agent that monitors the motivation and the vigor (Figure 2-a) of all professionals who are designated to a project and identifies a health condition, as shown in Figure 2-b, to determine how long this professional should be kept away.

As the degradation of the attributes of the professionals is continuous, if there was not a factor of probability associated to the agents, as soon as a professional's health measured below 90, this one would already be kept off for 3 days, preventing that the physical state get worse until a most critical situation were identified. In this case, the associated probability is a very low number, which avoids the occurrence of deviations and allows that the number of days off be different in most cases.

The agent which creates rumors or discussions between the professionals is a model-based agent. It notes the quantity of professionals in each project, the time elapsed and the quantity of errors in the project, the leadership and team work of each professional for, from time to time, inform the players if any of them is clashing with the team or if the staff is concerned with any factor linked to possible changes in the company organization or even rumors involving the project discontinuity.

To detect certain states, the agent must inform the player about what has been occurred and stores data on this report. Subsequently, if the environment perceptions related to these data have degraded and no corrective action has been registered, the agent will create some situation in the project that will result in lack of concentration or high concern in the professionals, thereby increasing the risk of poor performance of several other agents.

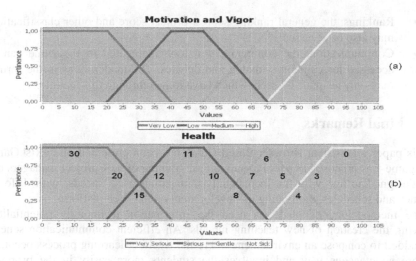

Fig. 2. Fuzzification and Defuzzification Graphs

The player is informed about the occurrence of any of these contingencies by means of messages in his inbox in addition to other reports located along the performance focus. The available message inbox is essential to maintain the player updated about the changes occurred in the project and it is one of the main communication tools included in the game.

7.3   Evaluation Module

Education is a kind of characterized service with a high intangibility degree. Contrary to the assets' quality, which can be measured objectively through indicators such as durability and defect number, the educational service quality has a more abstract and intangible nature [17]. It may be difficult an assessment of its efficacy or even the adequacy of its use.

In these cases some measures may be taken to verify if the student is making proper use of the subjects exposed and if the tool actually works according to its purpose. It is possible to assess the quality perceived by the users, by questioning them if the tool reached their expectations and if they have acquired the worked content, or to evaluate the real knowledge acquired by attributing to the specialists (teachers) the role to analyze the results obtained by means of tests or other evaluation methods.

The eRiskGame is enabled with a special module designed to help the teachers in the task of monitoring the progress of the trainees and interpret their knowledge, skills and actions, in view of the expected changes in behavior, proposed in the tool goals.

Among these options available in that module, the registered teacher has access to:

- Monitoring the players' actions: all acquisitions, recruitment or any changes that the player makes in the project is recorded and shown in some kind of an interactive list of daily events;
- Monitoring the project is progress: the teacher has access to productivity statistics and projects' advancement;

- Rankings: the general ranking scores, project score and other classifications may also be accessed;
- Communication: the communication tool aggregated to the game can be accessed for guidelines, dialog and debates. The moderations in the forums may only be made by users which have joined through this module.

8   Final Remarks

In this paper a Persistent Browser-Based Game has been presented, the eRiskGame. This game was proposed as a tool to support the training of new project managers and was designed in line with the increasingly demanding users' needs, with different routines and schedules, motivating its development on the Web platform.

The methodology adopted has used the information technology potentialities allowing the creation of new teaching models. An efficient communication scheme was added to compose an environment where the teaching-learning process occurs in a more spontaneous way and involves the students more easily in the proposed context. In addition, the proposed tool offers a Risk Management practical vision different from the traditional education patterns.

Some earnings are easily noticed when using a game totally designed on the Web and without the need for special software to access it, such as: time flexibility, cost reducing, space flexibility and less interference in work routine. The high accessibility level promoted by this serious game also allows user to start a session in a given place and resume the game from any other place, using any access device. Thus, even people with very dynamic routines can benefit from the use of this tool.

Concerning the sharing and the quality of information exchange, one of the characteristics of the distance education systems, especially those which make use of asynchronous communication tools, such as forums, is that both the teachers and students have the opportunity to ripen their ideas and consult sources beforehand, favoring the preparation for more productive discussions. Thus the exchanged knowledge is better prepared and facilitates the users' understanding with different levels of familiarity with the theme for that matter.

All these benefits make this tool an innovative learning environment with characteristics very important to reach and gather distinct publics, allowing a greater collaboration between students and teachers, and could even be a model for other educational tools involving the most distinct topics.

References

1. Project Management Institute: A Guide to the Project Management Body of Knowledge, 3rd edn. Newtown Square, Pennsylvania (2004)
2. Brewer, J.L.: Project managers: can we make them or just make them better? In: 6th Conference on Information Technology Education, pp. 167–173. ACM, New York (2005)
3. Ayas, K., Zeniuk, N.: Project-based learning: building communities of reflective practitioners. Management Learning 32(1), 61–76 (2003)
4. Hall, E.: Managing Risk: Methods for Software Systems Development, ch. 5. Addison-Wesley, Reading (1998)

5. Ould, M.A.: Managing Software Quality and Business Risk, ch. 5. John Wiley & Sons, Chichester (1999)
6. Sommerville, I.: Software Engineering (Update), 8th edn. International Computer Science. Addison-Wesley Longman Publishing Co., Inc., Boston (2006)
7. Pfleeger, S.L., Atlee, J.M.: Student Study Guide for Software Engineering: Theory and Practice, 4th edn. Prentice Hall Press, Upper Saddle River (2009)
8. Hsu, R.C., Liu, W.-C.: Project based learning as a pedagogical tool for embedded system education. In: Proceedings of IEEE 3rd International Conference on Information Technology: Research and Education, Hsinchu, Taiwan, pp. 362–366 (2005)
9. Yadav, S.S., Xiahou, J.: Integrated project based learning in software engineering education. In: International Conference on Educational and Network Technology, Qinhuangdao, China, pp. 34–36 (2010)
10. Persistent Browser-Based Game – Defining a genre, http://www.pbbg.org
11. Browser Games List, http://www.browsergameslist.com
12. Pontes, A.A.A., Mendes Neto, F.M., de Campos, G.A.L.: Multiagent System for Detecting Passive Students in Problem-. Based Learning. Advances in Soft Computing 71, 165–172 (2010)
13. Dantas, A.R., Barros, M.O., Werner, C.M.L.: A Simulation-Based Game for Project Management Experimental Learning. In: Proceedings of SEKE 16th International Conference on Software Engineering and Knowledge Engineering, Banff, Canada, pp. 19–24 (2004)
14. Agarwal, R., Umphress, D.: A flexible model for simulation of software development process. In: 48th Annual Southeast Regional Conference, pp. 1–4. ACM, New York (2010)
15. Navarro, E.O., van der Hoek, A.: SimSE: An interactive simulation game for software engineering education. In: Proceedings of CATE 7th IASTED International Conference on Computers and Advanced Technology in Education, Kauai, Hawaii (2004)
16. Drappa, A., Ludewig, J.: Simulation in software engineering training. In: 22nd International Conference on Software Engineering, pp. 199–208. ACM, New York (2000)
17. Zeithaml, V.A., Berry, L.L., Parasuraman, A.: The Behavioral Consequences of Service Quality. The Journal of Marketing 60(2), 31–46 (1996)

Assessing the Performance of Virtual Teams with Intelligent Agents

Mauro Nunes and Henrique O'Neill

Instituto Universitário de Lisboa (ISCTE-IUL), ADETTI-IUL, Avª das Forças Armadas,
1649-026 Lisboa, Portugal
{Mauro.Nunes,Henrique.Oneill}@iscte.pt

Abstract. This study explores the application of intelligent agent technology to the assessment of the performance of virtual teams. From the followed methodology it was possible to 1) create a formal model of agent-mediated team performance, the aTeam model, 2) develop and validate a platform for carrying out experiments, the Promus agent system, 3) use that platform in a test case, the Promus Beer Game experiment, and 4) evaluate these outcomes by running the experiment on user trials. Results show that the intelligent agents are able to perceive and critically evaluate a virtual team's performance.

Keywords: Virtual organizations, virtual teams, team performance, intelligent agents.

1 Introduction

Throughout time new organizational types have emerged, usually in an attempt to acquire a competitive edge. These new types are frequently based on radically transformed organizational structures and have assumed different names in the literature, often with adjectives like extended, networked, virtual or smart. In one way or another, all these terms have been used to express not only the flexibility of the structural boundaries, but also a strategic orientation based on dynamically extending or reducing the structure vertically and horizontally, to compete globally and take advantage of business opportunities.

As Powell et al. [1] point out, many organizations also have changed internal work processes to a team-oriented process, e.g., in the software industry, as the scope and complexity of task demands exceed the capability of the individual to perform. Team-based work systems are recognized as creating a more productive, creative and individually rewarding work environment [2].

Townsend et al. [3] underline the importance of recapturing the productive potential of team-based work in radically transformed organizations where frequently co-workers are geographically and/or organizationally dispersed. The adoption of a team approach in this case provides the foundation for moving from conventional face-to-face teams to virtual teams [4].

Based on a comprehensive review of research about human performance in team settings, Paris et al. [5] maintains that there is still a need to "develop more dynamic

G.D. Putnik and M.M. Cruz-Cunha (Eds.): ViNOrg 2011, CCIS 248, pp. 62–69, 2012.
© Springer-Verlag Berlin Heidelberg 2012

measurement systems that allow for on-line assessment of teamwork," particularly because the long-established observational methods (i.e., behavioural checklists or videotaped observation, etc.) have been insufficient to measure teamwork processes [6]. These methods are labour intensive and time consuming, which decreases the speed of analysis and reporting of team performance, becoming unsuitable for large-scale team settings and to fully capture the dynamic nature of teamwork. We believe that intelligent agent technology may offer a value-added contribution to such a measurement system and even extend it, with proactive performance assessment, intelligent analysis and feedback. Researchers have applied agent technology to different areas of teamwork, such as teamwork simulation, team communication and team selection/formation.

It should be noted that our approach is focused on the synergistic relationship between intelligent agents and teams composed by humans. This relationship is established with the purpose of assessing the team's performance. Agents will primarily support teamwork, rather than aiding on individual tasks, following findings from Lenox et al. [7], which suggest that the direct support of teamwork is more beneficial than aiding individual tasks.

To critically assess a team's performance, agents require a set of team performance measures. However, these measures must be adequate and, preferably, linked with a team performance model. Building on research that examined dynamic modelling of team functioning, Marks et al. [8] proposed a time-based conceptual framework of team processes, which can help measure team performance. Agents should use performance measures based on process and outcome variables, which have to be introduced into the reasoning mechanism. This reasoning must take into account not only previously established standard measure values, but also values from existing performance data (history), which will act as a dynamic reference value.

Our study seeks to establish where and how can intelligent agents help assessing a virtual team's performance. We have formalized a possible answer to this question by purposing an agent mediated team performance model – aTeam [9]. We have also implemented the Promus agent system [10], a test bed for evaluating the aTeam model. This paper describes the results obtained when intelligent agents where used for evaluating team performance using an experiment based on the Beer Game.

1.1   Related Work

From the literature, it is possible to identify work related to this research. The work from Lenox et al. [7] has some similarities to the proposed, notably, the use of agents to support team performance. However, in their study, no geographically dispersed teams are considered, which decreases the communication and coordination effort. The agents also work as specialized facilitators rather than representing each member working as a team, circumscribing the work of the intelligent agents to support and promote teamwork dimensions (Team situation awareness, Support behaviour, Communication and Team initiative/leadership) in a target identification task.

The approach from Chung et al.[6] towards the development of a real-time measurement system for teamwork skills is also related to our approach. They focus their work on assessing team processes used by a group of individuals responsible for jointly constructing a knowledge map. Team processes were measured according to a taxonomy developed from previous work [see 11]; likewise, we also measure team processes according to a similar taxonomy [see 8]. However, their system was not proactive towards team performance, rather just an automatic measurement system. Although a team member identity was anonymous, they were all collocated at the same time, whereas in our study we are imposing team member time dispersion, as it is a key characteristic in a Virtual Team.

The work from Miller and Volz [12] also relates to our study, in the sense that they use a model of teamwork to identify weaknesses in team interaction skills in a human trainee within a team of agents. Although their study's subject is focused on training mixed teams of agents and humans, they state that it could also be used as a tracking or monitoring tool for human teams.

2   The Promus Agent System and the Beer Game Experiment

The agent platform was built based on the generic requirements gathered from past experience and the specific requirements for a team assessment tool from Paris et al. [5]. It presents a unique set of team-oriented features (based on the aTeam model) like capturing team performance metrics and proactive analysis of team performance. It measures both processes and outcomes in order to ensure consistently effective performance [13].

The Promus agent system is organized in two major components, the Promus Server and Promus Client. The Promus Server design follows an object-oriented approach based on software design patterns. Special care was given to the requirements of scalability, extensibility and cohesion.

Promus agents evaluate performance using relative concepts between the standard high, average and low concepts. Specifically, the agent reasoning is based on fuzzy logic with linguistic variables to evaluate the performance measures. It enabled the agents to show some intelligent behaviour by critically assessing performance within a broad spectrum of concepts to which they were not programmed.

The Beer Game was selected as a test case, inspired by the approach from Rafaeli and Ravid [14], which used the game with virtual teams, and Kimbrough et al. [15], which had intelligent agents playing the game. It was developed by the Systems Dynamics Group of the Sloan School at MIT and has been described by Sterman [16]. The game simulates a distribution system where the team's objective is maximizing net profit by managing inventories appropriately in the face of uncertain demand. Players are linked in a distribution chain, depending on each other for the right flow of orders and goods. Each team member takes a position (Retailer, Wholesaler, Distributor or Factory) in the supply chain.

This role-playing simulation of an industrial production and distribution system was originally created as a board game and used to introduce students of management to the concepts of economic dynamics and computer simulation.

Over the past years, computerised versions of the game have been created, seeking to enrich this system dynamics experience. The adapted version of this study follows the original game specification, but with some enhancements to make it more suitable for the study of virtual teams. The following enhancements have been made:

- Day duration – A simulated day lasts at most 2 minutes. If no play is made, then a standard play is assumed and the game moves to the next day;
- Chat meetings – Online players can create chat meetings to discuss game issues and strategy;
- Player offline – On each day, a player is randomly set as offline. It can only communicate through mail, which is only delivered on the next day. This is used to emphasize the effects of time dispersion, a common characteristic of a virtual team;
- Total cost summary – Players have access to a summary of current team accumulated costs and the costs from the remaining players in the supply chain;
- Demand with a seasonal pattern – A more complex demand pattern was used in order to make the game harder and foster team cooperation.

Following McGrath's [17] task classification schema, the Beer Game task can be qualified as a decision-making task. The classification schema proposes that any group task can be categorized as belonging to one of four main types. These main task types, related to each other as the four quadrants of a circumference structure, are identified by the main performance process that each entails: to generate (ideas or plans), to choose (a correct answer or a preferred solution), to negotiate (conflicting views or interests), and to execute (in competition with an opponent or external performance standards). A decision-making task falls in the second quadrant, Choose.

The original Beer Game task is different from the traditional group decision tasks. In these tasks, each player is limited to its echelon on the supply chain, with little knowledge of what is happening up or down the chain. This was suitable for the system dynamics research, mostly because it enables one to study the economic effects of oscillation (large amplitude fluctuation in orders and inventories), amplification (amplitude and variance increase steadily through the supply chain) and phase-lag (order rate peaks later through the supply chain).

In the adaptation for the Promus Beer Game, players are not circumscribed to the echelon on the supply chain. This task can be viewed from two different perspectives:

1. Individual perspective – The goal is for the players to provide the best answer to demand while keeping a low inventory;
2. Group perspective – Players are linked in a distribution chain, depending on each other for the right flow of orders and goods. So, a holistic approach to the distribution problem is required.

Hence, in the Promus Beer Game experiment, there is a higher requirement for teamwork, only made possible through the introduced communication mechanisms (nonexistent in the original experiment).

The game interface was divided in two parts (Fig. 1). The part above the tabbed control provides the player with situational awareness, by displaying the current status of the remaining players (Playing, Offline or Disconnected), an event log, current available communications (chat and/or mail), the role in the supply chain and the current cost distribution.

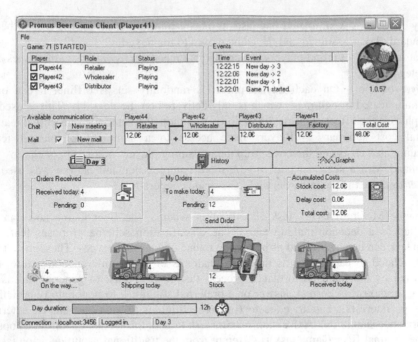

Fig. 1. Promus Beer Game main interface

3   Experiment Results

The Promus Beer Game implementation was used in four trials. The first three trials consisted of a challenge for undergraduate (Management) students, where in each trial, 20 participants in five teams played the game at the same time (60 participants in total). These trials were run on the same network of the Promus Server. The last trial consisted of a challenge for postgraduate (Logistics) students and had 12 participants in three teams. This trial was run on a remote location outside the Promus Server network.

Each trial was expected to take on average 1h10m (36 game days), and although the players were in the same room they were not allowed to engage in oral communication. Teams were randomly assembled for the duration of the trial. It was not possible to control if team members already knew each other or had previously worked together as a team. It was the first time that participants played the Beer Game.

3.1   Analysis

Promus Server successfully supported the trials, processing more than 22,500 system messages, generating 12,825 performance data records and 2,192 game plays.

The next table (table 1) sums up the performance evaluation of each game for the different trials. Trial t1 was used for platform training and fine-tuning. The number of performance warnings is shown at day 18 (halfway through the game) and day 36 in order to perceive performance evolution.

Table 1. Performance warnings per game

		#Warnings		Total Cost		
Trial	Game	Day 18	Day 36	Day 18	Day 36	Evaluation
t1	20	285		6.320,0 €		Training
	53	294		3.487,5 €		Training
	54	287		4.908,0 €		Training
	55	309		3.707,0 €		Training
	56	265		3.450,0 €		Training
t2	65	215		6.514,5 €	41.659,50 €	
	66	299	599	7.572,0 €	87.686,50 €	OK
	67	263	508	6.116,0 €	21.664,50 €	
t3	80	321	672	3.642,0 €	11.786,00 €	NOK
	81	271	611	3.366,5 €	24.171,50 €	
	82	261	561	5.585,0 €	18.079,50 €	
	83	250	582	3.986,0 €	17.789,50 €	
	84	266	501	7.608,0 €	41.965,50 €	
t4	85	321	686	5.154,5 €	24.217,00 €	
	86	320	675	5.601,0 €	21.815,00 €	
	87	341	721	5.385,0 €	47.257,50 €	OK
	88	280	611	3.785,5 €	18.527,50 €	
	89	322	641	8.992,0 €	18.636,00 €	

For trial t2 and t4 the fuzzy evaluation was able to reflect the team's performance by having a higher number of warnings on the games that had the highest total cost.

However, for trial t3 game 80 gets the highest number of warnings instead of game 84. If the outliers (games 80 and 84) were not considered then the performance evaluation would be correct. Looking closer at the performance measures from both games, this may be an example where flawed processes occasionally result in successful outcomes. Meaning that despite having better team processes in game 84, the followed game strategy did not achieve the best results. On the other hand, we also believe that the reasoning and the metrics capturing process can be improved.

3.2   Evaluation

The Promus agents are able to evaluate a team's performance based on the captured performance data. The performance evaluation process, using fuzzy logic, was able to reflect some of the team's performance traces, particularly in the form of performance warnings. While this was acceptable on a simple task like the Beer Game, it is not necessarily the behaviour in a real life situation. Even so, there is some evidence to show that agents are able to evaluate team performance as formalized in the aTeam model.

The Promus agent's performance feedback, based on the aTeam model using a drill-down approach, successfully helped break down a team's performance into a set of individual performances and specific performance measures. This has helped not only to identify potentially underperforming teams but also to trace back to the performance of team members, giving some evidence that the agent's performance feedback can help in determining potential underperforming teams. It also reveals that the quality of the performance feedback is very important, i.e., although a consolidated view of the results is necessary, it must also be possible to disaggregate the results into the respective contributing parts.

3.3   Limitations

This experiment has some limitations that must be considered before generalising the results. First, the experiment domain and test case do not take into account all the variables and constraints that are present in real life virtual team settings. This simplification however, enables the analysis to focus on the key aspects required by this study.

Having only students as participants in the experiment can also be considered a limitation, in the sense that they do not fully represent the target population for this case study. Conversely, trying to fully capture all the characteristics of a virtual team would be extremely difficult, if not impossible. For the purpose of this study, the sample used provided enough information, validating the research framework and proposed model.

4   Conclusions

Even though technology has been used extensively within virtual team settings, it still remains passive towards team performance. Hence, there is a need to adapt automation to team settings, not only automating the synthesis and interpretation of performance data, but also better measurement tools that can cope with high levels of complexity. This is where the application of the emerging agent technology may help.

Intelligent agent technology has been very helpful in different fields. However, it was unclear where and how this technology could be applied to the problem of managing team performance. This was the motivation for this study.

Unlike normal performance evaluation tools, the Promus agent platform conducts performance evaluation, using fuzzy logic, in real time, providing performance warnings while the task is being carried out. This potentially provides a higher degree of control to a team manager (a target client for this type of application), who can perceive how a team is currently performing and likely to perform in the future, hence acting almost as an early warning system.

Practical applications of this research can be used, for instance, in the evaluation of the performance of operators in a Call Center, where agents monitor the performance of each team of operators and provide real-time feedback to team managers, not only with potentially underperforming operators, but also with the work patterns of those that are better performing.

Acknowledgments. This work has been partially supported by ADETTI-IUL.

References

1. Powell, A., Piccoli, G., Ives, B.: Virtual Teams: A Review of Current Literature and Directions for Future Research. Database for Advances in Information Systems 35(6) (2004)
2. Sundstrom, E.: Supporting work team effectiveness: best management practices for fostering high performance. Jossey-Bass (1999)
3. Townsend, A.M., DeMarie, S.M., Hendrickson, A.R.: Virtual teams: Technology and the workplace of the future. Academy of Management Executive 12, 17–29 (1998)
4. Guzzo, R.A., Dickson, M.W.: TEAMS IN ORGANIZATIONS: Recent Research on Performance and Effectiveness. Annual Review of Psychology 47, 307–338 (1996)
5. Paris, C.R., Salas, E., Cannon-Bowers, J.A.: Teamwork in multi-person systems: a review and analysis. Ergonomics 43, 1052–1075 (2000)
6. Chung, G.K.W.K., O'Neil, H.F., Herl, H.E.: The use of computer-based collaborative knowledge mapping to measure team processes and team outcomes. Computers in Human Behavior 15, 463–493 (1999)
7. Lenox, T., Hahn, S., Lewis, M., Roth, E.: Improving performance: Should we support individuals or teams? In: Human Factors and Ergonomics Society 43rd Annual Meeting (HFES), Santa Monica, CA, pp. 223–227 (1999)
8. Marks, M.A., Mathieu, J.E., Zaccaro, S.J.: A temporally based framework and taxonomy of team processes. The Academy of Management Review 26, 356–376 (2001)
9. Nunes, M., O'Neill, H.: aTeam- Agent Mediated Team Performance Model. In: IADIS International Conference WWW/Internet, ICWI 2004, Madrid, Spain (2004)
10. Nunes, M., O'Neill, H.: The Promus Agent System, a tool to assess a virtual team's performance. In: International Conference Applied Computing, pp. 417–424. IADIS, Algarve (2005)
11. O'Neil, H.F.J., Chung, G., Brown, R.: Use of networked simulations as a context to measure team competencies. In: O'Neil, H.F.J. (ed.) Workforce Readiness: Competencies and Assessment, pp. 411–452. Erlbaum, Mahwah (1997)
12. Miller, M.S., Volz, R.A.: Training for Teamwork. In: 5th World Multi-Conference on Systemics, Cybernetics and Informatics, Orlando, Florida, pp. 52–57 (2001)
13. Meyers, C.: How the right team measures help teams excel. Harvard Business Review, 95–103 (1994)
14. Rafaeli, S., Ravid, G.: Information sharing as enabler for the virtual team: an experimental approach to assessing the role of electronic mail in disintermediation. Information Systems Journal 13, 191–206 (2003)
15. Kimbrough, S.O., Wu, D.J., Zhong, F.: Computers play the beer game: can artificial agents manage supply chains? Decision Support Systems 33, 323–333 (2002)
16. Sterman, J.D.: Modeling managerial behavior: Misperceptions of feedback in a dynamic decision making experiment. Management Science 35, 321–339 (1989)
17. McGrath, J.E.: Groups: Interaction and Performance. Prentice Hall, Englewood Cliffs (1984)

Combining Real and Virtual Research Environments through the Internet of Things

Dieter Uckelmann and Bernd Scholz-Reiter

University of Bremen, Hochschulring 20
28359 Bremen
{uck,bsr}@biba.uni-bremen.de

Abstract. Virtual Research Environments (VRE) have been researched in detail in the past years. However, the connection to and between real resources has not been focused on in detail. Connecting real and virtual worlds has been a major research topic though in the field of logistics. The Internet of Things has become a synonym for combining both worlds in logistics and beyond. It seems a straight forward approach to relate both fields of research and find synergies for a distributed logistic research lab environment. In a case scenario of the LogDynamics Lab at the University of Bremen the technical requirements of distributed logistic research communities and infrastructures that combine both, virtual and real world, are investigated.

Keywords: Virtual Research Communities, Internet of Things, Logistic Labs, Sustainable Business Models for Research Communities.

1 Introduction and Problem Statement

The access to VRE promises to address the dynamic changes in [1]:

- globalization and increased researcher mobility
- multidisciplinary nature of research
- changing roles of public and private research
- increased volume of research data
- changing nature of network technologies
- evolution of urban and work spaces development

However, in lab-based logistic research, there is a need to access real logistic objects and environments, including conveyors, robots, and different mobile technologies. Consequently, there are numerous research labs for logistics, Radio-frequency Identification (RFID) and the Internet of Things around the world that have built up considerable testing and demonstration infrastructures (see, e.g., www.autoidlabs.org, www.grfla.org). The necessary investments can be quite huge. The European Centre for Automatic Identification and Data Capture (AIDC) technologies, for example, received £5 million funding to set up a state-of-the-art technology demonstration area [2]. Investments in university research centers may be smaller, but there are ongoing investments through research projects that add to the pool of available technologies

G.D. Putnik and M.M. Cruz-Cunha (Eds.): ViNOrg 2011, CCIS 248, pp. 70–79, 2012.

over time. Unfortunately though, the usage time frame is quite often restricted to the run-time of a project. To maximize the value of the investment it would be necessary to integrate the acquired infrastructure in new research projects as well as in lectures. However, more often than not, the usage of the infrastructure is discontinued or slowly phased out after the end of the project. This trend is supported by time limited contracts for researchers that will usually leave the university as soon as they have received their PhD – thus taking part of the knowledge of how to operate the systems with them. Technicians with long-term contracts to even out this 'brain drain' are rare in times of limited university budgets.

At the same time, research in real environments represents only a small part of the overall research that is done in research projects. Fundamental research, process analysis, simulation and other methodologies are used upfront before trials, pilots, and demonstrations can be set up in the real environment. As a consequence, the internal degree of utilization of these expensive infrastructures again is quite low. Then again, there are researchers that do not have access to testing infrastructures at all. This may be the case for smaller universities and colleges that do not have the financial resources as well as for researchers from non-technical disciplines that do not have the technical expertise to install and operate these infrastructures.

New and different approaches need to be found to supply a higher degree of utilization for these infrastructures. In general, there are three different options how external researchers can access lab infrastructures. First, they may visit the lab facilities for the time of research. Second, mobile infrastructures may be shipped to the researcher. Third, remote access to the lab facilities may be given to the researcher, which is an option that aligns well with the concept of VRE – that is to use online tools for collaboration.

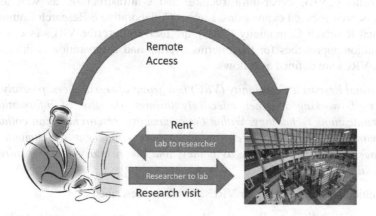

Fig. 1. Possible options to access distant lab infrastructures

Virtualization of physical research environments allows other researchers to access these available infrastructures, thus leading to better utilization while offering new opportunities for collaboration and synergies in VREs. Connecting virtual and real worlds is not a demand from research communities – it is a research domain that has become popular in logistics and beyond with the concept of the Internet of Things

[3], [4]. One of the core features of the Internet of Things is to provide visibility of the nature, status and location of objects, which may be used for VREs as well, specifically in logistics. Therefore, in this paper, a domain-specific platform to connect things for logistic research collaboration is favored for human-to-machine and machine-to-machine communication, whereas for human-to-human communication generic solutions may be used.

The Internet of Things by definition is not limited to internal (Intranet) or closed (Extranet) applications – it offers it services to a wider community [5]. A VRE in logistics should offer the same level of openness to other researchers. This does require open Internet-based interfaces as well as simple user agreements. Otherwise, access to real infrastructures requires financial support to operate, maintain and grow these infrastructures. While initial concepts and set-up can be established through public research funding, there is a need for a sustainable non-profit business model. This can be based on pay-per-use as well as on subscription models for remote access. E-Billing solutions offer possibilities to support both concepts in a flexible way.

In the LogDynamics Lab first steps towards a VRE have been taken through the integration of virtual control mechanisms, the integration of the EPCglobal Architecture [6] and e-billing mechanisms [7] to allow subscription as well as pay-per-use-based methods for accessing infrastructures, mobile objects and information. These achievements will be measured against the requirements for VREs.

2   Virtual Research Environments

Generic terms, such as Virtual Organization (VO), Collaborative Virtual Environments (CVE), cyber-infrastructure, and e-infrastructure, as well as more specific research-focused expressions, such as Collaborative e-Research Communities and Virtual Research Community (VRC), are used to describe VREs (see, e.g. [1]). The definition approaches for these terms overlap and a separation is difficult. For example, VRCs are defined as follows:

> *"A Virtual Research Community (VRC) is a group of researchers, possibly widely dispersed, working together effectively through the use of information and communications technology. Within the community, researchers can collaborate, communicate, share resources, access remote equipment or computers and produce results as effectively as if they, and the resources they require, were physically co-located"[1].*

The definition resembles those for VREs, which are described as:

> *"a set of online tools and other network resources and technologies interoperating with each other to support or enhance the processes of a wide range of research practitioners within and across disciplinary and institutional boundaries. A key characteristic of a VRE is that it facilitates collaboration amongst researchers and research teams providing them with more effective means of collaboratively collecting, manipulating and managing data, as well as collaborative knowledge creation" [8].*

While VRCs have a user focus, VREs are focused on the necessary infrastructures. Both definitions stress the importance of online tools and the collaboration – the willingness to cooperate is implied – across boundaries, such as disciplines, public and private institutions, and borders. Consequently, there has been a research focus for VRE on human interaction and connected IT-infrastructures (see Fig. 2). Some of the objectives that VREs aim to support include data production, data retrieval, data analysis, collaborative production of research outputs (e.g., publications), communication (e.g., with Web 2.0 functionality), research administration and project management [8].

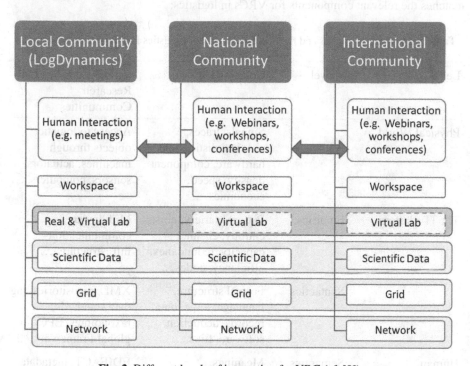

Fig. 2. Different levels of integration for VRC (cf. [9])

The lower three levels in Fig. 2., including the network, the grid (see, e.g. [9]) and the sharing of scientific data, have been united in research projects on VREs to achieve economies of scale and efficiency gains (cf. [10]). The fourth level includes physical infrastructures that go beyond network, grid, and data. A web-based application for accessing and controlling physical infrastructures has already been introduced in 1993[11]. However, the combination of multiple infrastructures in logistics labs requires additional efforts concerning integration and synchronization of machines. In logistics research we see an imbalance of research units that have access to a 'real' lab infrastructure and those that do not have direct access, yet could be enabled through corresponding virtual interfaces (see Fig. 2.). This approach fits well to the general concept of a VRC as it enables sharing resources through remote access *"to produce results as effectively as if they, and the resources they require, were physically co-located"* [1].

Information and communication technologies, therefore, play the most important role in VRCs. However, the requirements for these technologies in logistic VRCs need to be researched in more detail. Different levels of information technologies have already been researched in the field of semiotics long ago. Morris [12] distinguished between syntactics, semantics and pragmatics. These levels were extended in the field of organizational semiotics by Stamper [13], and Liu [14]. Stamper added physics, empirics, and social world and thus provided a theoretical foundation for the design and usage of computer-based information systems. Table 1 lists the six levels of semiotics as defined by Morris [12] and Stamper [13], and matches the relevant components for VRCs in logistics:

Table 1. Matching semiotics and the needs for a Virtual Logistics Lab Research Community

Level	Sub-level	Content [13]	Virtual Logistics Lab Research Communities
Physical World		Signals, traces, physical distinctions, hardware, component density, speed, economics, ...	Access to logistic objects through machines, actuators, sensors, computers, ...
The IT platform	Empirics	Pattern, variety, noise, entropy, channel capacity, redundancy, efficiency, codes, ...	Middleware, communication infrastructure, ...
	Syntactics	Formal structure, language, logic, data, records, deduction, software, files, ...	XML, repositories, tag data standards, taxonomies, EPC-global Framework, ...
Human information functions	Semantics	Meanings, propositions, validity, truth, signification, denotations, ...	EDIFACT, metadata, ontologies, semantic Web, ...
	Pragmatics	Intentions, communication, conversations, negotiations, ...	Web 2.0, Webinars, personalized information, financials, ...
	Social world	Beliefs, expectations, commitments, contracts, law, culture, ...	Contracts, legal frameworks, policies, user agreements, co-creation, trust, ...

The physical world relates to machines, actuators, sensors, and computers. Data (signals) are produced and communicated through corresponding middleware components. On the empirical level data is cleansed, for example through de-coding, filtering or redundancy reduction. On the syntactical level multiple tools are already available, such as XML, repositories, and more. Semantics remain an open issue for the VRCs, even though in some disciplines vocabularies and ontologies exist. On the level of pragmatics intentions need to be expressed and human interaction needs to be supported through corresponding online technologies, such as webinars, research blog and portal infrastructures. Existing systems should be integrated to avoid redundancy. Personalized and context-aware information is necessary to reduce the *available information* to *information as needed* in specific situations. Finally, the social level, according to Stamper [13], includes beliefs, expectations, commitments, contracts, law and culture. It is obvious that there are formal as well as informal aspects that need to be addressed. The formal part may be addressed through defined terms of use and information sharing contracts. The informal part is more difficult to address. Ethics in research need to be respected.

While these six levels need to be addressed in a holistic approach towards VRCs, there will be a focus on the specific topics for integrating lab infrastructures into a VRC, as the other issues have already been addressed in corresponding research on VRCs and VREs.

3   Technical Requirements

A closer look on the technical requirements for integration of real infrastructures is needed. There are three main topics that need to be considered: means for virtual access to the lab infrastructures, identification and tracking of logistic objects that move through these structures, and last, not least a tool to enable financial compensation for the maintenance and further development of these infrastructures. These three topics do not only provide the necessary fundament for virtual lab based research – they also represent a research topic in themselves. Additionally, there is a need to take generic requirements for VREs into account, such as user-friendliness and modularity. In order to set up a corresponding demonstrator at the LogDynamics Lab in Bremen, the mentioned three core-functionalities are being implemented and evaluated in respect to the generic requirements.

In logistics research the infrastructures are often referred to as 'labs'. Fortunately, the LogDynamics Lab at the University of Bremen is equipped with a large logistics infrastructure funded by the DFG, one of the largest research funding organizations in Germany. The virtualization of these labs requires remote control capacities, which are difficult to setup as harmonized interfaces to machines and testing equipment are missing. Industry effort for standardization such as promoted through the OPC Foundation (www.opcfoundation.org) and the Association for Standardization of Automation and Measuring Systems (www.asam.net) have failed so far to get broader support from research communities. One reason for this is the complexity of these infrastructures that may be appropriate for long-term production scenarios but not for agile research pilots. Lightweight interfaces are needed for researchers to enable quick developments and integrations. This is even more important for researchers from non-engineering disciplines that want to utilize these infrastructures for their research. Lightweight interfaces, such as RESTful APIs, are needed to allow researchers to access high-end infrastructure even in time-limited, short projects. Poor human-computer interfaces have been the biggest obstacle so far to motivate human to participate in VRCs [1]. Adaptability is another important design aspect that needs to be considered to address the unpredictable nature of research [15].

Within the Virtual Logistics Lab (VLL) – a student project at the University of Bremen – a flexible application has been developed that allows accessing, operating and controlling the core infrastructures of the LogDynamics Lab through corresponding web services. As standards for corresponding control software products' in remotely controlled laboratories are missing [16] a new web-based control interface has been developed as part of the VLL. The project has a two year time frame and will finish in July 2011. Experiments, such as RFID read tests, can be conducted with no need for the user to be present at the lab. VLL provides a flexible IT-infrastructure that allows remote control of machines through individual plug-ins that can be loaded and operated through web services. Currently, plug-ins for the automated buffer storage, the conveyor, a palletizer, an edgeware server (REVA) connecting to the RFID-infrastructure, a labeling machine, and a weighing and volume measuring device exist. The real experiments can be monitored via 5 web-cams.

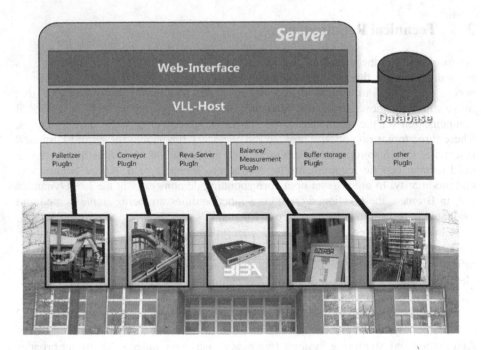

Fig. 3. The VLL architecture

Starting in summer a follow-up of the VLL project will focus on further integration with community supporting technologies. This will include an open REST API on the one hand as well as a community database on the other that makes the experimental data available to the research community to avoid redundant tests and to provide research data for further analysis.

In order to identify and track the logistic objects within this VRE, the EPCglobal Network is employed. The EPCglobal Network is one of the most promising approaches in the Internet of Things that builds on unique identification through RFID, integrates existing applications and provides access through query interfaces to relevant business data.

Finally, an e-billing infrastructure has been set up, that allows to bill any EPCglobal query [17], thus providing a pay-per-query mechanism. A combined login procedure for the EPCglobal query interface and the billing system is used to enable and simplify billable queries. In a further approach, this e-billing component will also be used in combination with the VLL to bill usage of the lab infrastructures in the future. A *"climate of trust amongst distributed members of research communities"* [1] is seen as a core requirement for VRCs, but trust does not pay for the maintenance and ongoing development of lab infrastructures. Means of balancing cost and benefits, such as the provided billing solution, are needed. Table 2 compares the current achievements with the generic requirements for VREs as required by Campolargo [9]:

Table 2. Compliance analysis of current achievements with generic requirements for VREs

Generic requirement [9]	VLL	EPCglobal Network (Fosstrak)	e-Billing (jBilling)
User friendly	Yes, Web-based	Yes, combined login procedure	
Adds value to the practice of the end users	Yes, access to remote logistic infrastructures, no need to setup and maintain own lab infrastructure	Yes, capture and query interfaces (information generation and access), no need to setup and maintain own EPCglobal infrastructure	Yes, pay-per-use vs. pay for infrastructure and maintenance
Modular	Yes, layered concept, separate plug-ins	Yes, similar to internet servers	No
Interoperable	Yes, may be used for other lab infrastructures	Yes, interoperable by design with other instances and business applications	Yes, e.g., with payment processors

Table 2. (*Continued*)

Extensible	Yes, extensible through plug-ins	Yes, but needs to go through standardization process	Yes, different options (e.g., rules)
Supportive of component orchestration as much as possible	Yes, scenario editor planned, REST API planned	Currently limited, e.g., only RFID and EPCglobal specifications allowed	Limited (private offering)
Distributed	Yes, possible through web-based concept	Yes, distributed environment by design (currently 2 instances running at the LogDynamics Lab)	Yes, partner concepts supported
Based on open standards	Partially (e.g., no support of OPC UA)	Yes, open source (Fosstrak), IP, standardized through GS1	Yes, open source (jBilling), Web-based
Secure	Yes, simple authentication	Yes, simple authentication	Yes, simple authentication
Customizable	Yes, through scenarios (scenario editor planned)	Yes (should be integrated with VLL scenarios)	Yes (should be integrated with VLL scenarios)
Compatible with other widely-used and -deployed systems	Yes (JAVA, Apache Wicket, Eclipse, trac, Extrem Programming)	Yes (MySQL, Tomcat)	Yes (MySQL, Tomcat)

4   Conclusion

Research on VREs and the Internet of Things have taken separate routes in the past. For virtualization of (logistic) lab infrastructures, it is a valid approach to combine both concepts. The EPCglobal Architecture allows to identify objects and to link additional information. Though this is still far from a holistic approach towards the Internet of Things, it is a first step towards increased visibility in logistic flows for VREs. Further functionality towards a VRE has been added at the LogDynamics Lab through the VLL project that allows remote control of the installed infrastructures and through billing integration to enable pay-per-use and subscription models to a logistic VRE. Comparing the current achievements with the generic requirements for VREs, it has been shown that most requirements have been addressed or will be addressed in the future. However, the willingness to pay for access to a logistic VRE will be crucial for sustainable operation of the virtual LogDynamics Lab.

References

1. OSI: Report of the Working Group on Virtual Research Communities for the OSI e-Infrastructure Steering Group,
   http://www.nesc.ac.uk/documents/OSI/vrc.pdf
2. Davies, M.: The Centre and what it is about,
   http://www.scnf.org.uk/members/presentations/shefoct06/the_centre_and_what_its_about.ppt
3. Fleisch, E., Mattern, F. (eds.): Das Internet der Dinge: Ubiquitous Computing und RFID in der Praxis: Visionen, Technologien, Anwendungen, Handlungsanleitungen. Springer, Berlin (2005)
4. Uckelmann, D., Harrison, M., Michahelles, F. (eds.): Architecting the Internet of Things. Springer, Berlin (2011)
5. Uckelmann, D., Harrison, M., Michahelles, F.: An Architectural Approach towards the Future Internet of Things. In: Uckelmann, D., Michahelles, F., Harrison, M. (eds.) Architecting the Internet of Things, pp. 1–24. Springer, Berlin (2011)
6. GS1: The EPCglobal architecture framework,
   http://www.epcglobalinc.org/standards/architecture/architecture_1_3-framework-20090319.pdf
7. Uckelmann, D.: A Billing integrated EPCglobal Network – Synchronisation of material, information and financial flows. In: Internet of Things 2010, Tokyo (2010)
8. Fraser, M.: Virtual Research Environments programme: Phase 2 roadmap,
   http://www.grids.ac.uk/twiki/pub/EResearch/VreRoadmap2/JISC-BP-VRE2-final.pdf
9. Campolargo, M.: 1st Virtual Forum on Global Research Communities,
   http://www.slidefinder.net/1/1st_Virtual_Forum_Global_Research/01_Mario_Campolargo_Global_Event/28807570
10. Bird, I., Jones, B., Kee, K.: The Organization and Management of Grid Infrastructures. Computer 42(1), 36–46 (2009)
11. Cox, M., Baruch, J.: Robotic Telescopes: An Interactive Exhibit on the World-Wide Web. In: 2nd Int. Conf. World-Wide Web, Chicago (1994)
12. Morris, C.: Foundations of the Theory of Signs. University of Chicago Press, Chicago (1938)
13. Stamper, R.: Information in Business and Administrative Systems. John Wiley and Sons, New York (1973)
14. Liu, K.: Semiotics in Information System Engineering. Cambridge Univeryity Press, New York (2000)
15. Dovey, M.: The Future of Virtual Research Environments. In: Dutton, W., Jeffreys, P. (eds.) World Wide Research: Reshaping the Sciences and Humanities, pp. 295–298. The MIT Press, Cambridge (2010)
16. Gröber, S., Vetter, M., Eckert, B., Jodl, H.-J.: Experimenting from a distance – remotely controlled laboratory (RCL). European Journal of Physics 28, 127–141 (2007)
17. Uckelmann, M., Harrison, M.: Integrated billing mechanisms in the Internet of Things to support information sharing and enable new business opportunities. International Journal of RF Technologies: Research and Applications 2(2), 73–90 (2010)

The Relevance of Results in Interpretive Research in Information Systems and Technology

Isabel Ferreira[1,2], Sílvia Ferreira[2], and Isabel Ramos[2,3]

[1] Polytechnic Institute of Cávado and Ave, Barcelos, Portugal
iferreira@ipca.pt
[2] Centro Algoritmi, University of Minho, Guimarães, Portugal
silviaggf@gmail.com
[3] University of Minho, Information Systems Department, Azurém
4800-058, Guimarães, Portugal
iramos@dsi.uminho.pt

Abstract. The rigor and relevance of the results is central to the process of scientific investigation, even in areas where the practice prevails, as is the case of the scientific area of information systems and technology. This issue is also particularly relevant when the underlying epistemological orientation is the interpretivism. Based on a literature review focused on interpretive research in the field of information systems and technology, we find that the generalization of research resulting under the interpretive paradigm are valid and are not exclusive to the positivist orientation. This paper explores the importance of interpretative research in the information systems and technology field. As a result we discuss the different perspectives around the generalization and its interpretation in an interpretative research, supporting the investigator in the grounds of validation of their results.

Keywords: Paradigms of science, interpretivism in IST research, results relevance, generalization.

1   Introduction

The rigor and usefulness of the researched topics are central in scientific research beyond the research process itself. In this sense, these concerns must be managed and aligned with the philosophical assumptions that best fit the way the investigator observes the regularities of the world. We must therefore reflect on the paradigm of the science underlying the research study.

The reflection on these issues assumes utmost importance in areas like engineering, where most of the time the phenomena associated with the use and development of information systems and technologies (IST) are treated. Here, the practice prevails, but the key to that scientific and technological knowledge to be produced is the definition of the research process based on a paradigm of science.

In recent years, scientific studies of the IST field were dominated by the positivist and engineering paradigms. However, the emergence of new research topics that can

G.D. Putnik and M.M. Cruz-Cunha (Eds.): ViNOrg 2011, CCIS 248, pp. 80–89, 2012.
© Springer-Verlag Berlin Heidelberg 2012

only be fully understood if studied in depth and for longer periods of time, such as organizational and systems design, organizational intervention, management information systems, technology development and their social implications, led to a paradigm shift and emergence of interpretivism in IST field research.

In this paper, presented to the First International Conference on Networked and Virtual Organizations, Emergent Technologies and Tools, we intended to call attention for the study of technological factors inserted in a social context and its impact on the individual, organization and society. These observations are crucial since most of the success factors, or failure, of technology projects are due to human factors rather than technological factors. In sum, we intend to reflect on a number of key issues that render the interpretive research relevant, as a philosophical orientation in the context of IST.

To achieve this objective we defined the following main questions to guide the literature review: (i) What is the influence of the interpretive paradigm research in IST field?; (ii) What issues arise when trying to reflect on the epistemological assumptions underlying the interpretive approach?; (iii) Will the Information Systems and Technologies become an emerging thinking? Emergency in what sense?; (iv)What is the relevance of interpretive research results?

To answer these questions, we started by conducting an exhaustive bibliography of the authors most relevant to the scientific area, identifying curriculum authors, books, book chapters, papers presented at conferences and published articles in scientific journals: David Avison, Robert Galliers, Michael Myers, Geoff Walsham, John Mingers, Richard Baskerville, Rudy Hirschheimer. This literature review was conducted by Scopus, Google Scholar, ISI Web of Knowledge. The documents research was made through the UM catalog, b-on; RCAAP, IEEExplore, Colcat.

Then, based on this extensive bibliography, we proceeded to the identification of the proceeds, the most relevant articles, identifying all those whose title refers to the following combination of words "research paradigms" and / or "information systems and technologies".

In section 2 we present the scientific area of IST as scientific and technological knowledge that emerged from the literature review performed. In Section 3, we discuss aspects related to the IST field as a convergence of knowledge and knowledge network. In Section 4, the discussion goes around the subject of IST field, as a knowledge network. The interpretivism as a research paradigm in the IST field is presented in Section 5. The generalization of results in interpretive research is discussed in Section 6. Finally, we present the conclusions.

2   IST, a Scientific and Technological Knowledge

The advance of science is dependent on how scientists communicate research results effectively to their peers, and, secondly, the willingness of academics not to apply these research results in developing new technologies and practices [1]. Research is therefore one of the most demanding resource of scientific endeavour. Communicating the results is the most extensive part of it. The final result of the activity designated as dissemination of scientific knowledge reflects the views of the scientific results published, hoping that they are applied downstream, helping to achieve a better quality of life, solving the world's problems.

Science and technology are, thus, an inter-performing cycle, feeding back to each other. The scientist makes intelligible what does the technician, and this, in turn, gives the science instruments and evidences [2].

Research and development (R & D) are human activities that aim to create, expand the frontiers of existing scientific knowledge with the goal of improving action on the world, resulting in a proceeding scientific and light of a particular epistemological orientation [3], [4], [5], [6], [7].

The understanding of science should not be limited and, according to Feibleman [8], we can't assume that science means technology. While science is the scientific knowledge about the regularities of the phenomena of the world determined by a particular paradigm of science (positivism or interpretivism), technology is knowledge on how to act in the world (know-how). The technology is the modus operandi, represented by a group of scientists interested in solving a problem set by the application of theory to practice [8]. According Fleibleman [8], though historically advances in technology have been made without the contributions of science, currently, the technology must be understood as an additional step of applied science, but without meaning to Skolimowski [9] a branch of applied science. It is therefore important to know the progress of technology so you can understand what technology is and, then, understand its meaning, the philosophy of technology (the structure and nature of technology).

Nowadays, technology has emancipated itself in a semi-autonomous cognitive domain. There are many connections between science and technology, but this system of inter-relationships should not be construed as a full dependency. Epistemologically, technology is one way of human knowledge and, accordingly, one must know the forms of relations with other forms of knowledge and not understanding it as dependent ways [9].

In Principia Cybernetica Web (2010), technology is the application of scientific knowledge to build or improve the infrastructure of agriculture, industry and daily life of man, i.e., an action on the world. According Feibleman [8], technology is man's reaction to the nature and circumstances. Produces and applies knowledge of tasks or situations in order to create effective artefacts that are both created and studied, the scientists can contribute to each activity - the design science, an important part of scientific knowledge, focused on the design of artefacts (constructs, models, methods and instantiations) to achieve goals of improving human conditions [10]. We are facing an understanding of technology as a result of scientific technological knowledge, explained by scientific theories and that scientific research can improve practices and real world problems and work [10].

Speaking about the IST, Lee and Baskerville [6], state that this is not just a science but a profession. By the early 80´s, last century, was considered a design activity applied to other disciplines of reference, or contributors disciplines as designation by Lee [11]. Today, despite some problems associated, asserts itself as a discipline of design science, first in a conventional perspective, consuming theories and methods of reference disciplines (contributors disciplines), but have also established itself a reference discipline [12].

At this stage of discussion, the important thing, according Hirscheim and Klein [13], there should be no disconnect between the world of professionals and the academic world. This concern is shared by Avison *et al* [14] [15], since they believe in the importance of practical research in IST and the impact of IST research in the practice.

3   IST, a Knowledge Network

IST, in terms of scientific area, are, according to McLean [16] and Avison *et al* [15], an inter-disciplinary knowledge, where the contributions to its development come from different disciplines, ranging from computer science, software engineering, organization science, management, economics, ethics, sociology, psychology, statistics, medicine, semiotics, systems thinking, among others. These contributions are identified as the foundation of the IS [14], [11].

According to the tenets of the emerging thinking presented by Santos [17], the IST field presents itself as an emerging thinking, the result of a convergence of knowledge. Baskerville and Myers [12], refers to this movement as a discipline of law (a reference to other discipline areas, particularly those who contributed to the maturity of the IS). The emerging term for these authors is understood not as the convergence of knowledge, but knowledge as a result of input from other areas of knowledge, forming a network of interpretivism emergence of IS research. Walsham [18] refers to this movement as a network of interpretivism in IS.

In recent years, there has also been an increase in contributions from management to IS research while there is a reduction in the focus of study by computer science. This trend shows the evolution of the research focus of the IS. The context of the IS is broad and includes important issues beyond the technology itself to include IS implementation, use, effectiveness, efficiency and their organizational and social impacts [15].

The technology is a significant change agent enabling organizational and individual quality within the organization. Rarely is the factor that limits the design of information systems or the cause of failure. The most likely factors to cause damage, or source of success, such as strategy, communication, control, users resistance are human factors and not technological factors [14].

This broader perspective of the object of study of the IS (the technological factors to human factors) is based on the understanding that this area of study influences and is influenced by a set of interrelated disciplines, the result, also, of the origin and academic formation of their researchers, embracing a plurality of research methods, countering the arguments that the IS field needs its own theory and thought [14][15].

The interdisciplinary and the study from the perspective of different paradigms (positivism to interpretivism) translate into a diversity of spoken problems [19], which according to Avison *et al* [15] make the IS an exciting and diverse discipline and a heterogeneous creative community [20]. But to other authors, this translates to a failure of focus, anxiety and identity crisis, and, accordingly, a confusing field of study, as described by Baskerville and Myers [12], Benbasat and Weber [19], Chekland and Holwell [21] and Davis [22].

As a result of interdisciplinary, Bacon and Fitzgerald [23] call attention to the importance of determining the central focus of IST research: the development, management and use of information for knowledge of work in an organizational context and of society, in particular, to be supported, or can be supported, enabled or facilitated by the IST. These authors add, moreover, that the science is information about knowledge, citizen satisfaction and performance management, expressed as: (i) nature of the data, information and knowledge; (ii) use of information in organizations; (iii) human-computer interface; (iv) relevance of information, value and costs; (v) data quality; (vi) knowledge management and organizational learning; (vii) semiotics (science that deals with the communication systems in human societies); (viii) IS research, theory and tools.

Avison *et al* [15], although considering understandable the concentration in the core themes of IS, they have the opinion that this view limits the potential of the discipline. The wide range of topics, theories and constructs make the IS a rich and interesting discipline, avoiding that researchers have a narrow vision of the discipline [14]. Understanding the diversity of issues to be tackled is important so that we can establish the relationships between different areas of reference used to explain the phenomena of IST, and so there is greater clarity around the description of this field.

These aspects are important for the IS gain some consistency and establishing itself as discipline [14], a discipline of law, which receives contributions from other sciences, but also that stated as a reference for other knowledge areas by virtue of having interest and value to researchers from other fields of knowledge [12]. It is essential to understand the diversity of theoretical foundations that are established among the various disciplines [19], in a multifaceted process, where researchers in IS, along with investigators from other areas of human potential, create a network of knowledge, of sharing understandings, breaking down boundaries, what Leguizamón calls the convergence of science, but without ignoring the traditional references of IS [12]. Today the IS face a new scenario, they can now serve themselves as a reference discipline for those areas that helped the early statement of IS as a discipline.

Being an emerging field, the scientific area of IST, whereas design science is the construction and evaluation of artefacts (constructs, models, methods or instantiations) designed and built by man to accomplish the purposes of Humans, in search of better Human living conditions in the organizational context, inter-organizational and society [10]. However, according to the authors [10], being the result of research in design science artefacts, it carries within itself some implications: (i) support building (perception, conception and implementation) and evaluation of theories of natural and social phenomena that suffer the impacts of technology; (ii) needs change and also the artefacts they built to meet those needs.

The construction of artefacts has increased, resulting in several phenomena to study. In consequence it becomes important to understand, critically assess the impacts of the artefacts of IST research results, so that building efforts are not wasted in the construction of low-impact artefacts already built.

4   The Interpretivism in IST Research

In the IST area, according to Klein and Myers [24], in recent years have seen the influence of interpretivism, helping researchers to understand the IST in social and organizational context - *"(...) the real world as a context for research (...)"* [14]. The emergence of new research topics, such as systems design, organizational intervention, management of IS and its social implications were instrumental in the emergence of interpretivism as a paradigm in IS research [18].

There is, currently, the paradigm shift in IS research, from positivism to interpretivism [25].

Positivism in IS research appears in the early periods of the 90's, when the focus of interest was the development of information systems in an orientation closer to computer science and software engineering, a not surprising aspect if we place the birth of IS in the computer science departments [14]. This dominant paradigm, considered by some authors as the paradigm of modern science, has some marks such as: (i) rationality; (ii) reductionism (the simplification paradigm); (iii) mechanistic; (iv) dissociation between subject/object, theory/practice, mind/body, *i.e.*, an objective reality or a real world exists independently of scientific researchers; (v) appreciation of what is quantifiable and scientifically feasible, using mathematics as a tool for validating knowledge; (vi) belief in the discovery of universal laws of general applicability to the functioning of the world; (vii) neutrality and objectivity of the investigator [5][6]. A *"(...) science simplifies the universe (simplicity) to meet him or know how it works (stability), as it is in reality (objectivity)"* [5].

The modern paradigm has provided a profound advancement of knowledge, but with it come new understandings of how scientific thinking and see the world, eventually contributing to the weakening of the pillars which supported itself [17].

Contemporary society is experiencing a transition between the epistemological paradigm of modern science - positivism and postmodern emerging paradigm (where the interpretivism is an expression), for which Santos [17] says are transition periods difficult to understand and go through. A paradigm shift in thinking about the world is lived to which Capra [26] designated the turning point between simplicity and complexity of observed phenomena; the jump from the explanation (hard science) to understanding (soft science) [27]. This brings a new concept of material and nature: instead of eternity, the history; instead of determinism the unpredictability; instead of the mechanism, the interpretation, spontaneity, the self-organization; reversibility to irreversibility and the evolution; the order and disorder; the need, the creativity and the accident. A contribute to a deep epistemological reflection on scientific knowledge [17], triggering, in a postmodern movement, the emergence of a new paradigm, the systemic thinking.

To Klein and Myers [24], investigation, according to this emerging philosophy, assumes that the knowledge of individual reality is gained, only, through social constructions such as language, consciousness, shared meanings, documents, tools and other artefacts. Such research focuses on the complexity of making human sense to the arising situation [28], which attempts to understand phenomena through the meanings that people attach to them [24].

As originally mentioned, the emerging paradigm has influenced the IST research, translated into a variety of problems under study, a variety of disciplines and theoretical frameworks of reference and the diversity of methods and techniques for collecting and analysing data [19].

The interpretivism is, in this respect, hailed as a valid approach for investigating IS in organizations and society, supported by pluralistic methodologies, mostly formed by researchers interested in human and social aspects of research in IS. And even the question of generalization, with all its implications in the acclamation of the research results, is not only valid in the context of positivism [18]. According to Walsham [29], the nature of generalization is different in the two research paradigms, positivism and interpretivism, but is not owned by just one of them.

5   The Generalization of the Results in Interpretive Research

The Oxford English Dictionary (1998), conceptualizes the term "*to generalize*" as "*form general concepts from particular cases*". Accordingly, the general does not need to have a quantitative or statistical dimension. The standard of statistical generalization based on sampling, as the only valid form of generalization should not be imposed. The statistical generalization is only one among other important notions of generalization. It is necessary to describe the different types of generalization, when methodologically contextualized in a different way. This means, that in a positivist context, generalization means to generalize a theory in different settings where the final result would be the achievement of universal laws governing all observed phenomena [6].

Because of the diversity of contexts in which scientists generalize (science of diversity - positivism and interpretivism), there is a variety of ways of conceptualizing the generalization. Generalization is a commitment from both the sciences, one on the widespread similarities in phenomena (positivism), other on the widespread differences in the phenomena (interpretivism) [6].

Considering the importance of the question, for the reasons and justification of the research results presented, it is considered appropriate to present, even if briefly, the framework presented by Lee and Baskerville [6]. These authors identify the different ways of generalization supporting, in that sense, the researchers, particularly those in the area of IS, to claim the generalization of their research results and thus their relevance.

An important aspect in the framework building is the distinction, in different notions of generalization, between theoretical statements and empirical statements. The empirical statements refer to data, measurements, observations or empirical descriptions or real-world phenomena. The theoretical statements posit the existence of entities and relationships that cannot be directly observed and, accordingly, can only be theorized. Both kinds of research, positivist and interpretive, deal with empirical statements (resulting from the observation of the investigator); they also include statements regarding the theory that the researcher uses to explain the observed phenomena [6]. Another important aspect is the differentiation between what the researcher generalizes from (generalizing from) and that the researcher is generalizing (generalizing to).

With reference to the definition of generalization, as provided in the Oxford English Dictionary, this can refer to the generalization from (generalizing from) particular cases to general notions (generalizing to), and the generalization from (generalizing from) a theory for the generalization (generalizing to) different configurations (generalizing to) [6].

Combining these two aspects, Lee and Baskerville [6] recognize that generalization can occur in four ways: (i) from empirical statements to empirical statements; (ii) from empirical statements to theoretical statements; (iii) from theoretical statements to empirical statements; (iv) statements from theoretical to theoretical statements.

Table 1. Framework of generalization

	Generalizing to empirical statements	Generalizing to theoretical statements
Generalizing from empirical statements	*EE* Generalizing from data for descriptions (measurements, observations, and other descriptions)	*ET* Generalizing from empirical descriptions (measurements, observations, and other descriptions) for the theory
Generalizing from theoretical statements	*TE* Generalizing from theory to empirical descriptions Generalizing a theory confirmed in a different field to another field descriptions.	*TT* Generalizing from concepts to theory. Generalizing a variable, or construct another concept for a theory

Font: Lee & Baskerville, 2003:233.

In consequence, the authors argue that the result of generalization (the general notions) can be theoretical statements or empirical demonstrations and the inputs for the generalization (instances, the particular cases) may also be theoretical statements or empirical claims.

Walsham [28] makes an illustration of the four types of generalizations using concrete examples, which are seen as explanations of particular phenomena derived from empirical interpretive research in specific settings in IS that may be useful in the future to other organizations and contexts.

6   Conclusion

It has been seen, in recent years, to an influence of interpretivism as epistemological orientation in IST research against of positivism. This research paradigm shift results, in part, from the emergence of new interest topics to the area of IST, namely the organizational and systems design, organizational intervention, management of information systems and their social implications. In this sense, there were several references in the literature that allowed answering the questions initially raised: (i) What is the influence of the interpretive paradigm research in IST? (ii) What issues arise when trying to reflect on the epistemological assumptions underlying the interpretative approach?

With the changing of point of interest of IST, we are witnessing a new form of the researcher to observe these objects of interest: to understand and critically contribute to the greater adoption and use of technology aimed at improving the living conditions of individuals, organizations and with impact on society.

Hirscheim and Klein [13], consider important this inter-relationship between the world of professionals and academia. Avison *et al* [14][15] highlight the importance of practice in IST research and the impact of IST research in practice.

Considering this perspective, in which scientific research can improve practices and real world problems and professional [10], we are witnessing an understanding of technology as a result of scientific technological knowledge, explained by scientific theories. Research in IST is based on theories and methods of reference disciplines (disciplines contributors), but it is itself also a reference discipline for other fields of study, especially those who contributed to its maturity [12][11]. The knowledge that results from input from other areas of knowledge translates into what Baskerville and Myers [12] describe the Emergence of Interpretivism in IS Research, which Walsham [18] calls its network of school interpretivism in IS. Are thus several references in the literature that supported the view around the question initially posed: (iii) Are the Technology and Information Systems an emerging thinking? Emergency, in what sense?

In any process of scientific research, the reasons for the viability of the results obtained are central thing, and as such, concern is also felt by researchers in the field of IST. This is particularly relevant when the underlying epistemological orientation is interpretivism. It soon raises doubts or criticism from the defenders of positivism, which argued in its favour only the generalization of results and, accordingly, the viability of them. Based on a literature review conducted, we reach the conclusion, reasoned that the generalization of research results under the interpretive paradigm are valid and not exclusive to the positivist orientation. Can be found, therefore, in reference literature explanations and arguments about the generalization of research results under the interpretive paradigm allowing, thus, answering the question initially posed: (iv) What is the relevance of interpretive research results?

There are a variety of ways of conceptualizing the generalization. Generalization is a commitment from both sciences, one on the similarities in widespread phenomena (positivism), one on the widespread differences in the phenomena (interpretivism) [6].

In sum, this article explores the importance of interpretative studies in the area of information systems and technology, highlighting the arguments presented by researchers around the generalization of the results and, accordingly, the relevance and validation.

References

1. Björk, B.C.: A model of scientific communication as a global distributed information system. disponível em (2006), http://informationr.net/ir/
2. Marconi, M., Lakatos, E.: Metodologia Científica, São Paulo, Atlas (2000)
3. Carvalho, J.A.: Metodologias de Investigação em Engenharia. Apontamentos da unidade curricular, do Programa Doutoral em Tecnologias e Sistemas de Informação, Universidade do Minho – Departamento de Sistemas de Informação (2009)
4. Blaikie, N.: Designing Social Research. Polity Press, Cambridge (2000)
5. Vasconcellos, M.J.E.: Pensamento Sistémico: o Novo Paradigma da Ciência, 7ª edn. Papirus Editora, São Paulo (2008)
6. Lee, A., Baskerville, R.: Generalizing Generalizability in Information Systems Research. Information Systems Research 14(3), 221–243 (2003)

7. Kumar, R.: Research methodology: a step-by-step guide for beginners. Sage, London (1999)
8. Feibleman, J.: Pure Science, Applied Science, and Technology: an Attempt at Definitions. In: Mitcham, C., Mackey, R. (eds.) Philosophy and Technology: Readings in the Philosophical Problems of Technology, pp. 33–41. The Free Press, NY (1983)
9. Skolimowski, H.: The Structure of Thinking in Technology. In: Mitcham, C., Mackey, R. (eds.) Philosophy and Technology: Readings in the Philosophical Problems of Technology, pp. 42–49. The Free Press, NY (1983, 1966)
10. March, S.T., Smith, G.F.: Design and natural science research on information tecnology. Elsevier Science 15, 251–266 (1995)
11. Lee, A.S.: Editorial, /W/SQuarter/y (25:1), pp. iii–vii (2001)
12. Baskerville, R., Myers, M.: Information Systems as a Reference Discipline. MIS Quarterly 26(1), 1–14 (2002)
13. Hiershheim, R., Klein, H.: Four Paradigm of Information Systems Development. Communication of the ACM 32(10), 1199–1216 (1989)
14. Avison, D., et al.: Reflection on information systems practice, education and a research: 10 years of the Information Systems Journal. Info Systems Journal 11, 3–22 (2001)
15. Avison, D., et al.: The beginnings of a new era: time to reflect on 17 years of the ISJ. Info Systems Journal 18, 5–21 (2008)
16. McLean, E.R.: Information Systems and Its Underlying Disciplines: a Summary of the Papers. Data Base Fall, pp. 3–6 (1982)
17. Santos, B.S.: Um discurso sobre as ciências. Edições Afrontamento, Porto (1985)
18. Walsham, G.: The Emergence of Interpretivism in IS Research. The management School. University of Lancaster. Lancaster LA1 4YX, UK (2001)
19. Benbasat, I., Weber, R.: Research Commentary: Rethinking "Diversit:y" in Information Systems Research. Information Systems Research 7(4), 389–399 (1996)
20. Swanson, E.B., Ramiller, N.C.: Information Systems Research Thematics: Submissions to A New Journal, 1987-1992. Information Systems Research 4(4), 299–330 (1993)
21. Checkland, P., Holwell, S.: Information, Systems and Information Systems: Making Sense of the Field. Wiley, Chichester (1998)
22. Davis, G.: Information Systems Conceptual Foundations: Looking Backward and Forward. In: Baskerville, R., Stage, J., DeGross, J. (eds.) Qrganizational and Social Perspectives on Information Technology, pp. 61–82. Kluwer, Boston (2000)
23. Bacon, C.J., Fitzgerald, B.: A Systemic Framework for the Fiel of Information Systems. The Data Base for Advances in Information Systems 32(2), 46–67 (2001)
24. Klein, H.K., Myers, M.: A set of Principles for Conduting and Evaluating Interpretative Field Studies in Information Systems. MIS Quarterly 23(1), 67–97 (1999)
25. Walsham, G.: Doing interpretive research. European Journal of Information Systems 15, 320–330 (2006)
26. Capra, F.: O Ponto de Mutação: A Ciência, a Sociedade e a Cultura Emergente, 25th edn. Cultrix, São Paulo (1982)
27. Vasconcellos, M.J.E.: Pensamento Sistémico: o Novo Paradigma da Ciência, 7ª edn. Papirus Editora, São Paulo (2008)
28. Kaplan, B., Maxwell, J.A.: Qualitative Research Methods for Evaluating Computer Information Systems. In: Anderson, J.G., Aydin, C.E., Jay, S.J. (eds.) Evaluating Health Care Information Systems: Methods and Applications, pp. 45–68. Sage, Thousand Oaks (1994)
29. Walsham, G.: Interpretive case studies in IS research: nature and method. Department of Management Science, The Management School, Lancaster University, Lancaster LA1 4YX, UK (1995)

Computer-Assisted Rehabilitation Program – Virtual Reality (CARP-VR): A Program for Cognitive Rehabilitation of Executive Dysfunction

Artemisa Rocha Dores[1,2,3], Irene Palmares Carvalho[4], Fernando Barbosa[5], Isabel Almeida[6], Sandra Guerreiro[6], Bruno Oliveira[7], Liliana de Sousa[1], and Alexandre Castro Caldas[8]

[1] Instituto de Ciências Biomédicas Abel Salazar, Universidade do Porto (ICBAS-UP), Lg. Prof. Abel Salazar nº 2. 4099-003 Porto, Portugal
desousa.l@netcabo.pt

[2] Escola Superior de Tecnologia da Saúde do Porto, Instituto Politécnico do Porto (ESTSP-IPP)
artemisa@estsp.ipp.pt

[3] LABRP, Faculdade de Psicologia e Ciências da Educação da Universidade do Porto (FPCEUP)

[4] Faculdade de Medicina da Universidade do Porto (FMUP)
irenec@med.up.pt

[5] Faculdade de Psicologia e Ciências da Educação da Universidade do Porto (FPCEUP)
fbarbosa@fpce.up.pt

[6] Centro de Reabilitação Profissional de Gaia (CRPG)
{isabel.almeida,sandra.guerreiro}@crpg.pt

[7] Faculdade de Ciências da Universidade do Porto (FCUP)
bruno.oliveira@dcc.fc.up.pt

[8] Instituto de Ciências da Saúde, Universidade Católica Portuguesa (ICS-UCP)
acastrocaldas@ics.lisboa.ucp.pt

Abstract. Every year millions of individuals sustain Acquired Brain Injury (ABI) often resulting in physical, cognitive and psychosocial deficits, leading to life-long changes in the quality of life of patients and their families. In the domain of rehabilitation, virtual-reality (VR) technology has assumed a crucial role in the creation of innovative assessment and training programs. The purpose of this study is to present the Computer-Assisted Rehabilitation Program (CARP-VR) after a brief review of the state of the art. CARP-VR was tailored to the rehabilitation of executive functioning and other related cognitive functions in patients with ABI. It consists of virtual environments that simulate real-life contexts in which patients perform various activities that are based on daily situations. The final version of CARP-VR is now ready to be employed, and tests have been designed to validate it as a tool for the rehabilitation of executive functioning and related cognitive functions.

Keywords: Virtual Reality, Cognitive Rehabilitation, Executive Dysfunction.

G.D. Putnik and M.M. Cruz-Cunha (Eds.): ViNOrg 2011, CCIS 248, pp. 90–100, 2012.
© Springer-Verlag Berlin Heidelberg 2012

1   The Neuropsychology of Executive Functions: From Cognitive Assessment to Cognitive Rehabilitation

Neuropsychology can be defined as the field of knowledge dedicated to the study of the neural mechanisms in its relations to cognitive functions and behavior. It is thus a field of neurosciences that involves cognitive sciences, behavior sciences and their interception [1].

In terms of pathological conditions, neuropsychology seeks the treatment of cognitive and behavior deficits resulting from changes in the functioning of the Central Nervous System (CNS). These dysfunctions may stem from an abnormal development of the nervous system or be acquired throughout the course of life. Regarding acquired injuries, neuropsychology has been confronted with new and demanding challenges resulting from life in modern societies. We are referring here to Acquired Brain Injury (ABI) resulting from Traumatic Brain Injury (TBI) or from neurological diseases, such as stroke. Traffic accidents or work-related accidents are frequently in the origin of TBIs, and a sedentary style of life is, among other causes, in the origin of stroke.

The considerable scientific, social and political advances of the last decades in developed countries have contributed to the development, in this area, of innovative prevention, acute-phase care and rehabilitation services. Despite these efforts, young, active adults continue to face the impossibility of providing continuity to their life projects, temporarily or permanently, as a result of ABI.

Among multiple cognitive deficits, such as those that affect visuospacial functions, attention or memory, we highlight the ones affecting executive functions (EF) for being particularly disabling. Dysfunction at the level of EF is usually called executive dysfunction or dysexecutive syndrome. Associated with the pre-frontal cortex, it appears, more than any other cognitive process, to determine the extension of patient recovery because, in case of dysfunction, all other systems may indirectly be affected [2].

Executive functioning is therefore a complex cognitive process that encompasses other cognitive processes. It refers to the cognitive capacities involved in behavior initiation, planning, sequencing, organization and regulation [3]. In addition to typically failing in the elaboration of the action plan, patients also have impulsive actions and difficulties in mental flexibility [4]. As a consequence, they display great limitations in daily-life activities.

Given the negative impact that executive dysfunction has in the life of patients and their families, it is surprising that only in recent years has it assumed a prominent place in the literature. Several factors may be in the origin of this delay, namely, the inexistence of clearly effective rehabilitation programs, the lack of theoretical consistency concerning the nature of EF, the diversity of deficits associated with it and the limited consciousness patients have concerning their deficits and the impact these have in their performances [5]. The limited ecological validity of neuropsychological tests targeting EF adds to these difficulties [6].

With respect to cognitive rehabilitation as a basic component of neuropsychological rehabilitation, an increasing number of reviews and scientific papers have suggested that it can bring significant benefits and give the quality of life back to patients and their relatives [7]. However, specific results of EF rehabilitation strategies, as evidence of its effects, even though gradually increasing, remain limited [8]. In spite of this, some strategies, such as problem-solving training and its application to people with TBI, or cognitive interventions that promote internalization and self-regulation strategies through self-monitoring and self-instruction have positive effects [9].

The development of new methods and EF rehabilitation tools grounded both in theory and in clinical practice, whose prescription can be based on ecological assessment, is a current requirement and the central subject of the work we propose. It will constitute a major contribution for research and for practice in this area [10].

2   The Advantages of VR in the Assessment and Rehabilitation of Executive Dysfunction

The above circumstances justify the inclusion of innovative technologies in the process of assessment and rehabilitation that may help to overcome some of the main limitations of current interventions. The democratization of information and communication technologies (ICT) made it possible for Virtual Reality (VR) to stop being a privilege of certain areas, such as the cinematographic industry, and be at the service of rehabilitation.

VR has been defined as "an advanced form of human-computer interface that allows the user to 'interact' with and become 'immersed' in a computer-generated environment in a naturalist fashion" [11]. "Sensory data generated by a computer system may be perceived as physical reality, especially when perception is enabled by use of the body in a manner similar to physical reality. The system ideally displays in all sensory modalities; fully encloses the person in these displays; tracks head position and orientation but also the movements of the whole body, determining the visual stereo and spatialised auditory displays as a function of this tracking" [12].

Three distinctive characteristics of VR are: presence, involvement and interaction. The first one refers to "the illusion of being in the rendered virtual place. When contingent events in the virtual world apparently relate directly to the participant, then further there is the illusion that what is occurring is real. Under these conditions participants tend to act and respond to the virtual reality as if it were real" [12]. Involvement can be defined as participation/persistence of the users in the task, or as their motivational degree. Finally, interaction is the capacity of the virtual environment (VE) to react to the user's action; the more the immediate environment changes in response to this action, the more interactive the VE is.

Thus this technology allows the creation of stimuli with identical properties to real ones. Its mere three-dimensionality confers an increased sensation of presence to the user, making laboratorial emulation of the reality possible. In fact, computer-generated VEs are more and more realistic.

The development of VR technology has increased considerably, with application in areas such as engineering, defense, medicine, education, entertainment, art, design, and visualization [13]. VR has also been successfully applied to some clinical domains in mental health, such as phobias, post-traumatic stress disorder, post-traumatic stress associated with traumatic brain accident, addictive behavior and other impulse disorders, panic disorder, eating disorders, disorders of the autism spectrum, cerebral palsy, attention deficit hyperactivity disorder, or even to increase the level of independence of the elderly. A review article also shows the effects of its use in people with intellectual incapacities, including in the promotion of important abilities for independent life, indicating that, with the exception of autism spectrum disorders, the distrust regarding transference of acquired competencies into real-life was unfounded [14].

More recently, VR technology has been applied to neuropsychological assessment and rehabilitation. Even though its applicability to this area was identified more than ten years ago [13], it seems to have attracted particular interest recently [15-20], including in Portugal [21-24]. Among the advantages of using VEs in cognitive assessment and rehabilitation, as well as in research, are the stimuli of easy manipulation and higher ecological validity inasmuch as they are more realistic than traditional stimuli.

Advantages of VR which make it possible to overcome the limitations of neuropsychological assessment through the traditional methods are: (1) the provision of real-world distractions and stressors; (2) increased interactivity and immersion; (3) enhanced flexibility and capacity for self-initiation and structuring of behavior; (4) better reliability and control; and (5) improved patient compliance and motivation [25]. Although these characteristics have been, until now, less explored in terms of rehabilitation, the advantages they brought to assessment are also applicable to the latter domain. Many authors have described the benefits that VR can bring to evaluation/rehabilitation, namely a more naturalistic or "real-life" environment, control of stimulus presentation and response measurement, safe assessment of hazardous situations, increased generalization of learning, increased standardization of rehabilitation protocols, and increased user participation [11].

Different cognitive functions, such as attention [20], memory [26], spatial transformation/reasoning [27], and executive functioning [6] have benefited from VR applications. A literature review concerning the use of VR in the assessment and rehabilitation of different cognitive processes such as spatial capacity and visual perception, attention, memory and executive functioning signals this technology's potential [4].

VR can bring additional benefits to rehabilitation, including the possibility of patients performing exercises at a distance, in the comfort and safety of their homes. Many patients still do not have immediate response from health services, remaining on waiting lists. Others can not benefit from therapy because of moving difficulties between their houses and health services. In these cases, VR may be the only possible solution. Additionally, it may allow the continuation of the rehabilitation program after patients are released. It operates as a networked and virtual organization, of which patients and therapists are part, with the goal of rehabilitation. Thus, VR does not come to replace the therapist. In the situations presented, monitoring the progression of the patient is essential, even if not presencial, for program planning, analysis and discussion of results. It is also desirable that such programs are integrated with other interventions, in order to provide a holistic approach to the patient.

The main difficulties for a generalized use of VR training in rehabilitation are still the selection of the adequate interaction devices and methods. The interaction methods must allow the navigation in detailed 3D environments and the manipulation of specific objects, always providing feedback information to the patient. This must be achieved in a way that can be considered natural and intuitive for several different users with diverse disabilities, backgrounds and practices. Even with the large diversity of available interaction gadgets (joysticks, mouse, gloves, trackers, etc.) and feedback media (image, sound, tactile stimuli), there is not a perfect solution that fits all the requirements and that can be considered easy to use and intuitive for all individuals with disabilities. Due to these difficulties, a usability test is being performed, addressing several different interaction solutions. This experimental work is described in section 5 and should be detailed in a forthcoming publication.

3   Computer-Assisted Rehabilitation Program – Virtual Reality (CARP-VR)

The current work has the main goal of studying the application of VR technology specifically in the area of rehabilitation of EF, but also in other cognitive functions such as visuospatial functions, attention and memory, in patients with ABI. CARP-VR consists of VEs that simulate real-life contexts (e.g., a house and a market) in which patients perform various activities that are based on daily situations (e.g., shopping). The tasks included in each activity have growing levels of complexity according to patients' performances.

3.1   The Development Process

The development of CARP-VR was based on the systematic review of scientific literature, expert consultation and the incorporation of changes resulting from refinement of the process itself. Our development process incorporates Sohlberg and Mateer's (1989) Model [2], specifications in the domain of rehabilitation, and considers the work of authors in the field of VR technology and serious games [28-29]. A detailed description of this proposal can be found in Dores, Carvalho and Castro Caldas (2009) [10]. For the first task, Theoretical Review and Practical Reflection, the Mateer (1999), Sohlberg and Geyer's (1986), and Ylvisaker's (1998) works provide theoretical support for the task of EF rehabilitation [30-32].

3.2   General Features

CARP-VR consists of two distinct environments. The first one, called Training Environment, is a house. The second one, the rehabilitation VE proper, is a car parking lot and a supermarket.

In the Training Environment, the patients can explore three different scenarios: Scenario 1 - storage room; Scenario 2 - dining room; Scenario 3 - bedroom.

In these scenarios the subjects need to solve different tasks of increasing complexity but low level of demand, because it is a training environment. The skills required are: recognition, sorting and problem solving, respectively.

In terms of the development process, the Training Environment aims to: (1) help decide the VE design, the hardware, the software and the visualization system to be used in the complete CARP-VR; (2) assess the degree of user satisfaction with it, first with healthy participants, then with ABI patients. In terms of its later use (as already part of the final CARP-VR), the Training Environment aims to allow patients to experience the VR technology and train navigation before beginning the rehabilitation program itself.

The structure of the Rehabilitation Environment consists of two phases: an assessment phase and a rehabilitation phase. The assessment phase will not be detailed here since it is the accomplishment of each rehabilitation task at the intermediate level. In addition to the rehabilitation task of each of the cognitive functions, we create different levels that are associated with them. These levels stem from the variation of a set of parameters that we now describe: Products' list (visible or not); List format (Auditory or Visual); Instructions (Yes/No - Y/N); Delayed start (Y/N); Repetition (Y/N); Error allowed (Y/N); Corrections (Y/N); Number of items to be purchased; Number of sections; Products' prices (Y/N); Supermarket map display (Y/N); Alarm (Y/N); Magic words – for the training of self-instruction, according to the *Goal Management Training* [33]; Time limit (Y/N); Temporal assessment; and Special Requirements (involving problem solving). These are articulated as to increase the difficulty of the tasks throughout the program.

4   System Architecture and Technical Specifications

CARP-VR is a real-time simulation of a supermarket in which patients can perform the tasks that they would normally do in such an environment. The simulation is powered by a real-time game engine, which grants an experience level similar to what is expected in a computer video game. This allows patients to fully interact freely with the objects in the supermarket, without any pre-computed paths or pre-established tasks.

The first version of the simulator was developed in C++ and used OGRE as the graphics engine. OGRE is "one of the most popular open-source graphics rendering engines, and has been used in a large number of production projects, in such diverse areas as games, simulators, educational software, interactive art, scientific visualization, and others" [34].

This graphics engine was chosen due to its recognized performance and because the available higher-level simulation engines, like NeoAxis Engine, version 0.9, NeoAxis Group, were not considered mature enough at the beginning of this project [35].

Later, the requirements for rapid preparation of several different simulation environments justified the evolution to a second version of the simulator. This new version was implemented in C# in order to take advantage of the NeoAxis Engine. NeoAxis is a proprietary game engine, free for non-commercial use that offers a fully integrated development environment for interactive simulation applications [35]. The use of the map editor, the object editor and other NeoAxis Engine high-level functionalities allowed a faster and more intuitive implementation of the required training environments [35].

4.1   Maps and Levels

All elements in the map, from shelves to individual products, were modeled in Autodesk Maya 2011, version 12.0, Autodesk, and then exported to the Ogre 3D format [36]. Once made available in the NeoAxis map editor, the different elements can be put in place according to their type. Shelves and other stationary elements are made static, to improve rendering, while products are assigned to a special interactive object.

In addition to objects, each map has a number of areas which allow the simulation to "know" if the patient visited those sections inside the supermarket. Also, special areas can be defined that allow a patient to perform specific tasks, like taking a ticket for the line in the meat section.

Once everything is in place — shelves, products and areas — the user can start to create levels. The levels are created in a special editor strictly designed for this purpose. Not only can the levels be edited, but the product and the areas can also be defined, and their properties, like price and category, can be assigned.

Each level is made of a number of tasks that the patient has to perform and complete successfully in order to progress in his/her rehabilitation.

These tasks were carefully crafted as the basic rules upon which all levels can be created. Beyond the most straightforward tasks that can be performed in a supermarket (e.g., select a product from a shelf and proceed to payment), other simpler rules were created to help patients in their rehabilitation process. These rules include the availability of aiding information, like the mini-map, the shopping list and the magic words, the amount of time available to complete all tasks, which includes the collection of the products and their payment, the amount of available money, which can be exact — according to the shopping list —, below or above needed, the areas that the user must visit and, of course, the shopping list. Also, the quantity of products to be acquired can be expressed. Each level has a textual description, shown to the patient upon level start, which contains the tasks that must be performed on that level. Also, an audio file can be supplied at each level, which will be played at the beginning of the level, providing this way an auditory description of the tasks at hand. Other auditory cues are available in the rehabilitation programme, like the right/wrong sound, or a sound stating that the patient chose a product not on the list.

In a more technical view, this editor was created with Windows Forms, API included in the .NET Framework, Microsoft [37] and data serialized using the facilities provided by the .NET Framework, version 4.0, Microsoft, 2010 [38].

4.2   Simulation

The simulation starts by asking the name of the patient and whether he should start from the previous level – the level where he was during the previous session – or from the beginning. This is the only area in the simulation designed to be accessed by the therapist. Thus, it is the only one that is based on a mouse model. From this point on, all interactions are based on joystick.

This interaction model was used in order to overcome the difficulties presented by patients, who, by the nature of their condition, are prone to co-ordination problems. The cart moves with joystick by moving its principal axes. By rotating the handle, the patient can look up and down. The same button is used for almost all actions: dialog box interaction — when a message box is shown —, and acquire a product. The help buttons, map, shopping list, return item to the shelf, are mapped to keys in the joystick so that the patient does not have to wonder with a cursor on the screen.

All acquired products are visible inside the cart, so the patient does not have to remember which products have already been bought. If the shopping list is available, any acquired product on the list will disappear from it, indicating that the product has been bought. Products not on the list can be either put in the cart or not, depending on the settings of each level.

Also, depending on the level settings, the user can put products back, by means of a dialog box, also controlled by joystick.

The simulation either ends once all products on the list have been bought, or once the patient reaches the payment area. In this case he has to successfully pay for the products in the cart. This is also determined by the level settings. A successful payment depends on getting all products from the shopping list and on the amount of money the patient has available.

If he/she has enough money, he must pay in cash. Otherwise, he can pay by credit card. Once the patient gets to the payment area, a dialog box appears with all the items he has in the cart, along with the cost of each one and the amount purchased, like in a real supermarket.

If the patient successfully completes the level, a new simulation will be presented with extra difficulty. In case of failure, the patient either repeats the level a number of times until he gets it done, or the difficulty level is lowered, depending on the settings of the map.

4.3   Storing Information

For each patient, at the very beginning of the treatment, biographic data are collected and stored in a MySQL database, MySQL Community Edition, version 5.5.11, available on site or remotely – for a more centralised management of the patients [39]. A separated application was developed in Java to manage patients' data, allowing the therapist to analyse the patient's biographic data and performance independently from the CARP-VR player or editor. In a near future, the CARP-VR player will store the performance data on the same database, associating each patient with his/her own statistical data, and will receive the last played level, allowing the patient to resume the therapy session -- at present, this feature is only available locally, in each computer where the CAPR-VR player is available. Once the CARP-VR player is able to upload data to the MySQL database, the independent Java application can be extended to show each patient's evolution graphically.

5   Usability Testing

Usability can be defined as "the extent to which a product can be used by specified users to achieve specified goals with effectiveness, efficiency and satisfaction in a specified context of use" [40]. Users' satisfaction in interacting with the product and this latter's utility have become crucial in today's software conception and development. Despite still quite often neglected, analysis of product usability can facilitate future users' acceptance of the application, performance and satisfaction [41-42]. We also consider users' motivation. Exploratory testing and evaluation, performed during program design and developmental stages by the development team and by healthy subjects allowed us to consolidate the functioning of the system, but do not necessarily ensure its adequacy to future users' real needs [43]. Thus we have conducted tests specifically with the population that CARP-VR targets. In this case, the different VEs developed have been independently tested in pilot studies, and results are presented elsewhere, as they are out of the scope of this paper. Results are promising, supporting the usability of the VR program and showing its relevance in subjects' motivation to participate in the rehabilitation process, which also reflects their satisfaction with it. They are presented in detail elsewhere, as they are out of the scope of this paper.

6   Ongoing Developments and Conclusion

Ongoing tests are designed to contribute to validate CARP-VR as a tool for the rehabilitation of EF and related cognitive functions. Results from pilot-studies contribute to the final version of the program in terms of its usability and subjects' motivation and satisfaction with it. The test of the final prototype is currently in progress with healthy subjects and subjects with pathology. The two groups will be compared and the overall results correlated with those obtained in traditional neuropsychological tests. In future work we expect to test the generalization of acquired skills to real-life tasks and the maintenance of acquired skills in follow-up studies. Hopefully, this work will enable clinicians to take advantage from VR technologies in the field of neuropsychological rehabilitation.

Acknowledgments. This project was possible in part due to a C&T research grant from the Foundation for Science and Technology (Reference SFRH/BD/28510/2006).

References

1. Cosenza, R.M., Fuentes, D., Malloy-Dinis, L.F.: A Evolução das Ideias sobre a Relação entre Cérebro, Comportamento e Cognição. In: Fuentes, D., Malloy-Diniz, L.F., Camargo, C.H.P., Cosenza, R.M., et al. (eds.) Neuropsicologia: Teoria e Prática, Artemed, Porto Alegre, pp. 15–19 (2010)
2. Sohlberg, M.M., Mateer, C.A.: Introduction to Cognitive Rehabilitation. Guildford Press, New York (1989)
3. Stuss, D.T., Benson, F.B.: The Frontal Lobes. Raven Press, New York (1986)
4. Rose, F.D., Brooks, B.M., Rizzo, A.A.: Virtual Reality in Brain Damage Rehabilitation: Review. Cyberpsychol. Behav. 8(3), 241–262 (2005)
5. McGlynn, S.M., Schacter, D.I.: Unawareness of Deficits in Neuropsychological Syndromes. J. Clin. Exp. Neuropsyc. 11, 143–205 (1989)
6. Odhuba, R.A.: Ecological Validity of Measures of Executive Functioning. Brit. J. Clin. Psychol. 44, 269–278 (2005)

7. Dores, A.R.: Reabilitação Cognitiva Através de Ambientes Virtuais. In: Santos, N.R., Lima, M.L., Melo, M.M., Candeias, A.A., Grácio, M.L., Calado, A.A. (eds.) VI Simpósio de Investigação em Psicologia, vol. 6, pp. 46–68. Universidade de Évora, Évora (2006)

8. Evans, J.J.: Rehabilitation of Executive Functioning: an Overview. In: Oddy, M., Worthington, A. (eds.) The Rehabilitation of Executive Disorders: A Guide to Theory and Practice, vol. 4, pp. 59–74. Oxford University Press, Oxford (2009)

9. Cicerone, K.D., Dahlberg, C., Malec, J.F., Langenbahn, D.M., Felicettti, T., et al.: Evidence-based Cognitive Rehabilitation: Updated Review of the Literature From 1998 Through 2002. Arch. Phys. Med. Rehab. 86, 1681–1692 (2005)

10. Dores, A.R., Carvalho, I., Castro-Caldas, A.: O Desenvolvimento de um Programa de Reabilitação Cognitiva com Recurso a Tecnologias Informáticas. In: Proceedings of VII Simpósio Nacional de Investigação em Psicologia, Braga, pp. 645–659 (2009)

11. Schultheis, M.T., Rizzo, A.A.: The Application of Virtual Reality in Rehabilitation. Rehabil. Psychol. 46, 296–311 (2001)

12. Slater, M., Perez-Marcos, D., Ehrsson, H.H., Sanchez-Vives, M.V.: Inducing Illusory Ownership of a Virtual Body. Front. Neurosci. 3, 214–220 (2009)

13. Stone, R.J.: Applications of Virtual Environments: an Overview. In: Stanney, K.M. (ed.) Handbook of Virtual Environments, pp. 827–856. Lawrence Erlbaum, Mahwah (2002)

14. Standen, P.J., Brown, D.J.: Virtual Reality in the Rehabilitation of People with Intellectual Disabilities: Review. Cyberpsychol. Behav. 8(3), 272–282 (2005)

15. Rose, F.D., Attree, E.A., Brooks, B.M., Leadbetter, A.G., Andrews, T.K.: Virtual Reality: an Ecologically Valid Tool for Assessment in Neurological Rehabilitation. Eur. J. Neurol. 3(supp.2), 131–132 (1996)

16. Carelli, L., Morganti, F., Poletti, B., Corra, B., Weiss, P.T., Silani, V., et al.: Post-stroke Cognitive Assessment and Rehabilitation: a New Ecological Virtual Reality Task. J. Neurol. 256, S32 (2009)

17. Christiansen, C., Abreu, B., Ottenbacher, K., Huffman, K., Masel, B., Culpepper, R.: Task Performance in Virtual Environments Used for Cognitive Rehabilitation After Traumatic Brain Injury. Arch. Phys. Med. Rehab. 79(8), 888–892 (1998)

18. Rizzo, A.A., Buckwalter, J.G., Neumann, U.: Virtual Reality and Cognitive Rehabilitation: a Brief Review of the Future. J. Head Trauma Rehab. 12(6), 1–15 (1997)

19. Sweeney, S., Kersel, D., Morris, R.G., Manly, T., Evans, J.J.: The Sensitivity of a Virtual Reality Task to Planning and Prospective Memory Impairments: Group Differences and the Efficacy of Periodic Alerts on Performance. Neuropsychol. Rehabil. 20(2), 239–263 (2010)

20. Rizzo, A.A., Schultheis, M.T., Kerns, K., Mateer, C.: Analysis of Assets for Virtual Reality Applications in Neuropsychology. Neuropsychol. Rehabil. 14(1/2), 207–239 (2004)

21. Dores, A.R., Guerreiro, S., Almeida, I., Castro-Caldas, A.: Reabilitação Cognitiva e Realidade Virtual: Uma parceria de sucesso? Educ. Méd. Int. 10(3), 187 (2007)

22. Dores, A.R., Guerreiro, S., Almeida, I., Castro-Caldas, A.: The Use of Virtual Reality in Cognitive Rehabilitation: an Exploratory Study. Neurorehab. Neural. Re. 22(5), 542 (2008)

23. Marques, A., Queirós, C., Rocha, N.: Metodologias de Reabilitação Cognitiva num Programa de Desenvolvimento Pessoal de Indivíduos com Doença Mental e Desempregados de Longa Duração. Psicologia, Saúde e Doença 7(1), 109–116 (2006)

24. Marques, A., Queirós, C., Rocha, N., Alves, J.: Realidade Virtual e Integrated Psychological Therapy na Reabilitação Cognitiva de Pessoas com Esquizofrenia. Saúde Mental 8(2), 11–15 (2006)

25. Penn, P., Rose, D., Johnson, D.: The Use of Virtual Reality in the Assessment and Rehabilitation of Executive Dysfunction. In: Oddy, M., Worthington, A. (eds.) The Rehabilitation of Executive Disorders: A Guide to Theory and Practice, vol. 14, pp. 255–268. Oxford University Press, Oxford (2009)

26. Brooks, B.M., Rose, F.D., Potter, J., Jayawardena, S., Morling, A.: Assessing stroke patients' prospective memory using virtual reality. Brain Injury 18(4), 391–401 (2004)

27. Rizzo, A.A., Buckwalter, J.G., Neumann, U., Kesselman, C., Thiebaux, M., Larson, P., Van Rooyen, A.: The Virtual Reality Mental Rotation Spatial Skills Project. Cyberpsychol. Behav. 1(2), 113–119 (1998)

28. Costa, R.M.: Ambientes Virtuais na Reabilitação Cognitiva de Pacientes Neurológicos e Psiquiátricos, Tese D.Sc, Coppe Sistemas e Computação. UFRJ, Rio de Janeiro (2000)

29. Machado, L.S., Moraes, R.M., Nunes, F.L.S.: Serious Games para Saúde e Treinamento Imersivo. In: Nunes, F.L.S., Machado, L.S., Pinho, M.S., Kirner, C. (eds.) Abordagens Práticas de Realidade Virtual e Aumentada, vol. 1, pp. 31–60. Sociedade Brasileira de Computação, Porto Alegre (2009)

30. Mateer, C.A.: The Rehabilitation of Executive Disorders. In: Stuss, D.T., Winocur, G., Robertson, I. (eds.) Cognitive Neurorehabilitation, pp. 314–332. Cambridge University Press, Cambridge (1999)

31. Sohlberg, M.M., Geyer, S.: Executive Function Behavioral Rating Scale (1986). In: Sohlberg, M.M., Mateer, C.A. (eds.) Introduction to Cognitive Rehabilitation, pp. 257–259. Guildford Press, New York (1989)

32. Ylvisaker, M.: Traumatic Brain Injury Rehabilitation: Children and Adolescents. Butterworth Heineman, Boston (1998)

33. Levine, B., Robertson, I.H., Clare, L., Carter, G., Hong, J., Wilson, B.A., Duncan, J., Stuss, D.T.: Rehabilitation of Executive Functioning: an Experimental-clinical Validation of Goal Management Training. J. Int. Neuropsych. Soc. 6, 299–312 (2000)

34. OGRE – Open Source 3D Graphics Engine, http://www.ogre3d.org

35. NeoAxis Game Engine – Development Tool for 3D Simulations, Visualizations and Games, http://www.neoaxisgroup.com

36. Autodesk Maya 2011, version 12.0, Autodesk, http://www.autodesk.com

37. Windows Forms, API included in the NET Framework, Microsoft, http://www.microsoft.com

38. NET Framework, version 4.0, Microsoft, http://www.microsoft.com

39. MySQL Community Edition, version 5.5.11, MySQL, http://www.mysql.com

40. ISO/DIS 9241-11, European Usability Support Centres

41. Carvalho, A.A.A.: Usability Testing of Educational Software: Methods, Techniques and Evaluators. In: Proceedings of 3° Simpósio Internacional de Informática Educativa. Escola Superior de Educação, Instituto Superior Politécnico de Viseu: CD-ROM, pp. 139–148 (2001) ISBN 972-98523-4-0

42. Carvalho, A.A.A.: Testes de Usabilidade: exigência supérflua ou necessidade? In: Proceedings of 5° Congresso da Sociedade Portuguesa das Ciências da Educação. Sociedade Portuguesa de Ciências da Educação, Lisboa, pp. 235–242 (2002)

43. Dores, A.R., Almeida, I., Guerreiro, S., Carvalho, I., Castro-Caldas, A., de Sousa, L.: Cognitive Rehabilitation of Brain Injured Patients with Dysexecutive Syndrome: The Test of a Prototype of a Virtual Environment. In: International Neuropsychological Society 2010 INS Mid-year Meeting, Poland, p. 30 (2010)

Recommendation of Learning Objects in an Ubiquitous Learning Environment through an Agent-Based Approach

Luiz Cláudio Nogueira da Silva[1,2], Francisco Milton Mendes Neto[1,2]
Luiz Jácome Júnior[2], and Raphael de Carvalho Muniz[2]

[1] Postgraduate Program in Computer Science, Rural Federal University of the Semi-Arid,
Mossoró - RN, Brazil
{luizclaudio,miltonmendes}@ufersa.edu.br
[2] Technological Center of Software Engineering, Rural Federal University of the Semi-Arid,
Mossoró - RN, Brazil
{luizjunior05,raphaeldecm}@gmail.com

Abstract. An ubiquitous learning environment provides students with a teaching method that would be not possible to be performed in a conventional web-based course. The use of learning objects in a standard way consists of an effective way to allow, among other features, content reuse and interoperability between different Learning Management Systems (LMS). Thus, these contents can be reassembled to create new content. However, a problem that occurs frequently is the unsuitability of the content to the context in which the student is inserted. A context-aware ubiquitous learning support environment allows students participating in this kind of course to receive content that suits their needs (available physical resources, preferences, geographic location, learning styles etc.). Thus, this paper presents an agent-based approach to context-aware recommendation of learning objects in order to enhance the learning process in ubiquitous learning.

Keywords: Distance Learning, Agents, Ubiquitous Learning, Learning Objects, Awareness Context Environments.

1 Introduction

Distance Education (DE) is a mode of teaching and learning which has been growing quite some years ago. The developments of computer networks, the improvement of the processing capability of personal computers and the advance of multimedia technologies, among other factors, contributed to the creation of this scenario. However, despite consisting of an effective teaching method, still presents some challenges, among which we highlight the need for a computerized support appropriate to the characteristics of each person. Through this support is possible to automate increasingly the process of learning, making the teacher a facilitator, ceasing to be the main source of information and passing to drive the learning process [1].

G.D. Putnik and M.M. Cruz-Cunha (Eds.): ViNOrg 2011, CCIS 248, pp. 101–110, 2012.

One of the ways to provide DE is through the use of mobile devices, this modality is known as mobile learning. This way of providing education allows that students and teachers can take advantage of the resources offered by mobile technologies. One of these benefits is the possibility to access, view and provide content irrespective of time and from any location [2].

However, even with the benefits offered by mobile learning, we should consider the particular characteristics of each student, including the resources of which he holds. This is necessary not only to provide content that meets the needs of students, but also to provide content in an appropriate way to the constraints of mobile devices since they have distinct and limited resources. In this context, arises the concept of context-aware environments. This kind of environment fits to the user, considering information provided by the own user, beyond those captured dynamically from his interaction with computing devices [3].

For the purpose of developing context-aware environments in the learning domain, called Ubiquitous Learning Environments (ULE) [4], it is essential that educational content be created in a standardized manner. Thus, it is possible that a Learning Management System (LMS) shows the contents properly and reuse content in different contexts and from different repositories. Furthermore, it is possible to combine different contents, which, in turn, improves the production process and, consequently, reduce its costs [5]. An effective way to standardize educational content is through the use of Learning Objects (LOs), which consist of small units of content that can be used, referenced and reused during a learning process [6, 7].

Given the relevance of the topic, the present work has as its general goal to provide a learning environment, through the use of mobile devices, to help and fit the needs of the students, according to characteristics of the context in which they are inserted.

This paper is divided into seven sections. Section 2 presents an overview of multiagent systems (MAS) to support learning. Section 3 describes the learning objects, as well as the standards used in their development. Section 4 presents the concepts and inherent characteristics in ubiquitous learning environments. Section 5 discusses related works. Section 6 describes the agent-based approach proposed in this paper and the role of each agent. The last section presents our final considerations and a discussion of future works.

2   Use of Agents in Learning Support Systems

In despite of different definitions of agents that can be found in the literature, there is still no consensus on the issue. However, it is possible to construct a concept from the definitions given by researchers.

According to [8], agents are autonomous software entities that perceive their environment through sensors and that act upon that environment through actuators, processing information and knowledge. A multiagent system (MAS), in turn, consists of a set of autonomous agents that collaborate to solve a problem which would be impossible to solve with just one agent.

Agents can be constructed in various ways. They can be agents of software or hardware, static or mobile, persistent or nonpersistent, reactive or cognitive. According to [1], one of the most important classifications of agents is in relation of them to be reactive or cognitive.

Reactive agents are agents that select actions to perform based solely on current perception, not considering the historical of perceptions. Since they do not have memory, they are unable to plan future actions [8, 1].

Also according to [8], another feature to be taken into consideration is the rationality, which is influenced by four factors: i) performance measure (defines the success criteria); ii) prior knowledge of the agent; iii) actions that the agent can perform; and iv) following perceptions captured by the agent so far.

Faced with these elements, it is possible to conceptualize a rational agent as one which, for each possible sequence of perceptions, selects an action that will maximize its performance measure, given the evidence provided by the sequence of perceptions and any internal knowledge of the agent [8]. Considering this definition, one can realize that is not always that a rational agent will make the best decision possible, but one that improves its performance measure.

Intelligent agents can perform various tasks in context-aware learning environments, such as i) monitoring the activities of the student in the learning environment, ii) automatically capture information from the dynamic context of the student, iii) recommend interest content for that student, among others. Before the increase in the number of students who interact with learning support systems, the use of agents to perform these tasks become extremely important, mainly due to the fact that they are complex tasks for the facilitators to manage from distance.

3   Learning Objects

An important concept regarding the educational content used in DE is the Learning Object (LO). According to Learning Technology Standard Committee - LTSC, from the Institute of Electrical and Electronics Engineers (IEEE), a LO is an educational material entity, digital or not, that can be used for learning, education or training [7].

Thus, a LO, beyond the content itself, has a structure containing metadata that allows, through its elements and attributes, describe its contents, its format, how that content is presented, beyond other information (content author, creation date, educational data, etc.). This metadata is created based on standard that will be presented later.

In summary, the central idea of the concept of LOs is to allow educational designers build relatively small educational components that can be used in different learning contexts. In other words, they are digital contents that enable or facilitate reaching an educational goal and their reusability [11].

Despite the benefits of using LOs, we should also consider the problems faced in creating digital LOs. [5] describes a series of difficulties that are faced while creating digital LOs: i) definition of the navigational structure; ii) adequacy of the contents of a print media to electronic media; iii) assistance to the pedagogical aspects of teaching; iv) integration of LO with different types of environments of DE; and v) high cost of authoring tools' licenses.

To solve these problems, we use LOs standards. According to [12], these standards are a way of organizing the data of a LO to provide communication between different computing environments, as well as ensure its accessibility and usability, and also provide interoperability.

The metadata standards are used in the resources' identification, aiding in the filtering of a search and retrieval of a record or a LO [12]. An example of the metadata's standard is the LOM (Learning Object Metadata) [7], which was developed by LTSC [6]. The purpose of this standard is to facilitate search, evaluation, acquisition and use of LOs, both by students and instructors, or even automated software processes. Data elements describe a LO and they are grouped into nine categories.

An integration standard, as the name implies, unifies in a reference model different types of standards, such as metadata standards, packaging, communication and interface, developed by other organizations [12]. The integration standard SCORM (Sharable Content Object Reference Model), developed by ADL (Advanced Distributed Learning) [10], integrates a set of technical standards, specifications and guidelines designated to attend the requirements of high level of SCORM - systems and accessible content, interoperable, durable and reusable. The content in SCORM standard can be distributed to students through any LMS that is compatible with and use the same version of SCORM [10].

In this paper we will use LOs developed according to the SCORM standard, both because it is a widespread standard and it is also composed of a series of other standards. Thus, we can enjoy the best benefits offered by each standard.

4   Ubiquitous Learning Environment

An ubiquitous learning environment may be understood as a context-aware mobile learning environment, providing most adaptive contents for learners. Context awareness describes a paradigm in which the context of a user is considered to define his profile [3, 14]. There is no consensus about the definition of "context". This one is specific of the application and the desired intention, requiring the identification of functions and properties of the individuals' domains [3, 13, 14].

In [3, 14], context is defined as information consisting of properties that combine each other to describe and characterize an entity and its role as a computer readable form.

The location is crucial to the context of the student in an environment for ubiquitous learning. However, the context includes more than just the location. A wide range of context factors combine themselves to form a context definition.

Almost all information available at the moment of interaction can be seen as contextual information, among which stand out [3, 15]: i) the various tasks required from users; ii) the wide range of devices that combine to create mobile systems with associated infrastructure services; iii) resources availability (e.g. battery status, screen size, network bandwidth, etc.); iv) resources in the neighborhood (e.g. accessible devices and servers); v) the physical situation (e.g. temperature, air quality, brightness level, noise etc.); vi) spatial information (e.g. location, orientation, velocity, acceleration etc.); vii) time information (e.g. time of day, date, season, etc.); and viii) physiological measures (e.g. blood pressure, heart rate, respiratory rate, muscle activity etc.).

The list above, though not exactly contain all the information that can be considered, is used to demonstrate the inherent complexity of the context, its specific nature of domain and difficulty to define and measure it [3]. In an attempt to reduce this complexity, [14] defines two general types of context: i) static context (named customization), which concerns a use case in which a user profile (context) is created manually and the user is actively involved in the process and having an element of control; and ii) dynamic context (named personalization), which refers to the condition in which the user is seen as passive, or at least with a little less control. In this case, the system monitors, analyze and react dynamically to user behavior and the role identified.

Many context-aware mobile learning applications (ubiquitous learning environments) use learning contexts in order to appropriately adjust or suggest content and activities for students [2]. However, these works do not consider the capabilities of mobile devices, what compromises a more precise definition of the context of students.

5   Related Work

Multiagent systems (MAS) have been widely used in educational environments. This technology can provide an aid to learning environments, making these environments more proactive and autonomous. MAS can be useful, for example, in developing a context-aware feature in a learning environment.

In [1], it is proposed an agent-based approach for detecting passive students in the problem-based learning (PBL) in virtual learning environments in order to detect and correct the presence of passive students, that are students who have difficulty of working in teams to solve a problem. Thus, this work aims to make the learning environment more pro-active, thus improving the learning process.

In [16], it is described a ubiquitous learning architecture for supporting student to learn English as foreign language in order to prepare for TOEFL (Test of English as a Foreign Language) test. The system provides adaptive content for different learners based on context-awareness, considering location, time, manner as well as learner's knowledge. This is possible through suggested topics as well as test questions. Besides, [16] also describes CAMLES (Context-Aware Mobile Learning English System) system prototype, that allows the learner to receive adaptive materials for TOEFL test anytime in anywhere with mobile phone.

We highlight, however, the difference of our work for the last one, since our approach consider the definition of context, beyond the student's profile information, information of available physical resources such as connection type, format (video, audio, etc.) supported by the mobile devices.

6   An Agent-Based Approach for Recommending Context-Aware Learning Objects

The agent-based approach proposed in this paper is presented in Figure 1.

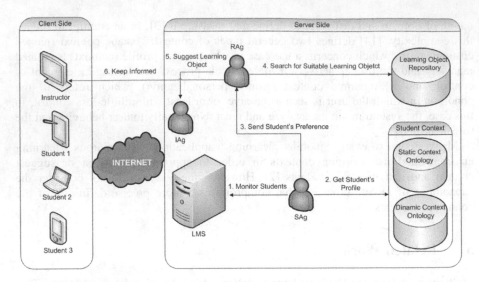

Fig. 1. Agent-based approach for recommending learning objects

According to the approach shown in Figure 1, three types of agents are proposed: Student Agent (SAg), Recommender Agent (RAg) and Interface Agent (IAg). The SAgs are responsible for monitoring the activity of students in the learning environment and send, to RAgs, static and dynamic information of the student's profile, recovered from the ontology of static and dynamic context respectively. The RAgs are responsible for identifying appropriate learning objects (LOs) to the student's context, according to both the information provided by SAgs and the learning objects available in the repository. Once identified this information, the RAgs inform both the IAg and the instructor. The IAg is responsible for presenting LOs selected in the best way for the student, considering the capabilities of his mobile device. The message exchange flow among agents can be seen in Figure 2, which contains the interaction model proposed in the MAS-CommonKADS+ methodology (see section 6.1).

6.1   Agent Model

The agents specification was performed by MAS - CommonKADS+, a methodology for modeling multiagent system, which consists in an extension to the traditional methodology MAS-CommonKADS [18]. This methodology describes the agents through spreadsheets, showing the details of the agents and their goals through CRC (Class-Responsibility-Collaborators) cards. Each CRC card is built to specify a particular agent. The agent goals are listed and the plans (actions that should be performed to achieve the goals) are described. It also identifies the knowledge that the agents own to perform their actions and the agents that collaborate in the execution of plans and services through which the interaction takes place among agents [19].

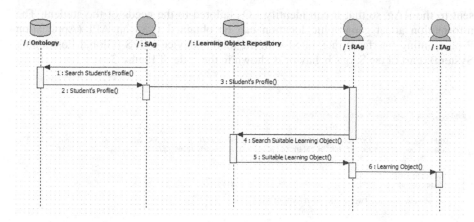

Fig. 2. Interaction model for communication among agents

The MAS-CommonKADS+ methodology, in its turn, proposes the integration of AML (Agent Modeling Language) to the MAS-CommonKADS methodology. It also suggests, among other things, the use of an interaction model to describe all the interactions among agents through the AML. This model is represented by sequence and communication diagrams, using AML diagrams [18].

6.2   Student Agent (SAg)

SAgs are intended to search, in both the static and the dynamic context ontologies of the students, the learning preferences that make up their profiles and dynamic information of the student context. To facilitate the comprehension of the behavior of SAg, Table 1 shows the CRC card of the SAg.

Table 1. CRC Card of the SAg

Agent: StudentAgent (SAg)			Class: mod_StudentAgent	
Goals	**Plans**	**Knowledge**	**Colaboration**	**Service**
Verifying student profile	Searching for a specified student profile	Student authentication	Student	Informing student profile

The SAg has a one shot behaviour, in charge of perceive the authentication of a student at LMS. While not finding any student, the agent remains in a locked state. If a new student logged into the LMS, the agent loads the student profile ontology model, and in looks for the preferences of this student. Then, the preferences information, in conjunction with information of the student geographical location, are sent to the RAg, so that it can identify LOs tailored to the needs of the student. The information about geographic location can be obtained from an API (Application Programming Interface) integrated with the mobile device's GPS (Global Positioning System). Part of the SAg's behavior is shown in the code of Figure 3.

```
package studentAgent;
import java.util.Iterator;

public class StudentAgent extends Agent {

    /* Represents the path to the ontology. */
    static final String ONTOLOGY_PATH = "file:"+System.getProperty("user.dir")+"/ontologies/StaticContext3.owl";
    static final String nsPrefixURI = "http://www.semanticweb.org/ontologies/2011/2/StaticContext.owl#";

    //(...)
    protected void setup (){
        System.out.println("Agente-estudante "+ getAID().getName() + " Executando");
        //Adds the behaviour that waits for a student
        addBehaviour(new WaitStudent(ONTOLOGY_PATH));
    }

    * The behaviour used by StudentAgent to search student profile.
    private class WaitStudent extends CyclicBehaviour{
        * Constructor: responsible for creating the models
        private WaitStudent (String ONTOLOGY_PATH){

        private MessageTemplate mt = MessageTemplate.MatchPerformative(ACLMessage.REQUEST);
        public void action(){
            //Waits only for REQUEST messages
            ACLMessage msg = myAgent.receive(mt);
            //if the message was received
            if (msg!=null){
                String title = msg.getContent();
                ACLMessage reply = msg.createReply();
```

Fig. 3. Part of the Student Agent source code in Java

6.3   Recommender Agent (RAg)

The RAg is responsible for detecting LOs appropriated to the context in which the student is inserted, according to provided by the SAgs and the metadata information of the available LOs in the repository. Once the student context characteristics have been identified, it communicates to the instructor and passes information from the LO to the Interface Agent (IAg). To facilitate the comprehension of the behavior of the RAg, Table 2 shows the CRC card of the RAg.

Table 2. CRC Card of the RAg

Agent: RecommenderAgent (RAg)			Class: mod_RecommenderAgent	
Goals	**Plans**	**Knowledge**	**Colaboration**	**Service**
Finding suitable learning objects	Searching for learning objects in the repository related to the student's profile	Student profile and learning objects repository	SAg	Informing suitable learning objects

6.4   Interface Agent (IAg)

The Interface Agent (IAg) aims to provide students with information as they progress in the distance learning course in which they are participating. This agent adjusts the type of message according to the device capabilities of the student. To facilitate the comprehension of the IAg's behavior, Table 3 shows the CRC card of the IAg.

Table 3. CRC Card of the IAg

Agent: InterfaceAgent (IAg)			Class: mod_InterfaceAgent	
Goals	**Plans**	**Knowledge**	**Colaboration**	**Service**
Showing learning objects in a suitable way	Checking the available resources for student	Suitable learning objects	RAg	Showing learning objects in a suitable way

7   Final Remarks

In this paper, we described the implementation of an agent-based approach for recommending learning objects in ubiquitous learning environments. The proposed solution aims to make the learning environment suitable to the student's needs. The agent-based approach presented here can be used together with any learning management system, once it has been developed as an independent software layer from the application. As further work, we intend to do a case study with a class of the computer science course to see the impact of the proposed agent-based approach in the content suitability.

References

1. Pontes, A.Á.A., Neto, F.M.M., de Campos, G.A.L.: Multiagent System for Detecting Passive Students in Problem-Based Learning. In: Demazeau, Y., Dignum, F., Corchado, J.M., Bajo, J., Corchuelo, R., Corchado, E., Fernández-Riverola, F., Julián, V.J., Pawlewski, P., Campbell, A. (eds.) Trends in PAAMS. AISC, vol. 71, pp. 165–172. Springer, Heidelberg (2010)
2. Yau, J.Y.-K., Joy, M.: A Context-Aware Personalized M-learning Application Based on M-learning Preferences. In: 6th IEEE International Conference on Wireless, Mobile and Ubiquitous Technologies in Education (WMUTE), pp. 11–18. IEEE Computer Society, Washington (2010)
3. Moore, P., Hu, B., Jackson, M., Wan, J.: Intelligent Context for Personalised M-Learning. In: International Conference on Complex, Intelligent and Software Intensive Systems, pp. 247–254. IEEE Computer Society, Los Alamitos (2009)
4. Zhao, X., Wan, X., Okamoto, T.: Adaptive Content Delivery in Ubiquitous Learning Environment. In: 6th IEEE International Conference on Wireless, Mobile and Ubiquitous Technologies in Education (WMUTE), pp. 19–26. IEEE Computer Society, Washington (2010)

5. Rodolpho, E.R.: Convergência digital de objetos de aprendizagem SCORM. Universidade Estadual de São Paulo Júlio de Mesquita Filho (UNESP), São José do Rio Preto, SP (2009)
6. Learning Technology Standards Committee (LTSC), http://ieeeltsc.org
7. Draft Standard for Learning Object Metadata IEEE Standard 1484.12.1, http://ltsc.ieee.org/wg12/files/LOM_1484_12_1_v1_Final_Draft.pdf
8. Russell, S.J., Norvig, P.: Articial Intelligence, a Modern Approach, 2nd edn. Prentice Hall (2003)
9. Caregnato, S.E., Mendes, R.M., de Souza, V.I. : A propriedade intelectual na elaboração de objetos de aprendizagem. In: Encontro Nacional de Ciência da Informação. Universidade Federal da Bahia, Salvador (2004)
10. Advanced Distributed Learning (ADL), http://www.adlnet.org
11. Castillo, S., Ayala, G.: ARMOLEO: An Architecture for Mobile Learning Objects. In: 18th International Conference on Electronics, Communications and Computers (CONIELECOMP), pp. 53–58. IEEE Computer Society, Los Alamitos (2008)
12. Dias, C.C.L., Kemczinski, A., de Lucena, S.V.S., Ferlin, J., da Hounsell, M.S.: Padrões abertos: aplicabilidade em Objetos de Aprendizagem (OAs). In: XX Simpósio Brasileiro de Informática na Educação, SBIE, Florianópolis (2009)
13. Moore, P., Hu, B.: A Context Framework with Ontology for Personalised and Cooperative Mobile Learning. In: Shen, W., Luo, J., Lin, Z., Barthès, J.-P.A., Hao, Q. (eds.) CSCWD. LNCS, vol. 4402, pp. 727–738. Springer, Heidelberg (2007)
14. Moore, P., Hu, B., Wan, J.: Smart-Context: A Context Ontology for Pervasive Mobile Computing. The Computer Journal 53, 191–207 (2008)
15. Schilit, B., Adams, N., Want, R.: Context-Aware Computing Applications. In: IEEE Workshop on Mobile Computing Systems and Applications (WMCSA), pp. 85–90. IEEE Computer Society, Santa Cruz (1994)
16. Nguyen, V.A., Pham, V.C., Ho, S.D.: A Context-Aware Mobile Learning Adaptive System for Supporting Foreigner Learning English. In: IEEE RIVF International Conference on Computing and Communication Technologies, Research, Innovation, and Vision for the Future (RIVF), Hanoi, Vietnam, pp. 1–6 (2010)
17. Yao, C.-B.: Adaptive Context aware and intelligent searching in mobile learning applications. In: The 2nd International Conference on Computer and Automation Engineering (ICCAE), Taipei, Taiwan, vol. 5, pp. 802–806 (2010)
18. de O. Morais II, M.J.: MAS-Commonkads+: Uma Extensão à Metodologia MAS-Commonkads para Suporte ao Projeto Dealhado de Sistemas Multiagentes Racionais. Masther Thesis. State University of the Ceará, Fortaleza, CE (2010)
19. Neto, F.M.M., de O. Morais II, M.J.: Multiagent System for Supporting the Knowledge Management in the Software Process. In: Ramachandran, M. (ed.) Knowledge Engineering for Software Development Life Cycles: Support Technologies and Applications, pp. 96–113. IGI Global, New York (2010)

A Survey of Student Satisfaction with Distance Learning at Faculty of Organizational Sciences, University of Belgrade

Maja Krsmanovic, Mladen Djuric, and Veljko Dmitrovic

Faculty of Organizational Sciences, University of Belgrade, Jove Ilica 154,
11000 Belgrade, Serbia
{Maja.Krsmanovic,Mladen.Djuric,Veljko.Dmitrovic}@Fon.rs

Abstract. With development of internet and following technologies, there is an increasing space for making education service more flexible. Also, Faculty of organizational sciences (FOS), University of Belgrade has recorded a growing number of students in last years. Among potential students, there is a significant group of those ones that are not able to attend classes regularly. These are some of the reasons why FOS decided to step into the accreditation process for distance learning curriculum. With the first generation of students attended distance learning program this year, it is important to get the information about their experiences. The paper aims to determine student satisfaction with web portal for distance learning, quality of deployed material, communication with teachers and peers and rules that shape distance learning system. The paper also analyses potential link of students' responses with their previous success expressed through the number of points for enrollment to FOS.

Keywords: Student satisfaction, distance learning, survey.

1   Introduction

Distance learning is a form of education that includes intensive application of electronic media and where the learning process is commonly separated in time and space.

One of the major advantages of distance learning compared to conventional forms of education is great flexibility. In traditional education student can't take courses at any time, but at the time determined by educational organization. Very important characteristic is physical presence and this can be a problem if student doesn't live near faculty. Students must also obey the schedule of classes which often can't be changed. In addition to correcting these deficiencies, distance learning is very flexible, stimulates creativity of students and affects on satisfaction, thus making the whole process more effective. Students can improve their knowledge at their own pace, at a place and time of their choice. It is believed that this way of study can make students more versatile, capable of living, allowing them to determine their pace of work and schedule of responsibilities.

Implementation of distance learning system improves capacities of educational organizations, while reducing costs of educational process. It also enables a more

G.D. Putnik and M.M. Cruz-Cunha (Eds.): ViNOrg 2011, CCIS 248, pp. 111–117, 2012.

even distribution of education by making the new educational programs available to areas outside the educational and economic centers. In addition, it allows the different institutions to have an access to foreign educational resources, which implies a higher quality of the acquired knowledge.

What has been recognized as a lack of distance learning process is that students have slower contact with professors than in traditional learning, where answers to the questions can be obtained immediately.

When it comes to students' satisfaction with distance learning mode, many autors have discussed it (Yi-Shun Wang, 2003; Pei-Chen Sun, Ray J. Tsai, Glenn Finger, Yueh-Yang Chen and Dowming Yeh, 2008; Sheng Liaw, 2008; George Bradford and Shelly Wyatt, 2010; Jen-Her Wu, Robert D. Tennyson and Tzyh-Lih Hsia 2010) and proved it as very important factor for distance learning process success.

2   Bases for Research

Although many authors emphasize the multiple benefits of distance learning systems, very few have dealt with the survey of attitudes of end users of such systems. The survey conducted for this study aims to determine the level of student satisfaction with the system of distance learning. Through 16 closed questions students expressed their satisfaction with the individual elements that make distance learning system. The Likert scale containing five levels was used. The elements that make this distance learning system are:

- Site functionality/clarity
- Site updating
- Clarity of the material
- Quantity of the material
- Tempo of lecturing (speed of giving students information)
- Understanding of the given tasks
- Variety in ways of comunication with lecturers
- Availability of the lecturer
- Success in comunication with students
- Relation between effort put in and number of points
- Possability of expressing an oppinion in the right way
- Timing the final exams in the classic way
- Discipline and motivation for work.

Questionnaire with which this research was conducted, in addition to 16 closed questions, contains another open question that gave students to express additional thoughts about this system. The questionnaire was sent by e-mail to all students of the first year of distance studies at the Faculty of Organizational Sciences (FOS), University of Belgrade. These are students of accredited study program of undergraduate study - Information systems and technologies. From 52 questionnaires sent, we received and processed 42 questionnaires that were correctly filled out, which is 80% of the population.

The structure of the sample by the two following criteria was unknown prior to research and is shown in Figure 1. First criterion includes points for enrollment to

FOS and the structure of sample by this criterion is shown at the left side of Figure 1. Second criterion is based on time that students have spent on the web site for distance learning and the structure of sample by this criterion is shown at the right side of Figure 1.

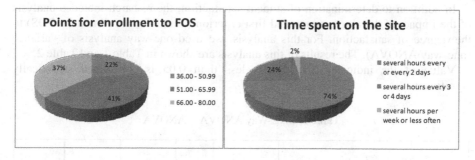

Fig. 1. The structure of the sample

3   Analysis of Results

Satisfaction of students with the individual elements that make distance learning system was determined by using One-Sample T test. The Mean Value of the degree of satisfaction of all students was taken as a value that indicates the total satisfaction of students with the individual elements of distance learning system. The results of this test are shown graphically in descending order in Figure 2.

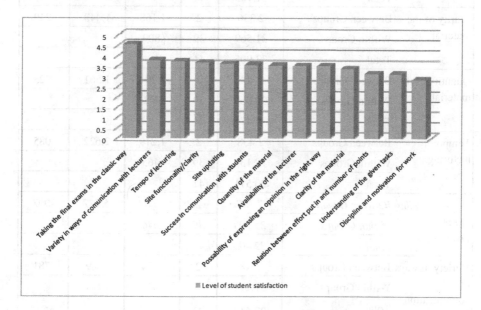

Fig. 2. Satisfaction of students with the individual elements of distance learning system

Students cited as the greatest benefits of distance learning the possibility to listen the lessons several times, at the time and place on their own choice according to their obligations and opportunities. On the other hand, students cited as the shortcomings a lack of interactivity and explanations by the teacher when a student doesn't understand what the teacher said.

In addition to determination of student satisfaction, the research includes analysis of the impact of the above mentioned first criterion (points for enrollment to FOS) to the degree of satisfaction. For this analysis, we used one-way analysis of variance (one-way ANOVA). The results of this analysis are shown in Table 1 and Table 2.

Value of the indicator Sig. that is less than 0.05 is considered statistically significant.

Table 1. ONE-Way ANOVA - ANOVA

		Sum of Squares	df	Mean Square	F	Sig.
Site functionality/ clarity	Between Groups	2.582	2	1.291	1.299	.284
	Within Groups	38.751	39	.994		
	Total	41.333	41			
Site updating	Between Groups	.242	2	.121	.218	.805
	Within Groups	21.663	39	.555		
	Total	21.905	41			
Clarity of the material	Between Groups	2.336	2	1.168	1.443	.249
	Within Groups	31.569	39	.809		
	Total	33.905	41			
Quantity of the material	Between Groups	2.408	2	1.204	1.561	.223
	Within Groups	30.069	39	.771		
	Total	32.476	41			
Tempo of lecturing	Between Groups	2.438	2	1.219	2.622	.085
	Within Groups	18.133	39	.465		
	Total	20.571	41			
Understa-nding of the given tasks	*Between Groups*	*7.207*	*2*	*3.603*	*5.577*	*.007*
	Within Groups	*25.198*	*39*	*.646*		
	Total	*32.405*	*41*			
Variety in ways of comunication with lecturers	Between Groups	.348	2	.174	.249	.781
	Within Groups	27.271	39	.699		
	Total	27.619	41			

Table 1. (*Continued*)

Availability of the lecturer	Between Groups	3.529	2	1.765	1.680	.200
	Within Groups	40.971	39	1.051		
	Total	44.500	41			
Success in comunication with students	Between Groups	1.754	2	.877	.733	.487
	Within Groups	46.651	39	1.196		
	Total	48.405	41			
Relation between effort put in and number of points	Between Groups	.713	2	.357	.328	.722
	Within Groups	42.429	39	1.088		
	Total	43.143	41			
Possability of expressing an oppinion in the right way	Between Groups	.784	2	.392	.335	.718
	Within Groups	45.716	39	1.172		
	Total	46.500	41			
Timing the final exams in the classic way	Between Groups	1.589	2	.795	1.358	.269
	Within Groups	22.816	39	.585		
	Total	24.405	41			
Discipline and motivation for work	Between Groups	4.382	2	2.191	1.599	.215
	Within Groups	53.451	39	1.371		
	Total	57.833	41			

Table 2. ONE-Way ANOVA - Multiple Comparisons - Tukey's HSD Test

Dependent Variable	(I) Points for enrollment to FOS	(J) Points for enrollment to FOS	Mean Difference (I-J)	Std. Error	Sig.	95% Confidence Interval	
						Lower Bound	Upper Bound
Understanding of The given tasks	1	2	-.182	.320	.837	-.96	.60
		3	-.967*	.328	.015	-1.77	-.17
	2	1	.182	.320	.837	-.60	.96
		3	-.784*	.285	.024	-1.48	-.09
	3	1	.967*	.328	.015	.17	1.77
		2	.784*	.285	.024	.09	1.48

* Indicates the existence of differences between groups

4   Interpretation of Results and Conclusions

Based on the results of the research conducted, we can conclude that the level of student satisfaction with the 12 elements (of 13) of the distance learning systems is above the average value (as an average value was taken the arithmetic mean of the possible values of the degree of student satisfaction and it is 3). For the majority of elements (9 of 13), according to the level of student satisfaction, values were within the interval [3.38 - 3.76], whereas the mean value (of all 13 elements) by the same criterion is 3.52.

Students are mostly satisfied (Mean = 4.54) by the fact that they may take the final examinations in the conventional way (in contact with teachers, along with the students that study in traditional system). On the other hand, the students are the least satisfied (Mean = 2.83) with the discipline and motivation to work in the distance learning system.

Life Orijentation Test (LOT), as a part of the ANOVA, shows a statistically significant difference at the level of Sig<0,05 among three categories of students by the previous success expressed by the number of points gained for enrollment to FOS. However, this difference can be observed only in one element - Understanding of the given tasks: F (2, 39) = 5577, Sig = 0.007.

Eta squared value as a quotient of Sum of Squares (Between Groups) and Sum of Squares (Total) for the reference element is 0.22 which indicates that the real difference between the means of the groups is large (each Eta squared value higher than 0.14 indicates the large real importance).

Subsequent comparisons using Tukey's HSD test indicate that (looking at the Understanding of the tasks given) the levels of student satisfaction in group 1 and group 2 differ on the level of student satisfaction in group 3 and that these differences are statistically significant as indicated by the corresponding values of Sig. that are less than 0.05. However, the levels of student satisfaction in group 1 and group 2 show no difference.

References

1. Adali, T.: Accreditation in e-learning: North Cyprus higher education case. Procedia Social and Behavioral Sciences 1, 2077–2080 (2009)
2. Deepwell, F.: Embedding Quality in e-Learning Implementation through evaluation. Educational Technology & Society 10(2), 34–43
3. Hornung-Prähauser, V., Mayringer, H.: How to assess the quality of online learning and teaching material? Salzburg Research Forschungsgesellschaft, Austria
4. Moussa, N., Moussa, S.: Quality assurance of e-learning in developing countries. Nonlinear Analysis 71, e32–e34 (2009)
5. Ramayah, T., Ahmad, N.H., Lo, M.-C.: The role of quality factors in intention to continue using an e-learning system in Malaysia. Procedia Social and Behavioral Sciences 2, 5422–5426 (2010)
6. Sun, P.-C., Tsai, R.J., Finger, G., Chen, Y.-Y., Yeh, D.: What drives a successful e-Learning? An empirical investigation of the critical factors influencing learner satisfaction. Computers & Education 50(4), 1183–1202 (2008)

7. Bradford, G., Wyatt, S.: Online learning and student satisfaction: Academic standing, ethnicity and their influence on facilitated learning, engagement, and information fluency. The Internet and Higher Education 13(3), 108–114 (2010)

8. Wang, Y.-S.: Assessment of learner satisfaction with asynchronous electronic learning systems. Information & Management 41(1), 75–86 (2003)

9. Wu, J.-H., Tennyson, R.D., Hsia, T.-L.: A study of student satisfaction in a blended e-learning system environment. Computers & Education 55(1), 155–164 (2010)

10. Liaw, S.-S.: Investigating students' perceived satisfaction, behavioral intention, and effectiveness of e-learning: A case study of the Blackboard system. Computers & Education 51(2), 864–873 (2008)

Proposal of a Computing Model Using GRID Resources for the JEM-EUSO Space Mission

J.A. Morales de los Ríos, M.D. Rodríguez Frías, L. del Peral,
H. Prieto, and G. Sáez-Cano[*]

SPace & AStroparticle (SPAS) Group, UAH, Madrid, Spain
{josealberto.morales,dolores.frias,luis.delperal,
hector.prietoa,lupe.saez}@uah.es

Abstract. For High Energy Physics (HEP) experiments the huge amount of data and complex analysis algorithms require the use of advanced GRID computational resources. Therefore, an exhaustive analysis of computational requirements and resources, in the frame of the GRID architecture, intended for the JEM-EUSO space mission software and computing infrastructure has been performed. Moreover solutions to account for the software and data repositories as well as a proper administrative organization are pointed out.

Keywords: Computing, GRID, JEM-EUSO, HEP.

1   Introduction

Detection of radiation from outside the Earth surface was discovered by Victor Hess in 1912 [1]. These high energy particles were called Cosmic Rays and still constitute a big challenge for physicists and astronomers. Huge progress has been made from both, the theoretical and the experimental points of view but fundamental questions are still open: where do they come from? ,how are they accelerated to such high energies? ,what is the composition of the highest energy cosmic rays?, how to interpret the features observed in the energy spectrum?, and so on. Furthermore, these questions are linked with each other, making it a rather complex problem.

For High Energy Physics (HEP) experiments the huge amount of data and complex analysis algorithms require the use of advanced GRID computational resources, but the use of these resources demands higher software complexity, highly specialized computing scientists, and sophisticated planning and organization. Here, JEM-EUSO is not an exception: huge quantities of data are required to simulate, validate and gather the results the scientific community expects from the experiment [2]. The computing model we are proposing is just the first step towards a GRID computing working properly for JEM-EUSO.

---

[*] For the JEM-EUSO collaboration.

G.D. Putnik and M.M. Cruz-Cunha (Eds.): ViNOrg 2011, CCIS 248, pp. 118–126, 2012.

2   The JEM-EUSO Mission

The "Japanese Experimental Module - Extreme Universe Space Observatory" (JEM-EUSO) is a worldwide collaboration led by RIKEN/JAXA, aiming to investigate the nature and origin of Ultra High Energy Cosmic Rays (UHECR) and Extreme High Energy Cosmic Rays (EHECR), i.e., charged particles, photons, neutrinos, with E > $5 \cdot 10^{19}$ eV and therefore opening the channel of high energy particle Astronomy [2].

JEM-EUSO will pioneer measurements of EHECR-induced Extensive Air Showers (EAS) from space, achieving accurate measurements of the primary energy, arrival direction and composition of EHECR, using a target volume far larger than is possible from the ground. Such measurements will shed light on the origin of EHECR, on the sources that are producing them, on the propagation environment from the source to the Earth, and, hopefully, on the particle physics mechanisms at energies well beyond the ones achievable in man-made laboratories.

Among the main goals of the proposed mission [2] are:

- The investigation of the highest energy processes in the Universe through the detection and analysis of the Extreme Energy Component of the Cosmic Radiation.
- To open the Channel of High Energy Neutrino Astronomy to probe the boundaries of the Extreme Universe and to investigate the nature and distribution of the EHECR sources. A spin-off is represented by the systematic surveillance of atmospheric phenomena (the atmosphere as a physics system, electrical discharges, and Meteors).

The fundamental obstacle to understand the nature and origin of EHECR is the lack of observational data. Therefore among the observational goals of JEM-EUSO are:

- To collect a large sample of EHECR in order to measure their energies, arrival directions, and composition;
- Make astronomical observations at extreme energies using charged particles, neutrinos, and/or gamma rays.

3   The JEM-EUSO Instrument

The JEM-EUSO instrument (Figure 1) consists of the main telescope, an atmosphere monitoring system, and a calibration system. The main telescope of the JEM-EUSO mission is an extremely-fast (~μs) and highly pixelized (~$3 \cdot 10^5$ pixels) digital camera with a large diameter (about 2.5m) and a wide Field of View (FoV) (±30°). It works in near-UV wavelength (330-400 nm) with single photon-counting mode. The telescope consists of four parts: the optics, the focal surface detector, its electronics, and the mechanical structure. The optics focuses the incident UV photons onto the focal surface with an angular resolution of 0.1 degree. The focal surface detector converts the incident photons to photo-electrons and then to electric pulses [3].

Two curved double sided Fresnel lenses with 2.65m external diameter, an intermediate curved precision Fresnel lens, and a pupil constitute "baseline" optics of the JEM-EUSO telescope. The Fresnel lenses provide a large-aperture, and a wide FoV as well as a low mass and a high UV light transmittance.

The combination of three Fresnel lenses provides a full FoV of 60° and an angular resolution of 0.1°. This resolution corresponds approximately to (0.75 - 0.87) km on the earth's surface, depending on the location inside the FoV in nadir pointing mode. The material of the lens is UV transmitting PMMA which has a high UV transparency in the wavelength from 330nm to 400nm.

The focal surface (FS) of JEM-EUSO is a sphere with about 2.7 m curvature radius, and it is covered with about 5,000 multi-anode photomultiplier tubes. The FS detector consists of Photo-Detector Modules (PDMs), each of which consists of nine Elementary Cells (ECs). The EC contains four units of the Multi-Anode Photomultipliers (MAPMTs). About 137 PDMs are arranged in the FS [3].

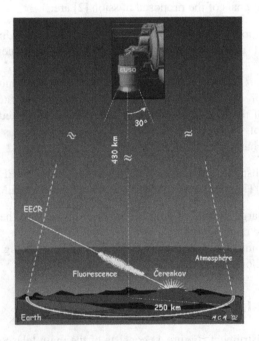

Fig. 1. Artistic view of JEM-EUSO looking downward the Earth's atmosphere by night

4   Computational Requirements

The JEM-EUSO mission needs to evaluate the full path of interactions of a cosmic ray while crossing the Earth's atmosphere towards the Earth's surface. To fully simulate all these processes a huge amount of software is required to account for all the stages of the air-shower and particle development. The injection in the Earth's atmosphere of the primary cosmic ray and the generation of the Extensive Air Shower; the simulation of the detector response; the reconstruction of the physics parameters of the primary cosmic ray from the JEM-EUSO observed data; and finally the backtracking of the particle from the Earth through the space to find the arrival direction of the primary cosmic ray [4].

Simulation of the EAS generated by the primary cosmic ray is a complex calculation made with Monte Carlo codes developed specially for this purpose by the Astroparticle community. The list of software for this includes; CORSIKA (COsmic Ray SImulator for KAscade experiment) [5], AIRES (AIR shower Extended Simulations) [6], CONEX [7] and users customized versions. Some primaries as ν or τ have to be simulated with other codes as PHYTIA, TAUOLA and HERWIG. To account for the simulation of the JEM-EUSO telescope and the event reconstruction, codes written by the collaboration have been developed. These official codes are ESAF (Euso Simulation and Analysis Framework) [8] and the Saitama code. Moreover, data analysis is done by macros in the ROOT [9] framework.

Once we have taken into account all the software listed above, we have to proceed to make a fully computational requirements study, first defining a set of Use-Cases Scenarios and then evaluating the needs for each set of tasks, like Monte-Carlo Simulation, RAW data and Analysis, Calibration tasks and resources for Unscheduled tasks made by the scientists working on the collaboration [10]. Monte-Carlo statistics have to be generated in an amount of 100 or 1000 time higher compared to collected real data (several thousand events with energy within UHECR are expected during JEM-EUSO operation). Based on several thousand real events, the Monte Carlo shower simulations should be around 100.000 to 1.000.000 events (where 1 simulated event = 28,8 TFLOPS using a Wheatstone test [11] and measuring the time needed by a MC software).

For the shower reconstruction and the detector simulation tasks, all the physicists of the collaboration are potentially involved as they might apply customized algorithms on data subsets. This way of performing analysis is called chaotic analysis. However additionally it is foreseen to perform scheduled analysis over the entire set of data. This scheduled analysis will group in each pass all the official algorithms. The time needed to analyze reconstructed events depends on the complexity of the analysis algorithm and on the overhead introduced by the GRID. The latter can only be predicted once the analysis on the GRID has been done with the final middleware and at the final scale. The processing power we have considered is an average value that can vary largely from one analysis to the other.

The MC-Simulation (Figure 2) is estimated using the performance measured with the average of several events using CORSIKA and estimating a base of 1M events needed, Raw data analysis is estimated to be around 28% of Monte Carlo based in our experience with software for data analysis. For Unscheduled tasks the estimation is the same for Raw data and Analysis, and calibration is estimated to be half the needs for Unscheduled tasks, but prioritized [19-21].

All data produced by the JEM-EUSO detector will be stored permanently (Figure 3) for the duration of the experiment. This includes the raw data, one or more copies of the raw data, one set of Monte-Carlo data, and reconstructed data from all reconstruction passes, analysis objects, calibration and monitoring data. A fraction of the produced data will be kept on short term storage, providing rapid access to data frequently processed and for I/O dominated tasks. The media for permanent and transient storage will be decided by the technology available [19-21].

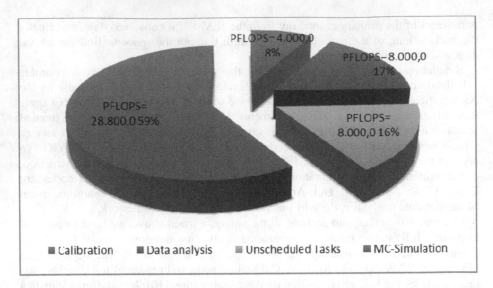

Fig. 2. CPU Requirements estimated in PFLOPS (PFLOPS = 1015 FLOPS) on a yearly based estimation [12-18]

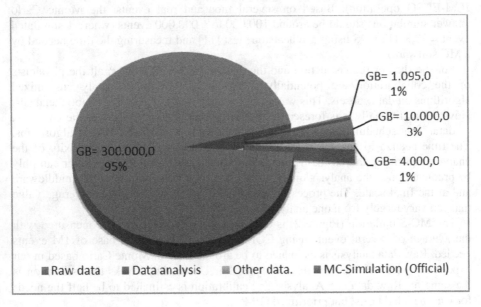

Fig. 3. Requirements for the Permanent Storage. Estimated in GB (Giga-Bytes = 109 Bytes). Yearly based estimation[12-18].

As we did for the CPU needs, Monte Carlo (where 1 event is around 300 MB, based in measurements made with the MC-Simulation software) is estimated for 1M events. The Data Analysis is estimated as 10 MB/event, but it depends on the

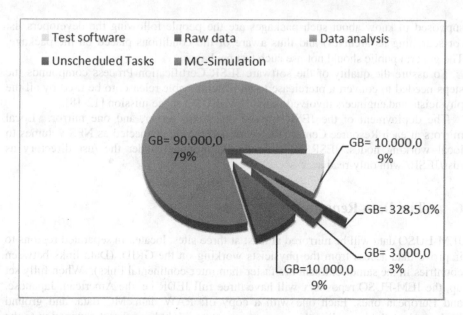

Fig. 4. Requirements for the Transient Storage. Estimated in GB (Giga-Bytes = 109 Bytes). Yearly based estimation [12-18].

software used and can vary a lot within the development of each analysis software; this number is just an estimation. Real data is estimated to 3 GB/day only, because that is limited to the telemetry data link of the ISS. Other data include storage space that has to be reserved for the calibration of the data and monitoring.

The requirements for transient storage (Figure 4) on fast access media depend on the computing model, the balance of available distributed processing resources and on the network bandwidth and occupancy. In the absence of GRID simulation tools, our estimations on needed transient storage capacities are based on the requirement to store on disks data that will be frequently accessed primarily through nonscheduled tasks. For an early estimation, the transient storage should have enough space to store 30% of the permanent storage for the MC-Simulation, the analysis tasks and the unscheduled tasks, plus additional storage for the software development test and user unscheduled tasks.

5   The Software Repository

The software repository (SR) compounds all the actions and resources needed to keep the software used in the collaboration organized, tested, and available to all the resources center and scientists participating in JEM-EUSO.

During the process of developing software and preparing a release, various packages are made available to the developer community for testing purposes. Special care should be taken to prevent non-developers to download and use nightly builds, snapshots, release candidates, or any other similar package. The only people who are supposed to know about such packages are the people following the developers list (or searching its archives) and thus aware of the conditions placed on the package. The general public should not use such test packages.

To assure the quality of the software JESR Certification Process compounds the steps needed to convert a prerelease to an official stable release, to be used by all the physicists and engineers involved in the JEM-EUSO space mission [12-18].

The deployment of the JESR foresee one main server, and one mirror. Local mirrors at each Resource Center (RC) with daily sync, connected as NFS volumes to local working nodes. JESR NFS should be mounted under the /usr directory as /usr/JESR/ with only-read access.

6   The Data Repository

JEM-EUSO data will be mirrored at least at three sites, located in separated regions to improve data access from the physicists working on the GRID. (Data links between countries in the same continent are faster than inter-continental links). When fully set up, the JEM-EUSO repository will have three full JEDR i.e. the American, Japanese, and European ones. Each one with a copy of: RAW data, MC data, and ground analysis data. Additionally other resources centers might have direct connection to the nearest JEDR with read access only.

For the files in the Data Repository a Catalog (Data Base) should be maintained to keep track of each file, and for faster searching. The catalog have different tables for each type of file; MC, Raw data and simulated/reconstructed data.

A table with the following MC data: Identifier, Primary Particle, Energy, Zenith angle, Azimuth angle, SW-Release, low-energy and high-energy hadronic interaction models, thinning, User, Site, latitude, longitude, and LFI (Logic File Identifier). A table for the raw data, containing: Identifier, time, date, post processed, ground-data analysis output identifier, and LFI as well as a table for simulated/reconstructed data, containing: Identifier, time, date, site, user, Mother-raw data identifier, and LFI [12-18].

The catalog is kept in one master site (any of the JEDR, to be defined) and mirrored to the others full JEDR. The catalog and the full JEDR will be synchronized daily. Moreover to access files on the JEDR two methods will be implemented, one for simple download, and other for direct work on the GRID.

In the simple download a toolkit (by simple software or a php web site, TBD), each physicists of the collaboration will have privileges to search the entire catalog and download the files selected. This option is simple and efficient but limited on the amount of data that the user can download daily for bandwidth limitations. For analysis that would require huge amounts of data (e.g., running a new program over of 3 months of raw data) a portion of the GRID is reserved for users [19-21].

For GRID work a simple program that receives the specs to search in the database as data cards, and outputs the LFI will do the work. So any physicist could write a simple script that first search the database for the files wanted, and then performs analysis on the files found. Both programs will be included on the JESR toolkit to provide all functionality to query, browse and download.

7   Administrative Organization and Virtual Organization

To separate development, production and users tasks JEM-EUSO will have 4 different VO (Virtual Organization) as shown in Figure 5, each one with separate privileges over the resources. The aim is to organize more efficiently the work in the GRID [19-21].

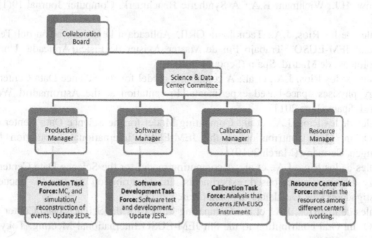

Fig. 5. Proposal for JEM-EUSO Science & Data Center administrative organization

Acknowledgements. The Spanish Consortium involved in the JEM-EUSO Space Mission are funded by MICINN under projects AYA2009-06037-E/ESP, AYA-ESP 2010-19082, CSD2009-00064 (Consolider MULTIDARK) and by Comunidad de Madrid (CAM) under project S2009/ESP-1496. J.A. Morales de los Ríos wants to acknowledge the University of Alcalá for his Phd fellowship. Moreover the authors want to acknowledge M. Ricci and A. Haungs for revision of the manuscript and useful comments.

References

1. Hess, V.F.: The Electrical Conductivity of the Atmosphere and Its Causes. Constable and Company (1928)
2. The JEM-EUSO Collaboration, http://jemeuso.riken.jp/en/index.html
3. Ebisuzaki, T., et al.: In: XVI International Symposium on Very High Energy Cosmic Ray Interactions ISVHECRI 2010, Batavia, IL, USA, June 28-July 2 (2010)
4. Bottai, S., et al.: Simulation and Data Analysis for EUSO. In: Proceedings of 28th ICRC, Tsukuba, p. 943 (2003)
5. Heck, D., Knapp, J., Capdevielle, J.N., Schatz, G., Thouw, T.: Forschungszentrum Karlsruhe Report FZKA 6019 (1998)
6. Sciutto, S.J.: The AIRES system for air shower simulations. In: An update, Contributed to 27th International Cosmic Ray Conferences (ICRC 2001), Hamburg, Germany, August 7-15 (2001)

7. Pierog, T., et al.: First results of fast one-dimensional hybrid simulation of EAS using CONEX. Nucl. Phys. Proc. Suppl. 151, 159–162 (2006)
8. Thea, A., et al.: The Euso Simulation and Analysis Framework. In: Proceedings of 29th ICRC, Pune, p. 104 (2005)
9. ROOT Homepage, http://root.cern.ch/
10. Espirito Santo, M.C., et al.: The EUSO Science Operations and Data Centre. In: Proceedings of 28th ICRC, Tsukuba, p. 1089 (2003)
11. Curnow, H.J., Wichman, B.A.: A Synthetic Benchmark. Computer Journal 19(1), 43–49 (1976)
12. Morales de los Rios, J.A.: Tecnología GRID Aplicada a la Colaboración del Telescopio Espacial JEM-EUSO., Trabajo Fin de Master. Máster de Física Aplicada, Universidad Complutense de Madrid, Spain (September 2010)
13. Morales de los Rios, J.A., et al.: A computing model for the Science Data Center of high energy physiscs space-based experiments. Presentation at the Astromadrid Workshop, Madrid, Spain (June 2011)
14. Morales de los Rios, J.A., et al.: Computing Model for the Science Data Center of JEM-EUSO. In: Oral Contribution to the JEM-EUSO International Simulation Meeting, Tübingen, Germany (March 2010)
15. Morales de los Rios, J.A., et al.: A computing model for the Science Data Center of high energy Physiscs space-based experiments. In: Contribution to the "I Encuentro de Investigadores CI3, Guadalajara, Spain (March 2011)
16. Morales de los Rios, J.A., et al.: Computing Model for the Science Data Center of JEM-EUSO. In: Oral contribution to the 8th JEM-EUSO International Meeting, Tokyo, Japan (December 2010)
17. Morales de los Rios, J.A., et al.: JEM-EUSO Computing Model. In: Oral Contribution to the Grid & E-Ciencia Workshop, Valencia, Spain (July 2010)
18. Morales de los Rios, J.A., et al.: JEM-EUSO Computing Model. In: Oral Contribution to the 7th JEM-EUSO International Meeting, Huntsville, Alabama, USA (June 2010)
19. Alice Technical Design Report, CERN-LHCC-2005-018, Alice TDR 021 (2005)
20. Alice Computing Model, CERN-LHCC-2004-028/G-086 (2005)
21. The ATLAS Computing Model, ATLAS TDR–017, CERN-LHCC-2005-022

Cloud Computing: Concepts, Technologies and Challenges

Abílio Cardoso[1] and Paulo Simões[2]

[1] Universidade Portucalense, Porto, Portugal
[2] CISUC-DEI, Universidade de Coimbra
abilioc@upt.pt, psimoes@dei.uc.pt

Abstract. An important revolution is taking place in information technology with the introduction of the cloud computing paradigm, which is expected to bring several new benefits and services to customers. Cloud computing makes it possible to detach the process of building the infrastructure and service delivery to end users by redefining the business models of software and hardware, so that customers stop purchasing goods to buying services. This paper presents the state of the art of cloud computing and discusses the key challenges of an ongoing research work, focused on the applicability of IT governance to the migration of existing systems to the cloud.

Keywords: Cloud computing.

1 Cloud Computing

Until recently, cloud computing was just a sounding expression in the field of Information Technology (IT), but with the crescent maturity of virtualization and the growing economic pressure on IT organizations to do more with fewer resources, cloud computing is proving to be the next big IT revolution.

1.1 What Is Cloud Computing?

The term cloud computing has emerged in the fourth quarter of 2007 on a collaborative project between IBM and Google [1,2], however, and despite being a topic about which much has been written, there is no consensual definition about what really mean the term cloud computing. As an illustration, Vaquero et al. [3] gathered a collection of 22 definitions of cloud computing appeared in 2008.

The National Institute of Standards and Technology (NIST) define cloud computing as:

"a model for enabling convenient, on-demand network access to a shared pool of configurable computing resources (e.g., networks, servers, storage, applications, and services) that can be rapidly provisioned and released with minimal management effort or service provider interaction" [4].

G.D. Putnik and M.M. Cruz-Cunha (Eds.): ViNOrg 2011, CCIS 248, pp. 127–136, 2012.
© Springer-Verlag Berlin Heidelberg 2012

This work follows this definition of cloud computing because it is recognized by several authors [5-9], it has a wide scope and because it includes the common features of the cloud computing paradigm.

A simple way to see the cloud computing is using the analogy with the traditional services of water, gas and electricity; there, users pay for using these services; in cloud computing, pay for the IT services they use. Cloud computing makes it possible to take apart the process of building infrastructure and services providing to end users, mainly because it is able to adopt a technology without first the need to make large investments.

1.2   Related Technologies

The cloud computing paradigm has a great contribution of grid computing, but also inherits characteristics from other computing paradigms such as distributed computing, utility computing, web 2.0 and web services. In the following paragraphs we will examine some of the technologies related to cloud computing.

Grid computing, a form of distributed computing where the resources of many networked computers are used to solve a single problem, is recognized by several authors [2, 10-13] as a predecessor of cloud computing. Taking advantage of the large amount of time that computers are on low workload, grid computing uses this downtime and its computing power for other purposes, such as scientific research and collaborative projects that require resources to achieve their objectives. It is usually necessary to use specific software, such as BOINC [14] or Globus Toolkit [15], among others, to enjoy the free resources on computers and share information so that it can be processed by various computers that are part of grid.

Dillon et al. [16] identify the following differences between grid and cloud computing: while grid computing derives its resources mainly by using the shares to form a virtual organization the cloud is usually owned by a single entity; the grid computing aims to provide maximum computing power for a task through shared resources while computing cloud is more suited to small and medium sized tasks; the grid computing is mainly used for scientific computing while cloud computing is more widely used in business applications; grid computing aims to achieve maximum computing power while in cloud computing we have computing as request.

Cloud computing as well as having a large contribution of grid computing also inherits characteristics from other computing paradigms such as **distributed computing** [1, 2], the possibility of running an application on multiple computers at the same time, **utility computing** [1, 10] business model where resources such as computing, storage and others are provided and charged such as electricity and **Web 2.0**. The cloud computing services are, by nature, **web services** which offer computing services on demand dynamically, and thus it is a natural evolution of Web 2.0 [17]. Cloud computing uses web services [1, 18] as the prevailing way to provide services to its users.

1.3   Characteristics

The **virtualization** is used in cloud computing in order to have on the same physical machine a variable number of virtual machines and as a practical and quick way of allocating resources. Virtualization allows the abstraction and isolation of lower-level functionality from the underlying hardware to allow portability of the higher level functions such as aggregation and sharing of physical resources [1]. The resources are made available to multiple clients located on the same infrastructure so there is a sharing for different customers in a **multi-tenant** architecture [9].

The cloud computing paradigm is **based on services**, since the resources of cloud, such as disk, computing, programming environment, applications, etc. are provided in the form of services. These services are made available with **ubiquitous access** and in a controlled manner so that it can provide multiple payment models allowing users to **pay for the use of resources**. The services are provided through **self-service** allowing the user to unilaterally afford computing power, storage, choose which operating system to use, etc. according to their needs, without requiring human interaction by the provider of cloud services in a **scalable** and **elastic** fashion giving the illusion that the available resources are infinite [19].

Much of the energy wasted by systems occurs when they are on hold. In fact, the typical usage of the servers is located usually between 20 and 30% in the remaining time in "pause" consume about 60% when at peak usage [20]. The services offered by cloud share a set of features that allow for **economies of scale** and energy.

1.4   Availability Models

The cloud is traditionally classified according to its availability in **public cloud** where the services of cloud computing are available over the Internet to users in general, either in a free or on a pay-by-use model. At the other end is the **private cloud** when the institution has its own data center with a large number of servers heavily using virtualization, self-provisioning and automated management of resources. The private clouds can benefit corporations that have invested in a huge computing power, bandwidth and network storage, improving the utilization of resources acquired, however, this model does not enjoy the full economic benefits of cloud computing, as the institution still have to maintain the resources even when they leave to be used.

In the **community cloud** model the services are available for a number of organizations that share common interests.

These models are not closed and it is therefore considered another model, **hybrid cloud** where infrastructure is formed by composition of cloud types above.

Recently, by the hand of the Amazon, another model emerged, the **Virtual Private Cloud** (VPC) [21], which set up a secure bridge between the user private infrastructure and the public cloud Amazon. This implementation is positioned between the public and private cloud. It is regarded as private because on the one hand, the connection between infrastructure and the cloud be conducted using a virtual private network (VPN), and secondly because the Amazon dedicate series isolated resource for this type of use [16].

1.5   Deployment Models

The architecture of cloud computing is divided into different layers described as Everything-as-a-Service, XaaS, being the most common division into three major groups, which define reference architectures for cloud computing solutions, according to the services they offer their users.

With **Infrastructure-as-a-Service**, IaaS, the user may have, upon request of processor resources, storage, networks and others from a provider. In this model, the user can also implement and execute software in general, including operating systems and applications. The user does not intervene in the management or control of resources in the cloud, but it controls the operating systems, storage and applications installed. Examples include Amazon EC2 [22] Amazon S3 [22] and Akamai [23]. In the **Platform-as-a-Service** model, PaaS, the users can implement the applications envisioned by them in the cloud, using the programming languages and tools offered by the service provider. The user does not intervene in the management or control of resources in the cloud having limited access to programming. Examples: Google Apps [24] and Force.com [25]. In the third model, **Software-as-a-Service**, SaaS, applications are executed on the cloud infrastructure of service provider and usually accessed using a Web browser The user does not own the application that uses remotely, has no responsibilities in infrastructure physical structure that hosts the application and does not intervene in the management or control of resources in the cloud. Examples of this model: Salesforce.com [26], Gmail and Facebook.

2   Challenges

Cloud computing offers many advantages, such as the ability to dynamically adjust the available resources according to needs, a great scalability in resource utilization, a reduced initial investment to launch new services, an easy access, but also has number of challenges that must be overcome by technology providers. Note however, that some of these challenges are old but in a new setting that can exacerbate the problem [27]. Among the challenges of cloud computing are emphasized:

Security: Security, privacy and integrity are some of the biggest concerns in the implementation and use of the paradigm of cloud computing [19]. A recent study [28] in which were surveyed over 500 executives and IT managers from 17 countries revealed that despite the benefits of cloud computing, executives have more confidence in internal systems than in cloud-based due to threats safety and loss control information. Another study [29] included in the ongoing investigation by the International Data Corporation IDC, where they questioned 244 IT managers shows that 74.6% of respondents pointed to security as the first challenge of the cloud. This issue could be minimized with data encryption, compliance with standards, service level agreements.

Service Availability: They are known the outages in access to services [19, 30, 31] of some cloud providers. These interruptions can lead to cascading problems in all the institutions working directly or indirectly with the provider. This challenge can be mitigated if users of cloud services establish service level agreements that guarantee the desired levels of availability.

Single Point of Failure: The cloud computing services are available through the Internet which can lead to another issue, the existence of single points of failure, namely if there is no access backup. Another single point of failure could exist if we use the same provider for all services. While a single provider is simple to manage it represents a single point of failure in case of a provider outage.

Standardization: While the technology of cloud computing is still under major development, key aspects standardization of the paradigm is a good starting point for a more accurate development. In April 2009, the Distributed Management Task Force (DMTF) created the Open Standards Incubator group formed by several companies, such as AMD, Cisco, citrus, IBM, Intel, Microsoft, among others, to develop an informal set of specifications for resource management in the cloud, especially taking into account the interoperability between private and public or hybrid clouds [32].

The International Telecommunication Union (ITU-T) has been in operation since May 2010, a Focus Group on cloud computing [33] to develop standards for cloud computing, particularly with regard to issues related to telecommunications. Malcolm Johnson, Director of the Telecommunication Standardization ITU-T regarding the need for the establishment of standards when forming the group to develop standards for cloud computing, said [34]: "The cloud is an exciting area of IT, where there is an series of protocols to be designed and rules to be adopted which will allow people to better management of digital assets. Our new focus group aims to bring some much needed clarity in the area".

Vinton Cerf [37], one of the architects of TCP/IP, also points out the need for the existence of standards for the handling of information between clouds of different providers, comparing the lack of standards in existence today in the cloud with the lack of communication existing in 1973 when there was no communication between different networks.

Recently IEEE created two working groups P2301 [35] and P2302 [36] for the development of standards for cloud computing. The first group will work on standardization of the cloud, portability and management, while the second group will work on interoperability between clouds.

Other standards under development include the Open Cloud Manifesto, Open Virtualization Format, Open Cloud Computing Interface and rusted Cloud.

Information Localization: The dynamic nature of cloud computing and data movement within the cloud of a single vendor may involve the transference of information between servers with different jurisdictions with different legislation, leading to fact that the client wants to know where the data is stored and restrict the transfer of information within the cloud provider, in order to avoid exposure to this variety of laws and regulations.

Information Retrieval: The retrieval of information from the cloud poses problems when the client wants to be assured that he can retrieve his information at any time, particularly at the end of the contract with the service provider, and without any cost or restriction. On the other side and if the customer wishes to switch to another cloud provider, the provider may charge for returning the information in a format different from that used in its cloud [38]. This is a worrying aspect, mainly in public clouds, where there may be a high risk of user being trapped to a single vendor lock-in.

Lack of Interoperability: The cloud computing offerings were not designed to be interoperable between different providers of cloud services. This lack of interoperability increases the chances of vendor lock-in, limiting the ability to escalate the clouds by different vendors [39] and makes it impossible the clouds work together. Among the various reasons for this lack of interoperability can be referred the use of distinct hypervisor and virtual machine technologies, different security standards and interfaces for management.

Legislation: Closely related with the two concerns above and with the hiring of cloud computing services is the lack of legislation. At present there are few legal precedents for liability in the cloud. It is essential to obtain appropriate legal advice to ensure that the contract specifies the areas where the service provider [40].

Change Management: is an essential process in any IT department being the guarantee that only authorized and carefully planned changes are carried out. The migration to cloud computing must take into account several issues, among them stand out the inventory of all applications, processes and data that will be deployed in order to compare the benefits and risks of the two solutions and a study of service providers to clarify the key challenges already identified in this section and adequacy.

With the large amount of resources it provides for developing and deploying applications, the paradigm of cloud computing is an important tool for the replacement and migration of many of the services until now available in the data center.

Service Level Agreement: The service level agreement, SLA, as a guarantee to the costumers, should provide, at least, the same confidence the costumers have in data centers. Prodan et al. [38], indicate the lack of service level agreements, SLA, as the first problem encountered in the cloud service providers that have evaluated.

Benchmarks: In order to be possible the comparison and performance evaluation between two or more clouds it is needed to have access to metrics that allow a cautious comparison. As stated in [38] these benchmarks currently were missing in cloud providers.

Costs: A company that invested in the implementation of an application and its data center will surely think twice before migrate to the cloud. They can make it, but not before at least capitalize their investments.

Chow et al. present in [41] some challenges posed by cloud computing. These include the easiness and low cost that information can be accessed emphasizing that an attack on a cloud service provider can provide the information and the ability to process the stolen information, the increasing number of authentication requests and the problems posed by data mash-ups.

3   Cloud Computing Adoption

With the large amount of resources provided for developing and deploying applications and services, the cloud paradigm is an important tool for the replacement of many services available in the traditional data center. Could the migration /outsourcing to this new model and the challenges it poses be solved with the help of IT governance techniques, namely the Information Technology Infrastructure Library, ITIL?

Taking into consideration by one hand the need to better satisfy users' needs with less resources and by other the advantages of cloud computing paradigm, a possible solution to some of the problems presented and to the migration to the cloud, is, in our believe, the use and adaptation of the ITIL. This is a part of a work in progress that tries to answer the question "The management techniques of IT services, such as ITIL, can be applied to the cloud computing paradigm and the migration of current systems for cloud computing?"

The issues of migrating to the cloud paradigm could be divided into two major groups: the first one that includes the client concerns and troubles, and the second that contains the problems the client should solve jointly with the provider. In figure 1 is presented the top level issues of this idea in a diagrammatic form.

After clarifying the truly reason why to move to the cloud and making the decision to migrate is essential to obtain a detailed list of all processes, services and applications, the data they use and the relations between them in order to identify which can be migrated and which should remain in-house. This list also includes the detailed needs of security for each process, application and data. Special attention must be taken with the institution core processes since special care should be observed in deciding to and moving these processes to outside of the organization. These processes generally should stay in-house. The information needed for this process could be produced with the help of ITIL, namely the Service Portfolio, the Service Catalog Management process of the Service Design book.

Another important point that the client should look is the communications with the cloud provider, such is, line speed, security, backup among others.

In order to coordinate all the phases of the outsourcing process to the cloud a special attention must be taken with the management of the whole process. Again this change management process could be accomplished with the good practices of ITIL, in particular with the change management process of the Service transition.

On the other side are the issues that the client should solve with the provider(s) collaboration which includes issues related with the services offered by the providers, the contract, i.e., responsibilities definition of the client and the provider, legislation, what rights have the client at the end of contract, etc. Also in this group we consider the complete and detailed definition of all costs involved in the provision of services, the service-level agreements (SLAs), that specifies exactly what and how a provider is expected to do things such as service control, performance monitoring, service evaluation, among others. The Financial Management process of the Service strategy and SLA management process of the Service Design respectively are another ITIL process that helps in costs management and SLA management and validation. With regard to the data special care should be taken with the importation and exportation of information to and from the cloud, the storage, the security and the standards used for the transfer of data.

With the applications moved and executed on the cloud attention must be taken with the security, updates, backups and importation and exportation of the applications to other environments.

The security, as already said is a big concern namely when the information goes to the outside of the organization. When moving to the cloud the issues of responsibility, the access management, the infrastructure, the logs, the standards used, the rules that the personnel like system administrators follow among others should be clarified with the provider. These issues could be minimized with the help of the ITIL process of Information Security Management of the Service Design book.

Last but not least the support which embraces communication with the provider problem solving, incident notification, incident solving, helpdesk and training among others. Once more ITIL, namely the Service Desk function of the Service Operation provides an important support to this issue.

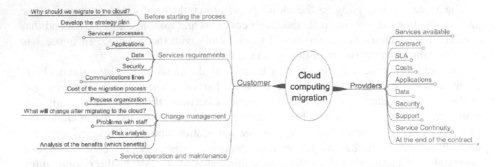

Fig. 1. Cloud adoption issues

4   Conclusion

The paradigm of cloud computing is increasingly proving to be a great revolution in technology infrastructure. The provision of computing power in a similar way to electricity, that is, as a service where you pay for what you consume, is finally being a reality. The adoption of the cloud computing paradigm poses issues that could be minimized with the adoption of the ITIL methodology.

References

1. Vouk, M.A.: Cloud computing: Issues, research and implementations. In: 30th International Conference on Information Technology Interfaces, ITI 2008, pp. 31–40 (June 2008)
2. Zhang, S., Zhang, S., Chen, X., Huo, X.: Cloud computing research and development trend. In: Second International Conference on Future Networks, ICFN 2010, pp. 93–97 (January 2010)
3. Vaquero, L.M., Rodero-Merino, L., Caceres, J., Lindner, M.: A break in the clouds: towards a cloud definition. SIGCOMM Comput. Commun. Rev. 39(1), 50–55 (2009)
4. Mell, P., Grance, T.: Cloud computing,
   http://csrc.nist.gov/groups/SNS/cloud-computing/
5. Chen, Y., Paxson, V., Katz, R.H.: What's new about cloud computing security? Technical Report UCB/EECS-2010-5, EECS Department, University of California, Berkeley (January 2010)
6. Grobauer, B., Walloschek, T., Stocker, E.: Understanding cloud-computing vulnerabilities. IEEE Security Privacy (99), 1 (2010)

7. Khajeh-Hosseini, A., Greenwood, D., Smith, J.W., Sommerville, I.: The Cloud Adoption Toolkit: Addressing the Challenges of Cloud Adoption in Enterprise. CoRR, abs/1003.3866 (May 2010)
8. Shimba, F.: Cloud Computing: Strategies for Cloud Computing Adoption. PhD thesis, Dublin Institute of Technology (2010)
9. Zhang, Q., Cheng, L., Boutaba, R.: Cloud computing: state-of-the art and research challenges. Journal of Internet Services and Applications 1, 7–18 (2010), doi:10.1007/s13174-010-0007-6
10. Foster, I., Zhao, Y., Raicu, I., Lu, S.: Cloud computing and grid computing 360-degree compared. In: 2008 Grid Computing Environments Workshop, pp. 1–10. IEEE (November 2008)
11. Nurmi, D., Wolski, R., Grzegorczyk, C., Obertelli, G., Soman, S., Youseff, L., Zagorodnov, D.: The eucalyptus opensource cloud-computing system. In: CCGRID 2009: Proceedings of the 2009 9th IEEE/ACM International Symposium on Cluster Computing and the Grid, pp. 124–131. IEEE Computer Society, Washington, DC, USA (2009)
12. Schwiegelshohn, U., Badia, R.M., Bubak, M., Danelutto, M., Dustdar, S., Gagliardi, F., Geiger, A., Hluchy, L., Kranzlmüller, D., Laure, E., Priol, T., Reinefeld, A., Resch, M., Reuter, A., Rienhoff, O., Rüter, T., Sloot, P., Talia, D., Ullmann, K., Yahyapour, R., von Voigt, G.: Perspectives on grid computing. In: Kranzlmüller, D., Reuter, A., Schwiegelshohn, U. (eds.) Perspectives Workshop: The Future of Grid Computing, Dagstuhl Seminar Proceedings, vol. 09082, Schloss Dagstuhl - Leibniz-Zentrum fuer Informatik, Germany (2009)
13. Sun Microsystems. Introduction to cloud computing architecture, White Paper, 1st edn. (June 2009), http://www.sun.com/featured-articles/CloudComputing.pdf
14. Boinc - open-source software for volunteer computing and grid computing, http://boinc.berkeley.edu/
15. Welcome to the globus toolkit homepage, http://www.globus.org/toolkit/
16. Dillon, T., Wu, C., Elizabeth, C.: Cloud computing: Issues and challenges. In: 24th IEEE International Conference on Advanced Information Networking and Applications (AINA 2010), April 20-23, pp. 27–33 (2010)
17. Wang, L., Von Laszewski, G., Younge, A., He, X., Kunze, M., Tao, J., Fu, C.: Cloud computing: A Perspective study. New Generation Computing 28(2), 137–146 (2010)
18. Stantchev, V.: Performance evaluation of cloud computing offerings. In: Third International Conference on Advanced Engineering Computing and Applications in Sciences, ADVCOMP 2009, October 11-16, pp. 187–192 (2009)
19. Armbrust, M., Fox, A., Griffith, R., Joseph, A.D., Katz, R.H., Konwinski, A., Lee, G., Patterson, D.A., Rabkin, A., Stoica, I., Zaharia, M.: Above the clouds: A berkeley view of cloud computing. Technical Report UCB/EECS-2009-28, EECS Department, University of California, Berkeley (February 2009)
20. Barroso, L.A., Hölzle, U.: The case for energy-proportional computing. Computer 40(12), 33–37 (2007)
21. Amazon Virtual Private Cloud (Amazon VPC) (beta), http://aws.amazon.com/vpc/
22. Amazon Elastic Compute Cloud (Amazon EC2), http://aws.amazon.com/ec2
23. What is akamai doing in the cloud?, http://www.akamai.com/cloud
24. Google apps, http://www.google.com/apps
25. Force.com: The leading cloud platform for business apps, http://www.salesforce.com/platform

26. Salesforce Customer Relationships Management (CRM) system,
    http://www.salesforce.com
27. Chow, R., Golle, P., Jakobsson, M., Shi, E., Staddon, J., Masuoka, R., Molina, J.:
    Controlling data in the cloud: outsourcing computation without outsourcing control. In:
    Proceedings of the 2009 ACM Workshop on Cloud Computing Security, CCSW 2009, pp.
    85–90. ACM, New York (2009)
28. Survey: Cloud Computing 'No Hype', But Fear of Security and Control Slowing
    Adoption,
    http://www.circleid.com/posts/20090226_cloud_computing_hype_
    security
29. Gens, F.: It cloud services user survey, pt.2: Top benefits & challenges,
    http://blogs.idc.com/ie/?p=210
30. Cruz, A.: Current gmail outage,
    http://googleblog.blogspot.com/2009/02/current-gmail-
    outage.html
31. The Amazon S3 Team. Amazon s3 availability event (July 20, 2008),
    http://status.aws.amazon.com/s3-20080720.html
32. DMTF to Develop Standards for Managing a Cloud Computing Environment,
    http://www.dmtf.org/about/cloud-incubator/DMTF_Cloud_
    Incubator_PR_FIN.pdf
33. Focus group on cloud computing (fg cloud), http://www.itu.int/ITU-T/focus
    groups/cloud/
34. Parkes, S.: Itu group to offer global view of cloud standardization,
    http://www.itu.int/ITU-/newslog/ITU+Group+To+Offer+Global+
    View+Of+Cloud+Standardization.aspx
35. IEEE Standards Association. P2301 - guide for cloud portability and interoperability profiles
    (cpip), http://standards.ieee.org/develop/project/2301.html
36. IEEE Standards Association. P2302 - standard for intercloud interoperability and federation
    (siif), http://standards.ieee.org/develop/project/2302.html
37. Krill, P.: Cerf urges standards for cloud computing (January),
    http://www.infoworld.com/d/cloud-computing/cerf-urges-
    standards-cloud-computing-817
38. Prodan, R., Ostermann, S.: A survey and taxonomy of infrastructure as a service and web
    hosting cloud providers. In: Proceedings of The 10th IEEE/ACM International Conference
    on Grid Computing, pp. 17–25 (October 2009)
39. Rochwerger, B., Breitgand, D., Levy, E., Galis, A., Nagin, K., Llorente, I., Montero, R.,
    Wolfsthal, Y., Elmroth, E., Caceres, J., et al.: The reservoir model and architecture for
    open federated cloud computing. IBM Systems Journal 53(4), 535–545 (2009)
40. ISACA. Cloud computing: Business benefits with security, governance and assurance
    perspectives,   http://www.isaca.org/Template.cfm?Section=Research&
    CONTENTID=53050&TEMPLATE=/ContentManagement/ContentDisplay.cfm
41. Chow, R., Golle, P., Jakobsson, M., Shi, E., Staddon, J., Masuoka, R., Molina, J.:
    Controlling data in the cloud: outsourcing computation without outsourcing control. In:
    Proceedings of the 2009 ACM Workshop on Cloud Computing Security, CCSW 2009, pp.
    85–90. ACM, New York (2009)

Orchestrating Inter-organisational Logistics Workflows on the Cloud

Bill Karakostas and Kamalendu Pal

School of Informatics, City University, London, UK
{billk,kam}@soi.city.ac.uk

Abstract. Cloud computing has made it possible to virtualise not only computing resources, but also whole business processes. A business process workflow that involves multiple participants can now be orchestrated on the Cloud using methods such as service virtualisation, message queues and dynamic message routing. This paper proposes a Cloud architecture for orchestrating inter-organisational logistics processes. The approach allows transport operators to streamline their processes by automating their workflow and to fulfill their reporting obligations to authorities. We illustrate this approach with a scenario of executing a export license application workflow on the Cloud.

Keywords: Cloud computing, inter-organisational workflow, logistics, message architecture.

1 Introduction

A logistics chain is a group of geographically distributed organisations that collaborate to move products between two locations [1]. Collaboration is not achievable however without communication. In logistics chains, electronic communications are mainly message based, where a message is encoded in EDIFACT, email, etc. A message carries data that convey information about the status of the logistics chain activities and is meant to be used for shared understanding amongst the participants and/or to trigger other activities.

Message based communications require a consensus on the format and content of the messages exchanged between sender and recipient. They also require that the recipient knows the electronic address of the sender. Both requirements become difficult to meet in virtual logistics chains where the participants do not know each other beforehand, and/or the membership of the logistics chain is dynamic as participants are added or removed as the logistics process takes place.

Cloud computing offers principles such as virtualization and elasticity of resources [2] that make it a promising paradigm to apply in the execution of virtual logistics chains. Clouds allow virtual services to be provided and accessed, while their physical details remain transparent to the service users. This provides flexibility as it allows logistics chain participants (and the services they provide) to come and go according to the status of the process. Other business benefits from Cloud based collaboration of logistics chains participants are discussed in [3].

G.D. Putnik and M.M. Cruz-Cunha (Eds.): ViNOrg 2011, CCIS 248, pp. 137–144, 2012.
© Springer-Verlag Berlin Heidelberg 2012

In this paper we build on the above idea, and describe a Cloud based architecture to support virtual logistics chain processes. The structure of the paper is as follows. Section 2 describes the main features and components of the Cloud logistics infrastructure. Section 3 illustrates the application of this infrastructure in a logistics scenario involving multiple participants. We conclude with an appraisal of the proposed approach and with plans for further research.

2   Cloud Infrastructure for Logistics Processes Management

A Cloud based infrastructure can help logistics chain participants to carry out collaborative processes and activities. It can do so by acting as a broker between participants and by allowing decoupled communications between them. Thus, the Cloud infrastructure acts as the orchestrator of the distributed business process. We propose that a Cloud based infrastructure for inter-organisational process management must provide the following types of services:

2.1   Naming and Identification Services

Every participating organisation needs to be uniquely identifiable in the logistics chain. One way to achieve that is to issue each participant with a globally unique identifier (UUID). UUIDs are attached to messages to uniquely identify their senders and sometimes the intended recipients. Although UUIDs are used across the logistics chain it is not a requirement that every participant knows the identities of other participants. Instead the Cloud can act as intermediary and connect two participants anonymously, if needed by using information about their respective roles or other context information (e.g. physical location) in their interaction.

2.2   Virtual Message Exchanges

It is important for every participant to receive messages from other participants in an efficient and fault tolerant manner that ensures that all messages are delivered to their intended recipients within specified timeframes. As performance and fault tolerance requirements cannot be guaranteed by typical messaging systems such as email, the Cloud must provide a dedicated message delivery service. Every participating organisation therefore is issued by the Cloud with a Virtual Exchange, similar to what proposed in [4]. This is similar in essence to a mail or messaging server, but with additional QoS capabilities such as guaranteed message delivery. Thus, participants can send messages to Exchanges belonging to other organisations. The messages received by the Exchange are routed to appropriate queues based on routing criteria such the sender of the message, its header, contents etc. All virtual Exchanges have unique names that can be explicitly specified as the destination of messages. This corresponds roughly to the idea of sending an email to a named recipient as opposed to broadcasting a general 'to whom it may concern' message.

2.3   Authentication and Authorisation Services

Only authorised organisations can participate in a given workflow. For this purpose they are issued by the Cloud with security tokens. Tokens' validity is restricted to a specific workflow instance only. Tokens are allocated to organisations according to their roles (see below) in the context of a workflow.

2.4   Role Management Services

In conjunction with security tokens, described above, roles define the possible messages that an organisation can send or receive in the context of a particular workflow. A Cloud registration service decides the possible roles an organization can assume.

2.5   Workflow Management Services

A workflow management services allows participants to enact and manage inter-organisational. workflow processes. . The Cloud supports different types of preconfigured workflow scenarios. An organisation can enact a workflow by sending one of pre-specified message types, instantiated with appropriate parameters, to the Cloud workflow management service. The service then starts the workflow and uses the initiator's Exchange to send messages regarding notifications and other updates about the process of the workflow.

2.6   Messaging and Message Routing Services

A message will always have one or more explicitly or implicitly defined recipients; these are identified by the Cloud service at runtime. Recipients therefore do not need to be explicitly specified in the message, and thus communications between workflow participants can be both asynchronous and anonymous. The Cloud service identifies the recipients of a message and routes it to their Exchanges.

2.7   Domain Specific Services

These are Cloud services that are domain specific, and apply to specific types of workflow. They can be for example, legal services, offering advice on specific activities pertaining to a workflow.

3   A Cloud-Based Inter-organisational Workflow Scenario

The scenario described in this section is adapted from [5] and applies to a product export process. The process starts when an organization acting as Supplier (role) has accepted the order from another organisation with role Customer, and prepares to ship the ordered product. If the Customer is in a country where an export license is required, the Supplier assumes also the role of Exporter and therefore needs to prepare appropriate export documents. The Exporter connects to the virtual Cloud workflow service for Export Applications and sends an export request message, thus triggering the appropriate workflow. By analysing the contents of the message to establish the country of origin and the type of product, the Cloud service identifies the appropriate Authority that handles the export applications and routes the message to its Exchange. The service also issues the exporter with a token corresponding to the new workflow. This token must now be attached to all received or sent messages concerning this workflow, to confirm their authenticity and relevance to this specific workflow. The Authority role is acted by a government authority such as the Export Control Organisation (*ECO* in the UK). This authority can operate for example, a message Exchange called *ExportControl*. Attached to this Exchange, the authority operates different queues for export license applications, inquiries etc. The Cloud service routes the Exporter's message to the above Exchange requesting an export license. The message contains the following fields:

- The UUID of the applicant (Exporter) and the corresponding security token
- References (URIs) to the shipment document and any other documents supporting the export application.
- A reference to the Exporter's own message Exchange that will receive the response from the Authority. The Exchange name is a unique URI such as *myExchange.mymessagebroker.mycompany.mydomain*.

By examining the message header, the Authority Exchange establishes that the message is an export license application and inserts it in its internal queue named *license_applications*. Subsequently, the message gets retrieved from the queue by another application (internal to the authority) and ultimately delivered to a person (such as a case officer) who process the application. When the application is examined, a response message is sent to the Exchange of the Exporter that contains:

- The security token corresponding to the relevant workflow
- A code describing the outcome of the application (e.g. "successful" or "unsuccessful").
- A URI for the export license. This is (a) digitally signed and (b) 'watermarked' using a hash of the Exporter's UUID and the security token. Thus, the export license's authenticity can be verified, but also the license cannot be reused for other purposes, i.e. it only is valid for the respective application and applicant.

Upon receipt of this message, the Exporter updates the status of the Export License application document with the new status, (e.g. "granted") and with a reference to the URI of the license. Using a similar approach, the Exporter requests (and eventually receives approval or rejection) for certificates such as:

- Health certificates (from Health Authority).
- Conformity certificate (from Import Health Authority).
- Certificate of Origin (from Chamber of Commerce), and others.

Table 1 shows some of the message Exchanges between participants in the above workflow.

Table 1. Messages Exchanges for export license workflow

Sender	Recipient	Message
Supplier	Customer	Packing Weight List/Delivery Note/Invoice
Supplier	Customs	Customs Product List /Customs Invoice, Certificate of Origin, Age certificates and batch codes, Invoice
Insurer	Supplier	Insurance certificate (for customer)
Supplier	Carrier/ shipper	Standard Shipping Note and Bill of Lading Instructions
Carrier/ shipper	Customer	Dispatch advice ('ship to')

The workflow ends when Customer records receipt of cleared goods at agreed location. The final message confirming receipt of the product is sent to the Supplier's Exchange.

During the above workflow, interaction between the systems of the participants is kept at a minimum consisting mainly of asynchronous message Exchanges. This in turn ensures minimum coupling and dependencies between such systems, and therefore more flexible and dynamic processes.

Figure 1 illustrates the Cloud architecture for the above scenario. Each of the identified participants (shipper, carrier, customs, etc.) operates an Exchange (shown as rounded shapes) to which queues are attached (rectangles with labels, attached to Exchange symbols). Although communications are shown as direct for clarity purposes, it is in fact the Cloud service that is responsible for routing the message from sender to recipient. Attached to each Exchange are 'systems' (shown as computer icons). These are internal systems of the participants such as ERP, warehouse and other logistics applications that are responsible for processing the messages received by the Exchanges. Organisations that do not operate Exchanges can still access messages using simple browser applications, through special purpose Internet gateways provided by the infrastructure.

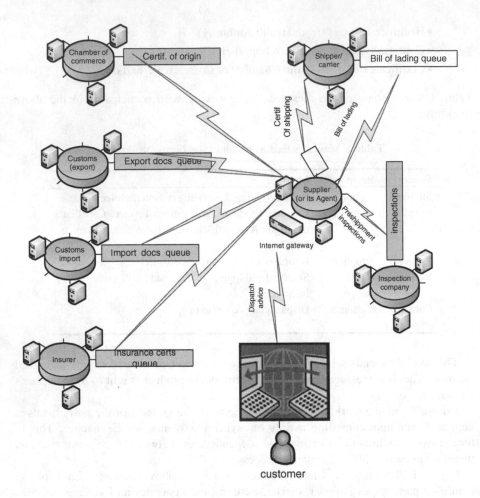

Fig. 1. Cloud architecture supporting logistics inter-organisational processes

4   Discussion

It has been noted in the research literature that the permanent building and dismantling of partnerships in inter-organisational business processes necessitates new kinds of flexible solutions [6]. We argue that such flexibility is made possible by a Cloud architecture such as the one described in this paper, that has potential benefits for stakeholders such as the national authorities involved in regulating and managing logistics, as well as for logistics service providers and users alike. The collaborative Cloud architecture can be seen as an evolution of the current effort to automate business to business and business to administration transactions by digitization. The Cloud simplifies this task by reducing the need of participants to install and maintain complex systems, and also the need to establish fixed (and therefore inflexible) digital links between organisations.

Some of the benefits for authorities involved in controlling or regulating logistics are:

•*Improved trader compliance*: merchants can submit correct and complete regulatory documentation on time and with fewer errors. This means that it's more likely an increased number of merchants will submit their documentation rather than avoid it.

• *Better security*: The approach supports better safety and security compliance by ensuring that all information is reported in systematic way, resulting in more secure and efficient trade procedures.

• *Increased integrity and transparency*: The Cloud maintains up to date procedural requirements and so reduces unintentional errors and increase trader compliance.

Some of the benefits for users (traders, carriers and other third parties) include:

• *Faster clearance and release:* The proposed service enables administrations to process information, documents and fees both faster and more accurately, so merchants should benefit from faster clearance and release times for goods.

• *Predictable application and explanation of rules*: The improved transparency and increased predictability of the legislation can reduce the potential for fraudulent behaviour.

• *Up to date information on rules and regulations*: This approach can provide the trading parties with up-to-date information regarding things such as import/export duties, tariff rates and other legal and procedural requirements.

In summary, this paper introduced a Cloud based architecture for automating inter-organisational processes and workflows in logistics chains, and illustrated it with an example from a UN/CEFACT process scenario. The Cloud architecture can be realized using off the shelf components and existing Cloud systems. The proposed infrastructure is not intended to replace the current systems of logistics participants:iIts aim is rather to augment such systems by making them Cloud enabled, and to enhance their communication capabilities.

The main obstacles for adopting the above described approach are likely to be political/cultural and economic rather than technological. One main issue for example, is who is going to fund the proposed Cloud infrastructure. Here different scenarios can be explored such as a joint government/private operation that is partly subsidised by government investment but is also subscription/fee funded. In this way a commercial organization can host the proposed Cloud infrastructure and run it as a commercial operation.

Acknowledgments. Research described in this paper has been partially sponsored by EU project e-Freight.

References

1. Christofer, M.: Logistics and Supply Chain Management: Creating Value - Adding Networks., 3rd edn. Financial Times/ Prentice Hall (2004)
2. Ko, R.K.L.: Cloud Computing in Plain English. Crossroads 169(3) (2010)

3. Karakostas, B., Katsoulakos, T.: Cloud Architecture for e-collaboration in the intermodal freight business. In: Proc. KMIS 2010: Internatonal Conference on Knowledge Management and Information Sharing, Valencia, Spain (2010)
4. Richardson, A.: Introduction to RabbitMQ An open source message broker that just works (2010), http://www.rabbitmq.com
5. UN/CEFACT, Reference Model of the International Supply Chain with special reference to Trade Facilitation and Trade Security Source: UN/CEFACT/TBG-International Trade Procedures and Business Process Analysis Groups (November 12, 2003)
6. Schmidt, R.: Flexible Support of Inter-Organizational Business Processes Using Web Services. In: Proc. Sixth Workshop on Business Process Modeling, Development, and Support (BPMDS 2005), Porto, Portugal (2005)

A Planning System Using a Four Level Approach for the Planning of Production in a Networked Organization

Wilhelm Dangelmaier and Dietrich Dürksen

Heinz Nixdorf Institute, University of Paderborn, Business Computing, Especially CIM,
Fürstenallee 11, 33102 Paderborn, Germany
{Wilhelm.Dangelmaier,Dietrich.Duerksen}@hni.uni-paderborn.de

Abstract. Planning of production in a networked organization is a challenge for many manufacturers in a globalized world. Optimal dimensioning of the network consisting of production sites and their economic interrelations is the overall planning task to be tackled. A system using a hierarchical four level approach to cope with this task is presented in this paper. The complex task is divided into four sub-tasks according to the time frame of the decisions, scope of consideration and the decision hierarchy of the company. These tasks are linked to a hierarchical overall process by adequate coordination processes. Mathematical optimization models are used to represent and solve the individual sub-problems. This process is implemented into a prototype planning system an evaluated using case studies.

Keywords: Networked production, hierarchical planning, dimensioning.

1 Introduction

This paper presents an approach for the planning of companywide production networks. It deals with the dimensioning and the configuration of the individual production sites with a given network structure. Dimensioning in general is the definition of all restrictions according to capacity and throughput and requires the consideration of time (cf. [1]). In the context of the planning of production networks this is the determination of the performance of the individual sites and actual flows inside of the network. The performance is determined under consideration of qualitative and quantitative capacity aspects. These aspects are specified in detail by the determination of required machinery and workforce.

2 Problem Statement

A production network consists of the production sites of a company that are connected by logistic interrelations. It is characterized by the distribution of production processes among several production sites leading to complex logistic interdependencies and an increased need of coordination (cf. [2]). Furthermore it cannot be regarded as fixed and unchangeable, because adjustments are required due to changes in surrounding conditions. Since initiated adjustments take effect in later

G.D. Putnik and M.M. Cruz-Cunha (Eds.): ViNOrg 2011, CCIS 248, pp. 145–154, 2012.
© Springer-Verlag Berlin Heidelberg 2012

periods only, it is not sufficient to react on changes in surrounding conditions when they occur. Therefore it is necessary to initiate adequate adjustments in advance to assure optimal production in a well configured network. Finding appropriate adjustment measures is to be carried out by planning. Planning can be defined as the anticipation of future events by systematic preparation of decisions and decision making (cf. [3]). The concept that documents the results of this process is called plan (cf. [1]).

Systematic preparation of decisions requires a formal definition of the planning task. Figure 1 shows the structure of the planning task of dimensioning of production networks. One of the prerequisites of the overall planning task is the current state of the production network. It is the starting point for the planning process and is given by the network structure consisting of production sites and their possible relationships. Further prerequisites are the future demands for the products and the surrounding conditions. The factual objective is the determination of an adequate dimensioning for the production network. Formal objectives are the requirements for the solution quality of the determined plan and the time needed to find the solution. The result is a plan that fulfills the factual and formal objectives and consists of determined qualitative and quantitative capacity requirements as well as required machinery and workforce. The planning method defines the decision making process. It uses a model of the production network that is supposed to be a formal representation of all relevant aspects of the production network according to the planning task. It includes a formal definition of the rules and parameters used by the planning method to find and evaluate alternatives.

Regarding the structure of the overall planning task four planning levels can be identified. Fig. 2 presents the planning levels and their hierarchical interaction. The task on top level of the hierarchy is the determination of qualitative capacity

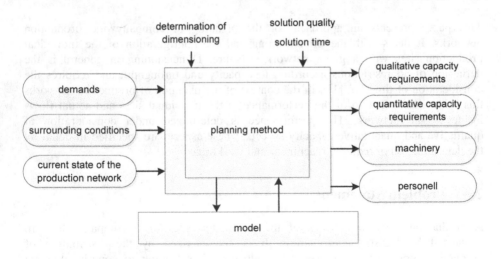

Fig. 1. Overall planning task

requirements, which determines the long-term performance of the production sites and the entire production network. This is done by assigning production processes to sites, which defines the products that can be produced at each production site. They build the framework for the decisions to be made on the second level, the determination of quantitative capacity requirements. At this level the task is to find a good or optimal distribution of the production to the locations based on the quantitative demand. Additionally, quantitative determination of flows in the network takes place. Based on these levels three and four are planned. On level three they are converted into machinery. With the objective of cost efficient fulfillment of demands decisions are made on the optimal development of machine assets and on the outsourcing of individual products. Machine capacities planned at this level and quantitative capacity requirements from level 2 are converted into workforce on level four. Therefore decisions on the employment and on the qualification of personnel have to be made. In addition to this top-down interaction the influence of subordinate levels on superordinate levels can be enabled by the anticipation of lower levels during the planning of higher levels. On the other hand it is possible to implement feedback loops.

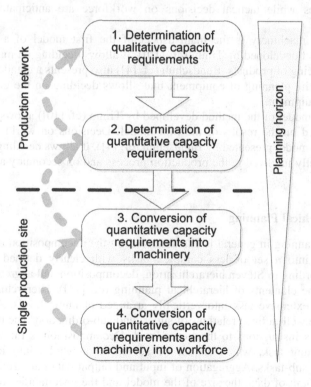

Fig. 2. Interaction of planning levels

3   State of the Art

3.1   Solution Methods for Dimension Planning

Qualitative capacity aspects are usually considered as a part of an extensive method. A model presented by Bundschuh (cf. [4]) includes qualitative aspects by the allocation of equipment to production sites. The allocated equipment defines the ability of a production site to produce a certain set of products. Kriesel (cf. [5]) presents a method for strategic location and production planning. His planning system allows decisions on productions sites, the allocation of production processes and products to production sites and the dimension of resources.

Quantitative capacity aspects can be found in different models for the optimization of production networks. A model presented by Henrich (cf. [6], [7]) allows the allocation of end products and quantities to production sites under consideration of capacity limits. Ferber (cf. [8], [7]) extends this model to allow the planning of capacities using capacity stages. Bihlmaier et al. (cf. [9]) develop a two stage stochastic optimization model for strategic and tactical production planning. The first stage focuses on strategic decisions like the allocation of products and quantities to production sites while tactical decisions on workforce are anticipated by linear approximation.

Planning of machinery is the main aspect of the first model of a hierarchical planning method developed by Timm (cf. [10]). It allows deciding on machine assets and on outsourcing of products. Bundschuh (cf. [4]) also presents a detailed version of the model for the planning of equipment that allows deciding on the extension and reduction of equipment.

The second model of the method developed by Timm (cf. [10]) allows deciding on workforce based on the results of the first model. Decisions on workforce are also included in the model presented by Bundschuh (cf. [4]). It allows deciding on primary personnel directly involved in the production process and on secondary and overhead personnel.

3.2   Hierarchical Planning

Hierarchical planning in general is characterized by the decomposition of a complex planning task into a set of less complex tasks with clearly defined hierarchical relations. According to Steven hierarchization, decomposition and aggregation can be identified as the elements of hierarchical planning (cf. [11]). Hierarchization is the division of an extensive task into vertically arranged planning levels. Among these levels there are well-defined relations of super- and sub-ordination. The upper level is allowed to pass instructions to the lower level. Decomposition is the division of a complex planning task, which cannot be solved as a whole, into less complex interdependent sub-tasks. Aggregation of input and output data into groups is used to reduce the amount of data, the size of the model and the uncertainties of the data. It can also be used to influence the type of decisions. Decomposition and hierarchization have to be performed under consideration of the decision hierarchy of the company to allow better acceptance of planning results (cf. [12]).

Schneeweiss [13] introduces a general characterization of hierarchical planning structures. A hierarchical planning system consists of "different kinds of subsystems having particular interrelations and outputs" [13]. One main characteristic of this system is the anticipation of the base-level by the top-level. According to this anticipation an optimal instruction is communicated to the base-level. Taking this instruction into account the base-level derives an optimal reaction that is passed to the top-level creating a feedback loop. This cycle is repeated until it results in a final decision.

4   Concept

4.1   Models for the Individual Levels

Mathematical optimization models have been defined for the individual planning levels. The presentation of entire models is out of scope of this paper, so only the objective functions of the models of the first and the second level are presented here. Table 1 presents a list of sets used in the models. The production sites of the production network to be planned are represented by the set of sites S. The Set of products E represents all end-products, components and parts that are produced. The set of technologies T represents the production processes in the production network with products being the input and the output of a technology.

Table 1. List of sets

Symbol	Definition
$P = \{p_0, \ldots, p_n\}$	Periods (period p_0 defines the initial state)
S	Production sites
E	Products
T	Technologies
G	Technology groups
$K = \{k_0, \ldots, k_n\}$	Capacity stages

Technologies with similar production processes are grouped to a technology group from the set of technology groups G.

The time structure and the granularity of the models are defined by the set of periods P with period p_0 being the initial state. Since the individual levels require different time structures and granularities the set P is valid in the context of the particular model only. The sets K, W and M represent the capacities to be planned at the different levels. Table 2 presents a list of all cost parameters of all models. Some parameters are relevant for several models; others are used for a single model only. Table 3 presents a list of the decision variables of all models.

Table 2. Cost parameters

Symbol	Definition
c_{tsp}^{T}	costs for technology t at site s in period p
c_{tsp}^{T+}	costs for adding technology t to site s in period p
c_{tsp}^{T-}	costs for removing technology t from site s in period p
c_{gsp}^{TG}	costs for technology group g at site s in period p
c_{gsp}^{TG+}	costs for adding technology group g to site s in period p
c_{gsp}^{TG-}	costs for removing technology group g from site s in period p
$c_{ess'p}^{LGfix}$	fixed costs for transportation of product e from site s to site s' in period p
c_{es}^{Pfix}	fixed costs for production of product e at site s
c_{es}^{Pvar}	variable costs for production of product e at site s
c_{ktsp}^{KS}	costs of capacity stage k of technology t at site s in period p
c_{kgsp}^{KSG}	costs of capacity stage k of technology group g at site s in period p
$c_{kk'ts}^{KA}$	costs for change from capacity stage k to stage k' of technology t at site s
$c_{kk'gs}^{KA}$	costs for change from capacity stage k to stage k' of technology group g at site s
$c_{ess'p}^{LG}$	costs for transportation of one unit of product e from site s to site s' in period p
c_{es}^{V}	penalty cost per unit of product e at site s for demands that exceeds available capacity

Table 3. Decision variables

Symbol	Definition
b_{tsp}^{T}	1 if technology t is assigned to site s in period p, else 0
b_{tsp}^{T+}	1 if technology t is added to site s in period p, else 0
b_{tsp}^{T-}	1 if technology t is removed from site s in period p, else 0
b_{gsp}^{TG}	1 if technology group g is assigned to site s in period p, else 0
b_{gsp}^{TG+}	1 if technology group g is added to site s in period p, else 0
b_{gsp}^{TG-}	1 if technology group g is removed from site s in period p, else 0
$b_{ess'p}^{LG}$	1 if transportation of product e from site s to site s' occurs in period p
b_{eps}^{EST}	1, if product e is produced at site s in period p, else 0
$b_{ess'p}^{LG}$	1, if product e is transported from site s to site s' in period p, else 0
b_{ktsp}^{KS}	1, if capacity stage k of technology t is selected at site s in period p, else 0
b_{kgsp}^{KSG}	1, if capacity stage k of technology group g is selected at site s in period p, else 0
$b_{kk'tsp}^{KA}$	1, if capacity is changed from stage k to stage k' for technology t at site s in period p, else 0
$b_{kk'gsp}^{KA}$	1, if capacity is changed from stage k to stage k' for technology group g at site s in period p, else 0
$x_{ess'p}^{LG}$	amount of product e transported from site s to site s' in period p
x_{esp}^{V}	amount of product e at site s in period p that exceeds available capacity

Model for the Determination of Qualitative Capacity Requirements

The objective of the determination of qualitative capacity requirements is to minimize the costs for the assignment of production processes to site, costs for changes in the assignment and logistic costs. Therefore the objective function (1) sums up the costs for technologies assigned, changes in the assignment of technologies, costs for technology groups assigned, changes in the assignment of technology groups and costs for transportation caused by the assignment. Additionally costs for the amount of any product that exceeds available capacities are added.

$$
\min z_1 = \sum_{p \in P} \left(\sum_{s \in S} \left(\sum_{t \in T} \left(b_{tsp}^T \cdot c_{tsp}^T + b_{tsp}^{T^+} \cdot c_{tsp}^{T^+} + b_{tsp}^{T^-} \cdot c_{tsp}^{T^-} \right) \right. \right.
$$
$$
+ \sum_{g \in G} \left(b_{gsp}^{TG} \cdot c_{gsp}^{TG} + b_{gsp}^{TG^+} \cdot c_{gsp}^{TG^+} + b_{gsp}^{TG^-} \cdot c_{gsp}^{TG^-} \right)
$$
$$
\left. \left. + \sum_{e \in E} \sum_{s' \in S} b_{ess'p}^{LG} \cdot c_{ess'p}^{LG\,fix} \right) + \sum_{e \in E} x_{ep}^V \cdot c_e^V \right) \tag{1}
$$

Model for the Determination of Quantitative Capacity Requirements

The objective of this planning level (2) is to minimize costs of production, transportation and capacities. Production costs consist of fixed production costs per product and variable production costs per unit. Transportation costs are calculated per unit of a product that is transported from one site to another. Costs for capacities consist of cost for chosen capacity stages for technologies and technology groups and for changes of capacity stages.

$$
\min z_2 = \sum_{p \in P} \sum_{s \in S} \left[\sum_{e \in E} \left(b_{esp}^{EST} \cdot c_{es}^{P\,fix} + x_{esp}^{EST} \cdot c_{es}^{P\,var} + x_{esp}^V \cdot c_{es}^V \right) \right.
$$
$$
+ \sum_{m=1}^{n^{ST}} x_{ess'p}^{LG} \cdot c_{ess'p}^{LG}
$$
$$
+ \sum_{t \in T} \sum_{k \in K} \left(b_{ktsp}^{KS} \cdot c_{ktsp}^{KS} + \sum_{k' \in K} b_{k'ktsp}^{KA} \cdot c_{k'kts}^{KA} \right)
$$
$$
\left. + \sum_{g \in G} \sum_{k \in K} \left(b_{kgsp}^{KSG} \cdot c_{kgsp}^{KSG} + \sum_{k' \in K} b_{k'kgsp}^{KAG} \cdot c_{k'kgs}^{KAG} \right) \right] \tag{2}
$$

4.2   Hierarchical Overall Process

Coordination Processes

In order to create a hierarchical overall process, coordination processes for anticipation, instruction and reaction are defined.

Anticipations: The determination of qualitative capacity demands anticipates the decisions of the second level by taking into account maximum capacities for production processes and production sites and local content quota for countries. Capacity stages used for the determination of quantitative capacity demands are an anticipation of available machine capacities and workforce, which are planned in detail on the subordinate levels. Machine capacities on level three include an anticipation of the availability of personnel.

Instructions: Planning results of the individual levels define the framework for subordinate levels and form the instruction of the upper level to the lower levels. The optimal allocation of production processes to production sites is the instruction passed from level one to level two. The allocation of products and quantities, which is one result of the model on level two, is the instruction passed from level two to subordinate levels. On level three decisions on machine assets and outsourcing are made and passed as instructions to level four.

Reactions: The definition of reactions requires the definition of a ratio indicating the need to react. Since the overall planning process and the individual levels have to ensure the production of all demands, the ratio of demands that cannot be produced using the determined plan is an adequate indicator. Its value based ratio of the objective function is used to allow the comparison of different products. Equation (3) shows the ratio for the second level. Additionally a threshold value K_2^{max}, is defined. A reaction occurs if the ratio of a plan is above the threshold value. Ratios and threshold values for levels three and four are defined in a similar way.

$$K_2 = \frac{\sum_{p \in P} \sum_{e \in E} \sum_{s \in S} x_{esp}^V \cdot c_{es}^V}{z_2} \tag{3}$$

Hierarchical Planning Procedure

The combination of the coordination processes described before results in a hierarchical planning procedure. On each level the corresponding mathematical optimization model is used to solve the planning task. On the first level production processes are assigned to production sites. This assignment is the instruction passed to the subordinate level, the determination of quantitative capacity requirements. Here quantitative capacity demands are determined by assigning products and quantities to production sites and passed as instruction to subordinate levels. If ratio K_2 exceeds the threshold value K_2^{max}, a feedback process is initiated allowing the adjustment of the parameters of level one for the next planning run. On level 3 quantitative capacity requirements are converted into machinery. Machine capacities planned at this level and quantitative capacity requirements are the instructions passed to level 4 and converted into workforce there.

5   Results

The approach presented in this paper was implemented into a software prototype to prove the usability for real world problems. This prototype is shown in figure 3. It consists of a database for input and output data, IBM ILOG CPLEX 12.1 to solve the optimization models and a Java program to build the model from input data using the CPLEX Java API. The program was parallelized to improve performance.

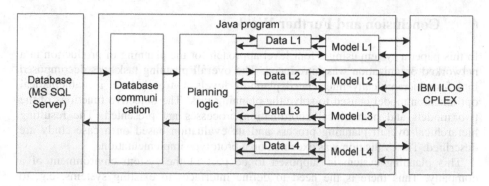

Fig. 3. Structure of the implemented system

This prototype was tested for different examples. One example is briefly presented below.

In this example 3794 products from 28 product groups are produced distributed to 7 production sites. A new site is going to start production in the second quarter of the first year planned. It is possible to allocate production processes of 41 products of product group 1 and 43 components of product group 1K to this site. At the beginning of quarter 3 of the second year the second part of the new site is going to start production. From then on the option to allocate production processes of 51 products of product group 2 and 40 components of product group 2K should be evaluated.

On the first level the allocation of production processes to the new production site and its effects on other parts of the production network were determined. A planning horizon of five years with a granularity of quarters was chosen for this level. The results showed the startup of production at the new site. Starting with the assignment of 42 processes in second quarter the number of processes assigned to the new site increases to 58 processes for the product groups 1 and 1K. A similar startup is planned for product groups 2 and 2K starting in third quarter of the second year.

Based on the allocation of production processes quantitative capacity requirements are determined by assigning production quantities to production sites. At this level a planning horizon of 24 months was chosen. The results showed that due to the assignment of quantities to the new site there is a drop in assigned quantities at two other sites producing the same products as the new one.

For one of the existing sites planning level three was executed to analyze the effects on the machinery of this site. At this site 32 machines are available to produce the demands for 434 products. Here a planning horizon of 52 weeks was chosen. Due to a high level of demands the results show a high utilization of machinery at this site. An extension of machinery is not necessary, because of the relieving effect of new site on the capacity situation.

In a last step workforce was planned for the same site. The results showed that the existing 173 employees are not sufficient and that it necessary to hire 12 additional employees. Additionally, 4 of the existing employees need to acquire a second qualification to allow flexible assignment.

6   Conclusion and Further Work

In this paper a system using a four level approach for the planning of production in a networked organization was introduced. The overall planning task was decomposed into four hierarchically interrelated planning levels. On each level a mathematical optimization model is used to solve the planning task. The objective functions of the two models and hierarchical coordination processes are presented. The resulting hierarchical overall planning process and its evaluation based on a case study are described. The evaluation was executed on a prototype implementation.

This planning system is supposed to be part of the system environment of a company. Thus there is the need to define interfaces to existing systems, e.g. to retrieve master data (products, bill of material etc.) needed as input for planning. There is also the need for a graphical user interface allowing a user-friendly control of the system, analyses of results and interaction with the system in the purpose of the hierarchical planning process. Thus a partial implementation of such a graphical user interface has been realized, but further extension is needed.

References

1. Dangelmaier, W.: Fertigungsplanung: Aufbau und Ablauf der Fertigung. Springer, Berlin (2001)
2. Kaphahn, A., Lücke, T.: Koordination interner Produktionsnetzwerke. In: Produktionsplanung und -Steuerung: Grundlagen, Gestaltung und Konzepte (2006)
3. Hahn, D.: Planung, strategische. In: Handwörterbuch der Produktionswirtschaft, Schäffer-Poeschel, Stuttgart (1996)
4. Bundschuh, M.J.: Modellgestützte strategische Planung von Produktionssystemen in der Automobilindustrie. Verlag Dr. Kovac, Hamburg (2008)
5. Kriesel, C.: Szenarioorientierte Unternehmenstrukturoptimierung - Strategische Standort- und Produktionsplanung. Heinz-Nixdorf-Institut, Universität Paderborn (2005)
6. Henrich, P.: Strategische Gestaltung von Produktionssystemen in der Automobilindustrie. Shaker, Aachen (2002)
7. Fleischmann, B., Ferber, S., Henrich, P.: Strategic Planning of BMW's Global Production Network. Interfaces 3(36) (2006)
8. Ferber, S.: Strategische Kapazitäts- und Investitionsplanung in der globalen Supply Chain eines Automobilherstellers. Shaker, Aachen (2005)
9. Bihlmaier, R., Koberstein, A., Obst, R.: Modeling and optimizing of strategic and tactical production planning in the automotive industry under uncertainty. OR Spectrum (31) (2008)
10. Timm, T.: Ein Verfahren zur hierarchischen Struktur-, Dimensions- und Material bedarfsplanung von Fertigungssystemen, Heinz-Nixdorf-Institut, Universität Paderborn (2009)
11. Steven, M.: Handbuch Produktion: Theorie- Management- Logistik- Controlling. Kohlhammer, Stuttgart (2007)
12. Stadtler, H.: Hierarchische Produktionsplanung. In: Handwörterbuch der Produktion swirtschaft, Schäffer-Poeschel, Stuttgart, pp. 631–641 (1996)
13. Schneeweiss, C.: Distributed Decision Making. Springer, Heidelberg (2003)

Resilience of Virtual and Networked Organizations: An Assessment

Zora Arsovski[1], Slavko Arsovski[2], Aleksandar Aleksic[2],
Miladin Stefanovic[2], and Danijela Tadic[2]

[1] Faculty of Economics,
University of Kragujevac, Djure Pucara, 34 000 Kragujevac, Serbia
zora@kg.ac.rs
[2] Faculty of Mechanical Engineering,
University of Kragujevac, Sestre Janjic 6, 34 000 Kragujevac, Serbia
{cqm,aaleksic,miladin,danijela}@kg.ac.rs

Abstract. Virtual organizations (VO) represent a future paradigm of business. Having in mind different types of perturbations in business today, from the economic crisis to the earthquakes in Japan and terrorists' actions, new business solutions have emerged in order to sustain development all over the world. As a new field in scientific research, organizational resilience needs to be investigated in the context of VOs. This paper has the intention to suggest a qualitative way to assess one dimension of organizational resilience in VOs and to establish directions for future work, emphasizing the importance of quantifying overall organizational resilience.

Keywords: Virtual organization, resilience, management of the keystone vulnerabilities, fuzzy model.

1   Introduction

Disruption in business has widened, it includes a traditional natural disaster and any event that disturbs this fast-paced operational flow — from an acquisition or organization's growth to a new government regulation or to a scheduled system upgrade. Many organizations today are made up of multiple, distributed members, temporarily linked together for competitive advantage, that share common value chains and business processes supported by distributed information technology. These organizations are virtual organizations (VO).

Efforts to improve the capacity for improvements and sustainability mechanisms of systems have often been an interesting theme of researchers and practitioners [1]. The practical concern for this topic is usually driven by events that have happened and can cause serious damage, either in one organization or in the industry as a whole. The motivation for organizations and VOs to prevent such events from happening again, in concrete cases is because they may result in severe losses (including equipment, funding, internal resources, even employees) [2]. New demands are invariably seen as translating into increased costs for organizations and VOs so they lead to challenges

G.D. Putnik and M.M. Cruz-Cunha (Eds.): ViNOrg 2011, CCIS 248, pp. 155–164, 2012.
© Springer-Verlag Berlin Heidelberg 2012

that should be overcome. Theoretically, the business paradigm called organizational resilience [3] should give answers on how to successfully overcome all kinds of disruptions and business threats.

Simply put, a resilience of virtual organizations (RVO) is characterized by dispersed people, knowledge, systems and workspaces. It is electronically integrated across employees, partners, buyers, suppliers, external sources and communities and deliberately designed to adjust quickly to misfortune, shock or major change. It must operate at full-speed, even in the face of adversity and caution. Organizational resilience has become a very interesting research area over the last two decades. There are significant research efforts [4], but this concept has to be explored more.

Legnick-Hall et al [5] proposed that an organization's capacity for resilience can be developed through strategically managing human resources. The goal is to create competencies among core employees, that when aggregated at the organizational level, make it possible for organizations to achieve the ability to respond in a resilient manner when they experience severe shocks. Authors started by reviewing three elements central to developing an organization's capacity for resilience (specific cognitive abilities, behavioral characteristics, and contextual conditions) and after that they identified the individual level employee contributions needed to achieve each of these elements.

VOs are usually global scale organizations, having business operations on a global level by using information and communication technology (ICT). That is why ICT represents one of the most sensitive parts of the VO resilience concept. VOs are based on information and on knowledge; with a simpler management structure, less bureaucracy, they seem to be more flexible than „classic" organizations [6]. This can be supported by the fact that information has a multiplier role, activating all economic sectors and it assists organizational optimization, raising productivity, while lowering costs. The central model of VO resilience which is proposed by Center for Quality – Faculty of Mechanical Engineering is presented in figure 1.

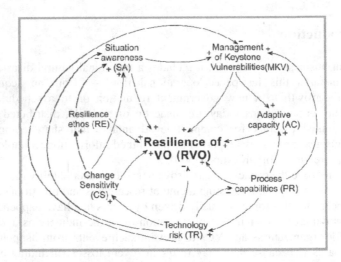

Fig. 1. Central model of VO resilience with the most influential factors (Change Sensitivity, Technology Risk and Process Robustness) and resilience indicators

Resilience of a VO is a very unexplored research area. The four dimensions of organizational resilience [7]: RE – Resilience Ethos, SA – Situation Awareness, KV – Keystone Vulnerabilities, AC – Adaptive Capacity.

As it is considered that some resilience indicators have the same value of importance for „classic" and virtual organizations, it is very important to clarify other more „sensitive" indicators. This model is very similar to the model of organizational resilience. Since the issue is VO resilience, the impact of three factors with the greatest influence is emphasized. These factors are: Change sensitivity, Technology risk, Process robustness.

VO resilience assessment is based on the four dimensions of organizational resilience and impact and inter relations of three listed factors should be examined by the type of VO. As it is a very complex task, presented here is a new model for the Management of the Keystone Vulnerabilities assessment based on the theory of fuzzy logic. This represents the first step in overall resilience assessment.

The contribution of this paper can be presented as follows:

1.   The correlation of resilience of „classic" and VO is analyzed for the first time,
2.   Relevant models of dependability, risk, safety, vulnerability and resilience are integrated into a new advanced model for resilience assessment.

The structure of this paper is organized as follows. The literature review of „classic" and VO resilience is presented in Section 2. The algorithm for VO resilience assessment is given in Section 3 and the case study is presented in Section 4. Section 5 sets the conclusions.

2   Problem Statement

The paper further explains the problem of the Management of the Keystone Vulnerabilities assessment in a medium manufacturing VO in an advanced defined period (for one year period). The solution of the considered problem directly influences the effectiveness of management towards goals. Nowadays, there is no defined methodological approach which can be used for VO resilience assessment, either in literature or in practice.

2.1   Notation

The notation used in this paper can be expressed as below:

i- indicator index, i=1,..,I,
I- number of indicators,
j- component index,
J - number of components of indicator I, i=1,..,I,
e-decision maker of management team index,
E-number of decision makers of management team,
k-part of VO index,
K-number of parts of VO,

$\tilde{w}{}^{e}_{ji}$ - a triangular fuzzy number $\left(x; l^{e}_{ji}, m^{e}_{ji}, u^{e}_{ji} \right)$ describing the relative importance of component j of indicator I, j=1,.., ; i=1,..,I according to judgment of decision maker e, e=1,...,E,

$\tilde{w}_{ji}$ - a discrete fuzzy number $\left(x; l_{ji}, m_{ji}, u_{ji} \right)$ describing the relative importance of component j of indicator I, j=1,.., ; i=1,..,I,

$\tilde{v}_{jk}$ - a triangular fuzzy number $\left(y; l_{jk}, m_{jk}, u_{jk} \right)$ describing the value of component j for part k of VO j=1,.., ; k=1,..,K,

$\tilde{V}_{i}$ - a discrete fuzzy number describing the weighted value of indicator I of whole VO, i=1,..,I

α -degree of membership functions,

$\overset{\sim}{MKV}$ - a discrete fuzzy number describing the weighted value of Management of the Keystone Vulnerabilities assessment of VO,

MKV - the scalar value of fuzzy number $\overset{\sim}{MKV}$.

2.2   Modeling of Indicators' Weights

All the components usually do not have the same importance. However, it can be assumed that one component in every part of the VO has equal importance. The relative importance of each component is subjectively assessed by a weighting coefficient, which is supposed to be a vague linguistic expression. A triangular fuzzy set is associated with each vague linguistic expression. For instance, the membership functions of the fuzzy terms which are used in this paper are: *very low importance*, *low importance*, *medium importance*, *high importance* and *very high importance*. The triangular fuzzy sets are defined on the almost integer scale [0-1], where 0 denotes the lowest relative importance and 1 denotes the highest relative importance: *very low importance* – (0,0,0.2), *low importance* – (0,0,0.4), *medium importance* – (0.3, 0.5, 0.7), *high importance* – (0.6,1,1), *very high importance* – (0.8, 1,1).

2.3   Fuzzy Delphi Method

The Delphi method accumulates and analyzes the results of anonymous experts (in this paper they are denoted as the management team [8]) that communicate in written, discussion and feedback formats on a particular topic. In this paper, the Delphi method is realized in the following phases.

Phase1. Every decision maker of the management team presents his assessment which is based on knowledge, experiences, available information, expertise, skills, etc. The team interprets their assessment in accordance with one of five defined linguistic expressions.

Phase2. Analysis of management team assessment is realized in the following steps:

(1) The mean value of assessment is calculated, $\tilde{w}{}^{I}_{ji}$, j=1,.., J_j; i=1,..,I, which is presented by a fuzzy number in compliance with fuzzy algebra rules [9].

(2) The distance $\tilde{w}{}^{I}_{ji}$ is calculated for every fuzzy number which has intersection $\tilde{w}{}^{I}_{ji}$ of the considered fuzzy numbers different from zero. The distance between two fuzzy numbers is a non-negative function as follows [10].

(3) Decision makers receive the results of analysis in written form.

Phase3. The management team gives their assessment in the second round with respect to the results acquired in the first round. The relative importance of component j, j=1,.., J_j; i=1,..,I in the second round is notated as $\tilde{w}{}^{II}_{ji}$. The analysis of results assessment in this round is performed like in Phase 2.

Phase4. Acquired result in the second round represents integrated expert opinions and strives to reach a consensus. *Phase 3* is normally repeated until a consensus is reached on a particular topic [11]. When consensus is reached , the relative importance of component j, j=1,.., J_j; i=1,..,I is notated as $\tilde{w}_{ji}$.

2.4   Modeling of Components' Values

Values of all defined components for each part of the VO cannot be stated quantitatively, as decision makers most often base their estimates on evidence data. In such cases, their values are adequately described by linguistic expressions. The number and types of linguistic expressions are defined by decision makers depending on their estimate.

In this paper, the fuzzy rating of each component value of each part of the VO is described by linguistic expressions which can be represented as a triangular fuzzy number. Values in the domain of these discrete fuzzy numbers belong to a real set within the interval [1-5]. Value 1, means the worst value of the component of organizational part k, and 5 means the most suitable value of the component of organizational part k, k=1,..,K of VO.

In this paper, the fuzzy rating of the management team can be described by using one of five linguistic expressions which are modeled by triangular fuzzy numbers: *low value* -(1,1,2), *fairly moderate value*-(1,2,3), *moderate value*-(1.5,3,4.5), *highly moderate value*-(3,4,5), and *high value*-- (4.5,5,5).

3   The Proposed Fuzzy Algorithm for the Management of the Keystone Vulnerabilities Assessment of the VO

The algorithm for the Management of the Keystone Vulnerabilities assessment of the VO is formally given as follows.

Step 1. By applying a modified Delphi method, calculate indicator weights which are described by triangular fuzzy numbers $\tilde{w}_{ji}$, $j=1,..,J_i$; $i=1,..,I$.

Step 2. Calculate weighted value of component j of the VO, $j=1,..,J_i$; $i=1,..,I$:

$$\tilde{V}_{ji} = \tilde{w}_{ji} \cdot \tilde{v}_{ji}$$

Step 3. Calculate weighted value of indicator i of the VO, $i=i,..,I$:

$$\tilde{V}_i = \frac{1}{J_i} \cdot \sum_{j=1}^{J_i} \tilde{V}_{ji}$$

Step 4. Rank of all $\tilde{V}_i$ in an increasing order and calculate the degree of belief that any $\tilde{V}_i{}'$, $i=1,...,I$, $i \neq i^*$, is higher than $\tilde{V}_i{}^*$ using the method in [12].

Step 5. Calculate weighted value of the Management of the Keystone Vulnerabilities of the VO:

$$\tilde{R} = \frac{1}{I} \cdot \sum_{i=1}^{I} \tilde{V}_i$$

4   Case Study

The subject of analysis is an organization from the automobile sector in Serbia which operates as a Full Service Supporter of the one international corporation involved in production and distribution of auto cosmetics for trucks, commercial vehicles and passenger vehicles. It is a medium sized organization. The business functions of marketing, design and development, manufacturing and selling are interconnected through the net and geographically allocated in Slovenia and Serbia. The products of this organization are embedded in different types of original equipment manufacturer-OEM (Renault, Peugeot, Volkswagen, BMW, Seat, etc.). The organization owns certifications of quality ISO 9001:2008 and ISO/TS 16949 and it is linked with its suppliers in supply chains for different OEMs through the sophisticated e-solutions. It has developed business relationships with more than 25 suppliers and two of the largest suppliers participate in 75% of procurement value. The three greatest buyers purchase 80% of total produced assets. Having in mind the many years of established good business relations, there is a high level of trust and loyalty among them. This VO has six different parts and the Management of the Keystone Vulnerabilities will be assessed for each of them. Indicators and components of the MKV in the VO are:

i=1, **System Risk management and Planning** j=1, Development j=2, Operational	i=5, **Connectivity** j=1, IS Architecture j=2, Redundancy of IS in Percentage
i=2, **System Exercises** j=1, Resources j=2, Procedures j=3, Training j=4, ICT Maintenance	i=6, **Robust Processes for Identifying & Analyzing Vulnerabilities** j=1, Staff competences for Identifying & Analyzing Vulnerabilities j=2, Management and compactness of the team for Identifying & Analyzing Vulnerabilities
i=3, **Internal Organizational Components** j=1, Physical j=2, Human j=3, Process	i=7, **Staff Engagement & Involvement** j=1, Profoundness of Staff Engagement & Involvement j=2, Awareness of Staff and their Involvement
i=4, **External Organizational Components** j=1, Physical j=2, Human j=3, Process	

Input data:

Compo nents	Relative importance	Assessed value given by management team
11	*low importance, medium importancex2, high importance, very high importance*	*moderate value (k=1,2), highly moderate value (k=3,4), high value(k=5)*
21	*medium importance, high importancex3, very high importance*	*highly moderate value (k=4,5), high value(k=1,2,3)*
12	*very low importancex3, low importance, medium importance*	*Low value (k=1), fairly moderate value(k=2,3), moderate value (k=4,5)*
22	*very low importance, low importancex2, medium importancex2*	*moderate value (k=1,2), highly moderate value (k=3,4,5)*
32	*low importance, medium importancex3, high importance*	*fairly moderate value (k=1), moderate value (k=2,3,4), highly moderate value (k=5)*
42	*low importance, medium importance, high importance, very high importancex2*	*fairly moderate value(k=1,2), moderate value (k=3,4), highly moderate value (k=5)*
13	*very low importance, medium importancex2, high importance, very high importance*	*fairly moderate value(k=1), moderate value (k=2,3,4), high value(k=5)*
23	*medium importance, high importance, very high importancex3*	*fairly moderate value(k=1,2), moderate value (k=3), highly moderate value (k=4,5)*

33	*very low importance, low importance, medium importancex2, very high importance*	*moderate value* (k=1), *highly moderate value* (k=2), *high value*(k=3,4,5)
14	*low importance, high importancex2, very high importancex2*	*moderate value* (k=1,2), *highly moderate value* (k=3), *high value*(k=4,5)
24	*very low importance, low importance, medium importance, high importance*	*fairly moderate value*(k=1,2), *moderate value* (k=3,4), *high value* (k=5)
34	*low importance, medium importance, very high importancex3*	*fairly moderate value*(k=1), *moderate value* (k=2,3,4), *highly moderate value* (k=5)
15	*low importance, medium importance, high importancex2, very high importance*	*fairly moderate value*(k=1,2,3) *highly moderate value* (k=4,5)
25	*medium importance, high importancex3, very high importance*	*moderate value* (k=1,2), *highly moderate value* (k=3), *high value* (k=4,5)
16	*very low importance, low importance, medium importancex2, high importance*	*moderate value* (k=1,2), *highly moderate value* (k=3), *high value* (k=4,5)
26	*very low importance, medium importancex2, high importance, very high importance*	*highly moderate value* (k=1), *high value* (k=2,3,4,5)
17	*medium importance, high importancex3, very high importance*	*fairly moderate value*(k=1,2), *moderate value* (k=3), *highly moderate value* (k=4), *high value* (k=5)
27	*low importance ,medium importancex2, high importance, very high importance*	*Low value* (k=1,5), *fairly moderate value*(k=2,3), *moderate value* (k=4)

The weights of components are acquired by the application of the modified Delphi method (in Phase 1):

$$\tilde{w}_{11} = (0.36, 0.6, 0.76), \tilde{w}_{21} = (0.68, 1, 1), \tilde{w}_{12} = (0.06, 0.1, 0.42),$$

$$\tilde{w}_{22} = (0.06, 0.1, 0.42), \tilde{w}_{32} = (0.3, 0.5, 0.7) \tilde{w}_{32} = (0.3, 0.5, 0.7),$$

$$\tilde{w}_{42} = (0.48, 0.8, 0.88), \tilde{w}_{13} = (0.36, 0.5, 0.78), \tilde{w}_{23} = (0.2, 0.4, 0.6),$$

$$\tilde{w}_{33} = (0.3, 0.5, 0.7), \tilde{w}_{14} = (0.58, 0.9, 0.94), \tilde{w}_{24} = (0.3, 0.5, 0.7),$$

$$\tilde{w}_{34} = (0.36, 0.6, 0.76), \tilde{w}_{15} = (0.42, 0.7, 0.82), \tilde{w}_{25} = (0.64, 0.82, 1),$$

$$\tilde{w}_{16} = (0.3, 0.5, 0.7), \tilde{w}_{26} = (0.42, 0.7, 0.82), \tilde{w}_{17} = (0.64, 0.82, 1),$$

$$\tilde{w}_{27} = (0.42, 0.7, 0.82)$$

By applying the procedure of the developed Algorithm (from Step 2 to Step 4), the following results are obtained and given in Table 1:

Table 1. The weighted values and rank of indicators

Indicators	$\alpha = 0$	$\alpha = 0.5$	$\alpha = 1$	Rank	The degree of belief that the indicator which is in second place is lower than the indicator which is in first place
i=1	0.342; 0.652	0.447; 0.602	0.56	7	
i=2	0.046;0.374	0.091;0.248	0.15	1	0.465
i=3	0.095;0.566	0.184;0.423	0.3	3	
i=4	0.102;0.574	0.199;0.443	0.327	4	
i=5	0.106;0.546	0.207;0.44	0.34	5	
i=6	0.171;0.725	0.286;0.567	0.43	6	
i=7	0.106;0.464	0.179;0.364	0.27	2	

By applying the expression (Step 5), the total assessed value of the Management of the Keystone Vulnerabilities of the VO is:

$$\widetilde{MKV} = (0.138, 0.34, 0.557)$$

4.1   Discussion

The rank of indicators which is presented in Table 1 is acquired by the application of the developed model. The indicator of Management of the Keystone Vulnerabilities of the VO which has the lowest value is i=2, System Exercises. The indicator which is placed in second place is i=7, Staff Engagement & Involvement. The measure of belief that the value of this indicator is lower than the value of indicator i=2, System Exercises is 0.465. Based on the acquired result, it can be concluded that the management team should direct their attention to implementation measures which are going to provide an increased value of System Exercises and Staff Engagement & Involvement. The indicator which has the greatest value and does not need to be in focus for the improvement of the management team is the indicator, System Risk management and Planning. In this way, the management team can quickly come to the realization of its primary goal – increasing the value of total resilience of the VO.

5   Conclusion

In order to improve a process in the shortest possible period of time, it is necessary that a management team undertake certain activities directed towards the highest priority of indicators and components of the treated indicators, i.e. the indicators that have the biggest influence on the VO's efficiency. The solution to this considered problem advocated in all defined processes of a company makes it the most critical factor for successful establishment of firms. In the literature and in practice, there are almost no methods which offer a solution to the given problem in an exact way.

In general, indicators ranking problems adhere to uncertain and imprecise data which are described by linguistic expressions. Modeling of linguistic expressions is based on the fuzzy set theory.

Beside the afore mentioned various advantages of the proposed approach for the ranking of indicators of a VO, this research work can be extended by adding more indicators, depending on: (1) the considered VO, (2) corporate policy, (3) business policy which is implemented within a VO, (4) internal and external changes, etc. We can hold that the indicators' rank is constant during one business year. Also, it should be mentioned that the proposed model presented in this paper can be easily extended to the analysis of other Management of Keystone Vulnerabilities of VOs.

Acknowledgments. The research presented in this paper was supported by the Ministry of Science and Technological Development of the Republic of Serbia, Grant III-44010, Title: Intelligent Systems for Software Product Development and Business Support based on Models.

References

1. Andre, P.M., Afgan, N.H., Carvalho, M.G.: Management System Sustainability (Based on QMS, EMS, H&S and Business Indicators) 3(5), 1–13 (2009)
2. Robb, D.: Building resilient organizations, OD practitioner. Journal of the Organization Development Network 32(3), 27–32 (2000)
3. McManus, S.: Organizational resilience in New Zealand, PhD thesis, University of Canterbury (2008)
4. Arsovski, S., Arsovski, Z., Andre, P., Stefanović, M.: Relation between organizational – and information resilience: a way for improvement of system capacity. International Journal for Quality Research 4(3), 205–214 (2010)
5. Legnick-Hall, C., Beck, T., Legnick-Hall, M.: Developing a capacity for organizational resilience through strategic human resource management. Human Resource Management Review (2010), doi:10.1016/j.hrmr.2010.07.001
6. Botezatu, C., Botezatu, C., Carutasu, G.: Virtual Enterprise Information System Requirements. In: International Conference Competitiveness and Stability in the Knowledge-Based Economy, Craiova, October 20–21 (2006)
7. Stephenson, A., Vargo, J., Seville, E.: The Australian Journal of Emergency Management 25(2), 27–32 (2010)
8. Robbins, S.P.: Management. Prentice Hall, New Jersy (1994)
9. Zimmermann: Fuzzy set Theory and its applications. Kluwer Nijhoff Publising, USA (1996)
10. Sadeghpour-Gilden, B., Gien, D.: La Distance-Dpq et le Cofficient de Correlation entre deux variables Aleatoires floues. In: Actes de LFA 2011, Monse-Belgium, pp. 97–102 (2010)
11. Chang, W., Wu, C.-R., Chen, H.-C.: Using expert technology to select unstable slicing machine to control wafer slicing quality via fuzzy AHP. Expert System with Applications 34(83), 2210–2220 (2008)
12. Dubois, D., Prade, H.: Decision-making under fuzziness. In: Gupta, M.M., Ragade, R.K., Yager, R.R. (eds.) Advances in Fuzzy Set Theory and Applications, pp. 279–302. Elsevier, North-Holland (1979)

Integration of Virtual and Networked Organization Using Server Oriented Architecture

Miladin Stefanovic[1], Slavko Arsovski[1], Zora Arsovski[2], Aleksandar Aleksic[1],
Snezana Nestic[1], Dragan Rajkovic[1], and Zoran Punosevac[3]

[1] Faculty of Mechanical Engineering, University of Kragujevac, SestreJanjic 6 34000
Kragujevac, Serbia
{miladin,cqm,aaleksic,s.nestic}@kg.ac.rs
[2] Faculty of Economics, University of Kragujevac, DjurePucaraStarog
3, 34000 Kragujevac, Serbia
zora@kg.ac.rs
[3] Higher School for Industrial Management, Krusevac, Serbia
zpunosevac1@nadlanu.com

Abstract. Virtual enterprise integration (VEI) is virtually the most critical
success factor for making virtual enterprise (VE) a real, competitive, and widely
implemented organizational and management concept. One of the possible
approaches in virtual enterprise integration is employment of web services. In
this paper we will present an approach for developing an SOA for VEI. The
general assumption of the suggested approach is that service oriented
architecture is based on business services and they mostly correspond to
exchanged documentation in a real business system. CASE tool for web service
specification is also presented.

Keywords: Virtual enterprise integration, web services, service oriented
architecture, documentation, quality system.

1 Introduction

VE is considered as a temporary organization in which various distributed business
partners form a cooperative network [1]. A virtual enterprise is a business model
(with many variants) in which different legally independent companies cooperate
electronically (mainly by means of the Internet) to offer better services to customers
that cannot be offered by one single member [2]. Virtual enterprise integration (VEI)
is virtually the most critical success factor for making virtual enterprise (VE) a real,
competitive, and widely implemented organizational and management concept.
However, according to many authors [1, 2, 3], the present solutions for VEI are either
insufficient or inexistent [3]. Many authors emphasize new business approaches, such
as resilience [4], in order to improve business solutions. The main mechanism, or tool,
for the processes of interaction improvement, is the computer and information
technology in a variety of specific technologies and aspects. On the other hand, there
is a difference between VEI and EI [5]. Understanding integration as a design process
is of the greatest importance for building a new generation of integration models for
VE [6].

G.D. Putnik and M.M. Cruz-Cunha (Eds.): ViNOrg 2011, CCIS 248, pp. 165–175, 2012.

Process integration spans all dimensions of virtuality. In many cases, the integration pertains to back-end or legacy applications. In other cases it also involves the integration of information or databases from multiple sources. In most cases it is a combination of the two. In fact, it is often the case that applications have their own repositories or databases.

The corresponding concept in virtual enterprises is the process. An organization is defined by its sets of enacted policies and procedures; so are virtual organizations. Processes are used to implement these policies and procedures. Processes define the control logic of the interactions and exchanges for particular goals. The process models include the various roles and relationships between participants. Processes also define the messages or documents that get processed at each step. Thus connectivity and integration needs not only to address process integration that uses the common interface technologies, but also to provide a direct representation and enactment of the exchange, control, and information flows between applications, human participants, or trading partners [7].

The scope of virtual enterprises can be summarized as follows [8]:

- Process Integration of applications within the same organization:
- Process Integration of organizations, applications, and content between different organizations in the same enterprise:
- Process Integration of Trading Partners.

Processes involve choreography of activities. These activities can be carried out by specific individuals; by specific organizational roles; by specific e-business roles; or specific applications. One of the main advantages of business process management is the separation of the operational or process logic from the application. In almost all applications there are processes and workflows. The application programming interfaces and the application packages themselves often embed or capture these processes.

In the integration of virtual enterprises there are different levels of integration. This paper advocates step by step procedure for integration on business process level as well as integration on application level using SOA (Service Oriented Architecture).). Some author [9] states that SOA could solve some important issues such as cooperatively usage of capabilities inherent to different technologies that can interact or could be controlled concurrently, other [10] states that usage of SOA architecture allows the reuse of existing software components as well as interconnection between remote positioned partners and entities.

The general assumption in this paper is that service oriented architecture is based on business services, and that business services are mostly adequate to exchanged documentation in real business system. The documentation of quality system (DQS) is identified as appropriate approach for description of business processes in business system and identification of exchanged documentation with business environment. In this paper we will present the approach for planning and specification of the Web Service for VEI, based on documentation of quality system which is a focus of this article. Configuration CASE tool to set up virtual enterprises based on SAO is also presented.

2   Business Process Integration in Virtual and Networked Organizations

At present, many enterprises experience difficulties in the formation and operation of virtual enterprises, especially concerning integration issues. There are many different approaches to definition of an architectural framework which aims to support the set-up and operation of virtual enterprises, associated methodologies, modeling frameworks, modeling languages [11]. A Number of different problems exist in operation, and integration of collaborative networked and / or virtual organization. As regards integration, different levels of integration could be separated. The lowest level of integration is, naturally, physical level of integration. This level of integration is needed to facilitate co-operating applications and enterprises. The second level of integration is application integration that is concerned with ICT (information and communication technology) support for interoperation between enterprise resources. On this level we have to deal with two different parts: standards in order to provide integration at the level of forms [12] and integration that provides that output of one application is meaningful to other applications [13]. The Third level of integration is business process that should provide common understanding of virtual enterprise about shared business processes. Modeling part is concerned with business process integration. In integration of virtual enterprises business process that for an interface between different organizations or organizational parts have the most importance. Different reference models provide means for definition and recognition of different business process that should be adopted and defined among different partners. The highest level of integration is inter-enterprise coordination, such as in supply chains or networks, or any other situation where enterprises need to coordinate with other entities.

In this paper we will deal with integration on the business process level which (Integration on the business process level) will contribute to further integration on application level. Virtual enterprises should have common understanding about shared business processes. Business processes in virtual enterprises are not carried out by a single enterprise. In collaborative networked organization or virtual organizations process interconnection mechanisms are necessary to coordinate geographically distributed business processes. Actually, existing business process modeling and enactment systems have been mainly developed to suit enterprise internal needs. Thus, most of these systems are not adapted to inter-enterprise cooperation.

Quality of business processes should maintain similar level of quality in all integrated collaborative network. Quality Management System is collective term for methods and techniques developed to ensure quality of processes in companies. QMS is represented by set of process descriptions, procedures and routines. Documentation of quality system is developed to support QMS and describe all necessary segments.

On the first place DQMS have to present processes in the business system. The documentation of the quality systems is selected as suitable approach to describe business processes in the real business organization. Also DQMS enables identification of exchange of business documentation between different part of organization, or between organization and business environment. Further business services in business organization are mostly adequate to exchanged documentation in real business system or between business system and other entities. Finally, business services should match to service oriented architecture (SOA).

According to approach AS2 [14] documentation of quality system is divided to: procedures, procedure, instruction, or direction (depending on complexity of activities and organizational level on which activities are defined or performed).

The procedures and templates are integral part of one scenario, for example: product development or marketing and sale. More functions and organization units from one company or parts of distributed organization units and well as a part of virtual enterprises are employed in realization of one scenario. The next step is definition of phases and functions, and definition of elements of each scenario and definition of information about elements of scenario. During the distribution of a function in specific phases, we have to define activities, documents, additional elements and connection between elements as well as input of data. This finally will be used for development of interfaces and application specification.

Integration of business process, analysis of documentation of quality system and accompanied diagrams should provide: identification and modeling of business services; identification and modeling of atomic business services; specification of composite business service (business services that consist of atomic business services); identification of communication between entities, and specification of deployment and execution of services.

In the first step procedures will be generalized as a business services. Some of the will be identified as atomic services and some of them as composite business services (composed of one or more atomic services). Outputs from procedures (reports) or input in procedure (reports, templates) could be generalized as exchanged data. Finally, specification and execution of services could be defined.

3   Methods for Development of Service Oriented Architecture for Application Integration

Service-oriented architectures (SOA) will form the basis of future information systems. Based on open XML standards, Web Services are service- oriented architectures that allow creating an abstract definition of a service, providing a concrete implementation of a service, publishing and finding a service, service instance selection, and interoperable service use. Different authors recognized the potential of web services and service oriented architecture for integration of virtual enterprises [15, 16]. Some authors advocate agents and web services [17]. Other authors suggest other approaches [18]. Generally [19] SOA contains three major components: service provider, service directory and customer service. On the other hand [20, 21] SOA is architecture oriented business application, which integrated processes which are integrated and shared through services.

Basic web services are being assembled to composite web services in order to directly support business processes. As some basic web services can be used in several composite web services, different business processes are influenced if ,for example, a web service is unavailable or if its signature changes.

Web services and SOA should provide high quality context for: enterprise integration and interoperability; distributed organization; model-based monitor and control; heterogeneous environments; open and dynamic structure; cooperation; integration of humans with software and hardware and resilience, agility, scalability and fault tolerance.

There are many different approaches in development of SOA, model – driven approach is one of them. One of the key issues is mapping of business processes to an SOA. Next step is usage of notation that will enable automated mapping to an execution language. Business Process Modeling Notation [OMG-BPMN] is very commonly used. In case of BPMN, the abovementioned automatic mapping is already defined for the Business Process Execution Language (BPEL) [22].

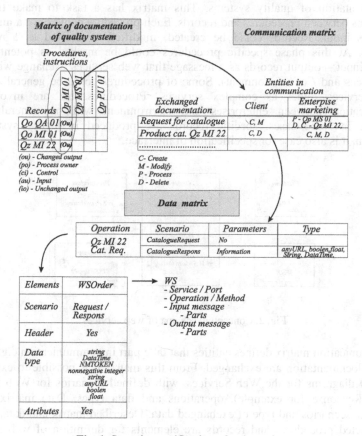

Fig. 1. Steps in specification of web service

As it was mentioned before that the general assumption is that service oriented architecture is based on business services and business services are adequate for exchange of documentation. Documentation of quality system could be identified as appropriate approach for identification of exchange of documentation in real business system or between different parts of enterprises or between enterprise and environment.

Mapping of business services to web services and service oriented architecture, according to this method has the following steps (Figure 1):

- Development of a matrix of documentation of quality system,
- Development of a communication matrix.
- Development of a data matrix, and
- Implementation and development of summary description of the Web Service.

Using above presented diagram we could easily isolate any specific entities and develop UML diagrams.

In the first step, according to Activity diagram (Figure 1) we can develop a matrix of documentation of quality systems. This matrix has a task to make traceable connections between procedures and records. Each procedure could have a number of records as input. Records could be created, modified or deleted as a result of procedure. At this phase specific procedures could be marked as potential web services (input – output records as a message that web services exchange with other web services and / or environment). Some of procedures could be generalized as a atomic services, other as complex services. Procedures that are involved in communication between enterprises and environment will be generalized as interfaces. In some cases, specific records are produced in legacy systems or application, it is also case for specification of interface.

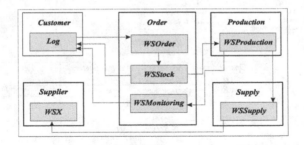

Fig. 2. Conceptual schema of web services

Communication matrix defines entities that take part in communication e.g. entities between documentation are exchanged. From this matrix it is possible to extract the sequential diagrams for the Web Services, with defined scenarios for Web Services (Request/Response for example), operations and data types. Data matrix, define operations, scenarios and type of exchanged data. Described matrix and data, derived from selected procedures and records are elements for definition of web services: scenario (request / response), header, data types and attributes. According to selected records in is possible to define input and output messages (with their parts).

Finally, analyzing all business services, all exchanged documentation (documentation of quality system) it is possible to get conceptual schema of web services (Figure 2). Presented approach enables: enterprise integration and interoperability, support for distributed organization, model-based monitor and control, support for heterogeneous environments, open and dynamic structure as well as resilience, agility, scalability and fault tolerance.

4   Configuration Case Tool for Virtual Enterprise Integration Based on SOA

Based on the general idea of analysis of flow of documentation of quality system, CASE tool was developed. Developed service oriented architecture is based on business services, and business service correspond to exchanged documentation. Development of CASE tools for specification of web services has been discussed by different authors [23, 24]. CASE tool presented in this paper is based on suggested approach of analysis of documentation of quality system.

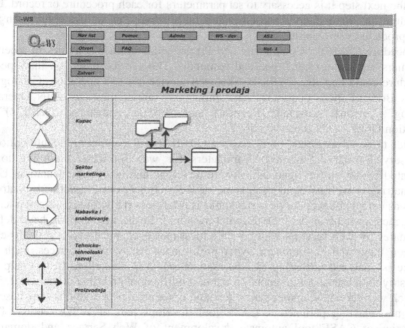

Fig. 3. Symbols and data flows (procedures and flows) for Marketing and sale scenario

The CASE tool was developed as tree layer web application. The main reasons for that is development of open, flexible structure. In development of this CASE tool following should be provided: understanding and presentation of existing services; presentation of needed information resources; definition of needed interfaces and presentation of existing interfaces; detailed presentation of process and their understanding; definition of new services and information for integration with legacy systems; definition or change of processes under influences of new services; easier implementation of new processes; easier selection of set of technologies and testing and evaluation.

Software solution enables definition of different scenarios with data flows and exchanged documentation. Using defined dialog box it is possible to develop new scenario, or open and modify existed scenarios.

In development of new scenario it is possible to set the name of scenario (Marketing and sale scenario, figure 3) and the entities included in the exchange of documentation. On the Figure 3 we have customer, marketing sector, supply, RD sector and production. Each sector could be entity in the same company or parts of collaborative networked organization or virtual organization (so boundaries between them could be interfaces between different business entities or inner-organizational borders). After definition of scenario, using drag and drop approach, specific diagrams could be created using notation according to AS2 methodology. Using symbols on the left bar it is possible to set different working activities (each activity is covered by quality procedure) as well as inputs and outputs.

In the next step it is necessary to set parameters for each procedure or record. Each procedure has a name, code and other general attributes, as well as connection with other procedures or records.

Procedure QpMI01 "Commercial and Propaganda" defines activities in receiving customers request for catalogue and respond. The service based on that specific procedure could be named WSSale. This web service has two operations Catalog and Order. Both of these operations have input and output messages - IN Operation Catalog – record "Customer Request" and "Product catalogue (QzMI22)", in operation Order – "Customer's order".

After these adjustments, users activate CASE tool for autonomy identification of web services and definition of parameters for web services. According to the presented model on the figure 3, software develops matrix of documentation. Using this matrix, as well as input data, some of the web services are defined as atomic, others as composite web services and some as interfaces (between existing application and legacy systems or between different systems). In the first step we have defined candidates for web services with possible messages exchanged between them self of between them and environment. After preliminary list of web services, each web service is analyzed according to input and output documentation. In this step it is necessary to define specific inputs, creation, modification and final outputs. After that for each web service scenario, parameters and types are defined. In this step, based on input and existing parameters, CASE tool develops part of WSDL code. These properties of CASE tool automate development of Web Service and domain of WSDL code development, and reduce or eliminate causes of errors in code. After set of specific parameters some of them could be adjusted manually. In this version following standard parts of WSDL code were included: header, xsd types, input message, output message, definition of ports, binding, SOAP, definition of RPC. Users need to manually set name space, elements names, soap address location.

5   Conclusion

In this paper the starting assumption was that service oriented architecture corresponds to business services on the one side. On the other hand, business services correspond to exchanged documentation in real business environment. Documentation of quality system is used for description of business processes. Integration on the business process level will contribute to further integration on application level. Integration of business process, analysis of documentation of quality system and accompanied diagrams should provide: identification and modeling of business, atomic and composite services as well as identification of communication between entities.   Mapping of business services to web services and service oriented architecture, according to this method has following steps: development of 3 matrices (documentation of quality system, communication and data matrix).

Suggested approach enables integration of virtual enterprises using exchange of documents (documents of quality system) as a basis. Since documentation of quality system align internal and external processes with standards and quality system recommendation different entities could benefit from this approach. Web Services through their robust ease of integration, flexibility, and support of XML vocabularies provide the appropriate platform to realize virtual enterprises. In addition suggested approach provides path for development of service oriented architecture for virtual enterprises.

Finally CASE tool for configuration of service oriented architecture is presented. Based on presented approach this CASE tool suggests list of web service that form service oriented architecture for virtual enterprises.

Presented software tool has following advantages:

- On the first place this CASE tool enables development of general view that helps integration of virtual enterprises. In the virtual as well as other enterprises exchanged documentation usually follows specific business services. This tool gives picture of general flow of documentation.
- Based on flow of documentation CASE tool provides general list of possible web services as a part of service oriented architecture. Since integration of virtual enterprises covers integration of heterogeneous and distributed resources web services provide suitable architectures.
- General list of web services provide general framework for adjustments and modifications. Each composite service could be divided or reconfigured as well as specific interfaces or connections to legacy systems.
- Each web service could be developed in general and standard parts of WSDL could be proposed by software. Additional configuration must be set manually.

This tool also has a number of limitations. In the first place it is in early phase of development and it could provide just a general web service architecture based on stated assumptions. Furthermore, automatisation of different advanced steps are on the low level.

Suggested approach shows benefit of implementation of quality management system in organization and development of documentation of quality system management as a basis for integration of internal processes, integration with other entities and communication between enterprises and environment. Implementation of QMS and DQM could be used for development of service oriented architecture for information integration of resources and entities.

Acknowledgment. Research presented in this paper was supported by Ministry of Science and Technological Development of Republic of Serbia, Grant III-44010, Title: Intelligent Systems for Software Product Development and Business Support based on Models.

References

1. Kim, T.Y., Lee, S., Kim, K., Kim, C.H.: Modeling framework for agile and interoperable virtual enterprises. Computers in Industry 57(3), 204–217 (2006)
2. Dorn, J., Hrastnik, P., Rainer, A.: Web Service Discovery and Composition for Virtual Enterprises. International Journal of Web Services Research 4(1), 23–39 (2007)
3. Putnik, G., Cunha, M.M.: Virtual enterprise integration: technological and organizational perspectives. Idea Group Inc. IGI (2005)
4. Arsovski, S., Arsovski, Z., Andre, P., Stefanović, M.: Relation between organizational – and information resilience: a way for improvement of system capacity. International Journal for Quality Research 4(3), 205–214 (2010)
5. Stefanović, M., Arsovski, S., Nestic, S., Aleksic, A.: Integration of Virtual Enterprises Using Service Oriented Architecture. International Journal for Quality Research 3(2), 1–7 (2009)
6. Jhingran, A.D., Mattos, N., Pirahesh, H.: Information integration: A research agenda. IBM Systems Journal 41(4), 555–562 (2002)
7. Panetto, H., Molina, A.: Enterprise integration and interoperability in manufacturing systems: Trends and issues. Computers in Industry 59(7), 641–646 (2008)
8. Camarinha-Matos, L.M., Afsarmanesh, H.: Infrastructures for Virtual Enterprises: a summary of achievements. In: Proceedings of PRO-VE 1999 - IFIP Int. Conf. On Infrastructures for Virtual Enterprises, pp. 483–490. Kluwer Academic Publishers, Porto (1999) ISBN 0-7923-8639-6
9. Gold-Bernstein, B., So, G.: Integration and SOA; Concepts, Technologies, and Best Practices, WebMethods (2006)
10. Feuerlich, G.: Enterprise SOA: What are the benefits and challenges? In: 4th Annual International Conference Systems Integration 2006, Prague, Czech Republic, June 11-13 (2006)
11. Zweger, A., Tølle, M., Vesterager, J.: VERAM: Virtual Enterprise Reference Architecture and Methodology. In: Karvonen, I., et al. (eds.) Global Engineering and Manufacturing in Enterprise Networks GLOBEMEN, pp. 17–38. Julkaisija Utgivare, Finland (2002)
12. Fuquan, S., Wang, L., Tingbin, C., Yunlong, Q.: Dynamic Information Integration of Virtual Enterprises Based on Web Services and J2EE. In: International Conference on Wireless Communications, Networking and Mobile Computing, New York, USA, pp. 6146–6149 (2007)
13. Jamroendararasame, K., Susuki, T., Tokuda, T.A.: Diagram Approach to Automatic Generation of JSP/Servlet Web Applications. In: Proc. of the 6th IASTED International Conference on Software Engineering and Applications, Boston, USA, pp. 292–297 (2002)
14. Arsovski, S., Arsovski, Z., Stefanovic, M.: An Approach of Information System Development in QMS Environment. Communication in Dependability and Quality Management, An International Journal 4(2), 144–152 (2001)
15. Baïnaa, K., Benalib, K., Godartb, C.: DISCOBOLE: A service architecture for interconnecting workflow processes. Computers in Industry 57(8-9), 768–777 (2006)
16. Protogeros, N. (ed.): Agents and Web Service Technologies in Virtual Enterprises. IGI Global (2008)
17. Petersen, S.A., Rao, J., Matskin, M.: Virtual Enterprise Formation supported by Agents and Web Services, illustrated edition. IGI Global (2007)
18. Stefanovic, M., Matijevic, M., Eric, M., Simic, V.: Method of design and specification of web services based on quality system documentation. Information Systems Frontiers 11(1), 75–86 (2009)

19. Booth, D., Haas, H., McCabe, F., Newcomer, E., Champion, M., Ferris, C., Orchard, D.: Web Services Architecture (2004), http://www.w3.org/TR/ws-arch/ (accessed: May 30, 2011)
20. Braswell, B., Dudley, C., Rieu, L., Smithson, M., Verma, T.: WebSphere Service Registry and Repository Handbook. IBM Redbooks publication (2007)
21. Weiss, P.: Modeling of Service-Oriented Architecture: Integration, Information (2010)
22. Schmit, A.B., Dustdar, S.: Model-driven Development of Web Service Transactions. In: 6th International Workshop on Technologies for E-Services, TES 2005, Trondheim, Norway (2005)
23. Grundy, J., Hosking, J.A.: Visual Language and Environment for Composing Web Services. In: Proceedings of the 2005 ACM/IEEE International Conference on Automated Software Engineering, Long Beach, CA, USA (2005)
24. Kassoff, M., Kato, D., Mohsin, W.: Creating GUIs for Web Services. IEEE Internet Computing 7(5), 66–73 (2003)

New Perspectives of Virtual Teams' Collaboration

Cosmina Aldea[1], Anca Draghici[1], and George Dragoi[2]

[1] "Politehnica" University of Timisoara, Faculty of Management, 14 Remus str,
300191 Timisoara, Romania
cosmina.aldea@yahoo.com, adraghici@eng.upt.ro
[2] "Politehnica" University of Bucharest, Faculty of Engineering in Foreign Languages,
PREMINV Research Center, Splaiul Independentei 313, Sector 6, 060042 Bucharest, Romania
dragoi.george23@gmail.com

Abstract. This article describes new perspectives in virtual teams' collaboration, to underline the actual trends and to identify their future development. These will be used for product lifecycle projects management and to diminish/avoid risks, to harmonize team members' competencies (compatibility issues) to attend success in project development. The tools used for communication and real time research-work will increase companies' competitiveness by optimizing the resources dedicated to different projects, teams and management systems. To improve the productivity and to facilitate the communication between projects team members, the new approach of virtual teams is based on the use of complex software platforms to improve collaborative design, learning and work processes.

Keywords: Virtual and Augmented Reality, Knowledge Base, Human Resource, Virtual Teams, Collaborative Design.

1 Introduction – Definitions Overview of Virtual Teams

Today, more definitions of virtual teams evolve from the first description of the concept made by Lipnack (1997). *"Virtual teams are live. They are most definitely teams, not electronic representations of the real thing. They are going digital, using the Internet and Intranets. Unlike conventional teams, a virtual team works across space, time, and organizational boundaries with links strengthened by webs of communication technologies"* [9].Gassmann and Von Zedtwitz (2003) defined *"virtual team as a group of people and sub-teams who interact through interdependent tasks guided by common purpose and work across links strengthened by information, communication, and transport technologies"* [8]. Powell et. al. (2004) define virtual teams "as groups of geographically, organizationally and/or time dispersed workers brought together by information and telecommunication technologies to accomplish one or more organizational tasks" [11]. Ale Ebrahimet. al. (2009) are more explicit in defining the virtual team: *"as small temporary groups of geographically, organizationally and/or time dispersed knowledge workers who coordinate their work predominantly with electronic information and communication technologies in order to accomplish one or more organization tasks"* [1].

G.D. Putnik and M.M. Cruz-Cunha (Eds.): ViNOrg 2011, CCIS 248, pp. 176–185, 2012.

Virtual teams' members have two major needs to be satisfied: on one hand, there are working needs (related to the distributed collaborative work) and on the other hand, there is an impetuous self-development need. Therefore, a virtual team is both an *organization-for-learning, and a learning organization*. Virtual team members can be seen as tele-workers in a networked enterprise, a cluster of personal desks or workbenches equipped to support various forms of collaborative work. The network might be the Internet, a real company's Intranet or Extranet [10].

Organizations build-up and encourage the development of virtual teams for better attend their global objectives/interests in the global economy. The changes in managing people have underlined, in the last years, the importance of virtual teams (created by the organization extension boundaries) for the global business management.

A virtual team is known as a geographically dispersed team and it consists of a group of individuals that work across time, space and organizational boundaries with links strengthened by webs of communication technology. Many references related to virtual teams' definition are focus on their *working process* (to get efficiency and effectiveness), *socio-human aspects*, problems of members interaction (communication, culture differences, building trust, awareness etc.) or definitions underline the *processes of their building and development* (birth, growing processes).

In the context of this article, virtual teams are considered those for collaborative design activities or so call, engineering virtual teams. The main ideas behind this research are related to: (1) efficient and effective virtual teams' improvement; (2) the role of the virtual team in the modern product design process; (3) the connection between virtual teams and virtual networks; (4) presentation of some software solutions that can be used to support collaborative work during the design process.

2   Virtual Teams for Virtual Product Design

A central point of future virtual team development is linked with collaboration and communication processes/systems efficiency and effectiveness increasing. This are based on consistent, integrated data settings and on tools that support the knowledge management processes at a large scale. Traditionally, only data about the designed product are stored, made available for the product development team and archived for later product development projects [6]. With product lifecycle management, data, information, knowledge and wisdom coming from all product lifecycle phases are to be integrated (including customers needs, design, manufacturing, sales, operation and service, end-of-life data about sold/installed products) [12]. Details are given in Figures 1 and 2.

An environment supporting collaborative design (Figure 1) by virtual teams would include the following components: (1) integrated data sets, including description of the product and all related processes, and including data collected from the lifecycle of this and other related products; (2) interface to detailed planning, analysis and simulation systems, as some of the product and process features needed to be derived from the collected data; (3) simulation and visualization engines, to obtain an virtual environment containing easy understandable representations of product features and scenarios; (4) multi-modal, intuitive user interfaces, which allow people to easily view and manipulate the product features (visualization tools are crucial for collaboration).

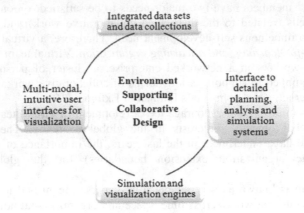

Fig. 1. Components for an Environment Supporting Collaborative Design

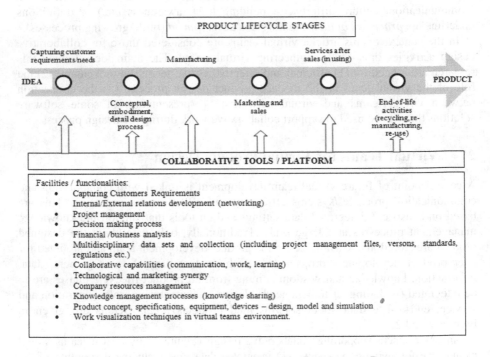

Fig. 2. Model Architecture of Virtual Product Development Process

In addition, there is a tremendous need for different competencies or expertise related to a large group/team of specialists (with different specializations, background, culture etc.) that have to interact together. Therefore, large design projects are developed by a virtual design team consists of members/teams that are geographically distributed locations [7] (i.e. the Airbus project in USA, Logan by

Renault project as a cooperation of Romania and France). Figure 2 shows an example of a general architecture for a virtual product development based on product lifecycle stages.

3   Virtual Teams as Virtual Network - Information Technology Support of Virtual Teams

To support the collaboration between members/groups/teams from different location, a virtual local area network has to be developed. This could be the primary stage of the virtual enterprise network development. Figure 3 shows a simplified model of a virtual network by consider different functional virtual teams join together based on Internet/Extranet/Intranet connections.

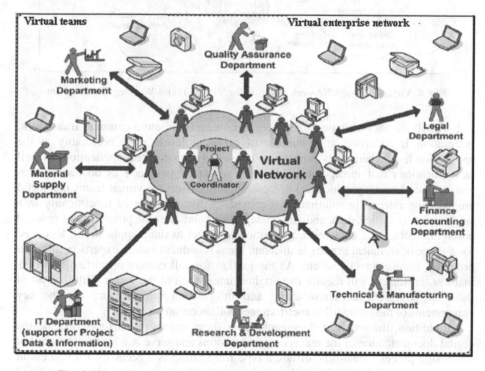

Fig. 3. Virtual Team for Project Development in a Virtual Business Network

It is widely understood that successful design is often a highly collaborative team based activity [9]. To be effective, a virtual team must be able to communicate, collaborate and coordinate its different resources, from and to a specific distance.

The following issues have been identified as crucial for collaborative work: (1) integration of different applications within the same organization; (2) integration of organizations, applications and content between different organizations in the same virtual enterprise (a presented solution is shown in Figure 4); (3) partners integration.

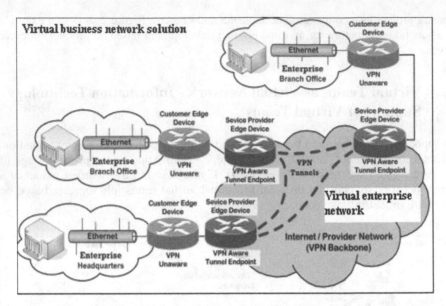

Fig. 4. Virtual Business Network Solution for Virtual Teams Working Environment

Formerly distinct activities are undergoing integration into a common framework. Integration is occurring at a number of different levels most noticeably at the application level where users expect ease of use between different applications as well as applications that incorporate a diversity of data types such as documents that embed spreadsheets, graphics and voice annotation. Users (as virtual teams members) are showing interest in solutions that provide a diverse range of functionality in a single network (voice, data, and video integration) and offer the possibility of reduced costs, i.e. less capital equipment acquisition (conduct to share application), less need for a range of technical experts in different areas (conduct to share experts in different projects), reduce travel cost etc. As the market for call centers on virtual networks matures, customers will require even tighter integration of the center with the rest of their business. The communications and information infrastructure are the key components of the Internet/Intranet/Extranet collaboration toolbox.

In addition, the archived documents from these collaboration tools become the digital documentation of the teams design decisions and serve at a historical record of the design process. Real-time different type file sharing is a necessity for successful virtual teams. With real-time file sharing, individual users can view the shared document on their screen, manipulate the files, and have the results immediately viewed by remote team members.

But, the availability of web collaboration tools is not enough to ensure the success, and also the virtual teams require, like all teams, a proper leadership and a management to establish clear objectives, define project procedures and team communication and collaboration. Virtual project management technique as well as additional guidance to keep the distributed team informed and engaged. In addition, before the virtual team project begins, the team must establish a management system, articulate the team's organization and develop a plan for operations [7].

In conclusion, virtual teams are deeply dependent of computer and telecommunication technologies. These technologies define the operational environment of any virtual team and thus come together to determine the *infrastructure* for collaborative working and learning.

Technologies that support virtual teams belong to three domains: (1) *Internet/Intranet systems* (provide important communicative and informational resources; allow members to achieve text, visual, audio and numerical data in user-friendly format); (2) *Collaborative Software* Systems (collaborative software are designed to augment both types of team work activities and to empower teamwork processes); (3) *Desktop Video Conferencing Systems* (the core system around which the rest of virtual team technologies are built).

The three infrastructure components, across which the virtual team interacts, provide technological empowerment to the virtual teams operation.

4   Comparison of Some Virtual Team Collaboration Tools

If the team is *100% virtual for the entire project's duration, organization must empower that team with the best tools,* it mustensure that the conference calls are aided with web tools and board sharing and it must establish consistent communication protocols and behavior [13].

The actual virtual teams are using complex software tools to collaborate and to develop new competitive products. During the project development process, there are used a lot of software tools that are capable of project management and real-time communication between project teams/members.

For the purpose of this paper, there have been analyze the following software used to improve collaborative work [3], [4], [5]. This analysis was done for didactical reasons, too.

*Skype*software allows meetings worldwide. Millions of individuals use Skype for audio and video calls frees, to send instant messages and files or for group meetings with other Skype users. Every day, people everywhere use low cost Skype calls to landline or mobile. Shortcomings: it is possible only between two people and cannot use shared applications or tools. Skype do not allow sharing application.

Marratech software allows meetings that are held in virtual meeting rooms available on a predefined server. Meeting rooms can vary depending of the type and number of participants and the meeting may be closed when an unwanted virtual meeting began. During the virtual meetings, initially there is no rigid assignment of roles; each participant has equal rights and can perform other roles. However, if desired, participants can be assigned with explicit roles as: moderator, presenter, student and listener.

WebEx makes sharing webcam video easy and intuitive (simple menus to navigate or manuals to read). If somebody from a team has a webcam enabled, just click the camera icon next to your name in the WebEx interface to start (or stop) sharing. Web conferencing allows members of a conference do almost anything they can do during face-to-face meetings. WebEx is able to: (1) hold a press conference; (2) demonstrate a product; (3) make a sales presentation; (4) conduct remote training; (5) collaborate on design [14].

Lotus Sametime is designed as a tool to announce the presence and instant transmission of messages (in a work team). Participants who begin an instant messaging meeting because they saw that the others are available at any given time, they can "improve" the exchange of information by adding an audio link to a streaming video, a white sheet and functionality for sharing application. In addition, they can pre-arrange meetings that are secured with a password.

Arel Spotlight software is based on planned meetings that are scheduled via a server. After creating a meeting, an e-mail that contains all the necessary information may be sent to each participant. Alternatively, they can create an instant meeting, other participants may then join using a particular Internet address (by calling Internet Explorer on your computer). Common applications such as CATIA can be share during demonstrations or working sessions.

Table 1. Comparison Between Information Technology Support Solutions

Functionality	Skype conference	Marratech	WebEx	Lotus Sametime	Arel Spotlight	Enovia 3DLive
Text transmitted	X	X	X	X	X	X
Sound transmitted	X	X	X	X	X	X
Video transmitted	X	X	X	X	X	X
Show/edit the content of whiteboards		X	X	X	X	X
Show the application	X	X	X	X	X	X
Share control of the application	X	X	X		X	X
Transmitting data by files	X		X		X	X
Inserting a comment			X			X
Combining calendars						
Show/edit calendar			X			
Show/edit list of media content			X		X	X
Conducting a opinion survey				X	X	
Show participation	X		X	X		X
Status record		X		X		X
Record succession	X	X	X	X	X	X
Record the whole session	X	X	X	X	X	X

Enovia 3DLive is a powerful product of Dassault for collaboration between virtual project teams. Easy to use, ENOVIA 3DLive provides a *virtual workspace* for reviewing product data and guiding contributors across heterogeneous information sources to the exact projects, people, and information necessary for efficient product development. With ENOVIA 3DLive all enterprise stakeholders are active participants in the product development process, employing the collective intelligence of all functional areas of a company as well as partners and suppliers. Users are involved in a visually rich, real-time environment where on-line virtual teams and communities are brought together quickly. Virtual teams can search, navigate, chat, perform co-reviews and collaborate on all aspects of the product, and all with just an Internet connection [15].

Table 1shows a brief analysis of the presented software for collaborative work, communication that are most used in virtual teams. This comparison was made using information from the vendors and users, but from our experiences gain in different projects when such software were available for use [2], [3], [4], [5].

A comparison between: Skype conference, Marratech, WebEx, Lotus Sametime, Arel Spotlight and Enovia 3DLive has been done by considering criteria related to their efficiency and effectiveness to support virtual teams work (share applications, data, information and knowledge; project management and collaborative learning) and communication functionalities.

5   Conclusion

When the number of task projects exceeds the capacity of a local project team, this will lead it to a delay in solving them and it will delay the launching of products on the market. In these circumstances, the only solution is to use virtual project teams, resulting in a reduction of work time, the contribution of knowledge from different areas of the world, new ideas and a further optimization of product quality.

Based on the results of the software analysis that facilitates the collaboration between virtual teams, it is demonstrated that the appearance of special programs for collaborating on a project, allows users to exchange information quickly and it leads to a decreased time required for developing and launching a product. It is highlighted that in the approach of virtual teams we must significantly consider the differences between software, which facilitates the access to information technologies, data storage and networking between participating teams at products development.

To be successful, virtual teams need a strategic framework in which to operate. They also, need good planning and in-depth project analysis, effective and accessible technologies, constant coaching, systematic fine-tuning, feedback processes and the full understanding that their success cannot be determined by a pre-designated set of communication technologies by itself. Virtual product development through virtual teams in virtual enterprises is a temporary alliance of teams who share the skills, abilities and resources in pursuit of a project and whose cooperation is supported by computer network and appropriate tools, skills and special applications software [12].

The software used for project management and for collaborative work should provide instant access to information and collaboration to support virtual teams members: (1) to improve time management and knowledge management activities;

(2) to improve collaboration, co-operation and integration; (3) to enhance revenue by responding swiftly and accurately by sharing products component information (costs, delivery date etc.) with stakeholders.

This research is based on our implication in national and international research projects related to virtual teams/network development. These assume our involvement in virtual engineering project teams (research and development teams), that have developed collaborative activities related to integrated design processes. In a chronological order, we present our research projects together with some lessons learned (example of good practice). In involvement in virtual engineering project teams (research and development teams), that have developed collaborative activities related to integrated design processes: we have learned (test and valid) the virtual teams characteristics and we started to use the videoconference system in a virtual engineering team at the international level (for project meetings and learning sessions) [3]. The wisdom gained was extend for the EMIRAcle organization (www. emiracle.eu). 2006-2008, The INPRO – Romanian Research Network for Integrated Product and Process Engineering (CEEX project, contr. no. 243/2006): we extend (developed and infrastructure built) the virtual engineering team characteristics at the national level and the communication system (Internet, Intranet, Extranet and videoconference system, www.eng.upt.ro/inpro/) [4], [5]. From 2008 to present, ECQA – European Certification and Qualification Association (www.ecqa.org): we extend our experience in the case of a virtual engineering team that develops e-learning programs that are recognized at the European level. Main experience have been gained in: Certified Integrated Design Engineer – iDesigner (FR/08/LLP-LdV/TOI/117025), ResEUr – Certified EU Researcher-Entrepreneur (503021-LLP-1-2009-1-BE-LEONARDO-LMP), dEUcert – Dissemination of European certification schema ECQA (505101-LLP-1-2009-1-AT-KA4-KA4MP) and Certified Business Process Manager – CertiBPM (LLP-LdV/TOI/10/RO/010).

Acknowledgments. This work was supported by the strategic grant POSDRU 107/1.5/S/77265, inside POSDRU Romania 2007-2013 co-financed by the European Social Fund – Investing in People.

References

1. Ale Ebrahim, N., Ahmed, S., Taha, Z.: Virtual R&D Teams in Small and Medium Enterprises: A Literature Review. Scientific Research and Essay 4(13), 1575–1590 (2009) (retrieved January 18, 2011)
2. Draghici, A., Draghici, G.: New Business Requirements in the Knowledge Based Society. In: Cunha, M.M., Putnik, G.D. (eds.) Advanced Technology for Business Integration: Social, Managerial and Organizational Dimension, pp. 209–241. Idea Group Publishing, USA (2006)
3. Draghici, A., Matta, N., Molcho, G., Draghici, G.: Networks of Excellence as Virtual Communities. In: Putnik, G.D., Cunha, M.M. (eds.) Encyclopedia of Networks and Virtual Organizations, pp. 1022–1030. Idea Group Publishing, USA (2007)

4. Draghici, A., Izvercianu, M., Draghici, G.: Managing Intra-national Virtual Team. The Case of Romanian Research Network – INPRO. In: Rusu, C., Badea, N. (eds.) Proceeding of the 5th International Conference Management of Technological Changes, vol. 1, pp. 481–490. Democritus University of Thrace, Greece (2007)

5. Draghici, A., Izvercianu, M., Draghici, G.: Building Virtual Teams in Research and Development Field of Activity. The Case of INPRO Virtual Network. In: Rusu, C., Badea, N. (eds.) Proceeding of the 5th International Conference Management of Technological Changes, vol. 1, pp. 491–500. Democritus University of Thrace, Greece (2007)

6. Dragoi, G., Cotet, C., Rosu, L., Rosu, S.M.: Internet/Intranet/Extranet-based systems in the CESICED Platform for Virtual Product Development Environment. In: Advances in Integrated Design and Manufacturing in Mechanical Engineering II, pp. 293–307. Springer, Heidelberg (2007)

7. Dragoi, G., Draghici, A., Rosu, S.M., Cotet, C.E.: Virtual Product Development in University-Enterprise Partnership. Information Resources Management Journal 23(3), 43–60 (2010)

8. Gassmann, O., Von Zedtwitz, M.: Trends and Determinants of Managing Virtual R&D Teams. R&D Management 33(3), 243–262 (2003)

9. Lipnack, J., Stamps, J.: Virtual Teams: Reaching Across Space, Time, and Organizations With Technology. John Wiley & Sons, New York (1997)

10. Michel, J.: The Many Facets of International Education of Engineers, Balkema, Rotterdam (2000)

11. Powell, A., Piccoli, G., Ives, B.: Virtual Teams: a Review of Current Literature and Directions for Future Research. In: The Data Base for Advances in Information Systems – vol. 35, p. 8 (Winter 2004)

12. Rosu, S.M., Dragoi, G.: VPN Solutions and Network Monitoring to Support Virtual Teams Work in Virtual Enterprises. Computer Science and Information System 8(1), 1–26 (2011)

13. Kohrell, D.: Agile Principle 6 – Face-to-Face Interaction (2011), http://blog.tapuniversity.com/2011/02/09/agile-principle-6-face-to-face-interaction/

14. CISCO Systems, http://www.webex.com

15. Enovia 3D Life brochure, http://www.3ds.com

Design of a Multi Agent Based Virtual Enterprise Framework for Sustainable Production

Bahram Lotfi Sadigh[1], H. Özgür Ünver[2], and S. Engin Kılıç[1]

[1] Middle East Technical University, Mechanical Engineering Department,
06531, Ankara, Turkey
Bahram.Lotfisadigh@gmail.com, enginK@metu.edu.tr
[2] TOBB Economics and Technology University, Mechanical Engineering Department,
06560, Ankara, Turkey
hounver@etu.edu.tr

Abstract. In this paper a Platform as a Service (PaaS) based multi agent virtual enterprise framework for sustainability is introduced which is designed in order to facilitate the collaboration between Small and Medium Sized Enterprises (SMEs) working in Aviation and Defense Cluster of OSTIM Organized Industrial Region in Ankara, Turkey. In order to enable SMEs to capture opportunities and design products collaboratively in a network, a Virtual Enterprise framework shall be developed. This framework also targets to improve sustainability for the SMEs in the breeding environment and prepare them for the forthcoming legislation regarding reduction of environmental impact, energy management and minimizing carbon emissions.

Keywords: Small and Medium Sized Enterprise (SME), Multi Agent Systems (MAS), Platform as a Service (PaaS), Sustainability, ODAGEM, Aviation and Defense Cluster.

1 Introduction

Collaboration is an imperative for SMEs to capture business opportunities in order to pursue common business targets. Virtual Enterprise (VE) is a collaboration framework between multiple business partners in a value chain to reach business goal(s) by sharing their fundamental capabilities using Information and Communication Technologies (ICT). In order to cope with turbulent business environments, mainly characterized by demand unpredictability, shortened product lifecycles, and intense cost pressures caused by dynamic and competitive markets, Virtual Enterprise platform is a key enabler. Our VE framework is particularly designed for collaboration of SMEs having different vertical competencies which are part of industry parks or clusters. SMEs collaborate within VE framework to develop new products with better quality and reduce market turbulence effects, with minimum investment. Collaboration promises flexible manufacturing advantages and empower SMEs to compete with large scale or multinational companies in the market without significant investments in their infrastructure. In order to make implementation of the

G.D. Putnik and M.M. Cruz-Cunha (Eds.): ViNOrg 2011, CCIS 248, pp. 186–195, 2012.
© Springer-Verlag Berlin Heidelberg 2012

proposed VE framework more flexible and reconfigurable, the VE platform will be developed with Multi Agent Systems (MAS) approach.

Ever increasing concerns regarding environmental and ecologic problems have pushed governments to produce new legislations in order to pressure manufacturers and enterprises to reduce their ecological footprint. For SMEs, to tackle these new governmental and public requirements is very difficult compared to large scale companies. Hence, sustainability is an important focus in our framework and we hope to help SMEs towards their environmental goals with this framework as well.

2   Related Works

It is obvious that producing a complex and competitive product is almost impossible by a single SME without collaboration with multiple partners. However this collaboration must stand on a firm and robust framework. Several frameworks have been proposed and examined for different phases and functionalities of VE. In order to define methods for existing applications and to inter-operate in a useful manner based on existing, emerging, de facto standards, "National Industrial Information Infrastructure Protocols (NIIIP)" provided an open, distributed and non-proprietary software infrastructure [1].

Leading studies and academic researches on VE goes back to early 90s. Barnett in 1994 presented a VE architecture based on object-oriented business process modeling approach [2].

A methodology for SME based VE network called Virtual Enterprise Methodology (VEM) has been developed by Burak Sari [3]. In this research VE concept was explained and based on this VE concept a structured methodology for VE framework and an ICT Reference as reference architecture for virtual enterprises has been developed [3].

Agile Manufacturing targets dexterous and reconfigurable organizational structures in order to respond dynamic and unpredictable market changes to develop cooperation among enterprises [4]. As Camarinha-Matos and Afsarmanesh stated in their paper, the main prerequisites to make a practical agile VE are flexibility, configurable base infrastructure and forming of breeding environments [5]. Aerts et al. have discussed that VE system flexibility would be enhanced using mobile agent-based ICT architecture. Use of mobile agents necessitates the preparation of an appropriate infrastructure by defining service bridges or docks for the cooperating enterprises [6].

Agent technology was first formed on the object-oriented paradigm [7]. Agents are autonomous entities which they have their own goal(s). Agents in relation with other agents and surrounding environment, considering both their internal and environmental conditions are capable of making appropriate decisions in their benefits and consequently bring flexibility and self-organizing characteristics to the system [8], [9], [10]. Solving more complex problems beyond the capability of a single agent requires multi agent systems to be used. In multi agent systems, agent interacts, communicate, and message each other and their surrounding environment through a network. Agents decide and react according to these communications and messaging in order to reach their pre-specified goals to persuade system actions in their desired direction [11].Implementing large amount of agents imposes high costs on the system so it's critical to choose appropriate entities to act as agents in the system [8], [9].

VE embeds distributed independent enterprises with various core competencies, and this is quite similar to Multi Agent Systems (MAS) and it can be modeled similarly [12]. In a VE, enterprises come together in a temporary consortium to share their competencies and skills in order to fulfill a business opportunity with the help of computer networks [13], [14]. Multi agent systems have been used to develop different aspects of distributed manufacturing systems like process planning and scheduling, supply chain management and so on [15].

Different MAS based inter enterprise integration architecture have been proposed by researchers but most of these architectures are ad hoc and they are not applicable generally for various systems and for practical purposes [16]. Designing, process planning, scheduling, supply chain management, network based collaboration among enterprises are the main areas to apply agent based systems. Rosenman et al proposed an open-system architecture for a collaborative CAD system supporting virtual product development called "Component Agent Design Oriented Model (CADOM)" in order to support dynamic virtual product development. CADOM is an information infrastructure to enable collaborative design [17], [18]. Another attempt on CAD/CAM systems and to improve reliability, agility, configurability of these systems using multi agent based modeling approach, has been studied by Shen et al. [19]. Two different intelligent approaches toward multi agent systems architecture has been compared in this research. With the aim of integrating various engineering tools (CAD/CAM, knowledge based systems) to open systems and enabling users to add/remove agents without stopping the progressing work, Distributed Intelligent Design Environment (DIDE) has been developed [19], [20]. The other agent based method which has been studied to enhance concurrent engineering concept in design and manufacturing is Meta Morphic approach. In this method soft hybrid agent types (resource and mediator agents) has been used and the main negotiation mechanism between agents is based on task decomposition and dynamically formed agent groups [19].

As Hales and Barker proposed in their paper, Virtuality index is an important criterion for enterprises to adopt virtual strategies. This index can be used for benchmarking the virtuality level of the enterprises and preparing a roadmap to increase this characteristic of the enterprise in order to ease those enterprises' contributions and partner shipment to virtual enterprise [21].

3   Proposed Concept VE Architecture

The main purpose of this research is to develop a multi agent virtual enterprise framework for SMEs utilizing ICT to collaborate for responding faster to market demands and improve their sustainability. Our framework has been designed targeting Defense and Aviation cluster in Organized Industrial Region (OSTIM) in Ankara. ODAGEM as a center of excellence was established in 2004 and is one of the Turkey's five centers of collaboration between university and industry. This center was established in Middle East Technical University (METU)-OSTIM techno-polis in order to improve the corporation between university and industry with the intention of development of the high tech R&D and education. This system has been proposed in a hybrid form. Here in this framework agents could be software or humans [22]. In our proposed conceptual VE architecture several agent types fulfill business functions those are needed for a VE to operate effectively. To manage business processes better and enhance orchestration of services to achieve better functionality this architecture is based on Service Oriented Architecture (SOA). Agents encapsulate different services which they have designed to execute, utilizing underlying SOA based environment.

The agents, which provide services, are classified in order to specify functions, their attributes and intelligence. Agents are able to accomplish business processes when they collaborate. Here in this framework, agents' targets are important from the green manufacturing point of view. This means that agents always keep an eye on green manufacturing criteria to fulfill their predetermined goals.

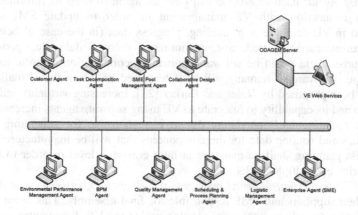

Fig. 1. Agent types in the Conceptual Framework

Types of agents (Fig.1), their functions and their special properties in our framework are described below:

Customer Agent; is the only agent which faces the customer. It accepts customers request for quote and collects all information regarding the customer requirements for the product.

Task Decomposer Agent; using engineering specifications and Bill of Materials (BOM), it decomposes downstream production process into tasks. These tasks will be published to Virtual Breeding Environment (VBE) as Request-for-Bids by VE management.

Collaborative Design Agent (CDA); takes customer requirements and transforms these requirements into engineering specifications and BOM tables. It enables design collaboration between partner companies in VE, utilizing a commercial design software package. After VE formation this agent will activate partner's accounts to enable them to take part in collaborative design process. If customer provides product design and related engineering specifications, CDA may be passive.

SME pool agent; is VBE management agent. This agent is responsible of new incoming SMEs registration or elimination of unqualified SMEs from the system. VBE actually is a pool of SMEs where potential SMEs for VE formation have been registered beforehand. In the case of capturing an opportunity ODAGEM asks for new bids by sending requests to all registered SMEs in this pool.

Environmental Performance Management Agent; as it has been described before, sustainability is one of the important issues in the future production systems. All manufacturers are required to reduce their ecological footprint as stated by the upcoming legislations. It will also be compulsory to imprint total energy consumption per product on their products to provide information to customers about their eco friendliness. Eco labeling is a way to take environmental concerns into account. This agent's main responsibility is to benchmark and rank SMEs in the pool regarding their sustainability measures such as energy consumption, carbon emissions and waste elimination and treatment conditions.

Enterprise Agent; each enterprise will have an agent to keep its information, and will be in connection with VE management in order to update SME's critical information in VE database (e.g. bidding, progress data (in the case of being a VE partner), current capacity used, cost, commitment, delivery date, etc.) periodically. This enterprise agent could be software, human or combination of both. Enterprise agent's type (software or human) will be determined based on the virtuality index which has been proposed by Hales and Barker [21]. Increasing virtuality index SME automation and its capability to integrate to VE using software agents increases.

Process Planning and Scheduling Agent; is responsible for generating detailed process plans and routing data for the components that will be manufactured. In this case process planning shall be managed at inter-company level in order to facilitate manufacturing by multiple SMEs.

Logistic Management Agent; manages the logistics between manufacturing partners, their suppliers and SME responsible for final assembly. This agent contains site information for all companies cooperating within the VE. It generates geographic routing information between partnering companies, and manages dynamic transportation routing. In this case also sustainability is important as transportation between firms should be done eco-efficiently.

Quality Management Agent; is responsible for inspection of parts or components. These components could be manufactured by partners, bought from suppliers or outsourced outside of VE.

4   Virtual Enterprise Phases

Virtual Enterprise life cycle consists of four different stages. After submission of an order from customer, an alliance among SMEs called "virtual enterprise" will be formed. In order to fulfill the customers' requirements, appropriate SMEs from VBE should be selected. According to the SMEs' ranking in VE management database and incoming bids from the pool members, suitable VE partners will be chosen. Nominated partners bidding will be gathered by VE management. An overall bid which is the collection of the total bids will be offered to the customer.

Next phase is design stage. It is quite obvious that if customer provides product design and engineering specifications directly, there would be no need for a collaborative design step and the system automatically will be passed to the operation phase. After design step, VE operation phase starts. In the operation stage, partners' performances will be tracked and supervised according to the master plan which has been prepared in the last step of the design stage. Periodic reporting of the activities is also performed in this phase. By the end of operation phase, product will be delivered to the customer. After receiving the customer's consent, payments will be finalized and service contract will be signed.

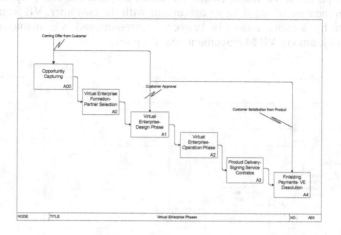

Fig. 2. VE Phases, IDEF0 Diagram of the Proposed Framework

Partners' past performances must be evaluated before VE dissolution and evaluation data must be updated in the system. Partner's performance is an important criterion in VE formation phase to choose most appropriate SMEs for the project. After this brief review about VE, different phases of VE as illustrated in Fig.2 are explained below in details.

Opportunity Capture; In order to increase benefits and enhance compatibility in today's dynamic market with intense competition among firms, enterprises should make use of arising opportunities from market analysis or direct request for quotes from customers. SMEs have to react fast and be ready to propose the most competitive bids to capture an opportunity. It seems that in some sectors (e.g. defense, aviation, automotive, etc.) there are always new opportunities for SMEs but benefiting from these chances is mostly beyond the capabilities of a single SME. To take advantage of such opportunities, SMEs need available and secure networks to collaborate with other SMEs with different core capabilities. By forming a VE, SMEs increase their competitiveness by sharing risks and complementing their capabilities to face ambiguous market environments.

VE formation; Virtual Enterprise Breeding Environment (VBE) is a group of interested firms which have registered in the VE database as potential partners for cooperation. Suitable SMEs will be selected from the SME pool in the VBE by VE management based on request for quote incoming from customers. SME selection is carried out based on different criteria. These criteria (e.g. cost, delivery time, commitment, skills, SMEs past performances in the earlier VEs, current used capacity, energy consumption ratio, and waste recycling /elimination performance, etc.) are kept in the system database for each SME in VBE and are updated periodically. According to the named criteria above, SMEs in VBE are ranked and benchmarked. After reception of a new request for quote from a customer, task decomposition process is completed, and decomposed tasks are sent to the VBE. Then incoming bids from SMEs are collected, based on these bids and SMEs performance data in the database, proper SMEs for partnership are chosen by VE manager. Selecting all partners, VE management calculates the total bid and proposes it to the customer. In the case of reaching an agreement with the customer, VE formation will be finalized by signing contracts between customer and VE management, and simultaneously, among VE Management and VE partners.

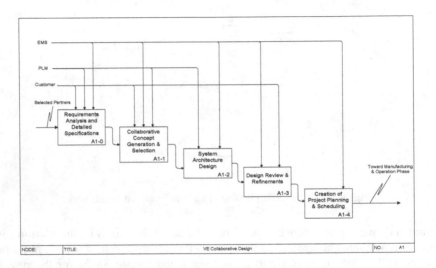

Fig. 3. IDEF0 Diagram of VE Collaborative Design

ODAGEM Centered Collaborative Design; In order to fulfill the design functionality and specifications of the ordered product, a collaborative design process is necessary (Fig.3).

In design phase partners analyze product requirements and clarify product specifications according to the customer needs. Following this step and based on the product requirements a collaborative concept design will be generated. To establish a professional collaborative design environment, it is required to use collaborative, secure and net based design tool which could be served through the network among the partners. This web based design software will be installed in the system server located in ODAGEM and VE partners and also customers will sign-in this (Platform as Service) PaaS based software remotely and design the product collaboratively. As this platform is internet based, use of it is independent of partners' operating system environments.

System architecture development is the next step of design process. In this step system structure will be developed and included system components, capabilities and their relations will be planned.

Succeeding step is design review and refinement of design specifications. In this step probable design problems or possible necessity for new partners will be considered again. Finally, based on generated concept design and system architecture project planning and scheduling will be developed and related Gantt charts will be created.

VE operation; In order to manage work progress and enhance orchestration between partners according to the master project plan and scheduling a robust, flexible and highly dynamic work flow management system is needed [23] (Fig.4).

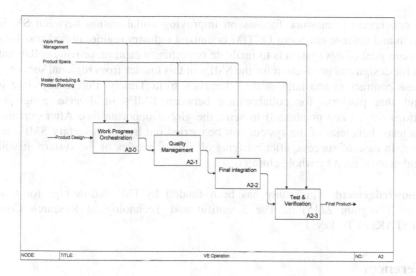

Fig. 4. IDEF0 Diagram of the VE Operation Phase

Manufactured components must be inspected to be checked if they are within specifications. Quality Control (QC), of individual components are responsibility of each partner SME, however VE Manager supervise and perform sampled inspections.

In order to finalize the production processes and produce final product, assembly process must be performed. To integrate all components, manufactured by partners in VE system and supplied by suppliers outside of VBE, all components must be transferred to the final integration plant.

Test and verification starts after final integration process. In this step product will be examined according to the customer's requirements and its functional specifications will be verified.

Product Delivery and Signing Service Contract; Product will be delivered to the customer after test and verification processes. Some products (particularly in defense industry) are needed to be assembled and be set up in the location where the customer asks. After product set up, there can be tests and demonstrations in the final location and customer approval about the product operation should be sought. In order to provide product technical services and maintenance during the operational life of the product, necessary service contract between customer and VE partners, should be signed. Final payments will be made afterwards and customer satisfaction about the product and service quality will be evaluated.

Performance Evaluation of VE partners; Before VE dissolution, partners' performances will be evaluated and this information will be stored in the system database. This information will be used in the next VE formations where a partner's past performance is used as criterion in future VE's partner selection processes.

5   Conclusion

This conceptual framework focuses on improving collaboration between SMEs in aviation and defense cluster of OSTIM organized industry region, in Ankara, Turkey. The main goal of this system is to facilitate opportunity capture, provide collaboration tools for design and production for the SMEs in this cluster from regional security and defense contractors and large scale enterprises from Turkey. Future objective is to extend this platform for collaboration between SMEs in diverse geographical locations (in Turkey or abroad) to seize the global opportunities. After performing alpha tests, beta tests of the system will be carried out by 3-4 voluntary SMEs in the cluster. In case of success, after ratifying all functionalities of the system, it will be extended to be used by whole cluster.

Acknowledgement. This study has been funded by PhD fellowships for foreign citizens (Program 2215) of The Scientific and Technological Research Council (TUBITAK) of Turkey.

References

1. NIIIP, http://www.niiip.org
2. Barnett, W., Presley, A., Johnson, M., Liles, D.: An Architecture for the Virtual Enterprise. In: IEEE International Conference on Systems, Man, and Cybernetics, San Antonio (1994)
3. Sari, B., Sen, T., Engin Kilic, S.: Formation of dynamic virtual enterprises and enterprise networks. Int. J. Adv. Manuf. Technol. 34, 1246–1262 (2007)
4. Sanchez, L.M., Nagi, R.: A Review of Agile Manufacturing Systems. Int. J. Prod. Res. 39(16), 3561–3600 (2001)
5. Camarinha-Matos, L.M., Afsarmanesh, H.: Elements of a Base VE Infrastructure. Int. J. Computers in Industry 51(2), 139–163 (2003)
6. Aerts, A.T.M., Szirbik, N.B., Goossenaerts, J.B.M.: A flexible, agent-based ICT architecture for virtual enterprises. Computers in Industry 49, 311–327 (2002)
7. Baker, A.D.: A Survey of Factory Control Algorithms That Can Be Implemented In A Multi-Agent Heterarchy: Dispatching, Scheduling, and Pull. Journal of Manufacturing Systems 17(4), 297–320 (1998)
8. Van Dyke, P.H.: Characterizing The Manufacturing Scheduling Problem. Journal of Manufacturing Systems 10(3), 241–259 (1991)

9. Cantamessa, M.: Hierarchical and Heterarchical Behavior in Agent-Based Manufacturing Systems. Computers in Industry 33(2-3), 305–316 (1997)
10. Bradshaw, J.M.: An Introduction to Software Agents. In: Bradshaw, J.M. (ed.) Software Agents, pp. 3–46. AAAI Press, Menlo Park (1997)
11. Wooldridge, P.: An Introduction to Multi Agent Systems. Addison-Wesley, Reading (2000)
12. Oprea, M.: The Agent-Based Virtual Enterprise. Economy Informatics (2003)
13. Camarinha-Matos, L.M., Afsarmanesh, H., Rabelo, R.J.: Infrastructure Developments for Agile Virtual Enterprises. Int. Journal of Computer Integrated Manufacturing 16(4-5) (June-August 2003) ISSN 0951-192X
14. Camarinha-Matos, L.M., Afsarmanesh, H.: Virtual Enterprise Modeling and Support Infrastructures: Applying Multi-agent System Approaches. In: Luck, M., Mařík, V., Štěpánková, O., Trappl, R. (eds.) ACAI 2001 and EASSS 2001. LNCS (LNAI), vol. 2086, pp. 335–364. Springer, Heidelberg (2001)
15. Shen, W., Norrie, D.H.: Agent Based Systems for Intelligent Manufacturing: A State of the Art Survey. Knowledge Information System 1(2), 129–156 (1999)
16. Nahm, Y.E., Ishikawa, H.: A Hybrid Multi-Agent System Architecture For Enterprise Integration Using Computer Networks. Robotics and Computer Integrated Manufacturing 21, 217–234 (2005)
17. Rosenman, M., Wang, F.: CADOM: A Component Agent Based Design Oriented Model for Collaborative Design. Res. Eng. Design 11(4), 193–205 (1999)
18. Rosenman, M., Wang, F.: A Component Agent Based Open CAD System for Collaborative Design. Automation in Construction 10(4), 383–397 (2001)
19. Shen, W., Maturana, F., Nerrie, D., Barthes, J.P.: Agent Based Approaches for Advanced CAD/CAM Systems. In: Proceeding of the Fifth Conference on CAD/Graphics, Shenzhen, China, pp. 609–615 (December 1997)
20. Shen, W., Barthès, J.-P.: An Experimental Environment for Exchanging Design Knowledge by Cognitive Agents. In: Mantyla, M., Finger, S., Tomiyama, T. (eds.) Knowledge Intensive CAD II, Chapman & Hall (1996)
21. Hales, K.R., Barker, J.R.: Searching For the Virtual Enterprise, Working Paper 1/100
22. Shen, W., Norrie, D.H.: Agent-Based Systems for Intelligent Manufacturing: A State-of-the-Art Survey. Knowledge and Information Systems 1(2), 129–156 (1999)
23. Aburukba, R., Ghenniwa, H., Shen, W.: Agent-Based Dynamic Scheduling Approach for Collaborative Manufacturing. In: Computer Supported Cooperative Work in Design, CSCWD 2007 (2007)

A Flexibility Reference Model to Achieve Leagility in Virtual Organizations

João Bastos[1], António Almeida[1], Américo Azevedo[1], and Paulo Ávila[2]

[1] INESC Porto & Faculdade de Engenharia da Universidade do Porto,
Rua Doutor Roberto Frias S/N
4200-465 Porto, Portugal
{joao.bastos,antonio.almeida,ala}@fe.up.pt
[2] ISEP Instituto Superior de Engenharia do Porto
Rua Dr. António Bernardino de Almeida, 431
4200-072 Porto, Portugal
psa@isep.ipp.pt

Abstract. The paper proposes a Flexibility Requirements Model and a Factory Templates Framework to support the dynamic Virtual Organization decision-makers in order to reach effective response to the emergent business opportunities ensuring profitability. Through the construction and analysis of the flexibility requirements model, the network managers can achieve and conceive better strategies to model and breed new dynamic VOs. This paper also presents the leagility concept as a new paradigm fit to equip the network management with a hybrid approach that better tackle the performance challenges imposed by the new and competitive business environments.

Keywords: Flexibility, Leagility, Virtual Organizations.

1   Introduction

Flexibility is an increasingly popular concept in modern times. Frequently, analysts assume that flexibility is essential to accommodate changes in the operating environment. Overall manufacturing systems that are flexible can use flexibility as an adaptive response to unpredictable events. Therefore, flexibility has been seen as the main answer for survival in markets characterized by frequent volume changes and evolutions in the technological requirements of products.

Building a definition of flexibility is not yet a straightforward process since definitions are distorted by particular management situations or specific problems. For the matter of this paper, Upton's definition is used [1]:

"Flexibility is the ability to change or react with little penalty in time, effort, cost or performance."

Most companies work on stable product categories produced in high volumes but, at the same time, they must deal with frequent product modifications and short product life-cycles. These constraints force the manufacturers to continuously evaluate their ability to change their manufacturing systems and the cost consequences related to

G.D. Putnik and M.M. Cruz-Cunha (Eds.): ViNOrg 2011, CCIS 248, pp. 196–206, 2012.
© Springer-Verlag Berlin Heidelberg 2012

those changes. This represents a complex issue in dynamic manufacturing contexts, such as the automotive, semiconductor, consumer electronics and high technological markets because the products are affected by frequent changes in volumes and technologies.

In fact, the customization of system flexibility provides economic advantages in terms of competitiveness, but, on the other hand, tuning the flexibility on the production problem reduces some of the safety margins, introduces investment costs and, in some cases, it can jeopardize the profitability of the firm.

Due to these constraints, a larger number of organizations increasingly confide in a brand new concept: Virtual Organizations (VO). A VO aggregates a group of distinct organizations that share resources and skills to achieve specific objectives and goals, but not necessarily limited just to one business alliance, and may have a regional or global focus.

In this context, the VOs can support the design and the production activities in order to improve the responsiveness and flexibility to meet the market demands. This derives from the ability to achieve a high degree of flexibility through different factories that can provide different processes, technologies and specific equipment specifically suited to reach the desirable "flexibility element" in each client order, or demand.

Alongside the concept of flexibility, in recent years another hybrid concept, leagility, has not been fully exploited in the context of supply chains and collaborative networked organizations.

In recent years, the concepts of "lean" and "agile" have aroused great interest in the research of supply chain management. The two paradigms that support this philosophy are presented as follows [2]:

- Leanness means developing a value stream to eliminate all waste, including time, and to ensure a level schedule.
- Agility means using market knowledge and a virtual corporation to exploit profitable opportunities in a volatile marketplace.

Recent researchers have advanced the idea that lean and agile systems coexist through the development of a theory of "leagile" manufacturing applied within a manufacturing system or supply chain. A leagile system has characteristics of both lean and agile systems, acting together in order to exploit market opportunities in a cost-efficient manner [3].

This paper addresses the use of the "leagile" philosophy within the context of dynamic Virtual Organizations coupled with the flexibility needs to motivate the decision-makers to improve the inter-organizational processes performance, thus assuring that the major goals behind the collaborative network formation are fulfilled.

Chapter two presents the flexibility concept in order to formalize the requirements model. The following chapter explains the leagile philosophy and its applicability in the context of dynamic Virtual Organizations. Chapter four addresses the definition of the VO and how the concepts of flexibility and leagility fit with the virtual organization management. Chapter five presents the Flexibility reference model proposed in the work and chapter six describe the technological approach for addressing the flexibility through the Factory Templates Framework. Finally, chapter seven presents final remarks and conclusions.

2   Flexibility Definition

A dominant feature in the academic literature is the use of taxonomies for flexibility, which classify different types of manufacturing flexibility elements. Table 1 presents a list of categories in order to typify the basic flexible categories relevant to dynamic Virtual Organizations.

These categories are useful in that they provide general "types" that can be used to distinguish one form or element of flexibility from another. This flexibility taxonomy is an important step to provide a better understanding of the overall flexibility concept.

Table 1. Categories for Flexibility

Categories	Ability...
Product	*change the product been made*
Routing	*modify the production routes*
Operation	*change manufacturing operations and activities*
Mix	*change product mix*
Volume	*alter production volumes*
Expansion	*add new nodes to the network*
State	*adapt to state and governmental regulations*

Another important aspect behind the flexibility concept involves its characterization (see fig. 1). For each flexibility element, it is necessary to establish the time period or time horizon in which the general period during which the changes will occur is defined. Associated with each flexibility element there are also four characterization elements: range, resolution, mobility and uniformity.

- Range has to do with the ability to put into effect or accommodate an interval on the dimension of the change; it defines the interval domain of variation of the flexibility element.
- Resolution defines how close the alternatives within the range of a given dimension are. Resolution increases with the number of possible alternatives if they are uniformly distributed within the range.
- Mobility reports the ability to provide mobility within the dimension of the change.
- Uniformity evaluates some performance measures within the range and costly evaluate their different positions inside the range of variation.

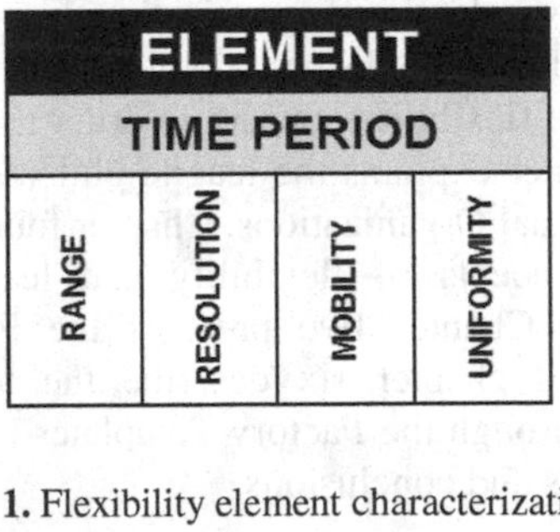

Fig. 1. Flexibility element characterization

Finally, the last feature associated with the flexibility concept is the definition of dimension. According to Terkaj [4], dimensions are general theoretical concepts that are embedded in the various forms of flexibility, which can be found in specific applications. For this reason, dimensions should not be measured, but should be treated as logical categories.

Table 2. Dimensions of Flexibility (adapted from [5])

Dimensions	Definition
Capacity	The system can execute the same operations at a different scale
Functionality	The system can execute different operations (different features, different levels of precision, etc.)
Process	The system can obtain the same result in different ways
Production Planning	The system can change the order of execution or the DVO node assignment to obtain the same result

The above mentioned definition of flexibility is therefore intended to support the construction of the flexibility requirements model in the context of the dynamic Virtual Organizations.

3   Leagile Concept

Womack and Jones [6] have stated that a manufacturing system employing the lean paradigm strives to operate with optimum resources to obtain an optimum performance. He also indicated that there are five basic principles behind lean thinking:

(1) specify value by product;
(2) identify the value stream for each product;
(3) make value flow without interruptions;
(4) pull value from the manufacturer; and
(5) pursue perfection.

Thus, lean is a methodology to develop a value stream for all products that seek to eliminate waste in several forms, such as: overproduction, waiting time, over processing, transport, inventories, defects and rework, focusing on an operational level.

On other hand, the expression "agile manufacturing" stems from the Agile Manufacturing Enterprise Forum at Lehigh University [7]. According to Lengyel, agile manufacturing is the ability of an enterprise to survive in a competitive environment with continuous and unanticipated change, and to respond quickly to fast changing markets that are driven by the customers valuing the products and services [8].

An agile manufacturing organization is, therefore, an organization that has the ability to succeed and reconfigure itself in a dynamic and competitive environment. It acts proactively in order to be a step ahead of the market needs and requirements.

Concurrently with the definitions of lean and agile, the concept of leagile emerged more recently. It constitutes a system in which the advantages of leanness and agility are combined. This concept was first introduced by Katayama and Bennett in 1999 for the manufacturing supply chains [9]). According to these authors, the leagility occurs in a supply chain when lean and agile manufacturers co-exist in the same network.

Aligned with this philosophy, it is possible to distinguish between the lean and agile portions of the supply chain because the lean manufacturers will have a fixed level of inventory produced in advance, whereas the agile manufacturers would be able to produce for orders varying in demand and product mix.

The co-existence of these two approaches is possible in networked organizations due to the fact that the lean manufacturers are separated from the agile manufacturers in the chain by means of a separation point referred to in the literature as the "decoupling point", as shown in Fig. 2.

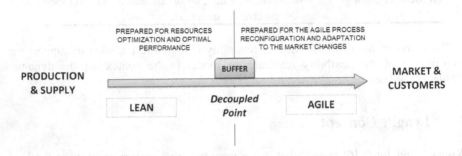

Fig. 2. Leagility in the manufacturing supply chain

This philosophy presents advantages in organizational terms. According to Van Assen [10], a decentralized organizational structure works best for agility because smaller, independent units can react to the environment more easily than a large, centralized structure. On the other hand, a lean organization performs better when there is a more stable environment and when steady material flow is created between the organization and the customers.

With this type of organization, the network is divided into a "back-end" part of the network that focuses on the production of physical products and/or services. And the "front-end" part of the network is aimed at the customer interface; it buys products from the back- end of the network, integrates them, and delivers them to the customers.

This organizational design thus seems ideally suited for a combination of the lean (production focused) and agile (customer focused) strategies, and it aligns with the vision of an agile network, thus being capable of dynamically reconfiguring itself as required to satisfy current market opportunities.

4   Dynamic Virtual Organizations

Today, it is increasingly common to see cases of collaboration among organizations that intend to integrate entities with similar or complementary competencies in order to design and / or produce new products and technological processes by sharing knowledge from their experience. Various forms of collaborative networks are applied in many areas and there are still various terminologies on this subject. In this context, Virtual Organizations (VO) aggregate a group of distinct organizations that share resources and skills to achieve specific objectives and goals. This is true when a group of organizations agree to adopt cooperation rules, common best practices, and mainly to share ICT infrastructures. Moreover, when a VO is established in a short-term to respond to an emerging market opportunity, during a short life-cycle, and dissolves when the goals are achieved, this is referred to as a dynamic Virtual Organization.

Nevertheless, this is really feasible whether it occurs within a VO Breeding Environment (figure 1). This means that the organizations and other supporting entities that adhered to a cooperation agreement based on medium- and long-term objectives, aim to increase their ability to form, design and implement temporary collaborations on the short-term, e.g., dynamic Virtual Organizations. The VBE concept is expressed in such forms as: industry cluster, industrial district, business ecosystems, inter-continental enterprise alliance, disaster rescue networks, virtual laboratory (e-science laboratory) and professional virtual community. Although the establishment of VBEs is increasing, there are still few such initiatives with proven experience and maturity [11].

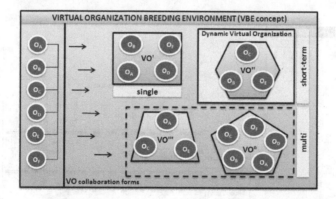

Fig. 3. VO Breeding Environment (VBE) – collaboration forms

The perspective of working together within the same extended infrastructure leads to the improvement of organizations' competitiveness. This can create high levels of synergy in terms of Business Strategy, New Product Development, Operations Management, among other concerns. Therefore, this makes it possible to select, agree and implement a dynamic VO as quickly as they can view market opportunities.

So, it is suitable that improving solutions in order to bring agility and flexibility through collaborative networks be an important place in the support of strategies for competitiveness [12]. In this context, the application of the flexibility and leagile concepts in the VOs can be an excellent strategy to reach those challenges, bringing better overall performance. They search for process improvement and adaptation to the emergent market changes. Indeed, the VO's scenario appears to be suitable for the application of these concepts.

However, collaboration implicates agreement among participants. This concern must be treated appropriately in order to plan and solve problem situations involving trustworthiness, sharing of resources and knowledge, and strategic alignment.

5   Requirements Model for Flexibility

Due to the competitive environments characteristics where the VOs perform, it is imperious that a strategic approach be defined for the decision-makers in order to provide potential characteristics enhancement for the network performance.

One of the basic elements of this strategic approach requires the comprehensive use of the flexibility concept as a fundamental aspect behind the design of dynamic collaborative networks. Flexibility is an intrinsic value that must be present in the role of decision-makers of Dynamic VOs during the entire collaboration life-cycle.

Flexibility improvement is frequently among the top concerns of manufacturing managers and is growing in importance; nevertheless this concept is somehow diffuse and ambiguous. So, this work seeks to address this problem especially in the VOs context by structuring the flexibility concept through a requirements model. Figure 4 presents the flexibility requirements model matrix.

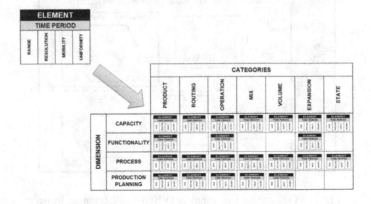

Fig. 4. Flexibility Requirements Model Matrix for Dynamic VOs

Using the concepts presented in Chapter two, it is proposed a matrix in which rows representing the dimension definitions, and in the columns the flexibility taxonomic categories. In the intersection of the rows and columns it is presented an abstract flexibility element that correlates the corresponding concepts from the dimension and flexibility categories where it is applicable for the dynamic VOs context.

Each of the abstract "flexibility element" is instantiated in a specific feature or ability that according to the decision-makers is relevant for the overall network performance.

At the same time the concept of leagility is convergent with primary motivations behind flexible dynamic VOs. Just as the VOs need these approaches to improve their performance also these concepts are fundamental to improve the competitiveness of organizations in VBE.

Another important aspect intended to address flexibility in dynamic VO's is related with the way the productions systems architecture are organized in order to flexibility and how they are depend in ICT technologies. The present research work proposes a new approach based on a Factory Templates Framework intended to help dynamic VO's stakeholders to conceive and implement adaptable and flexible VO's.

6   Factory Templates Framework

In contrast to other complex products, production systems and especially factories require an overall system architecture that allows them for continuous adaptation to the needs of customised products, the economic environment and the objectives behind the dynamic VO's. Consequently, in manufacturing, as in all complex systems, knowledge represents the key to maximising manufacturing success and the dynamics of this socio-technical system. This knowledge, which implicitly exists within the skills of workers, technicians and engineers, must be captured and stored within intelligence management systems, as well as being stimulated to flow between knowledge sources and all who seek knowledge in order to improve their work and optimise their processes. This exchange of knowledge between the different company's repositories within the VO's, must be structured and organized in a global reference model recognized by all the actors in the manufacturing processes as a Factory Templates Framework.

This Factory Templates Framework allows in the dynamic VO's the structuring and management of documents, best practices, methods, techniques, processes and knowledge, as well as manage constraints, goals and requirements following a concurrent engineering approach. In order to be successful, during the planning phase, the factory designer/manager must take into account different factors and issues such as: business goals, production facilities, human roles, information and control systems, energy efficiency as well as environmental and social issues.

Moreover, FT should support the process planning of the production systems at short, medium and long term, sharing with all the stakeholders involved in order to answer: *Which* are the goals to be achieved, *How* it is supposed to be done, *Who* is involved, *What* are the dates of start and end of each process and finally the reasons *Why* it should be done according to plan stipulation (Factory Planning support).

Therefore, it is not only important to design and monitor processes evaluating their flexibility, but also study its performance, looking for new paths to achieve better results inspired in the company's expertise acquired in the past. In line with this, the Factory Template Framework should support users to find answers to their problems, help them to develop the adequate level of flexibility, looking for the reasons that are affecting the system, and also supporting its improvement. Thus, two important functionalities should also be taken into account when exploring the Factory Template approach: Continuous Improvement and Performance Targets Management.

Moreover, using a feedback approach, the FT Framework is able to support the actual processes and activities performance analyses and assess their flexibility. Thus, the overall productions systems managers will be able to detect and visualize bottlenecks that affect negatively the whole VO's, and consequently, perform corrective actions in the specific low performance points in the network in order to improve the global performance. Done the corrective actions, it is essential that these new changes should be evaluated and the results confirmed, so they can be stored at Knowledge Repository and Best Practices databases.

With the Factory Templates approach it is expected that not only the dynamic VO's decision makers design their network processes faster, which are normally crucial and time expensive, but also improve the Virtual Organization overall flexibility and business goals alignment .

From the research work performed by this paper author's team, a new Factory Templates Framework was designed and currently its development and implementation phase is undergoing. From the performed work, the proposed Factory Templates framework is divided into 5 main modules:

- Workflow manager: composed of a workflow editor and engine, this module provides an intuitive interface that makes it easier for the Manufacturing Design to model approval based workflows. In this way, the WorkFlow Manager is responsible for the implementation of each process for each step of a VO life cycle stage, providing specific reports for each activity.
- FT Manager: this module is responsible for facilitating and assuring the correct creation of the overall product manufacturing process over the network, as well as deploying and controlling the life-cycle stages, guaranteeing that the planning sequence is accomplished. Once, the definition of the decoupling point for the leagile supply chain has been accepted as a potential competitive advantage, this will be crucial to overall VO manufacturing system planning support and execution.
- Performance Measurement: In this module, it is possible to measure all types of defined operational and logistic key performance indicators. By placing the evaluation results accessible to the rest of the network, this offers means to the decision makers in the VO's target low performance areas of the VO's and pursue improvement.
- Database Templates: this module is the Factory Template repository responsible for the storage of manufacturing process templates. In this repository it is not only stored the manufacturing processes and best practices implementations schemas.
- Best Practices Expert: this is the module responsible for the integration of the Factory Template with case based reasoning platform responsible for the search of the suitable Best Practices that best respond to the problem/solution that is being searched.

In order to simplify and guarantee a flexible architecture, a WebServices and an Open Data Base Connectivity approaches were used in order to support the global communication of the Factory Template Framework with the whole VO's network. Figure 5 presents the Factory Templates Framework UML module diagram.

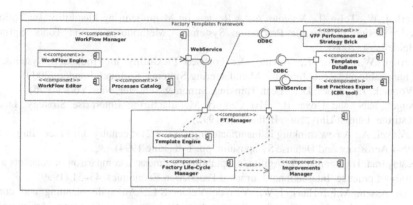

Fig. 5. Factory Template UML Diagram

7 Conclusions

The ideas presented in this paper intend to support Dynamic VO decision-makers in their management activities, allowing the effective response to the emergent business opportunities. The construction and analysis of the flexibility requirements model empowers the network managers through methods and tools in order to better formulize the strategies which can accomplish the short-term agreements so fit to the dynamic VOs concept.

The leagility philosophy it would in the perspective of the author's present competitive advantages to meet the challenges imposed by the new business environment. It provides both the efficiency associated with the lean concept, and the agility and proactivity associated with the agile manufacturing concept.

By the definition of a Flexibility Reference Model and further by the implementation of a Factory Templates Framework, the research team believes that is possible to provide managers of VO's networks with a conceptual and technological framework fit to the demands and challenges posed by a post-globalized market.

The outcomes expected with this approach seek to increase the organizations capabilities to strategically analyze and configure future networks with the abilities to ensure greater competitiveness and profitability.

References

1. Upton, D.M.: The Management of Manufacturing Flexibility. California Management Review 36(2), 72–89 (1994)
2. Fan, Q., Xu, X.J.: Research on Lean, Agile and Leagile Supply Chain. International Conference on Wireless Communications, Networking and Mobile Computing (2007)
3. Krishnamurthy, R., Yauch, C.A.: Leagile manufacturing: a proposed corporate infrastructure. International Journal of Operations & Production Management 27(6), 588–604 (2007)

4. Terkaj, W., Tolio, T., Valente, A.: A Review on Manufacturing Flexibility. In: Tolio, T. (ed.) Design of Flexible Production Systems – Methodologies and Tools. Springer, Heidelberg (2008)
5. Terkaj, W., Tolio, T., Valente, A.: Focused Flexibility in Production Systems. In: Changeable and Reconfigurable Manufacturing Systems. Springer, London (2009)
6. Womack, J.P., Jones, D.T.: Lean Thinking. Simon & Schuster, New York (1996)
7. Nagel, R.N. and Dove, R.: 21st Century Manufacturing Enterprise Strategy, Iacocca Institute. Lehigh University, Bethlehem (1992)
8. Lengyel, A.: A new thinking in manufacturing for the 21st century. In: Proceedings of the 1994 Aerospace and Defense Symposium, pp. 1–8 (June 1994)
9. Katayama, H., Bennett, D.: Agility, adaptability, leanness: a comparison of concepts and a study of practice. International Journal of Production Economics, 43–51 (1999)
10. Van Assen, M.F., Hans, E.W., Van de Velde, S.L.: An agile planning and control framework for customer-order driven discrete parts manufacturing environments. International Journal of Agile Management Systems 2(1), 16–23 (2000)
11. Camarinha-Matos, L.M., Afsarmanesh, H.: Collaborative Networks: reference modeling. Springer, New York (2008)
12. Faria, L., Azevedo, A.: Strategic Production Networks: the Approach of Small Textile Industry. In: Proceedings of 7th IFIP Working Conference on Virtual Enterprises No 64. Helsink (2006)

Effective Service Dynamic Packages for Ubiquitous Manufacturing System

Goran D. Putnik[1,3], Luís Ferreira[2], Vaibhav Shah[1,3], Zlata Putnik[3], Hélio Castro[1,3], Maria Manuela Cruz-Cunha[2,3], and Maria Leonilde R. Varela[1,3]

[1] University of Minho, School of Engineering, Campus de Azurém,
4800-158 Guimarães, Portugal
{putnikgd,vaibhav.shah,hcastro,leonilde}@dps.uminho.pt
[2] Polytechnic Institute of Cávado e Ave, School of Technology, Lugar do Aldão
4750-810 Vila Frescainha S. Martinho – Barcelos, Portugal
{lufer,mcunha}@ipca.pt
[3] University of Minho, CITEPE Research Centre, Campus de Azurém,
4800-158 Guimarães, Portugal
zlata.putnik@gmail.com

Abstract. This paper proposes a new integrated architecture for advanced manufacturing management with a Ubiquitous Management System (UMS) and a collection of adequate features to sustain it, where pragmatics on collaboration mechanisms prevails. The Market-of-Resources repository and its advanced brokering process will enable reliable interoperability, services dynamic packages and reconfiguration, as well as the (co-) management of production process, regardless information systems and using real-time collaboration mechanisms. This article contributes for building a logical model for UMS as well as an UML formalization for its supporting architecture

Keywords: Ubiquitous manufacturing systems, pragmatics, dynamic packages, interoperability, integration, effectiveness.

1 Introduction

Some very recent statements by people with high level responsibilities in the world demark the real and actual sensibility for future industrial requirements. Several points of views see the solution mainly based on getting more production capacity, using more resources, better efficiency, etc. However some others defend that the problem is not related only with deficient capacity but more with the incapacity to quickly adapt and react to, and we would say to act in the environment of, continuous market dynamic changes. In the future scenario of manufacturing the relation between customers, suppliers and companies will be transformed on virtual dependencies and ubiquitous services. Maybe arises new stakeholders and new rules for the game. The needed resources will be managed by another resources and the supplier of some material behaves as customer from another in a transparent way. One doesn't have space but has production. One doesn't have production but offers services to it. A new completely dynamic profile! The easiest way one adapts, we would say acts, the better he succeeds.

G.D. Putnik and M.M. Cruz-Cunha (Eds.): ViNOrg 2011, CCIS 248, pp. 207–219, 2012.
© Springer-Verlag Berlin Heidelberg 2012

This announced dynamics requires not only agile and efficient management processes, but information systems high interoperability, reconfigurable networks of production units (cells, plants, companies, etc.) and efficient and effective integrated collaborative tools to support the human participation on the process under an unpredictable business environment. Although the actual information systems follow initial specifications, those specifications are not aligned with human needs but business requirements, instead.

So the scope of this paper is to present a model for Effective Service Dynamic Packages (ESDP) applied to Ubiquitous Manufacturing Systems (UMS) and a set of new features to sustain it. The way the human-to-human interact through the system is improved with pragmatics support and an advanced resources brokering mechanisms is implemented on top of a Market-of-Resources, as meta-organization environment, allowing their dynamic and quick reconfigurations.

This paper continues as follows. Related research work is reviewed in Section 2. In Section 3 we outline the Effective Service Dynamic Packages proposal, exposing its organizational, logical and technical models. The supporting architecture is explored in Section 4 and finally, Section 5 presents future developments and concludes the paper.

2   Related Research Work

Manufacturing systems and processes have been subject for several scientific research and publications, mainly concerned with: a) production processes and stakeholders relation; b) support systems and c) workers and underlying behavior, ethical, social and organizational questions. All of them aiming the optimization (less costs) and improvement (more gains) of the manufacturing offer.

Since there is an emergent infrastructure (cloud) where each member (machine, process, user, etc.) is able to find and to get what he needs, where no one knows precisely his precedent or dependent, it seems clear that the next generation of Manufacturing information systems infrastructure will have to support more than flexibility/agility and integration. It must support collaboration services (Jaatun, Zhao, Rong, & Zhang, 2009) and, we say, ubiquitous (computation too) services. To sustain this point of view, follows relevant work references in the area.

Dynamic Packages

The Dynamic Packages (or Dynamic Packaging) concept is not really new. It was (indirectly) explored on communication protocols of computer network OSI model, where the DTP - Dynamic Packet Transport protocol proposed an optimized transport protocol suitable to improve the use of the bandwidth, packets transmission, etc. (CISCO, 2000). This efficiency improvement might have inspired developers and architects to adapt the same concept to business (software and process) area.

Although explored in several business areas (Cardoso & Lange, 2007), the essence of the concept represents nothing but searching mechanisms, an information system oriented perspective, which allows services to be dynamically selected. Ferreira, Putnik, Cunha, & Putnik (2011) already explored the concept and proposed its enrichment with collaborative functionalities. According to them, the resources (for services) can be dynamically discovered and purposed, but there must be possible the human (user) participation (interaction) on the final decision. A similar perception can be applied to manufacturing business.

But we must not confuse dynamic packaging with Dynamic Manufacture and Packaging, where predetermined proportions of some components are dynamically mixed in order to obtain a final product and then packaged to deliver to the customer. Also, we must not confuse it with Dynamic Manufacturing Environment where the control of the incoming materials, the manufacturing process control and the customer satisfaction are correlated trough the use of Quality Function Deployment (QFD) techniques and Knowledge Based Expert Systems (KBS) (Pearsall & Raines, 1994).

Considering this and seeing that manufacturing is evolving toward digitalization, we fill that future manufacturing, ever more information and knowledge oriented (Lan, Ding, Hong, Huang, & Lu, 2004), will needs to quickly reconfigure the production processes (schedules, machines availability and capacity, supply of material, human resources, etc.) since the agile, dynamic, integrated and distributed (virtual) network of companies, to which it will belong, regulated by a global and dynamic business model, will require it. In this situation the Dynamic Packages behavior needs to offer not only a set of possible resources or services (discovered by advanced brokering engines) but also to assure the contract between them towards the deadlines of products delivery.

Ubiquity, Open, Virtual and Cloud

Ubiquity	Virtual Enterprise	Open Manufacturing
Virtual Ubiquity	Open source	Virtual Organization
Virtual Hardware	Open Access	Virtual Capacity
Virtual Computing	Virtual	Virtual Development

We are convinced that there still exist some misplaced interpretations of emergent concepts of ubiquity, virtual and open. This misplacement becomes stronger with cloud computing architecture and related paradigms. Paraphrasing Dave Malcolm (2009), the interest in cloud computing is rampant across the entire IT industry and everyone has a different perspective and understanding of the technology.

Dynamic computing infrastructures, IT service-centric approach and self-service based usage model, are some of the announced supporting features of the cloud which makes clear that its main goal is to increase the capacity or add capabilities on the fly, without investing in new infrastructure or new software (Miller, 2008).

Running away from hardware virtualization, the services oriented architecture (SOA) and their web services brings virtual services (does not matter who and how are executed) and virtual development (Coppinger, 2007) at the top of "clichés" which need to be always available (ubiquitous) and able to be used according to their specifications (opened). Therefore manufacturing as a traditional evolving business activity must be integrated on this "infrastructure" just to take advantage of its potential.

The Open Manufacturing initiative (Christodoulou, 2011) already appeared to care these misplacements. It intends to reduce possible barriers to manufacturing innovation, focusing on procurement contract, grant, cooperative agreement, or other transaction supports. Again, we must not confuse the previous with the Open Access or Open (manufacturing) Source software which generally means no barriers to use and transform.

The Virtual Organizations are considered to be a mechanism to achieve significative returns increasing based on firms networks effects. The firms' network effects are directly related with network structure level and network technology level.

Considering the ubiquity and agreeing with Ferreira et al. (2010), the e-Business models forced enterprises to undertake important steps to their reorganization, both inside and outside the company. If the initial factor for this adaptation was the web, now it happens again with the Cloud (towards u-Business, the ubiquitous business). Cloud means no rigid structure and continuous reconfiguration. However, it is very difficult to archive real and useful collaboration between several (unknown) stakeholders, where the initial planning conditions can be changed, any time and for any reason.

So, Ubiquitous Manufacturing System (UMS) is represented, actually, as two qualitatively different paradigms. The first paradigm of UMS employs the ubiquitous computational systems to improve efficiency of the existing (organizationally "traditional") manufacturing systems, while the second paradigm implements UMS architecture and organization as a mapping of the concept of ubiquitous computational systems, not necessarily employing the ubiquitous computational systems in order to improve, not only the efficiency but, the effectiveness of the manufacturing system (G. Putnik, 2010).

We already see Virtual Ubiquity, but fortunately (or not) only for commercial companies' names.

Supporting Technologies

In ICT perspective we are facing a new era of architectures and paradigms. In nowadays services (web) are seen as the basic and main processing unity, as happened before with functions, modules, objects, components, etc. Services, inherent to Services Oriented Architecture (SOA), appeared to respond to portability (based on standards), processing autonomy (signatures), availability (discovered with UDDI) and interoperability (XML) properties of the new architecture systems.

Although offering new opportunities, web services demand new requirements as well. Since built in technology standards, they reduce significantly the required middleware for interoperability between heterogeneous systems. In business perspective, web services improved interaction inside the company as well as between others companies, their customers and suppliers. Paraphrasing Ari Bixhorn, from Microsoft[1], "The result is less information-technology complexity and significant cost savings".

Moving the same reasoning to manufacturing, manufactures can now easily communicate with all stakeholders, enabling better customer support and faster

---

[1] Ari Bixhorn is the Director of Web Services Strategy for Microsoft Corp.

time-to-market alignment. In summary, better product collaboration and consequent cost reduction.

Since SOA and web services enabled loose coupling as well as reusability and orchestration or governance architectures and services, they sustain their dynamic behavior and consequent response. The relation between partners is no more rigid point-to-point but, arbitrary, with several available services providers and consumers. Paraphrasing now Miko Matsumura[2], web services "is a way to map the capabilities of the network to the parameters of the request", given clearly focus to results and ignoring delivery details. So any common "No" result must be replaced by suggestions of alternatives.

As consequence of the webization of applications and process and the generalization of services implementation it is need now to orchestrate their utilization and establish their quality, even known that their supporting technology assures their interoperability and composition. It is necessary to find the answer to the question "how to compare services?".

To describe such properties we need to back again to ontologies and their capacity to semantic support. Thus it is possible to enrich services specification with more meta information, where semantic can be included. Web Services Modeling Ontologies (Bruijn, Fensel, & Keller, 2005) and Semantic Annotation for WSDL and XML Schema (Kopecký, 2007) are some efforts on that. "…by having a BOM Web service, any application on the manufacturing floor that is loosely coupled with the service has only to go to the Web service, rather than the BOM program installed at each application…" (Ahmed Mahmoud, Dell Vice President of ITGM- Information-Technology Global-Manufacturing)

The context now has several services, several enterprises and naturally several distinct architectures, so the need to integrate them is evident. Having this, an architecture which allows the interoperability between any application (or service) from any architecture model is a very intended purpose and critical goal which SOA tried to overcome. But to get that, web services need to be enhanced (T. Erl, 2007) and due to the dynamic behavior of this architectures (services availability and competence change easily) the overall architecture must react (to events) and behaves as an Event Driven Architecture (EDA), or better, as a Context-Aware Architecture (CAA), as suggested for ontologies (Kopecký, 2007), never ignoring that events are not all predictable (Hoof, 2006).

In this manufacturing system proposal we will need also to classify services and resources, since they must be cataloged in Market-of-Resources for posterior analyses under brokering and dynamic reconfiguration processes.

Lana (2004) already proposed a web manufacturing system to rapid product development based on rapid prototyping. However, since it is essentially a system oriented perspective, the collaborative features don't allow real-time participation and the dynamic reconfiguration is not specified as requirement. Sua(2005) proposed a Virtual Fab with a flexible and dynamic manufacturing service for virtual environment characterized by separation, transparency, simulation, and customization which does not represent our model of virtual enterprises. (Mostafaeipour & Roy,

---

[2] http://www.infravio.com

2011) explored e-Manufacturing with an Intelligent Management System, an integration proposal for existing manufacturing supporting software (CRM, ERP, SCM), being the middleware supported by web-based techniques, as is the case of the "intelligence" which is supported by agents. Focused on system autonomy, the dynamic reconfiguration and user participation on final decision are not specified.

On emergent corporate networks of Enterprise 2.0 (Newman & Thomas, 2009), a new buzz phrase promoting collaboration technologies (social networks, blogs, wikis and mashups) and software as a service (SaaS), the human represents the critical part on discussions, analyses and decisions. Thereby, tools for their communication and direct collaboration are critical requirements on new Multimodal and Rich Internet Applications and mobile devices are the main targets platforms for system architects and system developers. Information dissemination and disparate information consolidation have now real new tools.

Brokering and Market-of-Resources

Brokering is, by literature, a process executed by a broker who, in essence, means an act an agent does for other. However we intend to move its meaning to search and management area. According to (G. Putnik, 2001) a brokering process in manufacturing is much more than a search engine or information retrieval process. It is responsible for resources (cells, machines, persons, materials, etc.) selection, resources integration and scheduling, resource (dynamic) reconfiguration, resource monitoring, control and reliability analysis.

Considering this, the brokering will need high capacity to discover (search) resources as well high capacity and agility (dynamic behavior) to react to environment (Market-of-Resources) changes.

The main scientific contributions for brokering are focused on knowledge discovery. Accuracy and efficiency are well explored with agents, web services and matching algorithms technologies. Paraphrasing (Ferreira & Putnik, 2008), the "possibility to get useful information depends on the capacity to retrieve, search and interpret it". Selecting and ranking several results using collaborative-filtering (Silvia &Amandi, 2009); knowledge-based inference (Middleton, Shabolt, & De Roure, 2004); case-based reasoning and multi-criteria decision making of (Alptekin & Büyüközkan, 2011); data-mining over relational databases (Chaudhuri & Dayal, 1997); integrating data using patterns and markup languages (Hohpe & Woolf, 2004); adapting context-based multimodal adaptive systems (Höpken, Scheuringer, Linke, & Fuchs, 2008); etc. are all relevant initiatives. However, they only can "infer" new information from existing data, being the human perspective (information) impossible to get in this way.

The Market-of-Resources is a meta-organizational environment. It is an independent organizational entity (company) in the meta-organizational relationship with other independent organizational entities (companies), which form networked and virtual organizations, with the function of enabling their dynamic reconfigurations, through radical reduction of reconfiguration transaction costs and knowledge and intellectual protection (trust included) (G. D. Putnik & Cunha, 2005).

Communication, Collaboration and Pragmatics

Whenever two entities (systems, persons, applications, etc.) need to communicate there must be present the triad: transmitter, receiver and a channel to transmit the message. To collaborate they need the same communication model as well as mechanisms (tools) to work together. As Weaver (1949) sustained, after the confidence, the syntax for technical (accuracy), the semantics (meaning) for precision and the pragmatics (use) for effectiveness of the language (Morris, 1938), are the main critical factors for communication success. The same happens with the new collaboration tools.

But future communication tools (web, mobiles devices, etc.) and adhering information society show clearly that persons are rather easygoing, better related and share easily their point of view on decisions. However, this kind of relations needs to follow the functional specifications of actual software applications. Although the applications were developed to facilitate the human job and reduce his dependency, they cannot be fully functional to him, since the human behavior is very unpredictable. It can be easier to interact with someone but it is almost impossible to transmit a personal context interpretation, if one needs so.

Considering this, the emergent social collaboration tools are suitable to be integrated or adapted on future information systems. Since we consider critical to support direct human participation, pragmatic features will allow more collaboration and human interest alignment.

The fundamental, qualitative, differences between the pragmatics, semantics and syntactic, are virtually the best described by Carnap(1942), based on their degree of abstractness in relation to complete signs and semiosis:

"If in an investigation explicit reference is made to the speaker, or, to put it in more general terms, to the user of language, then we assign it to the field of pragmatics. . . If we abstract from the user of the language and analyze only the expressions and their designate, we are in the field of semantics. And if, finally, we abstract from the designate also and analyze only the relations between the expressions, we are in (logical) syntax." (Carnap, 1942, p. 9) (cited in (Recanati, 2004)).

So, the attempt to instruct new information systems with pragmatics in communication, will sustain their alignment with real customer's needs. The Pragmatic Web was the first technological tentative to instruct pragmatic aspects to existent syntactic and semantic web. However was not but some more meta-information to describe the meaning of the existent contents.

Different others experimental initiatives proposed collaboration mechanisms under semiotic frameworks but all of them tried, in a nutshell, to integrate existing technologies to get more advanced features and facilitate the human integration (use) in the system.

An ubiquitous system needs, besides the technological ubiquity support, a mechanisms to assure the customer's satisfaction, that is the system interoperability on the communicational level too. In complex and unpredictable scenarios, the user and the system need to be aligned and cooperate (collaborate) towards effective solutions.

If ones think that the main problem is a technical question, we think that two others dimensions need to be considered: a) the linguistic (Fromkin, 2000) used on the communication and b) the human behavior during the process. Thereby some more than technical arguments sustains the deficient alignment between Information systems, business and their user (human). Agreeing with (Ferreira et al., 2011) the human agency represents the strongest argument to depart systems from human satisfaction, since the systems do not support them.

For instance, the user does not always succeed his transmitted message and inversely, a transmitted message does not always mean communication. One cannot always interpret the intended meaning of the message transmitted. The ability to understand another speaker's intended meaning is called pragmatic competence (e.g. see (Mey, 1993)). So, having the capacity to communicate cannot be enough.

In another perspective, what happens if the context changes or the user move its interest to different results? The communication may had been perfect and well interpreted but now the intended results changed. This is common to human behavior.

In these and others situations, the system must give alternatives or allows interaction with the user. The system will (surely) need more information and the user will (surely) need different results. The effective manufacturing systems will work around this paradigm. All participating systems must be interoperable enough to allow agility and competence and work far away enough from the mechanical idiosyncrasy of common information systems.

3   Effective Service Dynamic Packages

This section presents the Effective Service Dynamic Packages (ESDP), an architecture proposal to handle effective service dynamic packages for Ubiquitous Manufacturing Systems, under Virtual Enterprise Organization model with high reconfiguration dynamics. It mainly supports: a) ubiquity, b) real-time collaboration for human-to-human interaction and c) dynamic reconfiguration.

ESDP Organizational Model

The traditional manufacturing process is not prepared to be supported by a Ubiquitous Manufacturing System (UMS), where the dynamic reconfiguration of processes and resources is required. Moreover, this new system to be effective must deal with dynamic and loosely coupled services, enabling enterprises with the sufficient agility to act quickly to effectively interact with dynamic environment.

This new "organization" will have traditional customers, providers and managers, but all of them advanced users, supported by specific information systems. There systems will be completely integrated with UMS and the *broker* and *Market-of-Resources*, the new stakeholders in the process, which will care of enabling the interoperability and resources ubiquity (anytime and anywhere availability) (Fig.1).

As we saw previously, the Open Manufacturing initiative (Christodoulou, 2011) tried to deal with manufacturing innovation obstacles. However, the ESDP goes a step further since it tries to be opened on usability, available on ubiquity and reconfigurable on dynamics. Effectiveness, indeed!

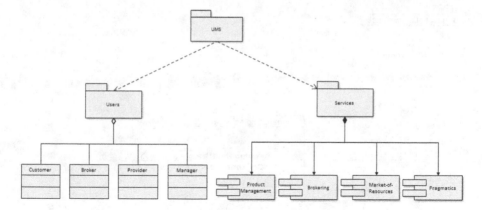

Fig. 1. UML ESDP Organizational Model

So the UMS effectiveness derives from the association of several interoperable services or components. The advantage for traditional Management Manufacturing Systems comes from the dynamic and advanced Brokering service; from the innovated repository Market-of-Resources, where any type of resource need to be registered and to register; and Pragmatics which responds for human-to-human interaction support.

Conceptually, this proposal represents further developments than other initiatives for manufacturing management. This model promotes a set of services and suitable technological features which allow their real-time governance, composition, selection, taking in consideration the user perspective.

Logical Model

Following the organizational model, the ESDP architecture comprises the following logical components: a) Product Management (PM), b) Brokering Engine (BE), c) Market-of-Resources (MoR) and d) Pragmatic Engine (PE). Fig.2 represents its UML architecture logical model.

The Product Management (PM) logical component acts as a traditional manufacturing management system, supporting the complete product life cycle. On the other hand, the Brokering Engine is the logical component responsible for the resources (services) dynamic selection and orchestration, that "best fit" product development requirements or expectations. It is responsible for reconfiguration management, assuring the permanent alignment among the Virtual Enterprise and the product development, as well. These resources are registered on the Market-of-Resources logical component which behaves as a repository to store, to catalogue (classify, qualify, ranking, etc.) and to regulate all kind of resources (cells, materials, plants, etc.). The human-to-human synchronous collaboration (video, audio, etc. and related auxiliary tools) which allows the natural involvement of the user on the co-creation/co-design (co-management) processes with other agents (humans) is the responsibility of the Pragmatic Engine logical component.

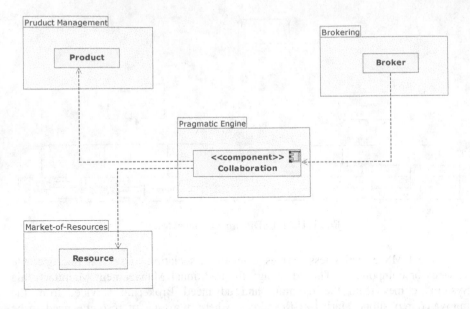

Fig. 2. UML Architecture Logical Model

4   ESDP Architecture

The ESDP global architecture (Fig.3) will be structured according to N-Tier pattern and functionally according to SOA/ESB and EDA patterns (Thomas Erl, 2009; Team, 2010), having multiple loosely coupling layers interacting and cooperating towards the system requirements satisfaction. The first tier – *Presentation* – prepares the results to be presented in the applications and supports *Collaboration* and *Pragmatics* mechanisms (co-creation). Almost all brokering process, its rules, algorithms and methods as well as the global system rules (profiles, authentication, security, etc.), will be implemented on the second tier of the architecture – *Business*, with a static collection of business services and a dynamic set of rules and process. SOA prevails on this level. All necessary interaction with the Market-of-Resources (resources repository) will be supported by the third tier – *Resources* – as well as any general databases interactions.

Technologically this architecture must support real-time collaboration (conversation) as well as asynchronous processing and information systems interoperability, enhancing the human interaction process which "behaves naturally" in the decision making on the resources (service) brokerage processes. This allows user to construct his proper resources planning considering his perception and contextual interpretation.

As previously described, the architecture will be layered, will support events (event-driven to assure reconfiguration and agility), and assure interoperability with services discovery and composition (service-oriented) following the Enterprise-Service-Bus pattern.

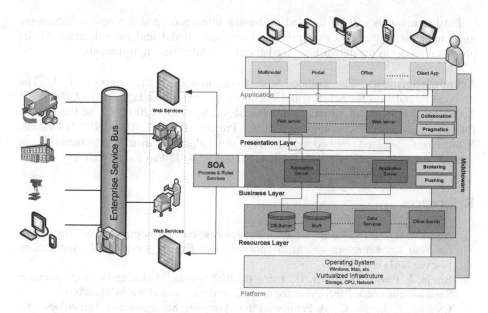

Fig. 3. ESDP Global Architecture

For brokering process there must be Web Processing Services (OCG, 2011) intervention, collaborating on dynamic resources selection from the Market-of-Resources.

Functionally, the architecture will be mainly supported by technological standards.

5   Conclusions and Future Research

The continuous emergence of new technologies and globalization of business activities requires continuous transformations on production processes and capacities towards efficiency and effectiveness.

From recent statements, the advanced manufacturing is a serious concern of world leaderships and several strategies are taking towards that. As they say, the technology needs to be more efficient but the processes need to change to get advantages of it. The proposed architecture in this paper responds well to these guidelines.

A new integrated architecture for advanced manufacturing management with a ubiquitous management system is proposed, and a set of new features to sustain it is established. An improved way to interact with the system on human-to-human pragmatic behavior is enabled and an advanced brokering mechanism to select and manage resources of Market-of-Resources is designed.

The architecture follows the SOA and ESB patterns, assuring the required interoperability and reconfiguration. The loosely coupled web services avoid the technological dependency and so, portability and expansibility of the system will be granted.

Further research will be focused on human interaction and the new collaborative tools inherent to the new enterprise and business model and on validation of the proposed model in the networked laboratorial and industrial environments.

Acknowledgements. The authors wish to acknowledge the support of: 1) The national Foundation for Science and Technology – FCT (Fundaçãopara a Ciência e a Tecnologia) scholarship, reference number SFRH/BD/49540/2009, 2) The Foundation for Science and Technology – FCT, Project PTDC/EME-GIN/102143/2008, 'Ubiquitous oriented embedded systems for globally distributed factories of manufacturing enterprises', 3) EUREKA, Project E! 4177-Pro-Factory UES.

References

1. Alptekin, G.I., Büyüközkan, G.: An integrated case-based reasoning and MCDM system for Web based tourism destination planning. In: Expert Systems with Applications, Elsevier (2011)
2. Bruijn, J., Fensel, D., Keller, U.: Using the Web Service Modelling Ontology to enable Semantic eBusiness. Paper Presented at the Communications of the ACM (2005)
3. Cardoso, J., Lange, C.: A Framework for Assessing Strategies and Technologies for Dynamic Packaging Applications in E-Tourism. Information Technology & Tourism 9(1), 27–44 (2007)
4. Carnap, R.: Introduction to semantics. Harvard University Press, Cambridge (1942)
5. Chaudhuri, S., Dayal, U.: An overview of data warehousing and OLAP technology. SIGMOD Rec. 26(1), 65–74 (1997)
6. Christodoulou, L.: Open Manufacturing: Defense Advanced Research Projects Agency, DARPA (2011)
7. CISCO, Dynamic Packet Transport Solution: CISCO Systems (2000)
8. Coppinger, R.: Cloud computing to enable virtual development (2007), http://www.flightglobal.com/articles/2010/04/27/340790/cloud-computing-to-enable-virtual-development.html (retrieved June 5, 2011)
9. Erl, T.: Service-Oriented Architecture; A field guide to integrate XML and Web Services. Prentice Hall, Alexandria (2007)
10. Erl, T.: SOA Design Patterns. Prentice Hall (2009)
11. Ferreira, L., Putnik, G.D.: Open Tourism Initiative, Tékhne, vol. VI, pp. 91–110. IPCA (2008)
12. Ferreira, L., Putnik, G.D., Cunha, M., Putnik, Z.: Towards effective Tourism Dynamic Packages. Information Resources Management Journal, IRMJ (2011)
13. Ferreira, L., Putnik, G.D., Cunha, M.M.: Disclosing the Tourism Dynamic Packages. Paper presented at the CENTERIS 2010 - Conference on Enterprise Information Systems (2010)
14. Fromkin, V.B.H.S.C., Szabolcsi, A., Stowell, T., Steriade, D.: Linguistics: An Introduction to Linguistic Theory. Blackwell, Oxford (2000)
15. Hohpe, G., Woolf, B.: Enterprise Integration Patterns: Designing, Building, and Deploying Messaging Solutions. Addison-Wesley, Boston (2004)
16. Hoof, J.: EDA extends SOA and why it is important. Journal (2006), http://soa-eda.blogspot.com/2006/11/how-eda-extends-soa-and-why-it-is.html (retrieved)

17. Höpken, W., Scheuringer, M., Linke, D., Fuchs, M.: Context-based Adaptation of Ubiquitous Web Applications in Tourism. In: O'Connor, P., Höpken, W., Gretzel, U. (eds.) Information and Communication Technologies in Tourism 2008, pp. 533–544. Springer, New York (2008)

18. Jaatun, M., Zhao, G., Rong, C., Zhang, X.: A Semantic Grid Oriented to E-Tourism. In: Jaatun, M.G., Zhao, G., Rong, C. (eds.) Cloud Computing. LNCS, vol. 5931, pp. 485–496. Springer, Heidelberg (2009)

19. Kopecký, J.: SAWSDL - Status and relation to WSMO, WSMO teleconference: Universität Innsbruck (2007)

20. Lan, H., Ding, Y., Hong, J., Huang, H., Lu, B.: A web-based manufacturing service system for rapid product development. Computers in Industry, 51–67 (2004)

21. Malcolm, D.: The five defining characteristics of cloud computing (2009), http://www.zdnet.com/news/the-five-defining-characteristics-of-cloud-computing/287001 (retrieved July 20, 2011)

22. Mey, J.L.: Pragmatics: An Introduction. Blackwell, Oxford (1993)

23. Miller, M.: Cloud Computing: Web-Based Applications That Change the Way You Work and Collaborate Online: Que (2008)

24. Morris, C.: Foundations of the theory of signs. In: Neurath, O., Carnap, R., Morris, C. (eds.) International Encyclopaedia of Unified Science I, pp. 77–138. University of Chicago Press, Chicago (1938)

25. Mostafaeipour, A., Roy, N.: Implementation of Web based Technique into the Intelligent Manufacturing System. International Journal of Computer Applications 17(6) (2011)

26. Newman, A.C., Thomas, J.G.: Enterprise 2.0 Implementation. MC Graw Hill (2009)

27. OCG. Web Processing Services. Open Geospatial Consortium (2011), http://www.opengeospatial.org/projects/groups/wps2.0swg (retrieved February 3, 2011)

28. Pearsall, K., Raines, B.: Dynamic Manufacturing Process Control. IEEE Transactions on Components, Packaging and Manufacturing 17 (1994)

29. Putnik, G.: BM_Virtual Enterprise Architecture Reference Model. In: Gunasekaran, A. (ed.) Agile Manufacturing: 21st Century Manufacturing Strategy, pp. 73–93. Elsevier Science Publ. (2001)

30. Putnik, G.: Ubiquitous Manufacturing Systems vs. Ubiquitous Manufacturing Systems: Two Paradigms. Paper Presented at the Proceedings of the CIRP ICME 2010 - 7th CIRP International Conference on Intelligent Computation In Manufacturing Engineering - Innovative and Cognitive Production Technology and Systems (2010)

31. Putnik, G.D., Cunha, M.M.: Virtual Enterprise Integration. IDEA Group Publishing (2005)

32. Recanati, F.: Pragmatics and semantics. In: Ward, L.R.H.G. (ed.) The Handbook of Pragmatics, Blackwell Publishing, Oxford (2004)

33. Shannon, C.E., Weaver, W.: A Mathematical Model of Communication. University of Illinois Press, Urbana (1949)

34. Sua, Y.-H., Guoa, R.-S., Chang, S.-C.: Virtual fab: an enabling framework and dynamic manufacturing service provision mechanism. Information & Management 42, 329–348 (2005)

35. Team, S. P.: SOA Patterns (2010), http://www.soapatterns.org/enterprise_service_bus.php (retrieved June 23, 2011)

Experimental Platform for Collaborative Inter and Intra Cellular Fuzzy Scheduling in an Ubiquitous Manufacturing System

Maria Leonilde R. Varela, Rui Barbosa, and Goran D. Putnik

Department of Production and Systems, School of Engineering, University of Minho,
Azurém Campus, 4800-058 Guimarães, Portugal
leonilde@dps.uminho.pt, rui_barbosa_1980@hotmail.com,
putnikgd@dps.uminho.pt

Abstract. The aim of manufacturing scheduling is the efficient allocation of machines and other resources to jobs, or operations within jobs, and the subsequent time phasing of these jobs on individual machines. Therefore, the scheduling of production processes of a distributed cellular manufacturing enterprise is one of the significant tasks to be performed to achieve competitive production, which means, e.g., to deliver products on time or to use resources efficiently and reduce production times. In this paper we propose a Web Platform for solving those kind of problems occurring either in intra or inter cellular manufacturing scenarios. Scheduling methods are local or remotely available through web services and can be easily and continuously incorporated in a distributed repository, which integrates XML-based components, belonging to a range of business partners, integrating a Virtual Enterprise, in the context of an Ubiquitous Manufacturing System. The scheduling data modeling and the data transferring processes are based on XML and related web technologies and decision-making is carried out through an interactive approach relying on fuzzy sets and user friendly interfaces for supporting cellular manufacturing scheduling.

Keywords: Collaborative Inter and Intra Cellular Manufacturing Scheduling, Ubiquitous Manufacturing System, Platform for user-friendly fuzzy decision-making.

1 Introduction

Manufacturing Scheduling results in a schedule that can be more or less detailed, in accordance to the intended objectives and the time horizon to be planned. Thus, there are cases where we are only interested in obtaining the sequence in which the jobs should be processed in certain machines of a manufacturing system, and others where we are interested in knowing the planned start and finish times of each operation of the jobs, to be processed on a set of machines. This double information completely defines a schedule or scheduling plan.

G.D. Putnik and M.M. Cruz-Cunha (Eds.): ViNOrg 2011, CCIS 248, pp. 220–229, 2012.
© Springer-Verlag Berlin Heidelberg 2012

There are many types of factors behind scheduling problems, like parameters for specifying job processing times, the definition of job ready times and machines availability, for job processing, among many other processing constraints result in a broad range of scheduling problems. So, there is a need to use a notation for problem representation, built upon a set of factors identified in the literature that enable defining a clear and objective problem categorization structure for representing real problem instances, belonging to those problem classes [1, 2, 3].

According to this notation the XML (eXtensible Markup Language) is used as a specification language for data modeling and processing. The main objective of this kind of specification is to make possible flexible communication among different scheduling methods providers through the Internet, based on a web platform for manufacturing scheduling support. Therefore, this specification contributes to the improvement of the scheduling processes, by allowing an easier selection of several alternative scheduling methods available for problem solving, as well as an easier maintenance of a distributed knowledge base.

In the proposed web platform, the SOAP protocol is used for the execution of implemented methods, local or remotely available through the Internet, within a Virtual Enterprise (VE), in terms of Web Services, for manufacturing scheduling purposes, implemented on MS.Net (http://www.microsoft.com/net/).

The effective and efficient resolution of scheduling problems begins with the identification of suitable scheduling methods to solve them. When there are alternative methods to solve a problem we can obtain alternative solutions, which should be evaluated against specified criteria or objectives to be reached, resulting in better supporting decision-making process for scheduling problems solving. Thus, we are able to properly solve a problem, through the execution of one or more scheduling methods and, subsequently, select the best solution provided by them.

For better system functionalities illustration an example will be given of the proposed scheduling decision-support platform, through an illustrative example, for solving a certain cellular manufacturing scheduling problem.

Such a platform also allows different users to share and to disseminate knowledge about manufacturing scheduling through the Internet, in the context of a VE, which is further described in the context of an Ubiquitous Manufacturing System (UMS). The proposed platform enables to easily specify scheduling problems and select methods for its resolution, as well as inserting new information about new scheduling methods and putting forward its implementations for problem solving, in an easy and interactive way, for remote invocation through the UMS environment. Moreover, fuzzy parameters are able to be specified for problem data definition, which enables even more flexibility on scheduling problems solving.

This paper is organized in 5 main sections. Section 2 presents some relevant information about the Ubiquitous Manufacturing System concept underlying to this work. Next, on section 3 the Inter and Intra cellular manufacturing scheduling scenario is briefly described, including some remarks about the importance of Collaboration and Fuzzy Decision-making, for enabling a suitable scheduling problems solving platform. After, on section 4, an illustration of the proposed platform for scheduling problems solving is provided, through an example of use. Finally, on section 5 a conclusion is presented.

2   Ubiquitous Manufacturing System

An Ubiquitous Manufacturing System (UMS) may be defined as an integrated manufacturing system characterized by an intensive replication of integrated resources, processes and software, spread through a globally distributed manufacturing environment, which aims at Manufacturing Systems Integration (MSI) and a collaborative-based management, as illustrated on Figure 1, which shows a platform for implementing these ideas and concepts in the scope of an on-going project, financed by "Fundação para a Ciência e Tecnologia" (FCT) (http://alfa.fct.mctes.pt/), under the subject of "Embedded Ubiquitous Systems for Globally Distributed Factories and Enterprises" (Ref. PTDC/EME-GIN/102143/2008) (http://alfa.fct.mctes.pt/apoios/projectos/consulta/vglobal_projecto?idProjecto=10214 3&idElemConcurso=2757). Although several different approaches and frameworks where already put forward by a widened range of contributions, arising from different authors worldwide, in the context of Virtual Enterprises management, there is still no single tool or package that can be termed as a Real-time Collaborative Management (RTCM) package. Therefore, the aim of this work consists on making a contribution for enabling a better integration of resources, processes, people and management functions, under the referred project arena, for improving the inter and intra cellular manufacturing scheduling decision-making process, incorporating a fuzzy-based approach into the proposed scheduling platform.

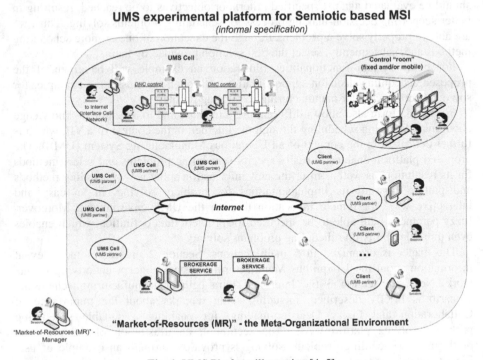

UMS experimental platform for Semiotic based MSI
(informal specification)

Fig. 1. UMS Platform illustration [4, 5]

The proposed scheduling platform, within the general UMS context aims at contributing to it in order to enable support to a "Market-of-Resources" (MR), which may be composed by an extended range of organizations to collaborate through RTCM, following an IT-based framework, where the manufacturing scheduling platform put forward in this paper consists on one important piece, which is process driven, i.e., enables an integrated use, based on cross-enterprise processes that integrate cross-enterprise application, and includes a centralized protected repository as well as a distributed one, for locally storing problems and solving methods information, on each business partner, in order to more accurately contribute to real-time collaborative manufacturing scheduling (RTCMS).

3   Inter and Intra Cellular Manufacturing Scheduling

Scheduling problems belong to a much broader class of combinatorial optimization problems, which, in many cases, are hard to solve, i. e. are NP-hard problems [6, 7]. In presence of a NP-hard problem we may try to relax some constraints imposed on the original problem and then solve the relaxed problem. The solution of the latter may be a good approximation to the solution of the original one. Many times we do not have a choice and have to draw upon what we may generally call approximation methods [6-11]. These include both, those, which we know how near their solutions may be from optimum ones and also a variety of heuristic methods, including those based on meta-heuristics, which are likely to achieve good solutions.

In order to execute the scheduling process it is necessary to clearly specify the problem to be solved. Scheduling problems have a set of characteristics that must be clearly and unequivocally defined.

Due to the existence of a great variety of scheduling problems there is a need for a formal and systematic manner of problem definition and representation that can serve as a basis for its classification. A framework for achieving this was developed by Varela [1-3], based on published work by other well-known authors [6-9, 11] and on some proposed extensions.

Good schedules strongly contribute to a company's success. This may mean meeting deadlines for accepted orders, low flow times, few ongoing jobs in the manufacturing system, low inventory levels, high resource utilization and, certainly, low production costs. All these objectives can be better satisfied through the execution of the most suitable scheduling methods available for the resolution of each particular problem.

Approaches to obtain good or at least satisfactory solutions, in acceptable time, within the context of Ubiquitous Manufacturing System (UMS) and Manufacturing Systems Integration (MSI) scenarios [4, 5] are based on the nowadays widely used local or neighborhood search techniques, and extended approaches, namely meta-heuristics, such as Genetic Algorithms, Simulated Annealing , and Tabu Search, which are also known as extended neighborhood search techniques and which usually perform well within a quick response requirement for, at least, reasonable solutions quality providing requisites.

Methods based on these heuristic or approximate approaches tend to provide good results in the available time to make decisions, reason why we decided to incorporate them in the scheduling web platform under development for supporting real-time, collaborative (inter and intra cellular) manufacturing scheduling (RTCMS).

RTCMS includes several stages. Each incremental progress from one stage will add towards mitigation of challenges that the next maturity stage may present. The three unique stages of RTCMS can be described based on a collaborative maturity principle, as follows:

1. Intra-enterprise RTCMS. An internal collaborative application within the walls of a VE. The VE is aligned based on processes with integrated applications supporting a business process based structure.
2. Inter-enterprise RTCMS. VEs that have achieved step 1 above integrate to provide a more collaborative environment through virtual projects, portfolios and teams sharing common goals and aligned to achieve single cross enterprise processes.
3. Just-in-time RTCMS. The highest level of collaboration based on a wide range of technology, were IT-based approaches, in general and Web Services in particular, as well as related technologies, namely based on XML, play an fundamental role, with no necessity of dedicated partnerships but standard industry process followed by industry players allowing just-in-time virtual collaboration. Established industry protocols and standards that have to be followed with Web Services acting as yellow pages, over the internet, allowing real-time information gathering and processing as well as real-time processes integration and management, namely in terms of manufacturing scheduling.

3.1   The Importance of Collaboration

Collaboration is being viewd as the next big wave after e-Commerce, digital commerce and several other variants that emerged in the last decades. Most of the previous concepts were considered to be technology to revolutionize businesses and related strategies. However, two key elements that these concepts lacked were related to the human aspect to make such concept successful. The first key element was related to captive audience, i.e., users of technology tools and the second to the actual adoption of such concepts, i.e., human behaviour. Users could utilize a new tool based on the latest technology, but their work metholodogy was still based on the old system. Moreover, people directly interact and share knowledge and experience for improving their know-how and thus more properly be able to solve problems on a real-time basis. Therefore, information and knowledge sharing and its optimal use based on collaborative team environment and integrated processes were missing. As such the same bottlenecks re-emerged: delay in the decision-making, lack of timely information, its access, visibility and dispersal and even worse, the absence of a constructive and progressive learning is still notorious. It could be wise to say that inherent to the human aspect captured above are the peocesses that humans follow. In majority of the cases, technology tools were introduced to work alongside existing processes and the integration of tools and processes was not tight. Technology was primarily used to streamline existing processes, but not to implement new processes that did not exist and which were needed to fill the gaps in existing processes [4].

In order to make a contribution to overcome the above referred difficulties and lacks, in this work we intend to enhance the importance of well-organized and working of manufacturing systems, in terms of appropriate requirements for enabling collaborative management, in terms of intra and inter cellular manufacturing scheduling, as illustrated on Figure 2, which in this specific case under consideration integrates four manufacturing cells, each one including two similar machine-centers, for jobs processing.

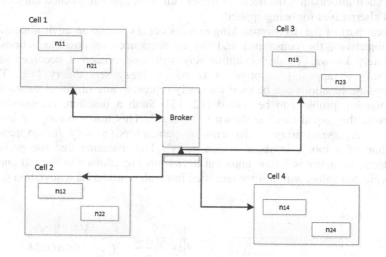

Fig. 2. Inter and intra-cellular scenarious within a VE

The manufacturing cells work integrated in a network, in the scope of a Meta-organization model, which implements the Ubiquitous Manufacturing System (UMS) context, previously described, were the brokering service plays an important role in several distinct aspects, namely in terms of assignment of orders received from clients to the working cells. Therefore, in this paper we intend to show how the scheduling decision-making, in the referred context of inter and intra cellular manufacturing can be enhanced through a proposed platform for Manufacturing Scheduling support, based on interoperability that arises from sharing scheduling knowledge within and across underlying manufacturing network of the UMS.

Moreover, we intend even to enhance this decision-making process by introducing collaboration principles based on uncertainty treated through fuzzy data specification and processing. In this context, either the integration and collaboration of humans than technology play fundamental roles to obtain enriched decisions in terms manufacturing scheduling solutions for the whole integrated manufacturing network, by using user-friendly scheduling platform interfaces, which enable to share information among the manufacturing cells, regarding each own manufacturing scenario as well as the general inter-cellular manufacturing one, occurring inside the VE, and therefore, enable to make supported decisions in a widened and integrated UMS context.

3.2   The Importance of Fuzzy Decision-Making

The main goal of a fuzzy solution approach is to find the solution or alternative decisions that may better satisfy and suite for each situation [12].
The proposed platform can be used as a support tool, for the decision-making process, by providing, in real-time, a range of alternative solutions to the decision maker, indicating the advantages and disadvantages (trade-offs) of each evaluated alternative. With such information the decision maker can depict an enlightened choice, among a set of alternatives for being applied.

Great part of the decision-making process occurs within an environment in which the objectives, the constraints and the consequences of possible actions are not accurately known. To deal quantitatively with imprecision it becomes sometimes necessary to appeal to approaches based on fuzzy sets theory [13]. Therefore, appropriate functions can be used for easily represent any fuzzified parameter of the optimization problem to be solved [12, 13]. Such a function, commonly used to represent the "equal case" is shown in Figure 3. This function can, for instance, be used to represent fuzzy coefficients or parameters, namely for expressing "the deadline of a job X is about 7 time units". This meaning that the preference of the decision maker is 7 time units but deviations are allowed to the left and right of the preferred value, within some specified interval, considering a deviation p_i.

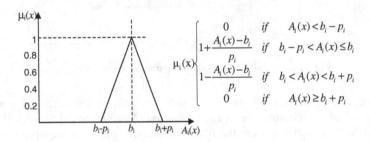

$$\mu_i(x) \begin{cases} 0 & if \quad A_i(x) < b_i - p_i \\ 1 + \dfrac{A_i(x) - b_i}{p_i} & if \quad b_i - p_i < A_i(x) \le b_i \\ 1 - \dfrac{A_i(x) - b_i}{p_i} & if \quad b_i < A_i(x) < b_i + p_i \\ 0 & if \quad A_i(x) \ge b_i + p_i \end{cases}$$

Fig. 3. Membership function illustration for "equal" fuzzy parameters

4   Illustration of Platform Usage

The main purpose of this work consists on trying to improve the scheduling problems solving process. Therefore, we decided to develop a web platform for scheduling decision support, based on Web Services and XML modeling and related technologies [14-18].

The main element of the web platform is an interface for introduction, validation, and transformation of manufacturing scheduling data.

The scheduling information is stored in XML documents. The XML and other documents are stored on a distributed data repository, spread through business partner within a VE, on a UMS network.

Some of the main advantages of XML based representation are its openness, simplicity and scalability [16, 17]. This is one of the main reasons why we decided to use it for developing our web platform.

The web platform uses XML for data storage and processing, for showing multiple views of the data and for representing complex data structures. Therefore, XML may guarantee the future utilization of data formats and the exchange of data structures, in order to enable web documents sharing and legacy systems integration [2, 3, 19].

The web platform is being implemented through Web Services (http://www.w3.org/TR/ws-arch/) using MS.Net and the SOAP protocol. This environment is heterogeneous as servers can use their own technology, i.e. use different implementation languages or/ and different operating systems. More detailed information about the SOAP protocol can be obtained from (http://www.w3.org/TR/soap/).

Figure 4 illustrates our proposed web platform. This platform encompasses several main functionalities, which include knowledge insertion, about scheduling problems and solving methods, and correspondent information searching. Users can make requests for visualizing scheduling problem classes and methods information or even browse information about other concepts presented through the platform. The data can be shown in different views, adequate for each specific request. The system also enables problem results presentation and storage on different formats, namely XML, Excel, TXT or PDF as well as uploading problem data files in these formats, besides direct problem data insertion and results presentation through the browser interface.

For a better system's functionalities illustration we will explain the resolution of an instance of cellular manufacturing scheduling problem, where a set of six jobs (n=6) are to be processed on a Cell (C) integrating two different machines (m=2), in order to minimize the total completion time of jobs (makespan or Cmax), which can be expressed in its general form by C,2|n|Cmax problem and solved through the Johnsons rule [20, 21]. As in this particular problem the Cell acts as a regular flow-shop system [20, 21] the general problem structure is similar to F,2|n|Cmax problem [1-3, 6, 7, 9, 11]. Once having executed the Johnson's rule, for the given problem instance, an optimal solution can be provided, in terms of optimal jobs processing sequence, on each machine of the Cell, the starting and finishing times of each job on each machine, namely through a Gantt chart, and some statistics, including Cmax, which in this example is equal to 84 time units. Figure 4 shows the web platform interface for solving problems occurring on manufacturing cells integrating only two machines and as we can notice, there are some other solving methods available for this type of cellular manufacturing environment, like the Jackson's or the McNaughton's methods or other sequencing procedures, based on priority rules, such as SPT (Shortest Processing Time), LPT (Longest Processing Time), EDD (Earliest Due Date) or LDD (Latest Due Date) [20, 21], among other meta-heuristics, based on genetic algorithms, tabu search and simulated annealing, which are still being implemented [1, 2, 6-11].

The platform interface enables to easily compare solutions obtained from the execution of several distinct methods, as well as performing slight differences on some problem data, based on fuzzy parameters, in order to quickly obtain slightly different problem scenarios, for a same base problem, without having to repeat the whole problem data insertion or uploading from a file.

In Figure 4 this kind of situation is illustrated through a value of 19 time units, for processing the second operation of job 1 (t2=19), on the right top of the platform's interface, marked in shadow, which can be defined as a fuzzy parameter, varying in an interval of, for instance, 2 time units to the left and to the right [12]. Therefore, the user can easily evaluate solutions obtained for slyly different problem instances, by running the same or some other method available through the platform and remotely invocated, on some machine belonging to the UMS network.

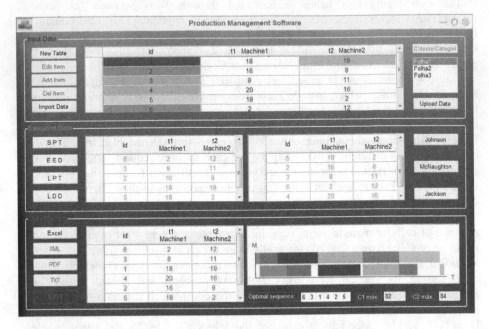

Fig. 4. Fuzzy Manufacturing Scheduling Platform Interface

5   Conclusions

In this paper a proposed platform for cellular manufacturing scheduling problems solving, either for intra or inter cellular manufacturing scenarios, which were presented and described. Concepts, related to problems and solving methods are modeled through XML and related technologies and methods are put available through an UMS network, where a set of business partners are dynamically integrated. The platform put forward enables remote invocation of problem solving methods within a Virtual Enterprise. Some of the important functionalities of the proposed platform include the ability to represent scheduling problems and more or less closely related problems specification, based on fuzzy parameters specification, either through some specific kind of file upload or direct data insertion through the platform's web interface.

In order to make possible flexible communication among different scheduling applications XML is used, not only for data modeling and storage but also for communication, in terms of problem data transmission among business partners of the VE, for remote methods' invocation and problem results providing on each Cell making a methods execution request. The XML-based scheduling data specification also contributes to the improvement of the scheduling processes by allowing an easy selection of several alternative methods available for problem solving, as well as an easy maintenance of a distributed XML-based repository and new methods incorporation, within an Ubiquitous Manufacturing System network.

Acknowledgements. The authors wish to acknowledge the support of: 1) The Foundation for Science and Technology – FCT, under the scope of the financed Project PTDC/EME-GIN/102143/2008, and 2) EUREKA, by the Project E!4177-Pro-Factory UES.

References

1. Varela, M.L.R.: Automatic Scheduling Algorithms Selection, Portugal: Msc. Thesis, University of Minho (1999)
2. Varela, M.L.R., Aparício, J.N., Carmo-Silva, S.: An XML Knowledge Base System for Scheduling Problems. In: Unger, H., Böhme, T., Mikler, A.R. (eds.) IICS 2002. LNCS, vol. 2346, pp. 63–74. Springer, Heidelberg (2002)
3. Varela, M.L.R., Aparício, J.N., Carmo-Silva, S.: Scheduling Problems Modeling with XML. In: Carvalho, J.C., et al. (eds.) International Meeting for Research in Logistics, pp. 897–909. International Meeting for Research in Logistics, Inc., Lisbon (2002)
4. Putnik, G.D.: BM_Virtual Enterprise Architecture Reference Model. Technical Report RT-CESP-GIS-2000-<GP-01>. Universidade do Minho, Portugal (2000b)
5. Putnik, G.D.: BM_Virtual Enterprise Architecture Reference Model. In: Gunasekaran, A. (ed.) Agile Manufacturing: 21st Century Manufacturing Strategy, pp. 73–93. Elsevier Science Publ., UK (2001)
6. Blazewicz, J., et al.: Scheduling Computer and Manufacturing Processes. Springer, Germany (1996)
7. Brucker, P.: Scheduling Algorithms. Springer, Germany (1995)
8. Jordan, C.: Batching and Scheduling. Springer, Germany (1996)
9. Graham, R.L., et al.: Optimisation and Approximation in Deterministic Sequencing and Scheduling: A survey. Annals of Discrete Mathematics (1979)
10. Artiba, A., Elmaghraby, S.E.: The Planning and Scheduling of Production Systems. Chapman & Hall, UK (1997)
11. Pinedo, M.: Scheduling Theory, Algorithms and Systems. Prentice-Hall Inc., USA (1995)
12. Ribeiro, R.A.R., Pires, F.: Fuzzy linear programming via simulated annealing. Kybernetica 35(1), 57–67 (1999)
13. Zadeh, B.L.: Fuzzy sets. Information and Control 8, 338–353 (1965)
14. Ceponkus, A., Hoodbhoy, F.: Applied XML. Wiley Computer Publishing, USA (1999)
15. Abiteboul, S., et al.: Data on the Web: From Relations to Semistructured Data and XML. Morgan Kaufmann Publishers, USA (2000)
16. Harper, F.: XML Standards and Tools. eXcelon Corporation, USA (2001)
17. Pardi, W.J.: XML: Enabling Next-generation Web Applications. Microsoft Press, USA (1999)
18. Carlson, D.: Modeling XML Applications with UML. Addison-Wesley, USA (2001); Laurent, S. S., et al.: Programming Web Services with XML-RPC. O'Reilly & Associates, Inc. (2001)
19. Goldberg, D.E.: Genetic Algorithms in Search, Optimization and Machine Learning. Addison-Wesley Publishing Company, Inc. (1989)
20. French, Sequencing and Scheduling – An Introduction to Mathematics of the Job-Shop. John Wiley and Sons, Inc. (1982)
21. Conway, R.W., Maxwell, W.L., Miller, L.W.: Theory of Scheduling. Addison-Wesley Publishing Company, Inc., England (1967)

P2P Decision Support System for Cooperative Electrical Energy Distribution Network Management

Gaspar Vieira, Maria Leonilde R. Varela, and Goran D. Putnik

Department of Production and Systems, School of Engineering, University of Minho,
Azurém Campus, 4800-058 Guimarães, Portugal
gaspar_vieira@hotmail.com, {leonilde,putnikgd}@dps.uminho.pt

Abstract. Nowadays, electricity distribution companies have already performed great investments in order to identify and calculate energy losses along the distribution network. Although that big effort, the applications and approaches for clearly identifying and solving the related problems still remain too poor and inefficient. The accurate identification and the precise calculation of electricity losses enables the clear specification of the critical points and segments in the networks and, consequently, the effective prioritization of actions and interventions in order to reduce those electricity losses and problems. Although some researchers and companies have already carried out work on this issue, the existing approaches focus almost only on empirical and probabilistic data. There is still a clear gap between real information and the considered one, which tends to be poor and imprecise. Due to this reality and the lack of appropriate software applications, in this paper we propose a P2P system for the management of the whole network of electricity distribution, from medium voltage down to low voltage, including billing and other functions processing on the transformation centers, electricity losses calculation and proposals for solving actions.

Keywords: Electrical energy, distribution network, P2P decision-support system, cooperative information and losses management.

1 Introduction

Energy efficiency measures can represent the difference between having power quality and affordable, or live with periods of energy shortage and/ or with poor quality. A major concern with environmental issues must also be considered during the management and decisions processes. Another big concern relies on minimizing network energy losses. This leads not only to higher revenues, but also to the improvement of the quality of the product offered to consumers. This can add value to the product helping to gain additional market, as well as turn possible postponing investments in expanding network capacity.

Although there are many methodologies in the literature with the purpose to manage an electrical distribution network by calculating the energy losses in a power distribution network in low voltage (LV), all of them have several "gaps" either in their development, often due to being based on empirical data and probability, and/ or

G.D. Putnik and M.M. Cruz-Cunha (Eds.): ViNOrg 2011, CCIS 248, pp. 230–240, 2012.

on its implementation, because although much discussion about energy losses has been carried out along the last decades, great improvements have not yet been implemented over the time in terms of the software development for supporting to manage electrical distribution networks, which makes it very difficult to make a comparison of what already exists in this area and what is clearly still necessary to be developed and researched, since unfortunately there is still not much information available.

Although the lack of information put available about this subject, some work is already being made and the work developed by [1] presents a software for calculating electricity losses in distribution networks, in terms of low voltage power, resulting in a flexible business tool, which allows the user to make calculations based on typical data for modeling their networks, based on measurements made on the ground. In [2] an approach is used based on expert systems, to assist in managing the distribution of LV power, knowing that these systems generally treat a very large variety of variables, many of which expressed through natural language, which turns the systems treatment strongly influenced by experience, trial, human perception and reasoning.

The work in [3] presents a methodology for calculating the energy losses in a secondary network, and a primary network as well as on distribution transformers, already implemented and in use at "CompanhiaPaulista de Força e Luz" (CPFL), in Brazil, along with the GISD system, which is a database for geo-referencing including engineering applications (Planning, Design, Maintenance and Operation).

In [4] the work presents an extensive discussion on fraud and non-technical losses in Brazil, through a set of collected papers analyzed, about resolutions and technical outcomes describing a systemic view on non-technical losses, by identifying the main types of fraud and theft and also shapes and equipment used to minimize or eliminate them. Finally, they analyzed the forms of combat which can also be applied to distributors in other countries. The work [5] presents a methodology and computational implementation for the calculation of technical losses in the various segments of a distribution system, and some comments about the most critical elements are made, also including some discussion about possible actions to reduce energy losses.

Moreover, the paper [6] presents the development of a 3D graphical interface based on virtual environments technology. The referred interface is intended to assist decision-making in a computer system for losses reduction in electrical energy distribution networks, but the authors refer that still some important work has to be carried out in order to be able to use the system.

The above mentioned gaps still remaining in energy distribution networks management motivated this work, were we put forward a decision-support system, which includes several functionalities, namely for electrical energy losses determination, which are described and included into two main categories: technical and non-technical ones, which are precisely identified and calculated [7, 8, 9].

Therefore, in this paper we put forward a methodology and computational implementation based on real data, obtained through telemetry instead of empirical and probabilistic data, which enables to obtain precise results, namely in terms of losses determination. Moreover, the proposed systems enables to clearly identify the losses in the distribution network points and activate a mechanism for analyzing and accurately solve the identified problems, by proposing corresponding repairing actions. The system architecture and its main functionalities are presented and briefly described in this paper. The system architecture follows a Peer-to-Peer (P2P) structure and includes a Data Base, where all relevant information, including parameters and data about diverse electrical energy losses types are stored, in order to enable an effective and efficient way to store information about electrical energy and its losses management. The main system functionalities also include modules for billing and payment processing, among others, including integration with other sub-systems.

2   Electrical Energy Distribution Network

The current system of electrical energy distribution is based on a large central power generation, which transmits power through systems of high voltage transmission, which is then distributed to other distribution systems in medium and low voltage. In general the energy flow is unidirectional and the power is checked and controlled by the center (s) in an order based on pre-defined requirements. The share of electrical energy distribution is a segment of the electrical system, consisting on the primary electrical networks (distribution networks of medium voltage) and secondary networks (distribution networks for low voltage). Electrical energy distribution companies are in charge about the construction, operation and maintenance of these networks.

The primary distribution networks are electrical circuits with three-phase three-wire (or simply three phase), connected at distribution substations and are usually built in the classes of voltage of 15 KV, 23 KV or 34.5 KV. In these classes of tension, the nominal operating voltage may be 11 KV, 12.6 KV, 13.2 KV, 13.8 KV, 21 KV, 23 KV, 33 KV and 34.5 KV. The levels of voltage: 13.8 KV and 34.5 KV are standardized by law; but other levels exist and continue to operate normally. Primary distribution networks, are installed with distribution transformers, fixed on poles, whose function is to lower the voltage level to the primary side voltage level (e.g., for download from 13.8 KV to 220 volts). The secondary distribution networks are electrical circuits with three-phase four wires (three phases and neutral), which typically operate at voltages (phase - phase / phase - neutral) 230/115 volts, 220/127 volts and 380/220 volts. These networks are connected to consumers, including residences, bakeries, shops, and so on, and also for street lighting. These networks serve the large consumption centers (namely, population and large industry, among others). Establishments such as large buildings, shops and markets consume more power, and require individual processors of 75 kva, 112.5 kva and 150 kva. In some cases, the tension between supplies is 380/220 volts or 440/254 volts.

The entire distribution system is protected by a system composed by circuit breakers at the substations where the primary networks are connected, and with key fuse in distribution transformers, which in case of short circuit switch off the power grid [10].

3   Systems Integration and Cooperative Network Management

3.1   P2P System Architecture and Integration with Sub-systems

The proposed system for managing an electrical energy distribution network includes a very comprehensive software architecture. The system architecture follows a Peer-to-Peer (P2P) structure (Figure 1) and includes a Data Base, where all relevant information, including parameters and data about diverse electrical energy losses types are stored, in order to enable an effective and efficient information and electrical energy losses management.

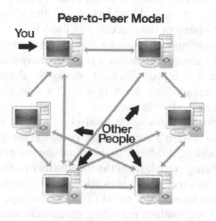

Fig. 1. Peer-to-peer framework

Emerging peer-to-peer technology and appropriate networks suite well to the increasingly decentralized nature of modern companies and their industrial and business processes, whether it is a single enterprise or a group of companies.

The P2P framework provides the capabilities that allow users, or peers, to directly interact with each other [11, 12]. The web application put forward within this work follows this P2P computing model. Therefore, it has the capability of allowing a direct-interaction between the peers, which turns the computing environment decentralized, namely in terms of storage, computations, messaging, security and distribution. One of the greatest benefits of this P2P network, in the context of this work, is to easily support the concept of community. Consequently, it is possible for users to organize themselves into groups that can collaborate and cooperate with each other in order to achieve a certain goal. In this context, this goal is to improve the resolution of energy distribution network management, providing a better decision-making support by enabling access to several different management approaches and energy distribution information. This is achieved, through a mechanism that allows them to share their energy distribution network management knowledge and solving procedures. The developed system is based on the principles of virtual enterprise (VE) [13, 14].

Within this VE, each peer can then be seen as a partner interested on solving energy distribution management problems and, whereby, looking for feasible solutions in the network, which is composed by a local knowledge base (KB) of each participating member. Whenever a member stores knowledge in his/her local KB, he/she is automatically contributing to the enrichment of the whole distributed knowledge repository that is available to all members of the company.

Some peers of the company can also act as super-peers. These special peers have the additional functionality of owning a list of the peers that belong to the VE. Such list contains information about the VE members and a flag that indicates the current state of each peer, which can be active or non-active. A super-peer also serves the purpose of configuring the P2P network as an open system, allowing any external user to join the company, or as a closed system, in the sense that only the nodes belonging to a certain company or domain can join the VE.

Each active peer is continuously waiting for requests from other peers or from browser-like users. When a request reaches a peer, it firstly asks to one of the super-peers for the list of other active peers. Next, it propagates the request to all the peers of that list. Once the replies have been returned, a compilation of the obtained solutions or actions is presented to the user.

One of the main purposes of this work consists on making a demonstration of the primary needs among the system's users and the common server, describing the input information for the supporting database. In this database information about the whole distribution network is being stored, from the transformer to the final consumer. This information comprises the secondary network, the connection extensions, micro-generation billing of Transformation Centers (TCs), the compensating reactive power and the various types of acquisitions regarding parameters readings on TCs and end consumers, in particular, estimated readings and company lectures, including manuals, telemetry readings and lectures by PDA.

The system's underlying database follows a relational-based model and was developed through SQL Server. SQL Server is a database management system (DBMS) for relational databases management, created by Microsoft, and consists on a platform for enabling reliable data manipulation. Moreover, it is a very robust platform and used for corporate systems about different dimensions (http://sqlserver-training.com/what-is-object-based-logical-model/). The relational databases contains three main components, a collection of data structures, especially links, tables or informally, a collection of operators, relational algebra and calculus and a collection of integrity constraints, defining the set of consistent states of the database and changes of states. The integrity constraints can be of four types, domain (also known as type), attribute, sward (relation variable) and restrictions on the database. Unlike the hierarchical and network-based approaches, in this development environment there are no links, and according to the principle of information, the whole information must be represented as given, and any attribute represents relationships between data sets. The relational databases allow users, including programmers, to write queries that were not anticipated by those who designed the database. With this, the relational databases can be used by multiple applications in a way that the original designers or programmers did not anticipate, which is especially important in databases that can be used for decades, moving a big amount of information, which contributed to turn the relational databases very popular, namely in different kind of business domains (http://www.bitpipe.com/tlist/Relational-Database-Management-Software.html). The database developed under the relational modeling paradigm, was "split" into various diagrams in the SQL server that will work linked together through their identity relations. Some important diagrams descriptions include information for the perception of the database schema, the transformer diagram, the network diagram about secondary liaison branch diagram, a diagram about micro-generation, an energy measurement diagram, a diagram for batteries capacitors, and also public lighting diagram, among others and three of the most important ones are going to be described next and illustrated through the Figures 2, 3 and 4.

System's Technical Connection and Communication. The technical diagram about connection and communication shows various kinds of electrical energy supply, the analyzer indicator in parallel, the hub, to serve as a connection to the final customer counters, the counters of Micro-BTE production and billing system and the TC. This diagram also describes the alerts that are sent via SMS, GPRS or email if the system detects the existence of any anomaly.

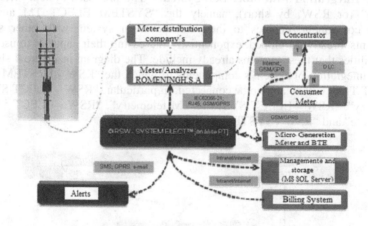

Fig. 2. Technical connection and communication

System's Communication with the Telemetry Sub-System. The diagram of communication between the "RSW System - SYSTEM ELECT TM análisePT" and "RSW - ELECT SYSTEM TM telemetry" is used to display the type of information sharing that exists between this two systems. The "RSW - ELECT SYSTEM TM telemetry" makes the collection of indicators readings, making a request to the hub. The hub enables to make a connection to the counters to collect the readings and send a reply with the indicator readings for the "RSW - ELECT SYSTEM TM telemetry", recording the same in this database. The "RSW - ELECT SYSTEM TM análisePT" enables the connection to the hub for the collection of indicator readings exactly in the same way as the "RSW - ELECT SYSTEM TM telemetry".

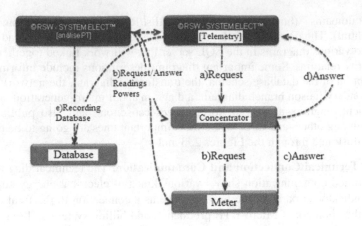

Fig. 3. Communication with the telemetry system

System's Integration with other Sub-Systems. The proposed system "Romeningh Software" (or RSW, by short), namely the "SYSTEM ELECT TM análisePT" system's component, enables to integrate the main system with other system's components already developed, exponentially increasing their capacity to use several functionalities that these systems already include. The diagram in Figure 4 shows the possible integration of system's components to which the "RSW - SYSTEM ELECT análisePT TM", will be able to be connected, in particular, "RSW - ELECT SYSTEM TM energy", "RSW - ELECT SYSTEM TM telemetry", "RSW - ELECT SYSTEM TM website" and "RSW - SYSTEM ELECT TM mobile".

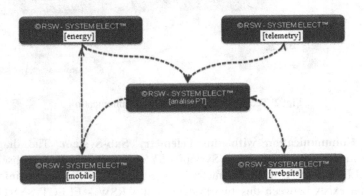

Fig. 4. Integration with other systems

3.2   Electrical Energy Network Management

Energy losses management consists on one of the major problems arising under the scope of electrical energy distribution networks. Therefore, it is of greatest importance to identify which portion of the losses may be included in the tariffs and charged to consumers. Technical losses are inherent to the process, and therefore assumed to be liable to pay. Besides of commercial losses, although being technical ones, this kind of losses conduct to the need of necessary investments in the energy network (maintenance, expansion of capacity, reconfiguration, upgrading, etc.). If these losses exist the problem of lack of maintenance of the electrical distribution network must be assessed and properly tackled.

Therefore, to be well succeeded on the energy losses reduction objective, there is a need for identifying and accessing the losses throughout the distribution system. Energy losses can be classified as to their origin and location [1]. Regarding their origin, a loss can be categorized into technical and non-technical one. A technique loss is the energy that is lost during distribution. This type of loss is inherent to the process and occurs on the materials and equipments used during the distribution, such as transformers, cables, and network connections, before the point of delivery. A non-technical loss is the energy actually delivered to the consumer, through their own or another distributor, but for some reason it was not billed, which are commonly associated with fraud energy consume, by some consumers in the network.

Moreover, the losses can be classified into global losses, losses in transmission and distribution losses. The global losses include losses in the generation, transmission and distribution. The transmission losses are associated with the systems for generation and transmission, distribution losses occur only in the distribution system.

The proposed system aims to take into account all these losses. Some important features are already implemented, namely the losses identification, along the electrical energy distribution network.

The proposed system was designed to enable managing the entire electrical energy network in a cooperative way. In this context, this systems enables the integration of several distinct sub-systems or system's components, linked with the main system's core, as described before, and also to perform different kind of actions on all those system's components, namely by putting a set of distinct queries, through an user-friendly way. Those actions, based on queries or other operations, along the energy distribution network, can also be enriched through the use of fuzzy parameters, which can be specified for several kind of purposes, namely for being able to more adequately treat the energy losses determination. For this purpose, fuzzy sets theory can be used, for defining those fuzzy parameters [15].

The main goal of a fuzzy solution approach is to find the solution or the alternative decision that better satisfies a situation that occurs under a fuzzy environment [15].

The implemented software can be used as a support tool, for the decision-making process, by providing, in real-time, a range of alternative solutions to the decision maker, indicating the advantages and disadvantages (trade-offs) of each evaluated alternative. With such information the decision maker can reach an enlightened choice of the best alternative for each application.

4   System Functionalities

The software was developed in Visual Basic 6.0, which serves as a connection to a relational database developed in SQL Server. Considering the applications to which this system is proposed it was necessary to develop a user-friendly and intuitive graphical interface, enabling the reading of data from a geo-referenced database.

Through the proposed system access to several sub-systems is possible namely for TC management, billing, characterization of all the electricity grid, energy losses determination, micro-generation, electrical energy data processing and the whole network management and different kind of reports about various relevant information gathering and several parameters processing that are useful regarding the use requirements of the system, which turns possible functionalities through this system.

Moreover, the network management menu enables to specify the main general and specific characteristics of the network. These features include the identification of distribution centers, namely transformation centers among other interactions.

Besides that, it is possible to identify the project type, in terms of ownership. The type of the installation can also be specified as an urban one or other kind, as well as its underlying construction model. In terms of client type, the system also enables to identify it, for example, as "micro-generation" client or other kind of client.

5   Conclusion

This work presented an ongoing project aimed to put forward a system for monitoring and managing an electrical energy distribution network. The system features allows the definition of an interface for each user, customizing and configuring the system according to his/her interests and needs, within a VE along the distribution network, through a P2P based architecture of the proposed system. The system may also to be easily adapted and new features may be implemented, according to future specific requirements. The work conducted so far allowed for the characterization of the distribution network, including the geodesic survey, the physical description in terms of infrastructure, the technical and behavioral characteristics of the network, and the assessment of connection points and ways of connecting networks and customers.

The implementation of the system and the collection of main information, mainly related to various types of losses, technical and non-technical ones have been a major effort required in this research and this phase is already in an advanced stage of development.

As a next step, in order to come to an effective analysis of the quality of customer service, by the operator of the distribution network, the system will be fully implemented. The main objective is to allow measuring and continuously localizing losses in order to obtain information about real-time behavior of the electrical energy distribution network, and thus about the power quality and the overall service provided to business partners and customers.

The ultimate goal of the system under development is to eventually offer various features that may help providing essential information about the quality of service to each individual customer, allowing them to be pro-active on the resolution of potential problems. Among the expected general benefits are the enhancement of the overall improvement in quality of service, the significant reduction in terms of response time to failures within the distribution network, in order to enable to better manage it and also enable a better customer service line. The quality of service is a current need of the markets; the system quality service intends to efficiently record all complains cuts and changes in delivery of consumption, among other situations. These data enable the customer to analyze and verify the service that is being provided as well the suppliers to express their needs for actions, by using manual or automatic processes. The system is being implemented to allow a continuous acquisition and recording on file of events that result in the detection of anomalies related to power quality and its losses management, among other important energy distribution control parameters. The information gathered can, therefore, be viewed in tables and/ or graphics, and thereafter generate reports in order to better support decision-making. The reports also can be sent directly to the printer and inserted into other windows applications or applications, and can also be accessed via Internet by using a web browser. Another important goal about the operation of this system is related to the possibility of being integrated with other systems or sub-systems, taking advantage of the potential it has for communicating through the Internet, based on web technology, for example, by implementing remote access to systems for data acquisition or even for using wireless technology.

Acknowledgements. The authors wish to acknowledge the support of: 1) The Foundation for Science and Technology – FCT, under the scope of the financed Project PTDC/EME-GIN/102143/2008, and 2) EUREKA, by the Project E!4177-Pro-Factory UES.

References

1. Strauch, M.T.: Desenvolvimento de metodologia para cálculo de perdas elétricas em redes de distribuição de baixa tensão. Dissertação de Mestrado, Universidade Salvador (2002/2007)
2. Todesco, J.L., Morales, A.B.T., Veloso, S.: Gestão da distribuição Secundária de energia eléctrica utilizando um sistema especialista. CELESC Brasil (2005)
3. Manhães, L.R.: Calculo de perdas com aplicação de curvas de cargas típicas de consumidores integradas a sistema gis. CPFL Brasil (2008)
4. Aranha, N., Edison, A.C., Coelho, J.: Combate às perdas não-técnicas no Brasil, Florianópolis (2008)
5. Méffe, A., et al.: Metodologia para definição dos níveis ótimos de perdas técnicas em sistemas de distribuição e priorização de obras para sua redução. Universidade de São Paulo, Brasil (2005)
6. Netto, A., et al.: Interface 3D para manipulação de dados em redes de distribuição de energia eléctrica (2002)
7. Méffe, A.: Metodologia para cálculo de perdas técnicas por segmento do sistema de distribuição. Dissertação de mestrado, Escola Politécnica da Universidade de São Paulo (2001)
8. Leão, R.: GTD – Geração, Transmissão e Distribuição de Energia Eléctrica. Universidade Federal do Ceará (2009)
9. http://www.erse.pt/pt/electricidade/factosenumeros/Paginas/Perdasnarededededistribuicao_PC.aspx
10. European Commission, European Technology Platform SmartGrids. Vision and Strategy for Europe's Electricity Networks of the Future. Directorate-General for Research, Sustainable Energy Systems (2006), http://www.smartgrids.eu

11. Papazoglou, M.P., Krämer, B., Yang, J.: Leveraging Web-Services and Peer-to-Peer Networks. In: Eder, J., Missikoff, M. (eds.) CAiSE 2003. LNCS, vol. 2681, pp. 485–501. Springer, Heidelberg (2003)
12. Terziyan, V., Zharko, A.: Semantic Web and Peer-to-Peer: Integration and Interoperability in Industry, Industrial Ontologies Group, MIT Department, University of Jyvaskyla, Finland
13. Putnik, G.D.: BM_Virtual Enterprise Architecture Reference Model. Technical Report RT-CESP-GIS-2000-<GP-01>. Universidade do Minho, Portugal (2000b)
14. Putnik, G.D.: BM_Virtual Enterprise Architecture Reference Model. In: Gunasekaran, A. (ed.) Agile Manufacturing: 21st Century Manufacturing Strategy, pp. 73–93. Elsevier Science Publ., UK (2001)
15. Ribeiro, R.A., Pires, F.M.: Fuzzy linear programming via simulated annealing. Kybernetica 35(1), 57–67 (1999)

Prototype Multiplex Communication System for Remote Control of Machine Tools

Vaibhav Shah, Goran D. Putnik, and Hélio Castro

Department of Production and Systems Engineering,
University of Minho, Guimarães, Portugal
{vaibhav.shah,putnikgd,hcastro}@dps.uminho.pt

Abstract. In transition from classical/traditional to modern manufacturing systems, a number of key improvements have occurred, including the ability to control a machine remotely, over Internet. The past approaches on implementing a remote control system have mostly focused on the remote controlling technology and much less on organizational aspects. The proposed work is focused on communication functionality as one of the key organizational aspects. This paper discusses a prototype implementation of communication functionality in remote control of machine tools, considering communication as an intrinsic organizational issue, aiming at improving the effectiveness of manufacturing systems integration.

Keywords: Remote CNC Operation, Networked Manufacturing Cell, Communication System.

1 Introduction

With the growing demand of modern day rapid and high-volume businesses and "international market" scenarios, an obvious need of new and innovative manufacturing methods has emerged. Today the geographic boundaries between a customer and a product or a product manufacturer have been greatly eliminated by new information and communication technologies (ICT) as well as computer integrated manufacturing (CIM) environments. The manufacturing industry has taken advantage of these new technologies in many areas of product development. However, there is still big scope for further development of distributed manufacturing, and indeed its industrial implementation. The possibility to do businesses with overseas clients has also created new "needs" as businesses are willing to take the maximum out of the available technologies, and collaboration among various activities such as planning, production, supply and others is very much critical, see e.g. [1], [2] and [3]. New business models are emerging as well. One such business/organizational model for the manufacturing system, involving global (or geographically distributed) partners is a Ubiquitous Manufacturing System (UMS) [4]. In a ubiquitous system for manufacturing, the manufacturing processes are expected to be executed "anytime, anywhere" in the system network and the client (customer or business client) and resource provider (manufacturer or plant owner) must be connected to each other through communication networks. Either distributed or ubiquitous manufacturing systems are the demand of the time. Hence the emerging

G.D. Putnik and M.M. Cruz-Cunha (Eds.): ViNOrg 2011, CCIS 248, pp. 241–252, 2012.
© Springer-Verlag Berlin Heidelberg 2012

need of capacity to remotely manufacture a product, to be more precise, the ability to remotely operate a machine.

And while speaking of distributed manufacturing systems, major challenges which have gained research focus include remote operation, web-based computer numerical control (CNC), real-time operation coordination among others [5], [6], [7], [8]. A lot of progress is seen in the area of virtual machine tools (VMT) and virtual manufacturing, based on virtual reality and web centric technologies [9]. The issue addressed in the presented work is about communication in a distributed/remotely controlled manufacturing system/cell. In our survey of the past research works focusing on communication system of remote CNC operations or distributed manufacturing systems, we have observed mainly two types of aspects, what we call, in the context of the presented work, as – 1) organizational communication and 2) operational communication. Organizational communication can be described as non-technical communication which is more about "business deals" and organizational integration, for e.g. finding resources or communication concerning logistic issues, information exchange in organizational structure and cooperation [10], [11], including assurance of full understanding of communicated information among the partners. While the "operational type" communication category includes technical communication or rather machine level communication, meaning commands being sent, low-level machine/resource requests being sent, parameter values being transmitted, machine tool coordinates being communicated and so on [7], [8], [12].

In the presented work, a "multiplexed" approach is presented, which combines and preserves functionalities and characteristics of both of the above types of communication. This work also represents the multiplex communication system prototype, developed as a part and one of the functionalities of a ubiquitous manufacturing system (UMS) [4], to integrate communication in remote machining or remotely operating machine tool. In the UMS architecture model, communication is an integral part of the system and is intertwined with the network functionalities connecting distantly located network partners through various levels of communication channels and the presented work exhibits the communication system as required in the aforementioned UMS architecture, implementing the multi-functional multi-channel communication system. Thus the communication functionality proposed here is called multiplex communication.

This is a contribution towards building a complete ubiquitous manufacturing system network and a virtual enterprise model in accordance with BM_Virtual Enterprise Architecture Reference Model (BM_VEARM) [13] where communication system for remote machining is an integrating element and feature of the network.

2   Communication Systems for Manufacturing Environment

2.1   Communication in a Distributed Manufacturing Environment

The technologically advanced models, such as those based on Wise-ShopFloor concept [7], or Virtual Reality Modeling Language (VRML) based models [8], [12], [14], focus on remote CNC operating, and are missing the human to human "direct" communication paradigm. By this we mean, although technologically well equipped to enable the remote controlling capacity of a distributed network, the information sharing and organizational communication aspects are missing in these types of models. Importance of coordination in a real-time distributed controller system has been proven already [15]. The coordination cost and negotiation iterations are vital parameters in the overall cost effectiveness of a distributed manufacturing system [16] and must be considered while designing such a system. A remotely controlled manufacturing plant requires a real-time coordination and communication is a key factor here. Information sharing among partners in a manufacturing network gives higher networking flexibility and effectiveness [17].

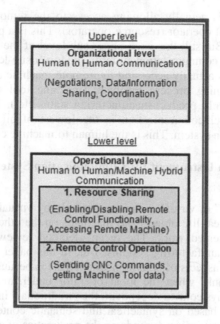

Fig. 1. Multiplex communication system levels for remote control

The proposed "multiplex" communication system levels are shown in Fig. 1.

In Fig. 1, multiple layers of the proposed multiplex communication system are shown. There are two main layers:

- "Upper" or "Organizational" level;
- "Lower" or "Operational" level.

Organizational Level. The Organizational level communication is a communication between two remote network users, hence a human-to-human communication involving "normal", "video chat" based communication. Role of this level of communication channel is for "higher" level coordination among network partners for co-construction of meanings and removing ambiguities along the information and data sharing, order placing, searching for resources etc.

Operational Level. In the Operational level, the communication is "hybrid" in a way that it involves communication between human and human plus human and machine. This is a lower level of communication, which follows the "contract" achieved through the upper level communication, when an operational channel between users/partners is established. Considering a CNC machine cell also has a local cell operator (resource operator), the communication would be between two human users (one locally with the cell, and another remotely) in the first place and then between the remote user and the cell/machine. Thus the Operational level communication channel is further separated in two sub-levels:

1.   Resource sharing;
2.   Remote control operation.

The resource sharing is actually allowing access to the remote user for the CNC machine cell by the cell operator (resource operator). This is a part of the operational level communication. But still this is an upper sub-level of the two sub-levels of the operational level of the communication system. The lower sub-level of the operational level communication is actually accessing the remote machine and sending/receiving commands and machining process feedback (machine tool coordinates, program execution progress details, product manufacturing status etc.). This second sub-level of the operational level communication is the lowest of all the channels of the multiple communication system. This is the human to machine communication.

2.2   Semiotics as an Instrument for Communication System in Manufacturing Operations

Moreover, the "feeling" of virtual existence, not only by virtual reality 3D interfaces [7], but by seeing the real-life objects and machines on the other end is also a matter of interest in the presented work. The recent detailed review [9] discusses many virtual reality based manufacturing systems. But, in this paper a special emphasis is given to the pragmatic aspects of communication. This is because the communication process is complete only when the local operator understands the remote user's message, which is always context dependent, the "traditional" information transaction based communication, based on syntactical and semantic contents only, is not fully effective. The full understanding depends on the pragmatics of communication too. In this sense, the human-to-human communication represents a co-creative process of the intended meaning of the message, removing wrong interpretations and ambiguities. Considering pragmatic aspects of communication, besides the usual semantic and syntactic aspects, makes this approach "semiotic based". The presented work is a step in the process of implementation of semiotics based integration [18] of distributed or ubiquitous manufacturing system as a non-traditional work environment. Semiotics based integration considers communication as a key instrument [18].

3   UMS Architecture and Functionality of Remotely Controlling Machine Tool

3.1   UMS Network Communication Architecture

In the above mentioned UMS network [4], mainly three types of user categories are defined: clients, brokers and resources (machining cells or machine programmers). The Fig. 2 shows UMS network user communication channels specification diagram.

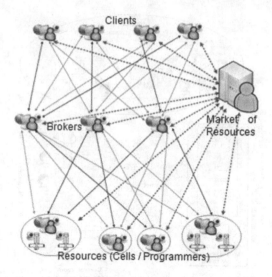

Fig. 2. A scheme of UMS network user communication channels

The three different categories of users of the system communicate with each other on organizational level, as between a "client" and a "broker" or a "broker" and a "resource" or a "client" and a "resource"; and on operational level (as between a "client" and a "resource" while operating on the resource's manufacturing cell. These functionalities have already been discussed and justified from semiotics point of view as well as communications point of view [18]. Also, in this UMS network, the role of "market of resources" is previously discussed [19] and its description is not in the scope of this paper.

Also, the remote controlling functionality has already been explained in detail [20].

3.2   A Remote Client Perspective

To better understand the requirement of the remote client, Fig. 3 shows an informal specification of the UMS architecture, excluding elements like brokers and the "market of resources" and focusing solely on a remote client – remote cell operation perspective.

The two highlighted circles in the Fig. 3 show a UMS cell and a client "control room" – the two ends of the communication channel.

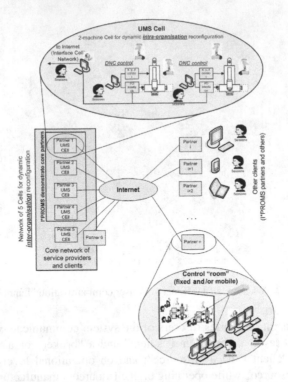

Fig. 3. UMS informal specification with remote client perspective

3.3   Manufacturing Cell in the UMS

Fig. 4 shows a typical manufacturing (machining) cell in the aforementioned ubiquitous manufacturing system. The cell configuration is previously defined [21] as well as the cell semiotics [18].

Fig. 4. A manufacturing cell installation

3.4   Remote Controlling Functionality

Once a connection between a client and a resource has been established by a broker, a direct communication takes place between the client and the resource (cell). The communication system architecture is shown in Fig. 5 for the client-resource "remote machining call" in the aforementioned ubiquitous manufacturing system.

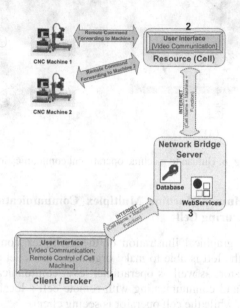

Fig. 5. Remote controlling functionality in the UMS architecture

4   Communication System as Integrated in the Remote Machining

4.1   Human to Machine Communication

Fig. 6 shows two images of client's interface and client's "control room" ambience. In Fig. 6 (a) the client's interface screen is showing the live video feed of remote CNC machine with operation control panel on the left. And in Fig. 6 (b), the photo shows client "control room" where client is operating the remote cell. The "organizational level" communication is missing in this model.

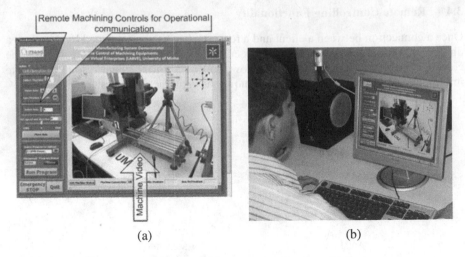

Fig. 6. Human to machine operational communication

4.2   Human to Human/Machine Multiplex Communication between Client and Manufacturing Cell

The Fig. 7 shows a graphical illustration of the multiplex communication system, where the client on the left is able to make organizational level communication with the remote cell operator, as well as operational level communication. The client, on his screen is seeing and communicating with remote cell's local operator as well as the remote machines, while the cell operator is seeing client.

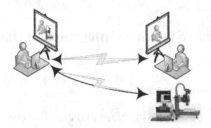

Fig. 7. Multiplex communication between a client and a manufacturing cell

Fig. 8 shows the two screens of client and resource operator and a photo from the client "control room" showing the client operating the resource remotely.

In Fig. 8 (a), the client's perspective of the remotely located cell in operation is visible (showing the client's interface) with various controls to operate on the cell machines to control the machine tool and also the focused video of the machine tool showing current position of the tool. This gives a full control to the client, while also watching what is exactly going on at the other end – the "Operational level" communication. Also, the communication controls on the window gives the client an ability to communicate and exchange information/data with the person on the resource/cell side – the "Organizational level" communication.

The Fig. 8 (b), on the other end, is what the cell's local operator is seeing while on the operation call with the remote client. The resource operator is communicating with the remote client with a video chat by being on the other end of the "Organizational level" communication.

The client screen is as seen in Fig. 8 (a), with video feed of the remote cell and the client operates on this remote cell while watching the real-time life-size picture as if being in that cell physically and operating on the machine piece and tool. This clearly gives the two remotely located users an ability of remote operation as well as two-way "multiplex" communication, which is absent in the traditional model shown in Fig. 6. The video communication+control functionality allows the two levels of the "multiplex" communication channel.

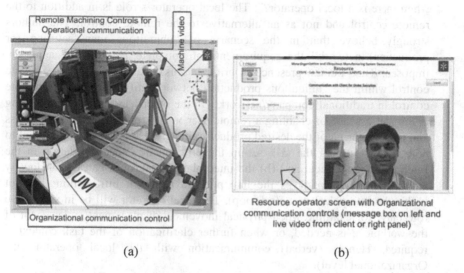

(a)   (b)

Fig. 8. Client – Resource remote operation and communication screens

5   Conclusion

The authors are proposing a new approach for integration of communication system in the remote control of manufacturing systems. Below are presented further explanations in form of answers to some pertinent questions:

1. "Why the architecture presented?": In usually implemented remote control systems the architectures are based on "client-server" model supporting only one type of communication between only two types of users. The architecture proposed is to facilitate three different types of users in the network, as per the proposed UMS model, with support of two types of communication channels – verbal and machine communication levels, justified as Organizational and Operational communications levels respectively. The proposed architecture

gives capacity of such multiplex communication system as it has possibility of including both the types of functionalities in single networking stream.

2. "How to handle the speed variation in the Internet?": The remote control of machine tool is performed on different hierarchical levels, namely the levels of "task control", "elementary movements" and "primitive functions" (following traditional hierarchical control model by [22]). On the "task control" level operations (sending/uploading machining programs) are not Internet critical; whereas lower levels, the "elementary movements" and "primitive functions" control levels (interpolation control levels), although technically possible to be carried out remotely, are not executed over the Internet, but by the normal local machine tool Control Unit, thus, the "the speed variation in the Internet" is not critical.

3. "Why the feedback of tool position and access to machine controls is needed when there is a local operator?": The local operator's role is in addition to the remote control and not as an alternative to the remote control. The authors strongly believe that in the scenario of "ubiquitous manufacturing (or production) network" the requirements of complete automation cannot be imposed. Thus human presence is critical. This "feature" makes the remote control within the "ubiquitous production network" different from the remote control in traditional company/network. On the other hand, remote controlling is the real essence of enabling a remote user to control the machining process and manufacturing of the desired products remotely. However, it is important to note (a) that during the task set-up the problematic "speed variation in the Internet" is not critical and (b) the interpolation control is carried out locally although the user receives the live position feedback information (but not within the interpolation control loop). The local operator will be in supportive role only, for example when physical movement/displacement/replacement of the workpiece is needed, or when further clarification of the task context is required. Hence, (verbal) communication with the local operator (the Organizational level).

4. "On thesemiotics instrument": Communication is the key aspect in a network of remote users as in the proposed architecture and approach. This is because, similarly as for full automation, in the scenario of "ubiquitous manufacturing (or production) network" the requirements of complete computer based interoperability of equipment cannot be imposed and much of the integration will rely on human-to-human communication. The proposed multiplex communication system emphasizes importance of live communication. Without the two users indulging in an exchange of contextual discussion clarifying meanings of desired action, the communication becomes "dead" and ineffective (see section 2.2). Wrong processes could be carried out or wrong parties might be selected for order, if the remote operations do not include the communication aspects of face-to-face communication (as by physical presence of both the parties) would have occurred. Hence the multiplex system with video chat.

The future work will address improving technological aspects of communication system, improving user-interfaces; and overcoming challenges such as transmission of multiple video-streams on the same communication channel, interoperability of multiple types of machine tools, and identification of human-to-human communication aspects relevant for semiotics based manufacturing system integration framework.

Acknowledgements. This work is being carried out by support of:

1. The national Foundation for Science and Technology – FCT (Fundaçãopara a Ciência e a Tecnologia) scholarship, reference number SFRH / BD / 62313 / 2009;
2. The FCT project "Ubiquitous oriented embedded systems for globally distributed factories of manufacturing enterprises", reference number PTDC/ EME-GIN/102143/2008; and
3. The EUREKA project "E! 4177 PRO-FACTORY UES".

References

1. Papastavrou, J., Nof, S.Y.: Decision integration fundamentals in distributed manufacturing topologies. IIE Transactions 24(3), 27–42 (1992)
2. Wei, L., Xiaoming, X., Zhongjun, Z.: Distributed cooperative scheduling for a job-shop. In: American Control Conference, Green Valley, AZ, USA, vol. 1, pp. 830–831 (1992)
3. Fujiwara, H., Inoue, T.: Optimal granularity and scheme of parallel test generation in a distributed system. IEEE Transactions on Parallel and Distributed Systems 6(7), 677–686 (1995)
4. Putnik, G., Raja, V., Szecsi, T., Oztemel, E., Kubat, C., Sluga, A., Butala, P.: I*PROMS Experimental Platform and Test-Bed for Research and Development of the Ubiquitous Manufacturing Systems (UMS). In: Proceedings of ICME-CIRP Conference, Naples (August 2008)
5. Dong, B., Qi, G., Gu, X., Wei, X.: Web service-oriented manufacturing resource applications for networked product development. Advanced Engineering Informatics 22, 282–295 (2008)
6. Iwamura, K., Seki, Y., Tanimizu, Y., Sugimura, N.: A study on a real-time scheduling of holonic manufacturing system - coordination among holons based on multiobjective optimization problem. In: Arai, E., Arai, T. (eds.) Mechatronics for Safety, Security and Dependability in a New Era, pp. 195–200. Elsevier, Oxford (2006)
7. Wang, L., Orban, P., Cunningham, A., Lang, S.: Remote real-time CNC machining for web-based manufacturing. Robotics and Computer-Integrated Manufacturing 20(6), 563–571 (2004)
8. Hanwu, H., Yueming, W.: Web-based virtual operating of CNC milling machine tools. Computers in Industry 60, 686–697 (2009)
9. Abdul Kadir, A., Xu, X., Hämmerle, E.: Virtual machine tools and virtual machining—A technological review. Robotics and Comput-Integrated Manufacturing (2010) (accepted), doi:10.1016/j.rcim.2010.10.003 (2011)
10. Yazici, H.J.: The role of communication in organizational change: an empirical investigation. Information & Management 39(7), 539–552 (2002)

11. Huang, C.-Y., Huang, T.-S., Chen, W.-L.: Communication protocols for order management in collaborative manufacturing. International Journal of Production Economics 122, 257–268 (2009)
12. Kao, Y.C., Cheng, H.Y., Chen, Y.C.: Development of a virtual controller integrating virtual and physical CNC. Materials Science Forum 505–507, 631–636 (2006)
13. Putnik, G.: BM_Virtual Enterprise Architecture Reference Model. In: Gunasekaran, A. (ed.) Agile Manufacturing: 21st Century Manufacturing Strategy, pp. 73–93. Elsevier Science Publ. (2001)
14. Seo, Y., Kim, D.-Y., Suh, S.-H.: Development of web-based CAM system. International Journal of Advanced Manufacturing Technology 28, 101–108 (2006)
15. Kelling, C., Henz, J., Hommel, G.: Design of a communication scheme for a distributed controller architecture using stochastic Petri nets, pp. 147–154. IEEE (1995) 0-8186-7099-1/95
16. Ceroni, J.A., Matsui, M., Nof, S.Y.: Communication-based coordination modeling in distributed manufacturing systems. International Journal of Production Economics 60-61, 281–287 (1999)
17. D'Amours, S., Montreuil, B., Lefrançois, P., Soumis, F.: Networked manufacturing: The impact of information sharing. International Journal of Production Economics 58, 63–79 (1999)
18. Putnik, G.D., Putnik, Z.: A semiotic framework for manufacturing systems integration - Part I: Generative integration model. International Journal of Computer Integrated Manufacturing 23(8), 691–709 (2010)
19. Cunha, M.M., Putnik, G.: Agile Virtual Enterprises: Implementation and Management Support, p. XX+380. IDEA Group Publishing, Hershey (2006)
20. Putnik, G.D., Shah, V., Castro, H., Cruz-Cunha, M.M.: The functionality of remote controlling in ubiquitous manufacturing systems demonstrator for I*PROMS "efm" showcase. Tekhne - Revista de Estudos Politécnicos/Polytechnical Studies Review, IX 15, 169–189 (2011)
21. Putnik, G.D., Shah, V., Sousa, R.M., Castro, H., Raja, V., Szecsi, T., Oztemel, E., Kubat, C.: A Software Architecture and Functionality of Remote Controlling in Ubiquitous Manufacturing Systems Demonstrator for I*PROMS "efm" Showcase. In: Proceedings of 6th International Symposium on Intelligent and Manufacturing Systems, Sakarya, Turkey, October 14-16, pp. 842–851 (2008)
22. Barbera, A.J., Albus, J.S., Fitzgerald, M.L.: Hierarchical Control of Robots using Microcomputers. In: Proceedings of the 9th Industrial Symposium on Industrial Robots (1979)

Process Reuse in Product Development with 5D Models: Concepts, Similarity Measures and Querying Techniques

Tomo Cerovšek

University of Ljubljana, Slovenia
tomo.cerovsek@fgg.uni-lj.si

Abstract. The goal of this paper is to establish a framework for process reuse in 'collaborative product development' (CPD) supported by 5D product models. 5D integrates 3D models with non-geometrical metadata, costs, and schedules. Concepts, formal definitions, and possible technical solutions are proposed for (1) the reuse of business processes in 'collaborative product development' and (2) the reuse of related models and data embedded in 5D models of products. Drawing from the analysis of product development processes and 5D models first-order logic statements for explicit and implicit process reuse are defined. The process reuse is proposed through process repositories, conceptualised workflows, the querying of process results (e.g., 3D VR models, procedures), and used production resources (i.e., labour, equipment, material, finance). This study may advance process reuse within complex design communities and inspire the development of systems for project managers and product engineers.

Keywords: Collaborative product development, 5D BIM, processes similarity measures, query formulation, workflow patterns, business process management.

1 Introduction

The development of engineering products, such as cars, buildings, and aircrafts is becoming increasingly complex. Engineers must manage increasing amounts of data in less time to develop more competitive, higher quality products. Therefore, new knowledge, methods, and software are being developed to improve the management of processes throughout the 'product life-cycle' (design, production, maintenance).

The '*5D product model*' is a recent advancement for the design of building products. A 5D model consistently integrates geometrical (3D) product data models with non-geometrical metadata, costs (4D), and schedules (5D). The development of a 5D model involves complex workflows (Fig. 1), e.g., the modelling of geometry with metadata and the integration with external databases, tools, and services.

A 5D model is particularly useful for the simulation of the production phase. Some advantages of 5D are: a schedule linked to a model, model-based *quantity take-off, sequencing and calculation of resources* (e.g., labour, material, equipment, and sub-contracting), and model-based *cost estimation*. In this way, engineers can better communicate designs to other stakeholders, maximise transparency, consistency, and product quality while minimising risks, change orders, production times and costs.

G.D. Putnik and M.M. Cruz-Cunha (Eds.): ViNOrg 2011, CCIS 248, pp. 253–262, 2012.
© Springer-Verlag Berlin Heidelberg 2012

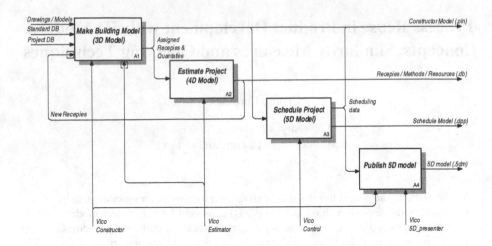

Fig. 1. A conceptual model of 'collaborative product development' with 5D models. Each activity (in rectangles) represents complex workflows (source: [1]).

1.1   The Motivation for Process Reuse

From the process perspective, we can divide any knowledge into two main categories: (1) *how,* process-knowledge and (2) *what,* process result-knowledge [2].

Note that the result of a 'collaborative product development' (CPD) process from Fig. 1 is a 5D model that includes processes (see also Section 3). In this situation, both types of knowledge (how and what) are processes that are candidates for reuse.

In contrast to the intuitive, the ad-hoc, reuse of parts non-process data and the ad-hoc reuse of parts of actual CPD and 5D model processes is not so straightforward. The problem is the media in which processes are executed and modelled–*important work-flows, actors, and tools* that lead to results may not be recorded. Table 1 gives standpoints that describe categories for reuse in CPD business process management.

Table 1. Process model standpoints important for the reuse of processes on different levels

Standpoint	Category	Capacity ...
Purpose	Document, Learn, Plan, Enact, BPR	...to manage business processes
Subject	Meta, Conceptual, Work-flow	...to model desired level of detail
Control	Active (enactment), Passive	...to describe/prescribe processes
End-users	Humans, Software, Hardware	...for an individual/group/network
Expressiveness	Available ontological constructs	...to model observed processes
Representation of a process	Alphanumerical, Matrix, Graphs, Arrows, Flow-Lines, Conditional diagramming, Swim lanes, Hybrid	...to use single/multiple types of representations and underlying communication channels
Decision phases	Identify, Capture, Analyse, Synthesise, Interpret, Act upon	...to handle complexity, structure, and reasoning of the problem
Management phases	Initiate, Plan, Execute, Control, Close processes	...to model material/information flow during the process stages

1.2 Related Work

The reuse of processes has been studied in many professional fields. The development efforts are justified by domain-specific requirements, which may include a variety of relevant standpoints, categories and capacities that are depicted in Table 1. Although, different methods may be used for process reuse [3], any development of a process reuse system must study at least the following *three essential issues*:

1. barriers and enablers to process reuse,
2. process reuse repositories, and
3. process similarity measures.

Barriers and enablers to process reuse. The barriers that prevent process reuse may be grouped into seven categories [4]: availability, rigidity, intellectual property rights, interoperability, difficult process discovery, highly limited process knowledge acquisition, and a lack of ranking for fragments of processes. Furthermore, researchers have identified special problems for process reuse in overly-restrictive procedures, incomprehensible processes [5], differences in process modelling techniques [6], or different uses of roles. The enablers for process reuse are the classification of a process [7], the use of controlled vocabularies [8], semantics with ontologies [9], and the advanced use of specialised workflow information search engines [10]. Technical components of software architectures that enable process reuse include the following functions: assess, cast, display, navigate, retrieve, adapt, and specify business processes [11, 12].

Process reuse repositories. The availability of processes is the first and most important prerequisite for process reuse. A repository may be described through six generic characteristics that determine the efficiency and effectiveness of process reuse: volume, ownership and access, format, metadata, structure, and dynamism. An important goal of any repository for process reuse is to assure that availability, relevancy and adaptability match specific methods. In software development, where reuse systems are more developed, a typical process reuse is often based on case-studies [13], process customisation [5] that is supported by process schema, and process adoption rules with process review. An important enabler is the observation of processes from different levels of abstractions [2, 14]. Since the processes can be used in a segmented manner or as wholes. The retrieval of processes should be made possible for different parts and/or granularities. The repository shall not force the use of overly restricted process but must provide the required traceability.

Process similarity measures. If we want to reuse, compare, or improve processes, we must be able to find and group similar processes. Therefore, we need process similarity measures. These measures may be adopted from the information retrieval (IR) of texts [15], linguistic analysis, graph-theory matching structural analysis, or other hybrid approaches. The similarity between process workflows can be categorised based on language or structure [16] and through iterative combined similarities of process names, input, and output [17]. Sometimes, it is more convenient to observe dissimilarities [18, 19]. The same similarity measures are used for the grouping (clustering) of processes, e.g., k-means clustering [6], hierarchical clustering [15], or structural clustering. The process reuse requires formal definitions.

2　Formal Definitions for Process Reuse

In this Section, first order logic descriptions for explicit and implicit reuse are given. In particular, we formally observe '*when and how*' issues related to process reuse.

2.1　Explicit Process Reuse

Time dependencies between modelled and actual processes are essential for reuse. Processes may be modelled before, during or after actual processes. Furthermore, modelled processes may target to and refer to processes at different times (see Fig. 2).

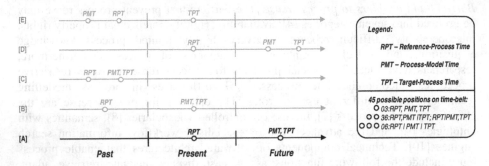

Fig. 2. The 'process reuse time-belt' illustrating variations of time-based dependencies among '*process-model time*' (PMT), '*reference-process time*' (RPT), and '*target-process time*' (TPT). Description of examples: [A] '*to-be*' and [B] '*as-is*' process models, as known from the BPR; [C] '*as-it-was*' process model; [D] '*transition*'; and [E] '*adapted*' process model. The models [A-D] are only a few that were chosen out 45 possible variations of the PMT, RPT, and TPT.

Any reference process can be explicitly reused (adapted) in target process if they are compatible. This compatibility can be measured with a distance. Mathematically, the distance d between the processes x and y is a measure that satisfies the criteria:

$$d(x,y) \geq 0, \; d(x,y) = 0 \text{ if and only if } x = y \qquad \text{(positive real number)} \qquad (1)$$

$$d(x,y) = d(y,x) \qquad \text{(symmetric)} \qquad (2)$$

$$d(x,z) \leq d(x,y) + d(y,z) \qquad \text{(triangle inequality)} \qquad (3)$$

Distances between the processes x and y may be Euclidian, angle-based distances, p-norms (e.g., block distance, Chebsyhev), or IR specific distances (e.g., Levinstein, Jaro-Winkler, Hammin, or Housdorff [20]). We can conclude that if a distance between two process models exists, then processes can be explicitly reused:

$$\forall x \forall y \exists d \; (Process(x) \wedge Process(y) \wedge Distance(x,y,d)) \leftrightarrow ExplicitReuse \; (x,y) \qquad (4)$$

Furthermore, if we assume that any two processes can be computationally compared, then one of the processes, or some of its parts, can be used as a query to retrieve other related processes.

2.2   Implicit Process Reuse

Implicit process reuse enables the retrieval and re-use of processes, although processes cannot be computationally, or in any other way, explicitly compared. As a solution to this problem, the following first order logic set of statements is defined:

$$\forall f \; (Feature(f) \wedge \exists q \; (Query(q) \rightarrow Can\_Match(f,q)) \rightarrow Searchable \; (f) \qquad (5)$$

$$\forall x \; (Process(x) \wedge \exists f \; (Searchable \; (f) \rightarrow Has\_Feature(x,f))) \rightarrow Searchable \; (x) \qquad (6)$$

$$\forall x \forall y \exists f \; (Has\_Feature(x,f) \wedge Has\_Feature(x,f) \leftrightarrow Are\_Similar(x,y,f) \qquad (7)$$

The first important implication is the searchable features that are linked to unsearchable items make unsearchable items searchable. This means that we are can still find and compare processes, although we do not know how the processes are assembled. The logical propositions (5), (6), and (7) relate to internal features and do not address external observations. We can define implicit searchability:

$$\exists m \; (Metadata(m) \wedge ((Has\_Metadata(x,m) \wedge Has\_Metadata(y,m))) \rightarrow \qquad (8)$$
$$Linked(x,y,CCV(m))$$

where x and y are arbitrary digital product content items or agents, and *CCV(m)* is a set of values from the common controlled vocabulary for metadata *m*.

$$\exists e \; (event(e) \wedge ((Has\_Event(x,e) \wedge Has\_Event(y,e))) \rightarrow Are\_Related(x,y,e) \qquad (9)$$

where an event *e* can be any event common to items x and y. It can be generalised:

$$\forall x \forall y \forall z \; (\exists a \; (Related(x,y,a)) \wedge \exists b \; (Related(y,z,b))) \leftrightarrow Related(x,z,y) \qquad (10)$$

where *a* and *b* can be any type of common parameters, features or objects. The logical propositions determine that two items are related if they have common features, metadata, or events. The implication of the second rule is used at Amazon.com where the interface can suggest additional items based on an event. The above definition also implies ternary relationships if we combine several items into one item. Note that the above definitions are recursive and very powerful because they can contain any type of relation.

$$\forall x \forall z \; (\neg Similarity(x,z)) \wedge \exists y \; ((Are\_Related(x,z,y)) \wedge (Similarity(x,y))) \rightarrow \qquad (11)$$
$$ImplicitSimilarity(x,z)$$

The statement above suggests a solution to the missing link between two compared items, i.e., what to do if there is no way to express similarity explicitly. The solution is an implicit transitive similarity that could allow end-users to search implicitly, although there is no direct relation between the two items. Therefore, it is important to know the content that may enable reuse in the context of CPD with 5D models.

3   Analysis of Content Enabling Process Reuse in CPD with 5D

In this Section, an overview of typical product and process data for process reuse in CPD with 5D is given.

3.1   Product Model Data

Product model data provide a BIM model that is a digital representation of a building and its components that are used in the process of CPD for visualisation, analyses, simulations, and project documentation. A BIM model is made by a BIM tool that has two main features [1]: (1) the modelling constructs are parametric 3D objects that represent real-world components with relationships and non-geometric meta-data; and (2) different views are integrated through a single data source that enables the constant synchronisation of views so that a change in one view is instantly reflected in other views (e.g., plans, sections, layouts, bills of quantities, views). Fig. 3 below shows an example of a BIM model, which results from the first activity in Fig. 1. The development of a building information model requires diverse tools and services.

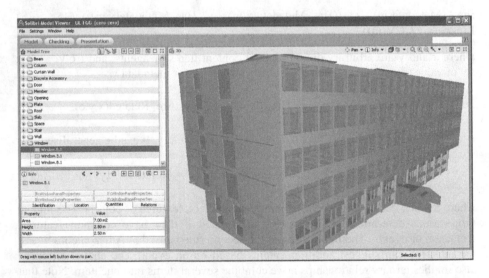

Fig. 3. Example of product model data: Building information model. Each element that is listed in upper left part of the window of a building is connected to a certain CPD process and each element is also linked to a task in specific location, which is a part of the integrated 5D model.

Once the 3D geometrical product model is developed, different concepts are linked to the product model data. This metadata describes the desired outcome of modelling (physical appearance) and the workflows that lead to these results. Quantities that are related to the digital equivalents are automatically calculated from the digital product model and linked to workflow data to form an integrated 5D model. Each digital element from Fig. 4 is linked to activities, as presented in Fig. 3, and are described in the next Section. Process reuse should enable the reuse of logic, structure and the adaptation to different audiences or the nature of the problems.

3.2   Process Model Data

Process model data in a 5D model is a location-based schedule (LBS) that determines the location for each activity. These locations are identified through 3D models and activity workflows that may be used for the planned production of a physical product (e.g., part of a building). The model-based estimation of the use of material, labour, equipment and subcontractors that depend on quantities are automatically calculated from a 3D model. The flow-chart in Fig. 4 illustrates a location-based process model that is important for both explicit and implicit process reuse. 5D models enable the reuse of location based process models.

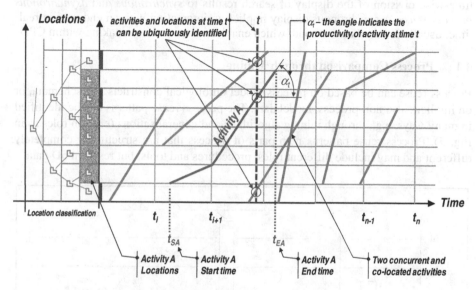

Fig. 4. The flow-chart as a source for process reuse. Flow-chart activities include times and locations that are hierarchically broken down. For example, for the "*Activity A*" (blue) start and end times for the activity (t_{SA} and t_{EA}) at particular locations can be identified on the chart, the angle of the activity line shows "*productivity*". The flow-chart enables the easy identification of concurrent and co-located activities. Note: each activity has its own workflow and resources.

The explicit reuse of flow-chart data can be easily defined. Note that only a small portion of the CPD can be captured or enacted through active process models. We are also interested in active processes that are modelled in a medium that captures all executed activities and has the ability to enact processes.

Table 2. Implicit process reuse in CPD

Implicit process reuse	Example	Font size and style
Process Input	Information	Data, Tools and Services
	Material	Labour, Material, Equipment
Process Output	Product	3D geometry with metadata
	Process	CPD/5D models workflows

4   Finding Candidate Processes for Reuse

Similarity can be measured objectively or subjectively. We assume that objective measures can be expressed mathematically, but subjective measures are descriptive. Objective similarity measures are expressed as norms or distances (see Section 2.1). Subjective similarity measures depend on personal observations, perceptions and beliefs. However, objective measures are often simplified subjective measures.

Therefore, every measure depends on a view that determines the observed properties. A property of process comparison may be grouped into two categories: mining and querying. Depending on the interface synchronicity, we could make a time-wise division of the display of search results to *synchronous* and *asynchronous process reuse*. A synchronous display implies an interaction with an end-user in real-time, usually in less than a second, which enables better decision making within CPD.

4.1   Process Comparison through Mining

Process reuse can be based on process model ontological constructs and schemata, or on implicit, also non-process, model data. The process reuse patterns can be identified in many ways, e.g., through mining algorithms and generalisations (e.g., on roles as in Fig. 5). Process reuse patterns map parts of process that are structurally completely different and may include different roles, procedures and tools, but result in 5D data.

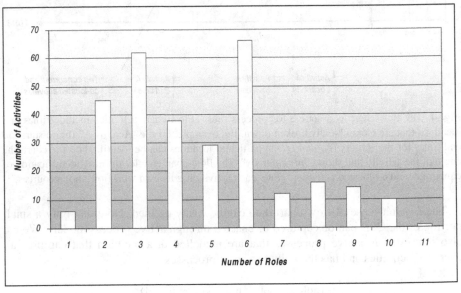

Fig. 5. Representation of overall CPD processes using a frequency diagram

The CPD processes with 5D models include product content that is often intra- or inter-linked in textual or non-textual form that may be unstructured or well structured, in native or open formats. To be able to find candidate processes from such data, queries should be formulated as text, graphics, or models that "represent" processes.

4.2   Querying for Similar Processes

The querying of processes in CPD with 5D should be based on input in the form of text, product model or process model data. To allow for better searching of process model data and process reuse we need better query formulation techniques, i.e. [21]:

- Query by Syntax. The syntax describes how language grammar is used and prescribes how words, symbols, or morphology may be combined to be properly understood. In general, we can divide syntax types into sequential and non-sequential. For example, we can use graphical symbols (e.g., diagrams) as a query that may not be processed sequentially. Any IR language must follow some syntax.
- Query by Example. Query by example was an early invention in database design that has evolved further into a widely adopted concept. It can be successfully applied to any type of search that uses some textual or non-textual object tat can be extracted from reference processes or process result data as a query example.
- Query by Template. Query by template is well established in digital libraries. A query by template implies the use of graphical representation and is especially useful when the document does not have a predefined, well-known data model.
- Query by Co-occurrence. Query patterns are created whenever querying is executed, whether through collaborative filtering or other co-occurrences, that are either determined through content or through information-seeking activities.

The quality of search results significantly improves process reuse with proper query refinement (e.g., with an extended use of controlled vocabularies). The location of process queries should be made available: (1) an application that is specialised for searching, (2) specific applications used in CPD, S or (3) generic API.

5   Conclusions

The level of process reuse today is similar to the level of the reuse of textual data decades ago. The reuse of textual data was advanced with growing amounts of textual data and better text IR techniques. We showed that process reuse in CPD is very promising, but it depends on the availability of large amounts of *process data* in standard representations (e.g., BPEL). The quantity of process data will drive the development of specialised crawlers, parsers, indexers, and analysers for processes. Therefore, the introduction of process repositories and business intelligence is crucial.

Process reuse within CPD with 5D requires combined similarity measures, more relevant implicit ranking with social interactions, and better end-user interfaces for query formulation and the display of process queries. The key to the improvement of process reuse in CPD is an in depth understanding of the engineering work and the engineer's information-seeking behaviour. Engineers exhibit, more than any other discipline, social and implicit information-seeking behaviour. The problem is that the majority of current solutions enable only explicit querying that is not sufficient. Process reuse in CPD with 5D requires new IR and process customisation techniques.

References

1. Cerovsek, T.: A review and outlook for a 'Building Information Model' (BIM): A multi-standpoint framework for technological development. Adv. Engineering Informatics 25, 224–244 (2011)
2. Cerovsek, T., Katranuschkov, P.: Active process reuse model for collaboration. ITcon - Journal of Information Technology in Construction 11, 467–488 (2006)
3. Maurizio, M.: Diversity in Reuse Processes. IEEE Software 17, 56–63 (2000)
4. Goderis, A., Sattler, U., Lord, P., Goble, C.: Seven Bottlenecks to Workflow Reuse and Repurposing, pp. 323–337 (2005)
5. Henninger, S.: An Environment for Reusing Software Processes. In: International Conference on Software Reuse, pp. 103–103 (1998)
6. Greco, G., Guzzo, A., Pontieri, L.: Mining taxonomies of process models. Data & Knowledge Engineering 67, 74–102 (2008)
7. Biplav, S.: Organizing Documented Processes. In: Debdoot, M. (ed.) IEEE International Conference on Services Computing, pp. 25–32 (2009)
8. Cerovsek, T.: Advancing Regulation Retrieval with Profiling, Controlled Vocabularies and Networked Services. In: ICAST 2009, pp. 257–264 (2009)
9. Philippe, R.: An Ontology-Based Support for Asset Design and Reuse. In: Corine, C. (ed.) International Conference on Computer Science, pp. 20–32 (2008)
10. Qihong, S.: WISE: A Workflow Information Search Engine. In: Peng, S., Yi, C. (eds.) International Conference on Data Engineering, pp. 1491–1494 (2009)
11. Zlatkin, S., Kaschek, R.: Towards Amplifying Business Process Reuse. In: Akoka, J., Liddle, S.W., Song, I.-Y., Bertolotto, M., Comyn-Wattiau, I., van den Heuvel, W.-J., Kolp, M., Trujillo, J., Kop, C., Mayr, H.C. (eds.) ER Workshops 2005. LNCS, vol. 3770, pp. 364–374. Springer, Heidelberg (2005)
12. Fiorini, S.T., Sampaio do Prado Leite, J.C., de Lucena, C.J.P.: Process Reuse Architecture. In: Dittrich, K.R., Geppert, A., Norrie, M. (eds.) CAiSE 2001. LNCS, vol. 2068, pp. 284–298. Springer, Heidelberg (2001)
13. Peter, J.F.: Reuse, Validation and Verification of System Development Processes. In: Ivica, C. (ed.) International Workshop on Database and Expert Systems Applications, pp. 300–300 (1999)
14. Xiaorong, X.: Improving the Reuse of ScientificWorkflows and Their By-products. In: Gregory, M. (ed.) IEEE Intl. Conference on Web Services, pp. 792–799 (2007)
15. Jae-Yoon, J.: Hierarchical Business Process Clustering, pp. 613–616 (2008)
16. Wombacher, A.: Evaluation of Technical Measures for Workflow Similarity Based on a Pilot Study. In: Meersman, R., Tari, Z. (eds.) OTM 2006. LNCS, vol. 4275, pp. 255–272. Springer, Heidelberg (2006)
17. Juntao, G.: On Measuring Semantic Similarity of Business Process Models. In: Li, Z. (ed.) International Conference on Interoperability for Enterprise Software and Applications, China, pp. 289–293 (2009)
18. Dijkman, R.M., Dumas, M., Ouyang, C.: Semantics and analysis of business process models in BPMN. Information and Software Technology 50, 1281–1294 (2008)
19. Remco, D.: A Classification of Differences between Similar Business Processes. In: IEEE Intl. Enterprise Distributed Object Computing Conference, pp. 37–37 (2007)
20. Vergeest, J.S.M., Spanjaard, S., Song, Y.: Directed mean Hausdorff distance of parameterized freeform shapes in 3D. The Visual Computer 19, 480–492 (2003)
21. Cerovsek, T.: On AEC Query Formulation Techniques. In: Zarli, A., Scherer, R. (eds.) ECPPM, pp. 269–278. Taylor & Francis Group, Sophia Antipolis (2008)

A Critiquing Mechanism in Engineering Machine Design

Kamalendu Pal and Bill Karakostas

School of Informatics
City University London
Northampton Square
London EC1V 0HB
{kam,billk}@soi.city.ac.uk

Abstract. This paper describes a critiquing mechanism in an engineering decision support system. The critiquing is placed in the context of a hybrid knowledge-based system, Mechanical Engineering Design Environment (MEDE), which exploits both rule-based reasoning and case-based reasoning to provide advice on machine design in a distributed environment. The embedded specific critiquing mechanism is presented and it role with the machine design-support environment is discussed. Finally the presented approach is compared with relevant research works.

Keywords: critiquing mechanism, decision support system, rule-based reasoning, case-based reasoning.

1   Introduction

As the practice of engineering design becomes multi-group decision making in nature, automated collaborative tools are becoming a viable option in order to support distributed engineering design. This research is motivated by recognition of trends towards globalization and its effect in engineering design. New information technology architectures, and in particular cloud computing [1] provides a new opportunity by which engineering designers can reach beyond a geographical region with minimal effort. Communications and discussions can be made much more efficient way by using distributed cloud technology and eliminating some of the engineering design related bottlenecks.

In reality, engineering design follows a sequence of events in which requirements of a problem are realized, alternative solutions are produced and evaluated. These activities sometime follow predefined sequential operations or concurrent operations. In order to complete these events, designers often consult standard engineering design data and use design related mathematical models; and make decisions at the different stages of design. Moreover designers often follow trial and error methods, in different stages of design process, to come up with a final design specification. To improve design decisions, it is necessary to carefully describe and measure design specific

G.D. Putnik and M.M. Cruz-Cunha (Eds.): ViNOrg 2011, CCIS 248, pp. 263–272, 2012.

criteria. In order to do this designers use different critiquing mechanisms (e.g. self-critiquing, group-critiquing) in a routine design practice. These critiquing mechanisms help to analyzing a design in the context of decision-making and provide feedback in order to improve the design. Feedback from critiquing mechanisms may generate design errors, point out incompleteness, advice alternatives, or provide heuristic suggestions. In other words, critiquing mechanism tries to help its end-users to make the necessary modifications by providing feedback or offer advice based upon knowledge of desirable behaviour early in the product development lifecycle.

Moreover on regular basis, engineering designers use domain specific knowledge for coordinating the design of classes of artifacts. By doing so, they accumulate a huge amount of problem solving soft skills (e.g. rule of thumb). This skill set helps designers to make relevant decisions at the time of need. In particular, defining efficient boundaries between the artifact's subsystems; making educated guesses about the required *degree of tolerance* needed to be used for individual subsystem design; and appropriate interface related issues between the subsystems.

In certain circumstances, designers often relied on previously solved design problems that are similar to new design case in hand. This problem solving process, where the past experiences are used in solving a new case, is known as case-based reasoning (CBR) [7], 12], [13], [14]. The main theme of CBR is based on the idea that past problem-solving experiences can be reused and learned from in solving new problems. A CBR system consists of a *case base* (which is the set of all cases that are known to system) and *an inferencing mechanism* to derive a solution from the stored cases [12]. The inferencing mechanism uses the knowledge stored in the *case base* and process user inputs, recall similar cases, retrieve the most similar cases, evaluate and adapt the retrieved cases and update the case base.

There are now several engineering design systems, produced in research, which are somewhat 'intelligent' in character; we refer to a selection of them in the later part of this paper. Most of them are case-based intelligent systems, and a few of them are based on other reasoning mechanisms (e.g. rule-based, model-based, neural-network based, and so on) [4], [8] instead. Both rules and cases are obviously required for engineering design problem while some systems are purpose-built to combine the two forms in an integrated environment. But almost all of them are in lack of distributed critiquing facility to finalize the design process in order to address the global trend.

What is needed, instead, is a knowledge-based engineering decision-support system that respects the relevant information expressed in the engineering product development rules, and that also come closer to the task that confronts the human designer: the analysis of clients' development request in terms of previously-designed product development specifications. These previously-decided design specifications are used for constructing valid justifications and used in supporting or opposing a design conflict. In an engineering design area, an explanation for a decision reached is often more important than the decision itself. Hence, the aim of the present research is to study the RBR and CBR in a hybrid architecture which can support the decision-outcome. For this research, a critiquing mechanism is used to support the automated **M**echanical **E**ngineering **D**esign **E**nvironment (**MEDE**), a hybrid system dealing with mechanical artifact design.

Before discussing the technical details, the basic concept of engineering design critiquing, and some important related issues in the context of engineering design are discussed. Next follows a short description of the domain of the research and the knowledge representation scheme. In particular developed software architecture of MEDE is presented in the next section. Moreover, how the system critiques the initial design specification is described by an example in the following section. Finally, the approach is compares with related research works and a set of concluding remarks are put forward in the last section.

2   Overview of Engineering Design Critiquing

Engineering design critiquing systems are aimed to help designers. In engineering design, often designers deal with physical artifact design and relevant process design. In general, engineering artifacts consist of a set of subcomponents. For example, design of a screw jack relates to the design of main screw, cup, locking nut, handle, body, and some other subcomponents, as shown in Fig. 1. The relationships between these design subcomponents are well defined by the engineering design theory. This type of design can be viewed as a component-based design where each component needs to design separately, and then put together to form a functional artifact.

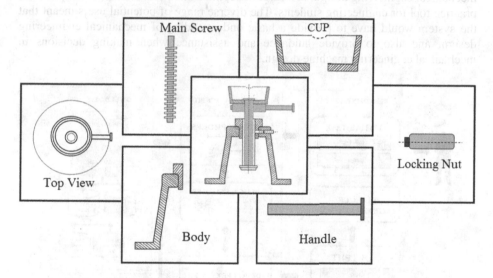

Fig. 1. Design components of screw jack

Moreover, engineering design is typically an iterative activity in nature. As designers progress through the series of decisions in order to complete the design, they realize more of the implications of the problem and the relevant features of the solution. This type of realization provides them to reevaluate previous decisions. In this process, designers create an initial part of the design, then evaluate the initial design and reflect on it. In reality, the designers try to design the subcomponents first and then put them together in a particular context to form the ultimate artefact. Based on the reflections, designers might change the initial design specifications, until they are ready to extend it further.

Therefore the main objective of this engineering design critiquing system is to develop an intelligent system which identify the human trend to error, and that help the human-decision-maker to improve personal task performance. The objective is not to machine detected instructions set for task performance, but of computer-supported judicious human decision-making. It is worth to remember that critiquing mechanism do not prevent errors directly; rather they suggest alternatives their human partners can execute to mitigate errors or find better solutions. One way to deal with such problems is to include automated critiquing mechanism in engineering design environment. Therefore, computer can play a collaborative role in helping to notice, criticize, and reduce human incorrect decision [16].

3   MEDE: A Framework for Engineering Design Process

The main idea behind the development of MEDE is to accommodate a readily-accessible source of advice for those who concerned with decision-making regarding mechanical engineering design, at a level of sophistication that would be acceptable in practice tool for engineering students. The diverse range of potential users meant that the system would have to provide a basic understanding of mechanical engineering design, and also to provide guidance and assistance when making decisions in mechanical engineering machine design.

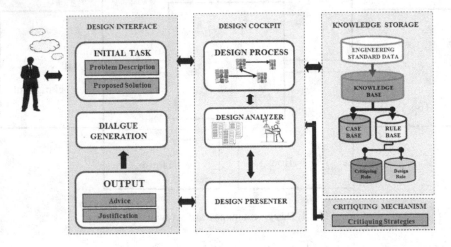

Fig. 2. Computational design environment of MEDE

The computational framework of MEDE is shown in Fig. 2. The decision support part of MEDE includes four major components: design interface, design cockpit, knowledge storage, and critiquing mechanism. The design interface component manages communications between the design engineer and the system. MEDE picks up the relevant facts of a new design case from a question-and-answer session with the user, and then generates its decision support through an interaction between the user and its own stock of knowledge of mechanical machine design.

The main function of design cockpit unit is to store the intermediate decisions, critique, and counter-critique and serves as a vehicle of sharing this information between the critiquing mechanism component and the user. The design cockpit component consists of design process unit, design analyzer, and design presenter. In design process unit, an initial design solution is generated based on the initial inputs from the user and by following its inbuilt design processes. The design analyzer tries to identify any error or miss judgment from the intermediate design solutions. The design analyzer uses the assistance of critiquing mechanism to detect incompleteness in the design and generate expert advice relevant to design decisions. The critiquing mechanism is based on a set of rules known as *critiquing rule*. The design presenter module generates the outputs to the designer of the problem and possible improvements. Output may take the form of message displayed in a dialogue-box, and it has got also the ability to provide justification of the critics. The feedback item enhances the designer's awareness of the status of the design, the justification provided enhances the designer's knowledge of the domain, and the designer is directed to amend problems, this in due time results in more knowledgeable designers and better designs that have fewer errors.

The knowledge base of MEDE consists of a *rule base* and a *case base*. The case base consists of a case storage of previous design specifications, a rule base repository, and relevant reasoning mechanisms. In rule base, it has got two different types of rules: design related rules and rules for intermediate design critiquing. MEDE also uses mechanical artifacts related engineering standard data. A considerable time has been spent in formalizing a particular area of machine-design-related decisions from textbook [9], in order to transform design knowledge to a production rule format. Production rule represents the knowledge in the way of "precondition-result" format, and these can be defined by using the Backus Normal Form (BNF) as follows:

```
<predication> ::= <predication name> [<variable>, …]
<operation> ::= <operation name> [<variable>, …]
<precondition> ::= null | <predication>
<metaresult> ::= <predication> | <operation>
<result> ::= null | <metaresult>
<production> ::= <result> ← <precondition>
<production system> ::= <production>, <production>, ….
```

A production rule example is given below which shows the design criteria of body thickness of a screw jack:

```
<production system> ::= <body feature> ← <the core module dimension>
<body> ::= <the core module dimension> | <relation dimension>
<body feature> ::= <the core module> | <operation>
<relation dimension> ::= <space relation> AND <dimension relation>
<dimension relation> ::= <body thickness = 0.25 * major diameter of main
  screw>
```

Based on the rule representation method, the rule-based reasoning process uses a step-by-step algorithm as follows:

Algorithm 1: Reasoning process based on rule

---

(1)   Initialize the rule base and input the initial parameters of the screw jack;

(2)   Search for the rule in which precondition is matched to the initial parameters. If found, then go to (3), if not, then go to (5);

(3)   If the result of the rule which was found in (2) was a conclusion, then add the conclusion to the design database, or if the result of the rule is an operation, then execute the operation, and make the rule;

(4)   Check and find out if the solution is in the design database, if yes, then end the solving process, if no, then go to (2);

(5)   Ask for more screw jack design information. If yes, go to (2), if not end the particular rule-based reasoning part;

(6)   If all the rules in the rule-base were used, then end the rule-based reasoning part of the system.

If the given facts of a new design case satisfy the conditions of the one of the production rules, MEDE can draw conclusion by applying that particular rule. However, in actual design cases, often designers obtained design specification from previously solved design instances. Therefore, MEDE needs to store case-based information also in its knowledge base.

In order to obtain the case-based design information, it is necessary to represent the previously-solved design specifications in some form that can be manipulated by programs. In this project, design cases are viewed as a set of nested objects. The overall organization of our case base is shown in Fig. 3, where CASE001 illustrates some of the structure that occurs in each of the case named in the left-hand part of the diagram.

The *case-definition* attribute refers to the unique characteristics associated with the case. The purpose of *case_index* attribute is to define which characteristics are to be used as indices. The *adaption_rule* attributes stand for the rules used to modify a retrieved case from the case base to make it fit for the current problem specifications. The rules used here are derived from domain knowledge, formulae and constraints. These rules are a subset of rules from MEDE's design rule base, as shown in Fig. 2.

The proposed architecture and function of the critiquing mechanism fit well in the paradigm of collaborative engineering design practice between a human designer and a computer. In addition, the knowledge storage can be viewed as expert in the field whom the engineering designer consults before making the final decision. The feedback and criticism mechanism provides a valuable support for human designer in order to make appropriate decision.

Fig. 3. Nested object case base: an example of information for one case

4   Scenario of Critiquing Facilities in MEDE

This section provides an example of MEDE's critiquing mechanism using a simple screw jack design related decisions. A screw jack needs to lift a maximum load of 6000 kgf through a height of 30 cm. The main screw of this screw jack is made of steel for which the maximum crushing yield stress is 3300 kgf/cm^2. A suitable factor of safety for calculating the safe load needs to be considered. The locking nut is made of gun-metal, whose allowable shear stress is 250 kgf /cm^2, and the allowable bearing pressure on screw threads is 100 kgf/cm^2. The nut is fixed in the cast-iron base and the screw is turned by means of handle inserted in suitable holes in the head of the screw. The design is be made so as to prevent the load from turning while raising the load. The co-efficient of friction of the threads and collar can be assumed as 0.14. In order to design and prepare the design specifications a design engineer could seek help from MEDE.

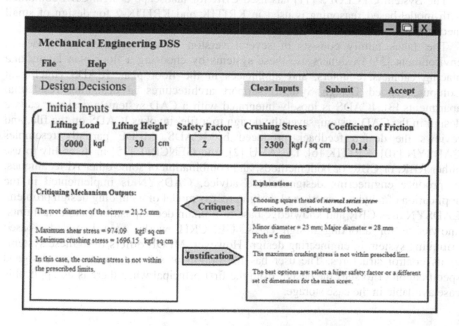

Fig. 4. An example of critiquing mechanism

In this example, the screw is subjected to direct compression and external turning moment. The core diameter of the screw may be calculated by considering compression only, so to take account of torsional shear; designer can take the load 25 to 30 percents greater. Therefore, the design load is going to be 7800 kgf (i.e. 1.3 x 6000). Assuming a safety factor of 2, designer could calculate the design specifications of the main screw and the other subcomponents by using different design formulas and number of important factors that need to be taken into consideration while making design specifications related decisions.

Fig. 4 shows an example of MEDE's critiquing mechanism for the above mentioned design problem. Once critiquing mechanisms generate different design related feedbacks, it then present appropriate justification information also in case of user needs. The designer may also follow guidelines to background domain knowledge relevant to the issue at hand and finalize the ultimate design specifications with the collaboration with MEDE.

5   Related Research

Several engineering design related knowledge-based systems have been constructed by exploring different artificial intelligent techniques (e.g. RBR, CBR, fuzzy logic, inductive learning, neural network and genetic algorithms) [8]. But majority of these systems failed to address the issue of critiquing mechanism. However, few systems have been built with some success in design critiquing. For examples, critics have been implemented to assist with the design of buildings, individual room layouts, computer programs, and so on.

The System CYCLOPS [11] has used CBR for landscape design. CBR combined with model-based reasoning is used in KRITIK and KRITIK-2 for design of small mechanical and electrical devices [6].

The Janus family consists of several version of a household kitchen design environment [5]. Designers use these systems by choosing a floor plan layout and placing cabinets, counters, and appliances in the floor plan. ICADS (Intelligent Computer Aided Design System) support architectures in designing residential apartments [3]. ICADS is loosely integrated with a CAD system: a designer edits a design in the CAD system, saves the design to a file, invokes ICADS on the file, and reviews the design feedback produced by ICADS. MEDE partially resembles CADSYN [10], KRITIK [6], DEJAVU [2], and GENCRIT [15] in its ability to use either RBR, or CBR, or both methods, and combination of some other AI techniques, to produce engineering design related advice. CADSYN is implemented in the application of a hybrid case-based design process model of a building design problem. CADSYN uses CBR and knowledge base of domain decomposition (and constraints) knowledge for adopting design cases. GENCRIT works as a knowledge-based critiquing system in engineering design. However, MEDE differs from these systems in its control structures. The user has the option of selecting previously designed specification or to start the design from the first principal when there is no applicable case available in the case storage.

6   Concluding Remark

We have introduced an engineering design framework based on hybrid knowledge-based and critiquing mechanism. We emphasized that both knowledge-based techniques and critiquing facilities are important for automated engineering design decision-support systems. The architecture of the proposed engineering design support system includes critiquing mechanisms, which collaborate with the user in making effective decisions. In other words, MEDE, rather than being completely autonomous, interacts with its user to form the final decision. We discussed the types of knowledge used by the critiquing mechanisms and the appropriate representation scheme for this knowledge.

In future work we will continue the themes of our current research and increase the functionality of current system by using appropriate collaborative graphical user interface. The identification of new theories of cognitive challenges may result in new features. We plan to explore issues of design rational in order to use our exiting critiquing framework in the other domains, for example real-world legal decision support systems. Moreover, one of the important issues we aim to concentrate in our future research is the opportunity of distributed cloud computing in engineering-design environment.

References

1. Armbrust, M., Fox, A., Griffith, R., Joseph, A., Katz, R., Konwinski, A., Lee, G., Patterson, D., Rabkin, A., Stoica, I., Zaharia, M.: A View of Cloud Computing. Communication of the ACM 53(4), 50–58 (2010)
2. Bardasz, T., Zeid, I.: DEJAVU: Case-Based Reasoning for Mechanical Design. AIEDAM 7(2), 111 (1993)
3. Chun, H., Lai, E.: Intelligent critic system for architectural design. IEEE Transactions on Knowledge and Data Engineering 9(4), 625–639 (1997)
4. Dym, C., Levitt, R.: Knowledge-Based Systems in Engineering. McGraw-Hill, New York (1991)
5. Fischer, G., McCall, R., Morch, A.: JANUS: Integrating hypertext with a knowledge-based design environment. In: Proceedings of the Hypertext 1989, Pittsburgh, PA, USA, pp. 105–117 (1989)
6. Goel, A., Bhatta, S., Stroulia, E.: KRITIK: An Early Case-Based Design System. In: Maher, M., Pu, P. (eds.) Issues and Applications of Case-Based Reasoning in Design, pp. 87–132. Erlbaum, Mahwah (1997)
7. Goel, A., Craw, S.: Design, Innovation and Case-Based Reasoning. Knowledge Engineering Review 20(3), 271–276 (2005)
8. Haymaker, J.: Opportunities for AI to improve Sustainable Building Design Processes. In: Spring Symposium on Artificial Intelligence and Sustainable Design, AAAI 2011, pp. 60–65 (2011)
9. Kutz, M.: Mechanical Engineers Handbook. John Wiley & Sons, Inc. (2006)
10. Maher, M., Zhang, D.: CADSYN: A case-based design process model. AIEDAM 7(2), 97 (1993)

11. Navinchandra, D.: Case-Based reasoning in CYCLOPS – a design problem solver. In: Proceedings DARPA Workshop on Case-Based Reasoning, p. 286 (1988)
12. Pal, K., Palmer, O.: A decision-support system for business acquisitions. Decision Support Systems 27, 411–429 (2000)
13. Pearce, M., Goel, A., Kolodner, J., Zimring, C., Sentosa, L., Billington, R.: Case-Based Decision Support: A Case Study in Architectural Design. IEEE Expert 7(5), 14–20 (1992)
14. Sycara, K., Navinchandra, D., Guttal, R., Koning, J., Narsimhan, S.: CADET: A Case Based Synthesis Tool for Engineering Design. Expert Systems 4(2), 157–188 (1991)
15. Shiva Kumar, H., Suresh, S., Krishnamoorthy, C., Fenves, S., Rajeev, S.: GENCRIT: A Tool for Knowledge-Based Critiquing in Engineering Design. AIEDAM 8(3), 239 (1994)
16. Silverman, B.: Survey of Expert Critiquing Systems; Practical and Theoretical Frontiers. CACM 35(4) (1992)

Modelling Languages Restrictions: A Comparative Study of ArchiMate and SOMF

João Gonçalves Henriques[1], Pedro Carmo Oliveira[2], and Miguel Mira da Silva[1]

[1] Instituto Superior Técnico, Portugal
{joaoltghenriques,mms}@ist.utl.pt
[2] INOV, Portugal
pedro.oliveira@inov.pt

Abstract. In today's IT projects, some specialists model architectures using ad hoc modelling languages in a recurrent way. Since those languages usually do not have defined rules or meta-models, and the majority of the people involved may not know such languages, misunderstandings and problems can arise. In this paper we tried to verify if there are any limitations in two well-known modelling languages, as we believe that the restrictions of today's modelling languages may be one of the causes of the use of ad hoc languages.

Keywords: IT-based services, information systems architectures, modelling languages, ArchiMate, SOMF.

1 Introduction

This paper is about modelling languages and information systems architectures. Motivated by some specialists recurrent practice of modelling architectures using ad hoc modelling languages, which we believe to be a problem, we decided to analyze and check for possible limitations of the currently used ones that could explain the previously referred to problem.

For this purpose we have studied and compared two well-known modelling languages, ArchiMate and SOMF, looking for limitations in modelling projects of multi-organizational integrated IT-based services. We have modelled in each of these languages four specific aspects which we think are crucial to this kind of projects. Afterwards, we analyzed the modelling artifacts in order to see if these were covered by both languages or if there were limitations in any of them.

We present the lessons learned with this process and, based on the conclusions, what we believe to be good ideas for future improvements in the two analyzed languages as well as for related future work.

2 Problem

We consider that the currently used modelling languages have shortcomings. Hence, such limitations might explain why some specialists use ad hoc languages for modelling their information systems architectures, instead of using the available

G.D. Putnik and M.M. Cruz-Cunha (Eds.): ViNOrg 2011, CCIS 248, pp. 273–282, 2012.

modelling languages. For example, in SPOCS [1], a large scale European Union project, some of the produced documents do not follow any existing language, but different sets of figures and elements defined by the several project architects, which causes greater confusion and incoherence.

As this can be a very broad problem to analyze, we will focus on the restrictions in modelling a specific type of project, mainly focused on *multi-organizational integrated IT-based services*, i.e. projects that integrate services provided by different organizations (public or otherwise).

This type of project has several characteristics that make it singular from a modelling point of view. First of all, the project's main outputs are what we call IT-based services, i.e. service supported by technology, usually provided by the Internet, but not fully automated. These higher level services, however, are supported by other services, some of them fully technological ones that can also be supported by other services and so on. Thus, one of the features of these projects is the existence of multiple layers or levels of services.

Another particular aspect of these projects is that they are multi-organizational. Their main goal is to integrate IT-based services from different organizations. These can be e-Government organizations, integrating their different services to make them more practical and simpler for the clients, or organizations along a supply chain that join their services so as to improve their efficiency. They can also include the case of multinational or very large organizations that wish to integrate the services provided by their different departments or offices. This multi-organizational aspect is very important for it requires the integration of systems with components owned by different organizations. Any modelling of these systems should represent this incorporation so everyone in the project can have a similar architecture vision as well as the perception of who has control over what.

The third important characteristic of these projects is that, since they are integration projects, they all represent a transformation of already existing systems. To integrate something that already exists requires the involved systems to develop. These same systems can already be in evolution by themselves, whether it is for the systems to be compliant with the integration or just an evolution completely disconnected from the integration project. This development should be represented in order for the stakeholders to understand how everything is at the moment and how it will be after the project's conclusion.

According to [2], organized networks of organizations, i.e. clusters of organizations that cooperate, with information and communication technology support - in order to achieve efficient product development, production, and marketing tasks - are referred to as collaborative networked organizations. On the other hand, virtual Organizations are defined as sets of independent organizations sharing skills and resources to achieve a common goal [3].

Based on these definitions we can say that projects mainly focused on *multi-organizational integrated IT-based services* involve either virtual or networked organizations.

Similarly, SPOCS can be considered a networked virtual organization, as all the involved entities form a collection of autonomous entities that behave as a single larger entity for the purpose of this project and they employ electronic means to transact business.

3   Related Work

In order to understand if there really are limitations on today's modelling languages we analysed two well-known ones that follow different paradigms, and compared them to find out if, as we believe, they have limitations.

3.1   ArchiMate

ArchiMate is an open and independent enterprise architecture modelling language. It supports the description, analysis and visualization of architectures across several business domains. It is an open standard adopted by the Open Group [4].

Being an enterprise architecture modelling language, ArchiMate focuses on the inter-domain relationships. Thus, it includes concepts for modelling both the global structure of each domain and the relations between different ones, in an easy to understand way, even for someone who is not an expert [5].

In order to be scalable, lightweight and easy to learn and understand, ArchiMate has a limited set of concepts, which follow a simple Framework that still provides a good structure for the architecture [6].

This Framework divides the architecture in three layers: business, application, and technology. In each layer the concepts are further divided into three aspects: behaviour, passive structure and active structure. Beside this distribution, ArchiMate also distinguishes between the systems external and internal views, clearly differentiating the external visible concepts, like relationships and interfaces, from the concepts and relationships that only matter internally [7].

3.2   SOMF

The Service-Oriented Modelling Framework is a service-oriented life cycle modelling methodology proposed by author Michael Bell [8]. This Framework is based on the service-oriented modelling paradigm. According to it, all software assets can be subject to modelling activities. Furthermore, all these assets are seen as services, i.e. service-oriented modelling elements, which are also evaluated by their contributions to service-oriented environments, according to its integration, collaboration, reuse and consumption capabilities.

In this modelling paradigm, services are treated depending on their life cycle state, which is divided into four categories: conceptual, analysis, design and solution services. However, throughout its life cycle a service can change its category.

The service-oriented modelling disciplines offer best practices, standards and policies in order to ease development activities throughout a service life cycle. Such disciplines allow us to identify in which processes the proper human resources are to be involved, such as when design and architectural artefacts, like diagrams and documents, are being produced.

SOMF services fall into three categories [9]:

- Atomic services: Fine grained services, usually indivisible software entities.
- Composite services: Structures that aggregate finer grain services that can be both atomic and composite.
- Service clusters: Group of related services, categorised by their similarities. They provide solutions to organizational problems.

SOMF modelling language allows the construction of three types of models: Analysis, design, and architecture models [10].

4   Case Study

The Simple Procedures Online for Cross-border Services (SPOCS) project is a European large-scale project for interoperability in the e-Government area. Its goal is to help carrying out the European Parliament services directive (2006/123/CE) [11].

The project aims at the implementation of a structure to create interoperability between entrepreneur support services from several European Union countries, so as to provide these entrepreneurs with online electronic services from any EU nation.

This case study was selected because it has all the characteristics of the type of project referred to in the problem section. Being both an e-Government project and a European scale project, SPOCS involves a great number of services, provided by several different organizations, including entities from different countries.

It will also bring a great deal of evolutionary changes to the already existing systems of the involved organizations. In order to properly visualize and analyze these changes, the architectural modelling should represent both the "As-Is" and "To-Be" perspectives.

Several applications will be developed mainly to provide technological support services. All these services will be aggregated to offer a higher level, implying several "layers" of services that should be properly represented when modelling the project architecture.

5   Experiments

We identified four common aspects that should be represented in the architecture of this kind of project and analyzed the four parts in both SOMF and ArchiMate to check if they had limitations. These functionalities are the representation of: different evolutionary stages; services specialization; ownership of assets; and services workflows.

5.1   Simultaneous Representation of Different Evolutionary Stages

In these projects we have an evolving architecture with a great number of changes occurring (but not all at the same time). Therefore, in order to have a good understanding of what will change and what is changing, it is important to represent all these alterations.

We tried to represent a part of SPOCS evolving architecture in SOMF and ArchiMate; the result was the following diagram:

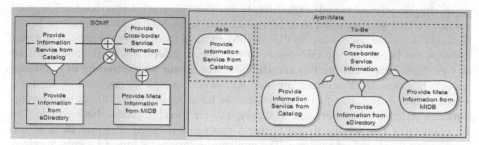

Fig. 1. Diagrams representing evolution diagrams in SOMF and ArchiMate

In this "proposition diagram for structural analysis" we see that the composite service "Provide Information from eDirectory" was decomposed from the "Provide Information Service from Catalog" and is now regarded as an autonomous service. Then, there is an aggregation activity involving the two now independent services and a third composite one named "Provide Meta Information from MIDB", incorporating all of them into the service cluster "Provide Cross-border Service Information".

To model the same thing in ArchiMate we had to make two different diagrams. So in the "As-is" diagram, we only have the "Provide Information Service from Catalog". In the "To-be" diagram we have the same service being aggregated into a newly created one along with other two new services.

5.2 Representation of Different Levels of Services

In modelling these projects the ability to represent several layers, or levels, of services with each layer generalizing the one below or specifying the one above is very important, because there are a great number of services that are integrated to create new higher level services. This ranges from technological low level services to business high level ones that are provided to the final costumers.

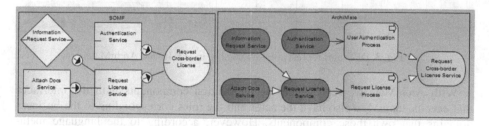

Fig. 2. Diagrams representing services specification diagrams in SOMF and ArchiMate

In order to test this capability, we modelled a hierarchy of SPOCS services using SOMF and starting in the higher level service available to the end client. In the diagram obtained, the analysis service Cluster "Request Cross-border License" is specialized into two analysis composite services, one of them being dedicated to two other analysis services, one composite and one atomic.

In the diagram obtained with ArchiMate, the "Request Cross-border License" service, which was regarded as a service cluster in SOMF, is now identified like a business layer one. According to the ArchiMate meta-model, any instance of a given concept can be specialized into others of the same concept. So, there should not be any problem in specialising this service, however, in our understanding of the meta-model, business layer services are not the same concept as application services. Furthermore, from our study of ArchiMate, we have not found any direct relationship between different layers services. The only way we found to model this example was by connecting this service to the business processes it fulfils and join them to the application layer services they use. The application service "Request License Service" is further specialized in two other application services.

5.3   Representation of Software Assets Ownership

The capacity to identify the ownership of software assets is vital to any multi-organizational project like SPOCS in order to understand who owns and is responsible and accountable for the involved systems artifacts. This perspective is also important to identify budgetary challenges that may arise.

We modelled three SPOCS project components, with the corresponding ownership in both SOMF and ArchiMate.

With SOMF we produced the following conceptual architecture diagram (Fig.3) in which the components are displayed like packaged technological assets and the organizations that own them are shown as business domains. The ownership of the components is explained by the use of the relationship "Owner of" that identifies the business domains as owners of the packaged technological assets.

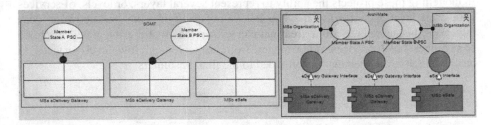

Fig. 3. Diagrams representing ownership in SOMF and ArchiMate

With ArchiMate we represented the application components with the interfaces that execute them. We also have the actor and the roles corresponding to the business domains that own those components. However, according to the language meta-model, none of the relationships that can exist between these concepts is related to ownership.

5.4   Service Workflows

In a service-oriented system, the execution is mainly focused on the consumed services. In that context, we believe that the architecture of such systems should represent their workflow.

We tried to model the execution flow of some SPOCS services in both SOMF and ArchiMate. In the diagram obtained in SOMF, the consumer, or client, requests the "Provide Cross-border Service Information" composite design service. The service then routes this request to the first service of the process, the Provide Service Information Service composite design, which handles and, afterwards, directs the same request to the next participating service, and so on, until the message is sent back to the starting service.

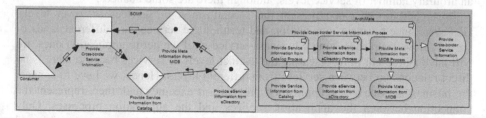

Fig. 4. Diagrams representing service workflow in SOMF and ArchiMate

In ArchiMate, instances of service can only be related to other instances through the relationships of composition, aggregation or specialization. Therefore, we could not directly model the routing of the requests between the services. Nevertheless, ArchiMate process concepts can have a trigger relationship connecting them. In addition, those processes might be associated to a service by a realization connector. So, in ArchiMate, a service workflow can only be implied through the use of process workflow, in which the processes are performed by services, and not directly represented.

6 Evaluations

In this section we present the results evaluation of the four carried out experiments in order to check which aspects are covered by SOMF and ArchiMate.

6.1 Simultaneous Representation of Different Evolutionary Stages

As it is possible to observe in figure 2, SOMF models' relationships represent some type of change. In the diagram, we have two composite analysis services, associated by a "decomposed" type connector. This means that the separated service used to be a part of the original one, but was parted through a decomposing activity. At the same time, we have those two composite analysis and a third analysis composite service connected to an analysis service cluster by a "generalized" relationship. Thus, these composite services, that used to be independent, are now aggregated into the analysis service cluster. So, with this diagram we can see how the services used to be and how they are now, i.e. we have both an "As-Is" and "To-Be" perspective on the same diagram.

From our understanding of the ArchiMate meta-model, there are no relationships similar to those. So, there are not relationships that allow different evolutionary perspectives to be represented in the same diagram. As a result, in order to develop different evolutionary stages in ArchiMate, we had to model two different diagrams, or viewpoints, one for the "As-Is" perspective and another for the "To-Be".

6.2   Representation of Different Levels of Services

Based on our results we can say that both languages have the capability to represent an arbitrary number of service levels, although there are some nuances.

In ArchiMate we can represent the specialization of services in lower levels. However, since business, application and technologic services are different kinds of service, if we keep specifying a business service until we get to application ones, we will have a problem in representing the distinct levels of services because there is no direct relationship between services from different layers. Hence, we have to connect the business service to the application processes it executes and, then, represent the connection between the application services and the application processes. Only through this indirect way can we represent a relationship between application and business services. The same is valid for technological services.

In conclusion, we can directly represent the specification (or the opposite, generalization) of a generic layer service, if the specific corresponding services are also from the same layer. If they belong to a different layer, though, this relationship can only be implied by the use of relationships between services and processes.

In SOMF we can keep specifying (or generalizing) generic services into more specific ones for an infinite number of times without any restrictions [12]. SOMF different types of services (atomic, composite or clusters) can be related amongst themselves by using specification or generalization.

6.3   Representation of Software Assets Ownership

Analyzing the produced diagrams, we can see that it is possible to represent the technological infrastructure domain of architecture both in SOMF and ArchiMate.

As we can see in figure 4, there is a connector that represents that a specific business domain owns a particular software asset. However, from our understanding and analysis of the ArchiMate meta-model, the same thing is not possible in ArchiMate which is an important capability that is also absent.

6.4   Service Workflows

In section 5.4, we presented the results produced when we tried to represent the execution flow of some SPOCS services in SOMF and ArchiMate. Analyzing those diagrams we realized that in both languages we can represent service workflows, but while in SOMF this is done directly, in ArchiMate service workflows can only be implied. This occurs because there is no relationship similar to a "trigger" between services in ArchiMate, and so we cannot directly represent the workflow. Nevertheless, since ArchiMate processes can be connected by a "trigger" relationship, and processes can be associated to services, we are able to have an indirect representation of the workflow.

In SOMF, by using "Circular Beams", we can represent a direct service workflow, although this type of connector may only be used when the service workflow is circular, i.e. the last service executed routes its messages to the first performed service, that then replies to the consumer.

7   Lessons Learned

Both analyzed languages (SOMF and ArchiMate) suffer from several limitations. We believe that it would be beneficial for architects if these limitations were addressed in future versions of both languages.

Furthermore, we learnt that in ArchiMate modelling language it is not possible to represent two different evolutionary perspectives at the same time, which could be added to ArchiMate with the inclusion of relationships that imply that something has changed like the "decomposed" and "aggregated" relationships that SOMF language provides.

Another drawback in ArchiMate is the lack of possibility to represent the ownership of the assets by the organization or department that actually owns them. A SOMF "owner of" type relationship could be considered as an addition to the ArchiMate meta-model so as to allow the ownership of assets.

There are still two other aspects that we believe could be added to ArchiMate meta-model, even if they are not actual restraints.

ArchiMate makes it possible to represent service workflows but in an indirect way. Then, we believe that adding some relationships like "triggers" between services would be beneficial for the language, since it would make it possible to explicitly represent service workflows.

We also believe that it would be interesting to add to the language meta-model "aggregation", "composition" and "specification" relationships between services from different layers. With this add-on, we could have a viewpoint from which visualization of the complete services hierarchy of a project is a reality.

Nevertheless, considering the four analyzed aspects, SOMF only has minor limitations. We observed that it is possible to represent service workflows, but merely if we represent the involved services as connected in a ring.

This may be explained because SOMF follows a service-oriented paradigm and the aspects that we focused on are important to projects dedicated to multi-organizational integrated IT-based services. This does not mean that SOMF has no other major limitations but simply means that we have not found any in the specific context of the four considered aspects. Likewise, SOMF might have major limitations representing non service-oriented projects.

8   Conclusion

Both ArchiMate and SOMF have some kind of limitation when modelling projects focused on multi-organizational integrated IT-based services.

Though we cannot extrapolate these conclusions to every modelling language, it is likely that the majority of current modelling languages have limitations in developing other kinds of project.

When a modelling language is created with the intent of modelling a specific kind of project, it is very likely that the selected language will have restrictions in modelling other projects, as we were able to observe in SOMF that did not have any major limitations in the four aspects we analysed for the SPOCS case study. However, it is, not the ideal language to model projects that are not service-oriented, since most of its diagrams cannot be represented.

If a modelling language is created to be as general as possible, like ArchiMate, it is likely that it will have limitations in some aspects that are very specific to a particular type of project. This explains the shortcomings of ArchiMate in representing the four aspects covered in chapter 5.

So, considering that it is likely that all languages will have limitations, when representing a specific kind of project, then, every systems architect would have to be an expert in several modelling languages in order to choose which to use to model a particular project. As this is not a tangible possibility, we can conclude that the limitations of the modelling languages lead some specialists to use ad hoc languages in order to model their information systems architectures.

A possible solution to this problem may be to keep including in more general modelling languages some concepts and capabilities from more specific modelling languages, thus reducing their limitations. Another solution to this problem could be to define a Framework with a set of criteria to help an architect decide which modelling language is the best to develop a specific project.

References

1. SPOCS: Single Procedures Online for Cross-border Services, http://eu-spocs.eu
2. Lavrac, N., Ljubic, P., Urbancic, T., Papa, G., Jermol, M., Bollhalter, S.: Trusted Model for Networked Organizations Using Reputation and Collaboration Estimates. IEEE Transactions on Systems, Man and Cibernetics – Part C: Applications and Reviews 37(3), 429–439 (2007)
3. Plisson, J., Ljubic, P., Mozetic, I., Lavrac, N.: Ontologies for Collaborative Networked Organizations. In: Putnic, D., Cunha, M. (eds.) Encyclopedia of Network and Virtual Organizations, vol. II G – PR, pp. 1128–1135. Information Science Reference, Hershey (2008)
4. ArchiMate, http://www.archimate.org
5. Berrisford, G., Lankhorst, M.: Using ArchiMate with an Architecture Method. Via Nova Architectura (2009)
6. ArchiMate 1.0 Specification, http://www.opengroup.org/archimate/doc/ts_archimate
7. Lankhorst, M.: Enterprise Architecture at Work: Modelling, Communication and Analysis. Springer, Heidelberg (2005)
8. Bell, M.: Service-Oriented Modeling: Service Analysis, Design and Architecture. Wiley, John & Sons (2008) (incorporated)
9. Orchel, M.: Service-Oriented Modeling Framework
10. Truyen, F.: Enacting the Service Oriented Modeling Framework using Enterprise Architect. Cephas Consulting Group (2010)
11. Directive 2006/123/EC of the European parliament and of the council December 12, 2006 on services in the internal market. Official Journal of the European Union (2006)
12. Bell, M.: SOA Modeling Patterns for Service-Oriented Discovery and Analysis. Wiley, John & Sons (2010) (incorporated)

Profiling and Framing Structures for Pervasive Information Systems Development

José Eduardo Fernandes[1], Ricardo J. Machado[2], and João Á. Carvalho[2]

[1] Polytechnic Institute of Bragança, School of Technology and Management,
Dept. of Informatics and Communications
5301-854 Bragança, Portugal
jef@ipb.pt

[2] Universidade do Minho, Escola de Engenharia, Dept. de Sistemas de Informação
4800-058 Guimarães, Portugal
{rmac,jac}@dsi.uminho.pt

Abstract. Pervasive computing is a research field of computing technology that aims to achieve a new computing paradigm. Software engineering has been, since its existence, subject of research and improvement in several areas of interest. Model-Based/Driven Development (MDD) constitutes an approach to software design and development that potentially contributes to: concepts closer to domain and reduction of semantic gaps; automation and less sensitivity to technological changes; capture of expert knowledge and reuse. This paper presents a profiling and framing structure approach for the development of Pervasive Information Systems (PIS). This profiling and framing structure allows the organization of the functionality that can be assigned to computational devices in a system and of the corresponding development structures and models, being. The proposed approach enables a structural approach to PIS development. The paper also presents a case study that allowed demonstrating the applicability of the approach.

Keywords: MDD, PIS, pervasive, ubiquitous, software engineering, process, information systems, architecture, framework.

1   Introduction

The dissemination of computing and heterogeneous devices and platforms, the high pace of technological innovations and volatile requirements, the size and complexity of software systems characterize the software development context today. This context challenges the way software is developed for emerging forms of information systems. Software Development Processes (SDPs), as well as generalized adoption of models, are fundamental to efficient development efforts of successful software systems.

Pervasive Computing, also called Ubiquitous Computing [1, 2], represents a new direction on the thinking about the integration and use of computers in people's lives. It aims to achieve a new computing paradigm, one in which there is a high degree of pervasiveness and availability of interconnected computing devices in the physical

G.D. Putnik and M.M. Cruz-Cunha (Eds.): ViNOrg 2011, CCIS 248, pp. 283–293, 2012.

environment. Widespread availability of affordable and innovative information technologies represents a potential opportunity for improvement/innovation on business processes or for enhancement of life quality of individuals. Among other things (such as social concerns), this opportunity promotes the attention to the efficiency and effectiveness of information management regarding to the way they acquire, process, store, retrieve, communicate, use, and share information. To take full benefits of the opportunities offered by modern information technologies, these devices need to be "appropriately integrated within organizational frameworks" [3]. Therefore, Pervasive Information Systems (PIS) [4] orchestrate these devices in order to achieve a set of well-established goals. In this way, PIS not only provide a solid basis to sustain the needed information to achieve effectiveness at both individual and organizational levels, but also leverages the investment on those information technologies or other organizational resources. In order to explore the potential offered by pervasive computing and to maximize the revenue of these kinds of systems, a PIS, as any other information system, must be designed, developed and deployed attending to its nature (these systems may potentially accommodate a large quantity of heterogeneous devices and be subject of frequent updates/evolutions).

This paper, further exploring the topic of software development for PIS, proposes an approach for profiling and framing functional profiles for PIS development, and presents a case study used for its applicability. This document structures its content as follows: section 1 introduces pervasive information systems, its issues and the benefits of a model-based/driven development based approach; section 2 gives insight into related research works and gives an overview of a development framework for PIS; section 3 presents the suggested approach; section 4 presents a case study wherein this approach is demonstrated; section 5 presents the conclusions and finishes this document.

2   Related Work

Software engineering has been, since its existence, subject of research and improvement in several areas of interest, such as software development processes (SDPs) whose process models evolved from waterfall and nowadays may assume several forms [5]. The development of large software systems is another area of interest that has been, for decades, subject of research work; several topics can be pointed out such as the exploration of issues related to the management of large scale software development [6, 7], software architecture [8-10], model-driven development [11, 12], among others. Not directly related with large projects, Medvidovic[13] points the relevance of software architecture in leveraging the pervasive and ubiquitous area. Model-Based/Driven Development (hereafter in this document, unless otherwise stated, simply referred as MDD) is another area that gains an increasing focus. MDD constitutes an approach to software design and development that strongly focuses and relies on models [14]. It automates, as much as possible, the transformation of models and the generation of the final code. This enables higher independence from the technological platform that supports the realization of the system.

MDD has the potential to offer key pathways that enable software developers to cope with complexity inherent to PIS. A proper PIS construction demands an approach that recognizes particularities of PIS and that benefit from MDD orientation. Research has been performed [15] to bring the application of MDD concepts and techniques to software of PIS. Fernandes et al. [4] suggest a conceptual development framework able to sustain an approach for software development of PIS that take into account MDD potential and PIS characteristics, particularly, heterogeneity and functional variability. The following paragraphs present a brief overview of this development framework.

The *development framework* [4] for PIS introduces and describes new conceptions framed on three perspectives of relevance to the development, called *dimensions*. Based in these dimensions, the development framework considers two additional main perspectives of development: one concerning the overall development process, and a second concerning to individual development processes. Fig. 1 illustrates a schema of the framework. The following paragraphs give an overview of these dimensions and development perspectives.

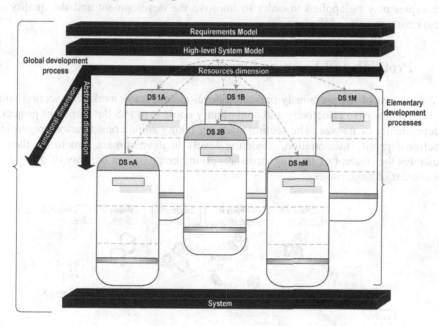

Fig. 1. Development framework for PIS

The three dimensions considered are: resources, functional, abstraction. The *resources dimension* sets up the several categories of devices with similar characteristics and capabilities. The *functional dimension* sets up the different functionality needed by the system and that can be assigned to resources in the system for its concretization. The assignment of a specific functional profile to a specific resource category results in a specific *functional profile instance* that is realized by devices in that resource category. Each functional profile instance has a corresponding *development structure* which embodies an elementary development process aiming to realize that instance. The *abstraction dimension* respects, in an MDD context, to the levels of abstraction that elementary development process may have (from platform-independent model (PIM), passing by platform-specific model (PSM), to generated code). The development framework structures the development in a global development process and several elementary development processes. The *global development process* is responsible for modeling requirements and for establishing high-level and global system models. Based on these models, it sets up functional profiles and categories of resources, as well as, high-level PIM for each functional profile instance that shall exist. The global development process has the responsibility for making all the necessary arrangements for integration of the several artifacts that result from elementary development processes and for final composition, testing, and deployment of the system. *Elementary development processes* are responsible for the software development of parts of the system that realize specific functionalities for specific categories of resources. For each of the development structures, an adequate software development process can be chosen, as long as it respects the principles of the approach globally adopted. MDD concepts and techniques may be applied in order to improve the development and the quality of those resulting parts of the system.

3   Profiling and Framing Structures

In the context of the previously presented development framework, this section aims to provide a way to effectively and consistently apply it in PIS development projects, independently of its size. The section starts by taking some considerations regarding functional profile instantiation, modeling levels in development structures; then it illustrates the concept of framing structure, giving emphasis on the way of using it in the context of large projects.

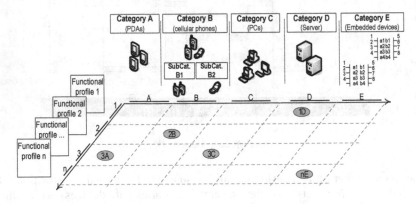

Fig. 2. Functional profile instances

The assignment of a functional profile to a resource corresponds to an instantiation of the functional profile, carrying the meaning of responsibility assignment to that resource. Fig. 2 illustrates an example of instances resulting from the assignment of functional profiles to resource categories.

The result of an instantiation process is an instance profile that has subjacent a kind of platform independent model (or depending of the perspective, it may be seen as a PSM) as it is expected to be later subject of possible model transformations into intermediate platform specific models (or eventually directly subject to code generation). Further development takes place based on this model, giving origin to a specific development structure related to that specific functional profile instance. Each development structure reflects a pathway of software development in order to realize a functional profile assigned to a category of resources. Fig. 5 illustrates these development structures as well, as the modeling levels that can be found inside them. These modeling levels respects to the abstraction dimension, one of the tree dimensions previously exposed. Depending from the point of view, an intermediate model can be seen as a PIM or a PSM: a model can be seen as a PSM when looking from a preceding higher abstraction model level, and can be seen as a PIM when looking from lower abstraction model level. For some development structures these levels may eventually not exist, as it is possible to directly generate the bottom-level PSM or even the code itself.

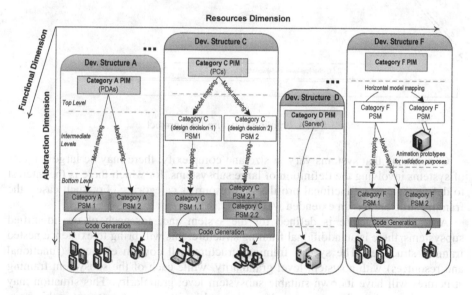

Fig. 3. Modeling levels in development structures (abstraction dimension)

Considering the schema of the development framework (Fig. 1) and the schemas related to functional profiles instantiation (Fig. 2 and Fig. 3 an overall conceptual representation of conceptions involved in the development framework can be schematized into a conceptual framing structure that allows the definition and framing of functional profile instances. This conceptual structure can be expressed by a schema similar to the one presented in Fig. 4. Fig. 4 illustrates the high-level and low-level models/specifications/artifacts (produced by starting and ending activities of the global development process). All relevant functional profiles are listed at the left side of the framing structure, and the resources categories identified are listed at the middle top. The definition of functional profile instances are signaled in the proper intersections of lines of functional profile with the columns of resource categories. For each functional profile instance there is an associated development framework (as depicted in Fig. 2 and Fig. 3; for each of these development frameworks there will be a corresponding elementary development process (as depicted by Fig. 1).

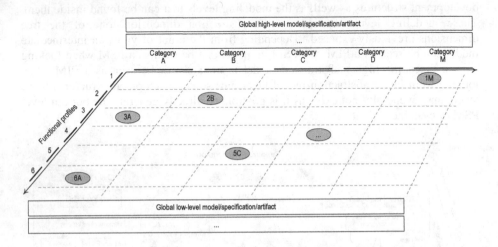

Fig. 4. Framing structure for a project

Considering that systems vary in size and complexity, there may be large projects of systems involving the definition of large subsystems, for which there is the interest to define their own functional profiles and resources categories. For such cases, the framing structure has an extended way of use.

A framing structure is defined for the system and, for each of the identified subsystems, there is an additional framing structure; this will bring to existence nested framing structures. The system framing structure will contain elements (functional and resources) with a system level granularity, while each of the subsystem framing structures will have its own suitable subsystem level granularity. This situation may be recursive and a subsystem may be composed by its own subsystems; is this case, for each of the subsystems, there will be again a corresponding framing structure that, at a certain point, will be a leaf framing structure containing final functional profiles and resource categories. The recursive nesting of framing structures allows dealing with any system size. In this process, each of the framing structures implicitly defines its own namespace for naming its constituent elements. Fig. 5 shows an example of the nesting of the framing structures to deal with the size of large projects.

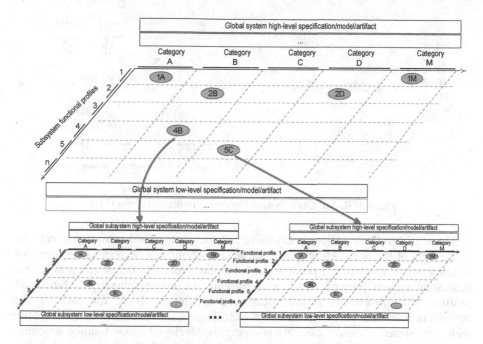

Fig. 5. Nesting of framing structures for large projects

4 The USE-ME-GOV Case Study

This section starts by briefly introducing the USE-ME.GOV (USability-drivEn open platform for MobilEGOVernment) project that aimed to create an open platform for mobile government services. Then, it illustrates the application of the development framework on this project. Attending to the project dimension and purpose/size of this paper, only a part of the model (where appropriate) will be used for illustration purposes (this does not affect the rationale to be taken for the whole model).

The USE-ME.GOV project [16] focused on the development of an open platform for mobile government services. This platform facilitates the access of authorities to the mobile market by allowing them to share common modules of the platform and to deal with multiple mobiles operators independently of each one's interface. USE-ME.GOV system general architecture is illustrated by Fig. 6.

The USE-ME.GOV Platform basically consists of two separate application system: (i) Core Platform, which is responsible for user's platform access, user and terminal management; (ii) Service Repository, which is a central registry of services. The USE-ME.GOV system also contains what is designated by "platform services". Platform services included in the USE-ME.GOV system are: (i) Context Provision and Aggregation Services; (ii) Localization Service; (iii) Content Provision and Aggregation Service. These services enable the use of user's context, user's localization, and access and aggregation of data form external sources.

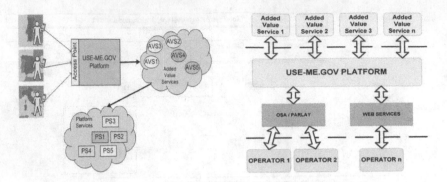

Fig. 6. USE-ME.GOV System General Architecture (from [17])

The USE-ME.GOV project is extensive and includes several subsystems services. In the light of the approach proposed, these subsystems can be seen as a system for which a whole development process can be applied. As such, the project will have a contextual system framing structure identifying the major subsystem's functional profiles and subsystem's resource category groupings. Then, for each of the subsystem functional profile instances (the crossing of subsystem's functional profile with subsystems' resources category grouping) is developed a new framing structure, at a subsystem level. In this framing structure the high-level model corresponds to the one regarding to the specific subsystem's functional profile instance in the preceding framing structure. In each subsystem's functional profile instance related framing structure, there will be functional profiles and resources categories, as expected (unless there is another level of subsystems, in which case, the rationale is applied again). The following paragraphs show the system framing structure of USE-ME.GOV.

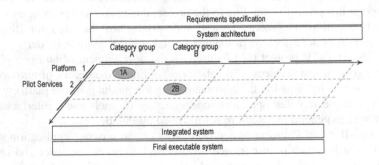

Fig. 7. Framing structure at system level for USE-ME.GOV project

For one of the identified subsystem's functional profile instances, the respective nested framing structure is illustrated. Further nested framing structures of this last one will not be presented here.

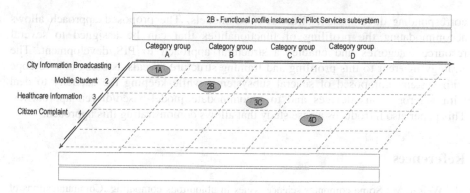

Fig. 8. Framing structure for Pilot Services subsystem of USE-ME.GOV

Fig. 7 illustrates the framing structure at the system level. It shows the subsystem's functional profile instances that get existence in the project. As it can be seen in Fig. 7, the framing structure has two major subsystem functional profiles: "Platform" and "Pilot Services". The resource categories related to subsystem functional profiles (as it also happens at the system level), have symbolic names of "Category group A", "Category group B", and so on. In these cases, it is acceptable to make no explicit identification/characterization of the resources categories. The framing structure assigns each of the subsystem functional profiles to only one resource group, giving origin to a single subsystem functional profile. The "Platform" and "Pilot Services" functional profile instances have also corresponding framing structures. Fig. 8 illustrates the framing structure related do "Pilot Services". The Pilot Services has several subsystems, one for each of the services of "Complaint Information Broadcasting", "Mobile Student", "Healthcare Information", and "Citizen Complaint". Again, as before in the preceding framing structure, there are resource category groups; for each of the subsystems, there will be again a corresponding framing structure. Symbolic names identify the several elements of the framing structure. Note that there is no conflict on the names used for resource categories groupings, functional profiles, or functional profiles instances as the framing structure implicitly defines a namespace.

5   Conclusion

Pervasive forms of information system are increasingly predominating on landscape of software systems development. Among others, resources heterogeneity, increased number of functionalities that may be simultaneously accomplished by distinct resources, high pace of changes on resources and requirements characterizes PIS. These have to be taken into account by a suitable approach to software development for PIS. This paper presents a profiling and framing structure approach for the development of PIS. This profiling and framing structure allows the organization of the functionality that can be assigned to computational devices in a system and of the corresponding development structures and models. The proposed approach allows accommodating the profiling of functionalities that can be assigned to several resource categories and enables a structural approach to PIS development. The strategy inherent to this profiling and framing structure reveals as being able to cope with systems composed of several subsystems, while keeping the capacity to deal with heterogeneous devices and to accommodate model-based/driven approaches. This paper also introduces a case study that allows demonstrating this approach.

References

1. Weiser, M.: Some computer science issues in ubiquitous computing. Communications of ACM 36, 75–84 (1993)
2. Weiser, M., Gold, R., Brown, J.S.: The origins of ubiquitous computing research at PARC in the late 1980s. IBM Systems Journal 38, 693–696 (1999)
3. Sage, A.P., Rouse, W.B.: Information Systems Frontiers in Knowledge Management. Information Systems Frontiers 1, 205–219 (1999)
4. Fernandes, J.E., Machado, R.J., Carvalho, J.Á.: Model-Driven Development for Pervasive Information Systems. In: Mostefaoui, S.K., Maamar, Z., Giaglis, G.M. (eds.) Advances in Ubiquitous Computing: Future Paradigms and Directions, pp. 45–82. IGI Publishing (2008)
5. Ruparelia, N.B.: Software development lifecycle models. SIGSOFT Softw. Eng. Notes 35, 8–13 (2010)
6. Kay, R.H.: The management and organization of large scale software development projects. In: Proceedings of the Spring Joint Computer Conference, May 14-16, pp. 425–433. ACM, Boston (1969)
7. Benincasa, G.P., Daneels, A., Heymans, P., Serre, C.: Engineering a Large Application Software Project: The Controls of the CERN PS Accelerator Complex. IEEE Transactions on Nuclear Science 32, 2029–2031 (1985)
8. Gorton, I., Liu, Y.: Advancing software architecture modeling for large scale heterogeneous systems. In: Proceedings of the FSE/SDP Workshop, FoSER 2010, pp. 143–148. ACM, Santa Fe (2010)
9. Mirakhorli, M., Sharifloo, A.A., Shams, F.: Architectural challenges of ultra large scale systems. In: Proceedings of the 2nd International Workshop on Ultra-Large-Scale Software-Intensive Systems, pp. 45–48. ACM, Leipzig (2008)
10. Laine, P.K.: The role of SW architecture in solving fundamental problems in object-oriented development of large embedded SW systems. In: Proceedings of the Working IEEE/IFIP Conference on Software Architecture, pp. 14–23 (2001)
11. Mattsson, A., Lundell, B., Lings, B., Fitzgerald, B.: Experiences from Representing Software Architecture in a Large Industrial Project Using Model Driven Development. In: Proceedings of SHARK-ADI 2007. IEEE Computer Society (2007)
12. Heijstek, W., Chaudron, M.R.V.: Empirical Investigations of Model Size, Complexity and Effort in a Large Scale, Distributed Model Driven Development Process. In: SEAA 2009, pp. 113–120 (2009)
13. Medvidovic, N.: Software architectures and embedded systems: a match made in heaven? IEEE Software 22, 83–86 (2005)

14. Fernandes, J.E., Machado, R.J., Carvalho, J.Á.: Model-Driven Methodologies for Pervasive Information Systems Development. In: Fernandes, J.M., Machado, R.J., Lilius, J., Porres, I. (eds.) MOMPES 2004, pp. 15–23. TUCS General Publication, Hamilton (2004)
15. Fernandes, J.E., Machado, R.J., Carvalho, J.Á.: Model-Driven Software Development for Pervasive Information Systems Implementation. In: Machado, R.J., e Abreu, F.B., da Cunha, P.R. (eds.) QUATIC 2007, pp. 218–222. IEEE Computer Society, Lisbon (2007)
16. USE-ME.GOV: Consortium Agreement - Annex I - Description of Work (2003)
17. USE-ME.GOV: D3.1 Recommendations (2006)

Seamless Information Integration in Network Enterprises Using MENTOR: Development of a Reference Ontology in Metrological Domain

Carlos A. Costa[1], António Monteiro[1],
Ricardo Gonçalves[2], and João Mendonça da Silva[1]

[1] CT2M – DEM - Universidade do Minho - Campus de Azurém,
4800-058 Guimarães, Portugal
{berto,jpmas,cmonteiro}@dem.uminho.pt
[2] UNL FCT Caparica,
2300 Monte da Caparica, Portugal
rg@uninova.pt

Abstract. Manufacturing teams face the challenge of integration and reuse of computational information systems and knowledge. Ontologies constitute a set of concepts, axioms and relationships describing a domain of interest. The distributed and heterogeneous nature of the organizations, in particular networked enterprises, led to the development of different ontologies for the same or overlapping areas, resulting in non-interoperability. This has become the basis for research methodologies to support a reference ontology, contributing to the standardization and development of ontologies within enterprises and virtual network, providing interoperability properties to intelligent systems. This paper extends the MENTOR methodology to support the development of reference ontology in the field of metrology. The aim is to maintain the different ontologies of each partner, providing networked enterprises with coherent interaction and unambiguous communication. A case study in the field of metrology is presented and the proposed methodology is demonstrated.

Keywords: Ontologies, metrology, measuring systems, intelligent manufacturing, interoperability.

1 Introduction

Nowadays, the global economy is driven by rapid innovation and short development schedules, with consumer´s expectative always increasing in terms of performance, quality and products' cost [1]. The management of expectations is the driving force for the strong industrial development, especially the technological development in production processes and manufacturing. In this context, computer support works as an aggregator of the multidisciplinary informational elements involved, contributing to increased automation and overall efficiency of manufacturing systems.

G.D. Putnik and M.M. Cruz-Cunha (Eds.): ViNOrg 2011, CCIS 248, pp. 294–303, 2012.

In parallel to manufacturing automation, and given the heterogeneous nature of the organizations involved, the teams face the challenge of integration and reuse of information, but non-interoperability and heterogeneity are main obstacles to such objective. The involvement of several organizations in nowadays product's lifecycle raises the complexity of the problem in terms of terminology and contexts, adopted product models and respective variables and computational data.

The absence of a common technical vocabulary among different partners is sometimes a source of conflicts that may result in non-interoperability between information systems. In this context, the establishment of the first edition of the VIM (International Metrology Vocabulary) was the first step towards the harmonization of terms and concepts in the field of metrology. Subsequently were presented other proposals and contributions, both from standards organizations and researchers,. However, given the diversity of the domain ontologies, not all concepts are covered, the issue remaining open therefore.

This led to research in methodologies to support a reference ontology. MENTOR methodology proposed by authors [2], is mainly intended to support an organization to adopt and build or reuse a reference ontology, particularly in this paper in the field of metrology. This reference ontology will improve semantic interoperability among the partners or companies concerning the contents of a standardized model of data representation, while allowing each partner to maintain its own ontology, providing consistent and unambiguous interaction.

MENTOR methodology proposed in this paper, is mainly intended to support an organization to adopt and build or reuse a reference ontology in the field of metrology. This reference ontology will improve semantic interoperability among the partners or companies concerning the contents of a standardized model of data representation, while allowing each partner to maintain its own ontology, providing consistent and unambiguous interaction.

The subsequent contents of this paper are organized as follows: Chapter 2 reports the flow of information in the inspection phases; Chapter 3 presents the MENTOR methodology for the development of a reference ontology, showing the benefits of its application; Chapter 4 presents a case study in the field of metrology and demonstrates the proposed methodology; Chapter 5 concludes this work.

2   Information Flow in Inspection Phases

During the inspection phases, the processes and the measurement systems need to be flexible and able to verify product compliance automatically, in order to validate the information corresponding to the design and manufacturing stages in a more integrated and adjustable process in time [3]. The variety of systems and software available contribute to a heterogeneous use that may result in problems of application and interoperability.

The first edition of the VIM published by ISO in 1984 [4] contributed with the main set of harmonizing concepts and terms in metrology. Some other documents and updates followed, in order to harmonize concepts and terminology within the measurement field,. Based on VIM, Abran A. and. Sellami A. [5], established a model of the concepts and sub-concepts presented therein, aiming in particular to illustrate the various levels of abstraction. However, this modelling does not yet cover all the concepts; it needs to be completed in order to ensure full coherence and consistency of representation.

Another important issue, since it may compromise the automatic planning, inspection and assembly of mechanical components is related to the geometric tolerance. Requicha and Chan [6] proposed a constructive solid geometry (CSG) based scheme, allowing the representation of surface features with tolerances and other associated attributes. Additional developments in the domain may be found in [4, 5, 6, 7].

The continuous diffusion of CAD/CAM fostered the Integrated Measurement Process (IMP), in parallel to manufacturing automation, to integrate the control and data sharing, facilitating the flow in good manufacturing systems, and easy, fast and reliable inspections. Feng presented a model for planning the dimensional control that provides the bridge between design and dimensional control of the manufactured products, summarizing some functional requirements and activities of IMP [8]. The additional performance and functional requirements may affect the planning and development of the IMP´s activities. Tsai and Cutkosky proposed a model of representation and reasoning for geometric tolerances in project [9]. Hong and Chang [10] reported that, although many efforts have been made towards shaping the representation of geometric tolerances, the field of research is still relevant and active.

Zhao X. et al [11] say that the modelling across an enterprise is viable due to the advances in Internet technologies and increasing integration requirements from industry. In this context, these authors present a model representation of geometric tolerances stratified by level of compliance. The model has as its main objective to allow an unambiguous communication among different application domains in an enterprise, and thus, to promote interoperability. The model uses the widely applied ASME Y14.5M-1994 as its foundation layer, supplemented with additional geometric tolerances information defined by DMIS and STEP to form the corresponding conformance layers that support IMP.

The development and diffusion of CAD/CAM systems and IMP led to the release of ISO/IEC 14598 series [12]. These standards series established the general requirements for measurement methods and quality assessment of software products, and may also be used along the development and maintenance phases. Sharing the same terminology of ISO/IEC 9126 [13], this series is mainly concentrated in setting the concepts in the field of measurement and in the establishment of requirements, recommendations and guidelines for supporting the measurement process. The SQuaRE project [14], based on the standards of ISO/IEC 14958 and ISO / IEC 9126 series, has its main focus on convergence, consistency and unambiguous concepts to avoid conflicts and promote interoperability. ISO/IEC 25000:2001 [15], was presented as the final result of convergence project between the standards referred and contains an explanation of the transition between them and SQuaRE, also providing information on how to use the ISO/IEC 9126 and 14598 series, in their earlier form.

The automatic assessment of compliance of organizations, products and processes for ISO 9000 led Henry Kim [16] to propose a formal model of ontology for enterprise quality. In despite its general character, the model also contains a sub-ontology of terms and concepts of measurement.

García et al. [17] identifies similarities, differences and conflicts in terminology and presents a unified approach, with the main objective of contributing to the harmonization of different standards of measurement software. Subsequently, the authors of [18] propose a basic Software Measurement Ontology (SMO) aiming the harmonization of the different software measurement proposals and standards, by providing a coherent set of common concepts used in software measurement. This ontology is also aligned with the VIM, although semantic interoperability problems still remain to be solved [19, 20].

Recently, the development of ontologies, as promising techniques with capabilities to solve semantic issues, has been addressed by important companies, research and scientific community. Thus, each company is struggling to develop competencies at this ontological level, but inevitably different perspectives will lead to different final results, achieving different ontologies in the same business domain in the end [21]. One possible solution is to have a reference ontology for a specific domain that all the domain enterprises should share in their business, using a mediator in the interface between the reference and the proprietary.

3   MENTOR: Methodology for Reference Ontology Development

A reference ontology development may follow the MENTOR methodology, which is adopted in this work. Its main objective is to help an organization to adopt, reuse and/or build, a domain reference ontology, through several main steps as semantic comparisons, basic lexicon establishment, mappings among ontologies and other operations on knowledge based representations [2]. This methodology considered the state-of-the-art in terms of ontologies merging and concatenation (and applications and tools as well [22-25]) butt trends in the research field [26,27]. This method was fully detailed in recent authors' publication [2]. In a quick overview, Fig. 1 (left) depicts the state diagram of the lexicon settlement phase.

The terminology gathering step concerns to the process of collecting all relevant terms (action 1.2) in a previously defined specific domain (action 1.1). All the participants in the process should give their inputs. There is no rule from where the terms should come: they are related with the domain established. Tools for automatic extraction of domain related terms can be found, but there is always need of a human checking before closing the terms list to avoid missing any domain terms. All the terms provided from the contributors are acceptable in this step (action 1.2). Nobody has authority to erase other's participant term. The term should be collected with reference to the contributor in order that each contributor provides term's annotation in the next step (action 2.1).

In the Glossary Building step (step 2) a glossary in the domain is defined, starting with annotations attribution (action 2.1) to the terms collected, to be provided by each contributor. After having all the terms provided with annotations, it proceeds to the terms revision cycle (actions: 2.2; 2.3 and 2.4), in which a multi-language dictionary (action 2.0) may be used if the organization members don't use the same natural language. The dictionary would help translations to the language agreed for the reference ontology. The terms revision process can have semantic and syntactic cases of mismatches (action 2.3), recorded as a semantic mismatch for future mappings using the proposed Mediator Ontology (MO). After a careful revision of all the terms (action 2.2) with a successful agreement (action 2.4) in their meaning consolidation, the glossary is defined from the terminology list in the domain specified. Another output from this process is the semantic mismatch records (action 2.3): this is made using the Mediator Ontology.

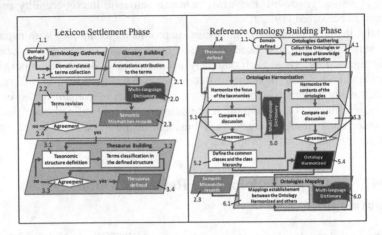

Fig. 1. MENTOR Phases and steps

The Thesaurus Building step (step 3) is composed by a cycle where firstly, the knowledge engineers define a taxonomic structure (action 3.1) from the glossary terms, establishing some as thesaurus node terms. Secondly, the other terms are classified to the right paths in the existent taxonomic structure (action 3.2). If there is an agreement (action 3.3) in the structure and in the terms classified, the thesaurus is defined (action 3.4). If not, the cycle starts again from the taxonomic structure definition (action 3.1). The thesaurus defined will enhance the ontology harmonization process in the next phase.

The Reference Ontology Building phase - Phase 2 (steps: 4; 5 and 6) is the phase where the reference ontology is built and the semantic mappings between the organizational ontologies and the reference one is established. Figure 3 (right part) describes this phase. The first step comprehends ontologies gathering (action 4.1) in the previously domain defined (action 1.1). Other types of knowledge representation can be used as input for the harmonization ontologies process together with the thesaurus defined (action 3.4) in the previous phase. The harmonization method for building ontologies, proposes the development of a single harmonized Ontology in two cycles (actions: 5.1 and 5.3) where first the structure is discussed until having agreement on it (action 5.1), resulting in the definition of the common classes and the class hierarchy (action 5.2), and then the same process for the ontology contents definition (action 5.3) is followed. From this process new semantic conflicts risk to arise. After agreement, the resolution could be recorded in the Mediator Ontology for further mapping establishments. With all the agreements accomplished, the harmonized ontology is finalized (action 5.4) together with the mapping tables (action

6.1), describing the ontological relationships between the harmonized ontology and each one of the individual ontologies through the use of the semantic mismatches records (action 2.3). Semantic difficulties related to the natural language of the potential users of the harmonized ontology are likely to happen. To assist on it, the ontology is complemented with a multi-language dictionary where a set of normalized tokens gives the reference to the corresponding concepts and definitions in different native languages (actions 5.0 and 6.0).

4   A Metrological Case Study

The competitive and demanding digital world of manufacturing business has led SMEs to consider the search for products in electronic format as an important method for parts selection and supply. Within networked enterprises, this is a major achievement, since new possibilities arise, like information retrieval, tasks automation and knowledge capture and re-use. Metrological stage is commonly an intermediary task, evaluating design conformance and manufacturing performance.

Considering the specific example of measuring a mechanical component, many product data models may be provided from different CAD applications, each one usually representing its specifications in different formats, with heterogeneous contents and classification. In common, most of them diverge from available advisory ISO standard designations or VIM vocabulary as described in previous section. Thus, the need to align applications and semantics to exchange products data, emerged as a priority to solve the dilemma. Fig. 2 describes the validating scenario, where a set of enterprises agreed to work together to supply a big common client with various mechanical parts which are built collaboratively.

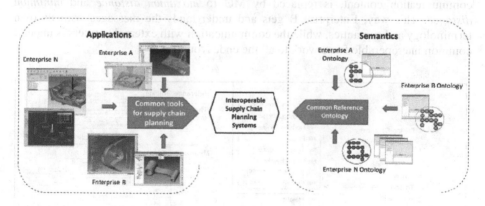

Fig. 2. Case study and validating scenario

The first step is to follow a methodology (e.g. VALTE - left side of Fig. 2), which will guide the applications evaluation activities [2], thus determining interoperability level.

In the second step, to establish a common semantic level it is developed a reference ontology to the endeavours that are working together (right part of Fig. 2). The

MENTOR methodology is used to develop such reference ontology. During the reference ontology building phase, it is produced a mediator ontology which records, and if necessary translates, all the semantic operations performed in this process. Fig. 3a shows a subset of the terms used by a Reference Ontology concerning the mechanical domain. In this example, when enterprise B receives a request of a "Hexagonal Bolt" with a "M16 diameter", the message is translated to a "hexagonal head Bolt" with a "Thread=Metric" with a "nominal diameter=16" assisted by terms included in the reference ontology. Although these mappings are relatively smooth to operate at Classes level, the complexity increases when going deeper in the established hierarchic semantics. Now, it was found that Enterprise B has two terms that Reference Ontology doesn't consider, which are Maximum Distance and Minimum Distance. It was found too that an Enterprise C, acting in the same domain of interest, has also the term Tolerance not considered in the reference ontology.

During the harmonization phase, domain engineers from both enterprises decided to use them as reference. Thus, the concepts Maximum Distance and Minimum Distance, used as a property, by enterprise B, may result in non-interoperability relatively to enterprise C. The same may occur due the term Tolerance used by the last one. Hence, three new additional concepts were created in reference ontology: Maximum Diameter, Minimum Diameter and Circularity. The first two defined in ISO 1101 Annex B as the maximum and minimum allowable variability in the process or characteristic in analysis; and the last concept defined by the difference between the radius of two concentric circles, whose value must be less or equal than the tolerance. MO logs all this operations, keeping the consistency between the ontologies. The example of Fig. 3b explains what happens in Enterprise B side when using the MO to translate messages according to reference ontology. The *maximum diameter* and *minimum diameter* reference concepts, which appear in the communication content, is replaced by MO to *maximum distance* and *minimum distance*. This way, Enterprise B gets and understands the messages with its own terminology and semantics, while the communication with external partners is under a common interoperable framework to all the endeavours.

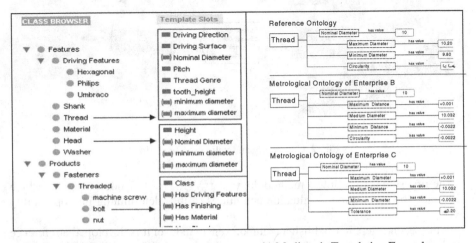

Fig. 3. a) Reference Ontology overview.   b) Mediator's Translation Example.

One immediate advantage of the use of MO, is that the method enables the computational systems of any enterprise to smoothly communicate with external parties as it was using the Reference Ontology. This is also the main motivation that enterprises may consider to adopt the Reference Ontology building process, independently of their domain expertise. To ensure the interoperability between the systems (i.e., the third step on this case study) Conformance Testing (CT) is applied to the exchanged files. Based on the defined methodology for CT, the architecture shown in the Fig. 4, is used to validate such files. The architecture was designed based in web-services, able to receive the files in XML format and checking them against the reference testing model using an Application Engine developed in JAVA, SAX, Schematron and XALAN.

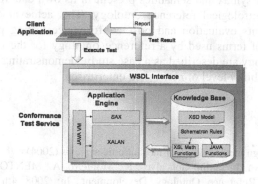

Fig. 4. Architecture for CT system validation [25]

Using the CT the user can check the files against the defined models, ensuring its correct implementation. The CT checks the XML against syntactic and semantic rules and sends back the detected errors enabling its correction. Following the same example as described before, if an attribute is defined that, in the "Thread" entity is named "nominal diameter" with a value 10, must be related to 10.20 and 9.80 (maximum and minimum diameters), and the system detects a relation which have "nominal diameter=10" with 10.25 as a *maximum diameter*, the CT with the semantic rules will detect the error reporting it to the user. With CT executed to its XML files, the next step is the application of the IC. To apply IC, the user will analyze and modify the test files, sent by the IC system, and send it back to evaluation. After checking all the files, defined in the ATS for IC, the user receives the confirmation that his system is interoperable. With all the ATS executed (CT ATS and IC ATS), the system´s validation can ensure that both systems are in conformance with the model defined and are interoperable with others systems of this type.

5   Conclusions

Within networked enterprises, agreement on a reference ontology is presented as a contribution to promote interoperability, herein focused in the field of metrology. The reference ontology appears to meet the needs of the globalization of markets and manufacturing systems, enabling communication with each partner operating in the same domain in a consistent and unequivocal way. The reference ontology aims to improve interoperability between the companies involved, respecting proprietary standard models for data representation.

Those models, in order to ensure full coherence and consistency of data representation, granted contributions by several researchers, as well as major international organizations for standardization in the area.

The paper proposes the use of the MENTOR methodology to reinforce computational systems communication in what Inspection terminology respects, within a set of manufacturing enterprises working together, to seamless communicate between each other. Through this methodology, they are enabled to understand each other using its own syntax and semantics present in its own data representation when supported by a metrological reference ontology. This achievement is assessed by software components evaluation and post conformance testing procedures. In this context, a subset of terms used by a reference ontology for the mechanical domain and related metrology are described as a case study, demonstrating the contribution to increase interoperability level of networked enterprises.

References

1. VDI 2206: Design methodology for mechatronic systems (2004)
2. Sarraipa, J., Silva, J., Jardim-Goncalves, R., Monteiro, A.: MENTOR – A Methodology for Enterprise Reference Ontology Development. In: 2008 4th International IEEE Conference on Intelligent Systems (2008)
3. Pereira, P.H., Hocken, R.J.: Characterization and compensation of dynamic errors of a scanning coordinate measuring machine. Precision Engineering (2006)
4. http://www.inmetro.gov.br/metcientifica/vim/vimGum.asp
5. Abran, A., Sellami, A.: Initial modelling of the measurement concepts in the ISO vocabulary of terms in metrology. In: Proc. of IWSM 2002, Magdeburg, Germany (2002)
6. Requicha, A.A.G., Chan, S.C.: Representation of geometric features, tolerances, and attributes in solid models based on constructive geometry. IEEE Journal of Robotics and Automation RA-2(3), 156–166 (1986)
7. Turner, J.U.: Relative positioning of parts in assembly using mathematical programming. Computer-Aided Design 22(7), 394–400 (1990)
8. Feng, S.C.: A dimensional inspection planning activity model. Journal of Engineering Design and Automation 2(4), 253–267 (1996); Special issue on Tolerance and Metrology for Precision Manufacturing
9. Tsai, J.C., Cutkosky, M.R.: Representation and reasoning of geometric tolerances in design. Cambridge Journals 11(04) (1997), http://journals.cambridge.org/action/displayAbstract?fromPage=online&aid=4203944
10. Hong, Y.S., Chang, T.-C.: A comprehensive review of tolerancing research. International Journal of Production Research 40(11), 2425–2460 (2002)
11. Zhao, X., Pasupathy, T.K., Wilhelm, R.: Modeling and representation of geometric tolerances information in integrated measurement processes. Journal Computers in Industry 57(4), 319–330 (2006)

12. ISO/IEC, ISO/IEC 14598:2001: Software Engineering - Product Evaluation. International Standards Organization, Genova, Switzerland (2001)
13. ISO/IEC, ISO/IEC 9126:2001: Software Engineering - Product Quality. International Standards Organization, Genova, Switzerland (2001)
14. Azuma, M.: SQuaRE: The next generation of the ISO/IEC 9126 and 14598 International Standards series on software product quality. In: Proc. of European Software Control and Metrics (ESCOM) , London, England (April 2001)
15. ISO/IEC, ISO/IEC 25000:2005: Software engineering — Software product Quality Requirements and Evaluation (SQuaRE) — Guide to SQuaRE. International Standards Organization, Genova, Switzerland (2001)
16. Kim, H.M.: Representing and Reasoning about Quality using Enterprise Models, PhD thesis, Dept. Mechanical and Industrial Engineering, University of Toronto, Canada (1999)
17. García, F., Bertoa, M.F., Calero, C., Vallecillo, A., Ruiz, F., Piatinni, M., Genero, M.: Towards a Consistent Terminology for Software Measurement. Information and Software Technology (June 27, 2005)
18. García, F., Bertoa, M.F., Calero, C., Vallecillo, A., Ruiz, F., Piatinni, M., Genero, M.: Efective Use of Ontologies in Software Measurement. The Knowledge Engineering Review (2008)
19. Drejer, A., Gudmundsson, A.: Exploring the concept of multiple product development via an action research project. Integrated Manufacturing Systems 14(3), 208–220 (2003)
20. Silva, J.P.M.A., Jardim-Goncalves, R., Monteiro, A.C., Steiger-Garcao, A.: Make the most of interoperability along PLC stages: A framework based on multilevel integration, DETC 2004-57733, Salt Lake City, Utah, USA (September 2004)
21. Jardim-Goncalves, R., Sarraipa, J., Agostinho, C., Panetto, H.: Knowledge Framework for Intelligent Manufacturing Systems. International Journal of Intelligent Manufacturing (2009)
22. Fernandez, M., Gomez-Perez, A., Juristo, N.: METHONTOLOGY: From Ontological Art Towards Ontological Engineering. In: Symposium on Ontological Engineering of AAAI, Stanford, California, pp. 33–40 (1997)
23. Stumme, G., Madche, A.: FCA-Merge: Bottom-up merging of ontologies. In: 7th Intl. Conf. on Artificial Intelligence (IJCAI 2001), Seattle, WA, pp. 225–230 (2001)
24. Noy, N.F., Musen, M.A.: The PROMPT Suite: Interactive Tools for Ontology Merging and Mapping. International Journal of Human-Computer Studies 59(6), 983–1024 (2003)
25. Gangemi, A., Pisanelli, D.M., Steve, G.: An Overview of the ONIONS Project: Applying Ontologies to the Integration of Medical Terminologies. Data & Knowledge Engineering 31, 183–220 (1999)
26. Uschold, M., King, M.: Towards a methodology for building ontologies. In: Proceedings IJCAI 1995 Workshop on Basic Ontological Issues in Knowledge Sharing, Montreal, Canada (1995)
27. De Nicola, A., Missikoff, M., Navigli, R.: A Proposal for a Unified Process for Ontology Building: UPON. In: Andersen, K.V., Debenham, J., Wagner, R. (eds.) DEXA 2005. LNCS, vol. 3588, pp. 655–664. Springer, Heidelberg (2005)

Smart Communities and Networked Organizations

Steven L. Goldman[*]

Departments of Philosophy and History, Lehigh University,
15 University Drive, Bethlehem PA 18015, USA
slg2@lehigh.edu

Abstract. The reduction in human interaction costs enabled by social computing technologies has created opportunities for companies to reduce the cost of growth and of innovation both by getting much more value out of their own personnel and by using people they do not employ to create value for them, either gratis, or for a fee to be paid only after the value is created. Recognition of these opportunities is driving business reorganization by "early adopter" companies pursuing the benefits to be derived from business applications of social computing. These benefits are anchored in the growing centrality to wealth creation of continuous innovation. Continuous innovation, in turn, is critically dependent on tacit interactions among people, that is, on interactions that provide access to implicit, as well as explicit, knowledge, information, experience and expertise possessed by possibly very large numbers of people, who may be widely distributed, organizationally, and even globally.

Keywords: Smart communities, agility, social computing, tacit interactions.

1   Introduction

Since the turn of the 21st century, new kinds of self-organizing online communities – among them, Napster, MySpace, Facebook, Flickr, YouTube, the World of Warcraft, Second Life, Twitter and the blogosphere -- have grown with startling rapidity. These communities have proven to be a rich source of tacit interactions, that is, interactions that provide access to implicit, as well as explicit, knowledge, information, experience and expertise, possessed by widely distributed individuals [Libert and Spector, 2008]. The challenge to companies is to develop business applications of opportunistically mobilized online communities that can exploit tacit interactions to nurture wealth creation for the mobilizing companies [Shuen, 2008]. There have always been communities, of course, and they are always valuable to their members. Social computing, however, is enabling the mobilization of new kinds of business value-creation communities, "smart communities", that are the cornerstone of an emerging second-generation agile business paradigm.

Smart communities aggregate and integrate tacit interactions on behalf of wealth creation for companies that mobilize them. Though they can take many forms, all

---

[*] This essay is based on an earlier collaboration with Lehigh University Professors Roger N. Nagel and Brian Davison of the Computer Science and Engineering Department.

G.D. Putnik and M.M. Cruz-Cunha (Eds.): ViNOrg 2011, CCIS 248, pp. 304–315, 2012.

allow companies to exploit human and physical resources not owned by them and/or to utilize resources they do own far more effectively than now. Smart communities are intrinsically boundaryless organizationally, but they *are* bounded [Fung et al, 2008]. Their boundaries are determined by the goal for the sake of which each community is mobilized and supported. The goal, in turn, determines which type of community to mobilize, the resources it will need, and the form of its facilitation. This article provides brief descriptions of how some companies are already using smart communities to create value. It also explores some of the questions that companies must address if they are to harvest the value latent in smart communities by adopting new business strategies, models, and operations.

2   Introducing Smart Communities

Competitive pressures in the 1990s, and the utilization of new, digital, information and communication technologies, forced a recognition of how *much* people mattered to a company's bottom line. They also revealed how much potential for greater profitability, growth and innovation remained untapped in their workforces because of traditional forms of business organization and management that inhibited collaboration by inhibiting open information sharing [Goldman et al, 1995]. While new technologies *enabled* collaboration, the way that businesses were organized did not always *allow* it [Lencioni, 2006; Ackoff et al, 2006].

For companies that reorganized to facilitate collaboration, work evolved from individuals working within managerial "silos" to people working collaboratively in cross-functional internal teams, in cross-enterprise teams, and in business networks [Shuman et al, 2001]. Sharing knowledge and information in these ways reduced the costs of some existing processes, but it also stimulated the invention of new business strategies, new business models, and new markets for new kinds of high value goods and services. Legacy organizational problems, however, and limitations of the first generation of digital collaboration technologies, made the transition to the original conceptualization of an agile business paradigm difficult for many established enterprises [Goldman et al, 1995; Preiss et al, 1996].

The recent introduction of more powerful, more usable, and much lower cost collaboration technologies, collectively called social computing technologies, is making this transition easier, cheaper, and more effective, thus more available to many more companies [Scoble and Israel, 2006]. At the same time, intensive global collaborative work is being driven by factors identified in Friedman's *The World is Flat* [Friedman, 2006]. These factors make collaboration not only intrinsically desirable, but a necessity if a company is to remain competitive. Concurrently, the continuing evolution of the Internet as a platform for collaborative business applications has made the routine mobilization of smart communities practical.

The distinctiveness of smart communities compared to cross-functional teams and networks is that the members of smart communities do not need to be known to one another, or to management, in advance of the community's mobilization. Smart communities can be self-organizing in response to management-set objectives, and they have a participation lifetime determined by those objectives. The convergence of Enterprise 2.0/Web 2.0 technologies and innovative social computing technologies allows people to share knowledge, know-how, expertise and experience in powerful new ways [Chesbrough, 2005; Chesbrough, 2006]. In retrospect, the first "wave" of what would come to be called social computing hit businesses in the 1990s. It included e-mail, digital calendar keeping and group scheduling, discussion forums, and first generation groupware. A following second wave included early virtual collaborative workspaces and Web conferencing, instant messaging, enterprise portals, and personal Web sites. The third wave is proving the most powerful of all. It includes blogs, wikis, mashups, file sharing, RSS feeds, texting, Twitter, social networking and profiles, social bookmarking, ratings and comments, virtual environments, and far more sophisticated collaborative workspaces and Web conferencing [Tapscott, 2006; Howe, 2008].

Exploiting this new, digitally supercharged, interaction-intensive environment requires harnessing to a concrete business problem the specific knowledge, experience, and expertise distributed among typically unrelated and previously unidentified individuals. Prior to being connected together in a smart community, its members would be unaware of the problem the community was being asked to solve, and unaware that they possessed knowledge relevant to solving it. That problem, furthermore, might be loosely formulated and the means for reaching it left unspecified. The precise specification of both means and ends thus become emergent properties of the interactivity that makes up a smart community.

2.1   Operational Smart Communities

The objective of any smart community is the creation of new value for a company out of the focused, collective engagement of it's self-selected members, who may work for that company or may not. Smart communities thus extend the concept of smart business networks, whose members, by contrast, are carefully selected in advance for their competence in executing precisely specified means to achieve well-defined goals [Goldman et al, 2009; Janneck et al, 2008; Nagel et al, 2004]. Established early adopter firms, among them Cisco, Procter and Gamble, and IBM, and a host of younger companies like eBay and Amazon, Google and InnoCentive, are proving the substantial benefits that flow from smart communities-based strategies, processes, and products. They also reflect alternative approaches to mobilizing smart communities [Ogle, 2007].

2.2   Tournament-Style Innovation Communities

The Goldcorp, Navteq, and Netflix stories are by now well-known illustrations of the power of smart communities to create value via open innovation processes. The Goldcorp Challenge, with prize money totaling roughly half a million dollars, was announced in 2000 by Goldcorp CEO Rob McEwen. McEwen posted the company's previously highly proprietary geological data on its Web site and invited all comers to study the data and predict where on Goldcorp's land the company was likely to find new sources of gold. McEwen knew nothing about gold mining when he took over the moribund gold producer, but he was inspired by a lecture on the open source software process behind Linux to open the Goldcorp site identification process to the public. His Challenge quickly generated recommendations to dig in 110 locations, 55 of which had not previously been identified by Goldcorp's own geologists, and 80% of these new locations yielded a total of 8 million ounces of gold. As a result, Goldcorp was transformed into a major gold mining company, with steadily increasing production from mines in North, Central and South America.

One lesson to be learned from the Goldcorp initiative is that promiscuous open communities -- promiscuous because anyone can join, without prior certification or credentialing -- with appropriate motivation and complemented by people with the relevant expertise, in this case Goldcorp's own geologists, can shortcut the innovation process, and at lower cost than traditional approaches to innovation. The self-organized smart community that Goldcorp mobilized was built on a hub and spoke model: the members studied the data and responded to Goldcorp with their recommendations. The Navteq and Netflix Challenges illustrate variations on this theme.

In 2003, Navteq, then an independent producer of digital map data, now owned by Nokia, announced the Navteq Challenge. This continues as an annual event in which Navteq distributes millions of dollars in cash, licensing agreements, and equipment to participants who invent location-enabled applications based on digital map and dynamic positioning data for cell phones and other handheld wireless devices. Like Goldcorp, Navteq mobilized an open community, in the sense of a community whose members were not known to Navteq management in advance. Unlike Goldcorp, however, it was not a promiscuous community. Challenge candidates had to establish to Navteq's satisfaction that they were plausibly competent to come up with new applications in order to receive contest materials.

In effect, Navteq's prize money precipitated a smart community of software innovators focused on creating applications that would add to Navteq's revenues. Some members of this community are established software developers, but participation is also, and importantly, open to competent newcomers with clever ideas. Navteq's mobilization of a smart community also differs from Goldcorp's in being renewed annually and in using the Navteq Challenge to leverage Navteq's position in an ecosystem of symbiotically related hardware and software companies offering products and services keyed to global positioning data. Navteq thus used a smart community of its own to enhance the value of the web of companies to which it belongs, on a win-win basis.

The Goldcorp and Navteq Challenges posed loosely specified goals: find gold; create innovative GPS data applications. The Netflix Prize, by contrast, specified a precise goal and a limited timeframe in which to achieve it. In October 2006, Netflix announced a $1 million prize for anyone who, by October 2011, could produce an algorithm for predicting the success of film recommendations to customers, based on each customer's past and present choices, that was at least 10% more successful than Netflix's in-house algorithm, called Cinematch. In the interim, Netflix awarded a $50,000 Progress Prize each year to any contestant who beat the previous year's best by at least 1%. The 2007 Progress Prize winner, for example, was the KorBell team, whose algorithm was 8.43% better than Cinematch-based recommendations.

By September 2008, over 39,000 contestants from 179 countries, organized into 3739 teams, had submitted over 30,000 valid programs and the top ten teams for 2008 were between 8.44 and 9.15% more successful than Cinematch. In 2009, two years ahead of schedule, the full prize was awarded to an enhanced Bellkor Pragmatic

Chaos team, who submitted their winning algorithm just twenty minutes ahead of an algorithm by The Ensemble team that also beat Cinematch by more than 10%.

The Netflix Prize community, like Goldcorp's, was promiscuous, but Netflix posed a very specific problem with very specific requirements for an acceptable solution: it had to be at least 10% more accurate in a company-generated test case than the Netflix algorithm, it had to be published in an open forum, and the publication had to include a natural language explanation of how the algorithm worked. While opening the community to all comers, Netflix management wanted to be sure that the winning algorithm was not a fluke. Subjecting the algorithm to public scrutiny -- including scrutiny by any interested members of the computing science community and members of the losing teams looking for a flaw – is yet another way of mobilizing a smart community on behalf of a company's own interests. In this case, a self-motivated solution-checking smart community formed by itself that needed no financial incentive at all to do the job required by Netflix!

2.3   A Facilitated Innovation Community

InnoCentive was founded in 2001 as the world's first open innovation community marketplace, spun off from an internal Eli Lilly exercise in community-style open innovation. Today, InnoCentive is a dynamic, evolving, for-profit innovation broker, selling both internal and external community mobilization services to its client companies. InnoCentive adds extra value for its clients by offering them the services of its own community of full-time consulting engineers and scientists who can help clients formulate problems and filter submitted solutions. The major difference between InnoCentive's use of community and the preceding instances is that the problems to be solved are not InnoCentive's problems.

2.4   Internal Innovation Communities

Ace Hardware management initiated a network linking 300 dealers for the more efficient transfer of product experience and business information between and among the company and those 300 dealers. As they did so, however, and at the instigation of Ace retail hardware store owners themselves, the network evolved into a workplace smart community of over 5000 Ace Hardware retail stores. This expanded community allowed retail store personnel to post problems they were having, exchange ideas and experiences, and bring the collective wisdom of thousands of people to bear on problems from the corporate level down to those of a local store. The resulting smart community led to increases in store sales that were much greater than the cost of the IT resources needed to support this community.

Bell Canada initiated a pilot study of how Social Network Analysis could be used to create internal workplace communities. Fourteen low- to middle-managers, selected for their commitment, passion and competitiveness, were asked to identify the co-workers they felt worked to the standards they set for themselves. The result was a 2500-member internal best practices community across Bell Canada sites that led to major increases in employee and customer satisfaction ratings. Best Buy created a similar smart workplace community, called Blue Shirt Nation, for its employees, who spontaneously responded by using the resource to share experience, advice, successes and failures, boosting morale and store sales.

In 2005, Intel implemented a company-wide smart community initiative developed on his own by employee Josh Bancroft to capture and share personnel experience and expertise. Three years later, on a completely voluntary basis, the resulting Intelpedia had over 20,000 pages, was growing at the rate of 800 new pages a month, and registered 200,000 views per day, company wide. All of these figures are much higher today. Advanced Micro Devices, British Petroleum (BP), Cisco and IBM are among scores of companies that are using immersive 3-D virtual environments as platforms for recruiting, training, disseminating information to employees, running simulations, and for interactive virtual co-location of globally distributed members of agile collaboration teams.

In addition to such smart internal communities, a growing number of organizations are using virtual reality environments to create external communities that complement internal ones. Universities are creating presences on Second Life, primarily for purposes of recruiting, but some are also using these virtual facilities for teaching purposes. Other companies, among them Peugeot and Toyota, are using Second Life to engage customers in product design, development and evolution.

2.5   Mixed Internal-External Innovation Communities

In 2000, Procter and Gamble's CEO A.G. Lafley committed the company to an open innovation model, supplementing P&G's internal R&D capability with its staff of 7500. By 2006, the community of outsiders that it invited to propose new products, or solutions to production problems, was responsible for more than a third of all new P&G products and for some 80% of products that were commercial successes. P&G's Web home page reveals how fully integrated this model is into its routine operations and corporate management has become an evangelist for open community approaches to innovation. In addition, P&G supports VocalPoint -- a managed online community of 500,000 mothers who spread information by (digital) word of mouth on products in relevant P&G markets -- as well as Tremor, a community of 250,000 teenagers who post their experiences with competitor products, P&G products, and teen trends in markets of interest to P&G. Learning to manage these communities has itself led to a new revenue stream for P&G, which now sells customer-based, word of mouth marketing services to other companies.

One P&G lesson is the importance of the CEO in driving down into the organization the inescapability of a commitment to a community-based strategy. Lafley, like Rob McEwen, inherited a major in-house R&D capability with an expectation that it *would* be invented here, but both made opening the innovation process to a community of strangers stick. Second, the open community approach to innovation was integrated into the existing Procter and Gamble R&D capability, it did not displace it. Third, P&G's experience teaches that an open community whose members are unknown, self-selected, and change unpredictably can be a stable platform for sustained growth even for a very large corporation.

Lego's Mindstorms product family mobilized a customer-based open community to drive product development, applications and innovation. SAP's Ecosystem is yet another variation of this theme, helping customers find the distributed expertise they need to solve problems, grow, innovate, and form partnerships and networks. What generates growth for SAP customers generates growth for SAP in the process. SugarCRM is a leading customer relations management software package that was developed by its user community and offered free over the Internet, with millions of downloads. Users use the software, announce bugs and post repairs, develop extensions, all for the good of the community, and to the benefit of the company. The paradigm of this was Linux, of course, which has steadily grown to become a major force in corporate computing and, for a "free" operating system, has spawned a highly profitable ecosystem of companies engaged in Linux development, implementation, and application that collectively generate billions of dollars a year in revenues.

2.6   Internal *and* External Innovation Communities

Google has been a smart community-intensive company from the start, treating its employees as a pool of talent to be continually reconfigured to create new value. The company ideal is for that talent to be routinely self-configuring in response to new ideas and challenges, and to that end personnel are allotted 20% of their time for pursuing new solutions to existing problems or new kinds of Google products and services. Gmail, Google Earth, Google Maps, Orkut, Google News and Adsense are some of the products of this "free thinking" time for personnel. New ideas are routinely posted to Google's elaborate intranet, called MOMA, for open evaluation and ranking, with a high ranking guaranteeing serious managerial attention [Stross, 2008].

All Google personnel are required to maintain highly detailed, and self-critical, professional profiles, updated weekly on OKR (Objectives and Key Results) forms. In addition to the usual background education and pre-Google experience, these profiles must include all past and current work experience at Google, along with a self-evaluation of that individual's contributions to the projects they have worked on, a description of projects they would like to work on, and identification of near and middle-term goals. The profiles are open to the entire Google community. To assure that personnel maintain their profiles, OKRs are the sole basis for employee performance evaluation by management.

Google, as well as Amazon (especially its Amazon Web Services division) and eBay, thrive on their ability to precipitate latent communities into actual ones in order to use them as platforms for revenue-generating services. Cisco and IBM, along with Microsoft, H-P, Oracle, and a rapidly growing number of established and start-up companies are pursuing business strategies based on selling smart community-mobilization tools and consulting services to other companies. They are also integrating smart communities into their own operations.

Like Navteq, but on a much larger scale, Cisco's strategy is to leverage its position in a global ecosystem of Internet users to create platforms for Cisco's own growth. The market space it has carved out is as a critical enabler of mobilizing smart communities for its clients by making inter-operability routine, from its packet switches to its communication solution services and its Internet-based collaboration tools. To that end, Cisco acquired WebEx to extend, and integrate, its VoIP and Internet video conferencing capabilities into TelePresence. Cisco acquired PostPath, an email software developer, and Jabber, a seller of secure commercial messaging solutions, aiming at providing an open, unified communications platform for smart community-supporting corporate and inter-corporate messaging services, a platform that will be compatible with existing choices of messaging software from Google, AIM, Microsoft, and Yahoo; hence the focus on interoperability.

Cisco's promotion of community mobilization products and services for others is complemented by its own internal smart community platform, called I-Zone, or Idea Zone, within its Emerging Technologies Group. This is an open internal community in which anyone can propose ideas for new products, markets or processes, and have them critiqued by other members of the community for further development. Since 2007 Cisco has supported an I-Prize competition whose finalists get to develop full-fledged business models for funding by Cisco as new ventures. IBM's InnovationJam similarly stimulates the formation of a smart community aimed at identifying the ten highest ranked proposals for new IBM business ventures [Baker, 2008].

IBM, too, is committed to selling smart communities-based collaboration tools and services and has similarly positioned itself as a provider of community mobilization infrastructure products. Closed systems, IBM argues, 'interfere with business agility'. Silo-like, closed information systems need to give way to unified information solutions. This is made possible by IBM-provided tools for creating internal and external smart communities that allow their members to instantly, easily and securely share knowledge and expertise. Such IBM products as Lotus Connections, UC2 (unified collaboration and communication), Jazz (collaborative software development), FileNet Team Collaboration Manager, and PassItOn (for retaining the knowledge of retiring personnel) show IBM's commitment to positioning itself in this market.

Apple's iPod, iPhone and iPad exemplify a strategy of mobilizing user communities around a product that then serves as a platform for delivering a stream of revenue-generating content and services created by collateral communities of providers. Apple is positioned at the hub of continually evolving complementary user and content provider communities who generate wealth for Apple as they provide value to one another. The success of this strategy is reflected in the billions of downloads of applications and a growing range of content from Apple's Web site, and of course in the awesome revenues that flow into Apple's coffers.

Among a growing number of revenue generating web service products, Amazon's Mechanical Turk is particularly illustrative of a community mobilization-based business model. Mechanical Turk is a globally open marketplace in which Workers can perform tasks for Requesters, with Amazon receiving a percentage of the fee. Mechanical Turk evolved into a commercial product for Amazon out of an internal need: eliminating duplicate Web pages on Amazon's own sites. Amazon CEO Jeff Bezos' decision to open the company's vast databases of customers and products to third party developers has made this information a platform for well over a thousand merchants, from whose profitable use of these databases Amazon derives substantial revenues.

Angie's List and Craigslist are highly profitable businesses based on online communities, in both cases inspired early on by the selfless help phenomenon: people freely offering to share their own experiences with strangers having related problems. Craigslist, which boasts over 12 *billion* page views a month, charges a fee for job listings and generates revenues from advertising, but allows free merchandise sale listings. Angie's List, which focuses on home repair service contractors and has expanded to include health care providers, generates its revenues from a membership fee. Both Lists provide tools for members to share experience, advice, and recommendations; and people freely display the spirit that makes smart communities work, including scores of active special interest communities comprised of past, present, and potential clients.

Threadless Tees and Brewtopia are additional examples of profitable companies that exist solely because of having created user communities that develop their products for them for their own gratification at no direct cost to the companies. Threadless Tees sells t-shirts designed by people who visit its Web site. Threadless Tees provides the design software and visitors can create any design they like. All designs are posted on the Web site where viewers can rank them and order them, with popular designs selling many thousands of copies, all at no design or marketing cost to Threadless Tees. Its community does it all! Brewtopia is an Australian seller of custom-branded beer, water and wine. It began with a customer community-generated beer recipe that became a commercial success and word of mouth propelled the company to grow and Brewtopia to prosper.

2.7   Unleashing Tacit Interactions

Whatever the approach to smart communities, maximizing tacit interactions, interactions that stimulate people to share knowledge, know-how, expertise or experience with others "promiscuously", is the goal. But the ability to use social computing, information synthesis and knowledge management tools to achieve this goal does not come naturally to traditional organizations. There is a "legacy" problem, inherited from the original industrial corporations – vertically integrated, centrally administered, hierarchically organized -- of silo-like organizational structures that inhibit even open internal communities [Raymond, 1999; Li and Bernoff, 2008]. There is also the legacy value of solving an organization's problems by using the organization's own resources, which inhibits mobilizing external communities, except as a last resort, implying an admission of failure or defeat.

Leveraging tacit interactions by means of smart communities is proving to be a powerful source of value creation and hence of competitive advantage. It is rapidly becoming a differentiation factor among companies in explicitly knowledge-based industries, in which it is obvious that the more knowledge available the better, but also in industries that seem less knowledge-intensive, like mining and manufacturing. In all cases, however, gaining access to previously untapped/unavailable knowledge, know-how and experience can create value, as the sample illustrations above reveal. In a smart community-based business environment, knowledge, relationship management, and information integration technologies are sources of competitive advantage. Together, they accelerate innovation, optimize resource utilization, and dramatically reduce concept-to-cash time [Shirky, 2008].

These same community-enabling capabilities also allow companies large and small to change the business ecosystems within which they compete, and even to create new ecosystems by changing their relationships to the companies in their ecosystem or changing the companies to which they are related. One illustration of this strategy was Apple's creation of a legal music distribution system via the coupling of iTunes to its family of iPods. The iPod went from competing against other music players as a piece of hardware in the mp3 music player ecosystem, to dominating a new music download ecosystem, one that has generated billions of dollars in revenues for Apple. Apple then extended this to relationships with film and TV content owners and most recently to relationships with book publishers in order to make the iPad competitive with Amazon's kindle.

The role of senior management in creating an organizational culture of mutual cooperation based on sharing knowledge an experience is twofold. Senior management sets the rules by which the organization operates -- IBM, Apple, Google, Bloomberg, are widely publicized examples – and these rules are reinforced by the metrics employed to incentivize, evaluate and reward personnel. If a cooperative and collaborative work ethic is not already the norm in an organization, if sharing and trust are not perceived as intrinsically valuable, they will not become the norm and they will not be valued unless the existing evaluation and reward metrics are changed. Second, senior management, having planted the seeds for a culture of mutual cooperation, must nurture them by providing the resources necessary for communities to flourish; and management must channel sharing and trust, cooperation and collaboration so that they accomplish management approved objectives that benefit the organization and its bottom line [Livingston and Solis, 2007].

3   Conclusion

A new kind of enterprise is emerging whose strategies and business models are centered in the first resort on mobilizing and carefully managing an evolving portfolio of smart communities. Smart communities-based business strategies are a necessary condition of competitiveness today because the increasingly intensive globalization of commerce puts a premium on knowledge, know-how and experience as applied to innovation and to the optimal execution of business processes. Not only is it increasingly difficult for one company, however large, to do it all, no one company today *is* doing it all!

The common denominator of smart communities of whatever kind is that their value lies in their potential for unanticipated, emergent, outcomes. Smart communities excel at solving problems that are loosely specified, and at creating solutions to problems that have not been specified in advance at all. They excel, in other words, at innovation and at creative solutions to problems. The justification for expending resources and effort on behalf of mobilizing smart communities is the promise that their agility will unleash positive emergent outcomes, outcomes whose benefits will far outweigh the expended resources and effort.

The "engine" of the positive emergent outcomes produced by smart communities is the tacit interactions that foster among all community members. To be smart, a community must be an interactive collaborative workspace in which *everyone* perceives themselves to be an actual or potential knowledge worker, not just individuals with formal credentials as such. That is, everyone participating in a smart community must feel stimulated to contribute to the community's goal whatever relevant knowledge, know-how, experience or expertise they possess [Srowiecki, 2004; Gloor, 2006].

In the mass production paradigm, the "clock speed" of knowledge, information and marketplace change was slow enough for companies to accommodate these changes by building factories that reduced unit production cost to the lowest possible level. In the 1990s, agility was a response to unprecedented increases in the clock speed of information, knowledge and marketplace change, especially as driven by the relentless accumulation of innovations in information, communication and production technologies [Goldman et al, 1995]. Today, smart communities are a means of more easily gaining access to much more of the knowledge and experience possessed by individuals by opening business processes and objectives to large numbers of people [Slowinski, 2005]. What people know that could be valuable to solving a particular problem is often tacit, unarticulated and too diffuse to use. Currently available social networking technologies are to such tacit knowledge what an imaginary technology would be to concentrating diffusely distributed deposits of gold or platinum or oil. Suddenly, what was desirable and very valuable but uneconomical, becomes available.

References

1. Ackoff, R.L., Magidson, J., Addison, H.J.: Idealized Design: Creating an Organization's Future. Wharton School Publishing, Upper Saddle River (2006)
2. Baker, S.: The Numerati. Houghton Mifflin, New York (2008)
3. Chesbrough, H.: Open Innovation: The New Imperative for Creating and Profiting from Technology. Harvard Business School, Cambridge (2005)
4. Chesbrough, H.: Open Business Models: How to thrive in the New Innovation Landscape. Harvard Business School, Cambridge (2006)
5. Friedman, T.L.: The World is Flat, Release 3.0. Farrar, Strauss and Giroux, New York (2006)
6. Fung, V.K., Fung, W.K., Wind, Y.: Competing in A Flat World: Building Enterprises for A Borderless World. Wharton School Publishing, Upper Saddle River (2008)
7. Gloor, P.A.: Swarm Creativity. Oxford University Press, New York (2006)
8. Goldman, S.L., Nagel, R.N., Preiss, K.P.: Agile Competitors and Virtual Organizations. Van Nostrand Reinhardt, New York (1995)
9. Goldman, S.L., Nagel, R.N., Davison, B.D., Schmid, P.S.: Next Generation Agility: Smart Business Networks and Smart Communities. In: Vervest, P.H.M., van Liere, D.W., Zheng, L. (eds.) The Network Experience. Springer, New York (2009)
10. Howe, J.: Crowdsourcing. Crown Business, New York (2008)
11. Janneck, C., Nagel, R.N., Schmid, P.D., Jarret, D.R., Connolly, M.L., Moll, M.A.: Smart Business Networks: Core Concepts and Characteristics. In: Vervest, P.H.M., van Hech, E., Preiss, K.P. (eds.) Smart Business Networking. Erasmus University, Rotterdam (2008)
12. Lencioni, P.M.: Silos, Politics and Turf Wars. Jossey-Bass, San Francisco (2006)
13. Li, C., Bernoff, J.: Groundswell: Winning in a world Transformed by Social Technologies. Harvard Business School, Cambridge (2008)
14. Libert, B., Spector, J.: We Are Smarter Than Me. Wharton School Publishing, Upper Saddle River (2008)
15. Livingston, G., Solis, B.: Now Is Gone - A Primer on New Media for Executives and Entrepreneurs. Bartleby Press, Savage (2007)
16. Nagel, R.N., Walters, J.P., Gurevich, G., Schmid, P.D.: Smart Business Networks Enable Strategic Opportunities Not Found in Traditional Business Networking. In: Vervest, P.H.M., van Hech, E., Preiss, K.P., Pau, L.-F. (eds.) Smart Business Networks. Springer, New York (2004)

17. Ogle, R.: Smart World: Breakthrough Creativity and The New Science of Ideas. Harvard Business School, Cambridge (2007)
18. Preiss, K.P., Nagel, R.N., Goldman, S.L.: Cooperate to Compete. Van Nostrand Reinhardt, New York (1996)
19. Raymond, E.S.: The Cathedral and the Bazaar. O'Reilly, Cambridge (1999)
20. Scoble, R., Israel, S.: Naked Conversations: How Blogs are Changing the Way Businesses Talk with Customers. John Wiley, Hoboken (2006)
21. Shirky, C.: Here Comes Everybody: The Power of Organizing without Organizations. Penguin Press, NY (2008)
22. Shuen, A.: Web 2.0: A Strategy Guide. O'Reilly Media, Inc., Sebastopol (2008)
23. Shuman, J., Twombly, J., Rottenberg, D.: Collaborative Communities: Partnering for Profit in The Networked Economy. Dearborn Trade, Dearborn (2001)
24. Slowinski, G.: Reinventing Corporate Growth. Alliance Management Group Inc., Gladstone (2005)
25. Stross, R.: Planet Google-One Company's Audacious Plan to Organize Everything We Know. Free Press, San Francisco (2008)
26. Surowiecki, J.: The Wisdom of Crowds. Random House, New York (2004)
27. Tapscott, D., Williams, A.D.: Wikinomics: How Mass Collaboration Changes Everything. Penguin, New York (2006)

A Platform for Agile Virtual Enterprise Synthesis

António Arrais-Castro, Maria Leonilde R. Varela, and Goran D. Putnik

Department of Production and Systems, School of Engineering, University of Minho,
Azurém Campus, 4800-058 Guimarães, Portugal
arraiscastro@gmail.com, {leonilde,putnikgd}@dps.uminho.pt

Abstract. Today, competitive pressures require companies to be very fast in introducing new products, to have short production lead times to manufacture and deliver products to customers and to be permanently aligned with the market. Product life-cycles tend to shorten. Even the dynamically reconfigurable global networked structures corresponding to the recent approach of the Agile/ Virtual Enterprise (A/VE) organizational model tend to last a shorter time while becoming more dynamic in their structural reconfiguration. The ability of fast reconfigurability is a requirement that the enterprises corresponding to this A/VE model must satisfy to assure a permanent alignment of the network with the market as highlighted in the paper. The paper defines and discusses the main concepts and features concerning a proposed platform for A/VE synthesis, based on reconfiguration dynamics to help quantify, analyze and manage A/VE, within the context of Ubiquitous Manufacturing System.

Keywords: Platform, Agile/ Virtual Enterprise synthesis and reconfigurability, Ubiquitous Manufacturing System.

1   Introduction

Agile/ Virtual Enterprises (A/VE) play a permanently growing important role in the today's global market scenario, therefore it is becoming increasingly more emergent to be able to easily and dynamically be able to configure and re-configure an Agile/ Virtual Enterprise (A/VE), in terms of collaborative members, in order to maintain updated existing manufacturing networks and, therefore, enable to better support managing them. This recognition was the main motivation for this work, in order to contribute to putting forward a platform for A/VE synthesis. In this paper the propose and briefly describe such a platform and present the underlying architecture and main expected functionalities, which will also be briefly described.

In order to more clearly expose the proposed platform for A/VE synthesis this paper will include a section for briefly refer to the Agile/Virtual Enterprise concept used and also some literature review about this subject and some existing approaches. Next the proposed platform is going to be described, in terms of the underlying A/VE model and associated functionalities.

G.D. Putnik and M.M. Cruz-Cunha (Eds.): ViNOrg 2011, CCIS 248, pp. 316–326, 2012.

2   Agile/ Virtual Enterprise Model

The Agile/ Virtual Enterprise model relies on dynamically reconfigurable collaborative networks, with extremely high performances, strongly time-oriented while highly focused on cost and quality, in permanent alignment with the market, and strongly supported by information and communication technology. Networking and reconfiguration dynamics are the main characteristics of this model, which claim for enabling and supporting environments, assuring cost-effective integration in useful time and preventing the risk of leakage of private information about products or processes. Some existing technologies and Internet-based environments can partially support this organizational model, but the reconfiguration dynamics can only be assured by environments able to manage, control, and enable virtual enterprise creation, operation and reconfiguration.

With the proposed IT-based platform, organizations interested on embracing a Meta-organization model will be able to successfully collaborate since the partnering enterprises will work as a seamless extended enterprise, all following a single unified process and not disjointed and fragmented processes that are only integrated via data bridges with no process or information intelligence. Figure 1 depicts this inter-connectivity spread through a globally distributed manufacturing environment.

Fast change, uncertainty, and strong competition are challenges of the actual worldwide economic context. Competitiveness is a main requirement of enterprises, whose satisfaction requires the definition of new organizational concepts, with extremely high performances that are strongly time-oriented while highly focused on cost and quality. Several factors appear as supreme factors of competitiveness: (1) the organizations' capability to achieve and explore competitive advantages in synergy, by using or integrating the optimal available resources for the functions that the organization undertakes; (2) the capability of fast adaptability to the market; together with (3) the capability of managing all business processes independently of distance, to be achieved through an Agile/Virtual Enterprise (A/VE) organizational model, in the context of Ubiquitous Manufacturing System network, characterized by a market of resources intensively spread through a globally distributed market [1, 2].

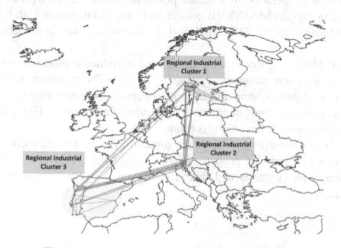

Fig. 1. Network of manufacturing sub-networks [1]

3   Platform for Virtual Enterprise Synthesis

3.1   Previous Work

A dynamic and reconfigurable supply chain is a critical tool for the implementation of agile Agile/Virtual Enterprises and for supporting mass customization business models, where products are created on a build-to-order basis. Synchronization at the supply chain level is required to support customer driven business operations, where the unique circumstances associated with each ordering and production scenario are considered, instead of adopting mechanical and automated workflow procedures, which are essentially process driven. Ghiassi and Spera [3] classify synchronized supply chain management as a new paradigm to provide a competitive strategy for customer-centric business environments. Lu and Wang [4] also address the benefits of synchronized supply chain management systems.

Chen, et al. [5] propose a multi-tier multi-agent architecture for collaborative production. They use tier agents to represent enterprises and site agents to represent local production units. The authors illustrate the application of this model in the TFT-LCD industry, typically divided into three segments (TFT array, cell and module assembly). At each segment different manufacturing sites are involved. Each segment is in fact an instance of a multi-site production system. The authors propose handling each enterprise using tier agents. Each tier agent interacts with other tier agents to handle order acceptance, order coordination and order cancelation.

Ghiassi and Spera [3] propose LEAP, a distributed system for companies that may have many plants spread over a wide geographic region, making many products, which they sell in many different markets. The authors developed a mathematical model that updates demand quantities continuously using forecasting techniques. The production plan is continuously updated to reflect the revised demand data up to the final scheduling of the production run.

Rabelo and Camarinha-Matos [6] developed HOLOS, a distributed multi-agent system that uses cooperation to schedule production inside an enterprise. The system was adopted in project MASSYVE project and further integrated with the federated information management DIMS/FIMS [7], extending the approach to virtual enterprises.

Moreover, Malucelli, Rocha and Oliveira [8] introduce a platform for facilitating the partner's selection automatic process – ForEV. The platform is implemented through a Multi-Agent System and includes a negotiation protocol – Q-Negotiation - through multi-criteria and distributed constraint formalisms. The platform also includes a reinforcement learning algorithm.

Although many contributions were put forward over the past years, we did not yet come across a platform for properly enable a truly integrated approach for Agile/Virtual Enterprises synthesis and this is the main motivation for carrying out the present work.

3.2   Proposed AVESP

In this paper we propose an Agile/ Virtual Enterprise Synthesis Platform (AVESP). The proposed AVESP features a multi-agent distributed architecture, using software agents and web services.

Software Agents

Software agents are defined as atomic computer programs that can accomplish a task or activity on behalf of the user and without constant human intervention [9]. These software modules can be bound to a specific execution environment - stationary agents - or they can have the capacity to transport itself to other execution environments, along with supporting data - mobile agents [3, 9].

Genersereth et al [10] propose three categories for software agent classification: deliberative agents (that support their decisions on symbolic reasoning, using a symbolic model of the environment; they engage in planning and negotiation in order to achieve coordination with other agents); reactive agents (that do not have any internal symbolic models of the environment, and act using a stimulus/ response type of behavior); and hybrid (a mix of deliberative and reactive models, based on a hierarchy of behavior layers, that can be further increased in response of external events).

Nwana [9] enumerates a list of three primary attributes, which agents should exhibit: autonomy (so that it executes its tasks without human intervention); proactiviness (in order to take decisions based on opportunity); cooperativeness or social ability (in order to interact with other software agents or human users); learning ability (agents should learn as they react and/ or interact with their external environment). From these three key characteristics they derive four types of agents: collaborative agents, collaborative learning agents, interface agents and smart agents.

Multi Agent Systems

Several authors propose using Software Agents to model distributed supply chains. The supply chain can be modeled as a set of intelligent software agents that interact in planning and executing processes, each being assigned to different tasks and responsibilities. A system built upon a set of multiple agents that interact this way is a multi-agent system (MAS). A multi-agent system is a loosely coupled network of software agents that interact to solve problems that are beyond the individual capacities or knowledge [4].

Rocha [11] defines MAS as a set of agents that combine their individual competences and work collaboratively, in order to fulfill a common objective.

Lu and Wang [4] propose a framework for supply chain management using multiple agents. The authors assign each agent to one of four different categories: customer centric agents (responsible for managing customer information), product-centric agents (responsible for utilizing the customer information and identify what the customer needs), supplier-centric agents (responsible for choosing the best suppliers for acquiring raw materials or components) and logistic-centric agents (responsible for dispatching materials and products for the manufacturer).

Jennings [12] considers that Multi-agent systems can form the fundamental building blocks for software systems, even if the software systems do not themselves require any agent-like behaviors. Huhns [13] enumerates several key characteristics of multi-agent systems: agent based modules more closely represent real-world things; modules can negotiate with each other; modules can enter into social commitments to collaborate; modules can volunteer to be part of a software system: modules can "change their mind" about the results of collaboration.

Using multiple agents that cooperate as members of a virtual workforce will support distributed order management, production scheduling and monitoring. In order to execute these functions the agents will need to implement bi-directional communication with each business partner. The agents will need to obtain capacity information from factories, assign production schedules, receive exception notifications, and so on. This means that part of the information the system needs will be distributed among several systems, potentially heterogeneous, that live inside each participating business. Agents will communication with these systems using XML and Web services.

XML and Web Services

XML turned into the universal integration language. In 2001 Bill Gates wrote "just as the Web revolutionized how users talk to applications, XML transforms how applications talk to each other" [14]. The web evolved into a transactional platform, with an architecture geared towards intelligently exchanging information between applications. Web Services play a key role in this transactional behavior, working as loosely coupled software components that provide business functionality through the Internet using standard based technologies (like SOAP and XML). Web Services are considered as self-contained, self-describing, modular applications that can be published, located, and invoked across the Web.

Web Services can be used along with software agents. For example, a software agent can analyze requests and determine how to fit them with Web Services. Web Services would, in turn, interact with external software systems (for example, internal ERPs or APS systems). Software agents can also interpret and contextualize results of invoked services.

Agents are typically cooperative and communicative, knowing about other agents and being able to interact with them, whereas Web Services are essentially passive until they are invoked, knowing little about its consumers. There are several works on incorporating agents into web service based systems [15, 16, 17].

The relationship between Web Services and software agents can be symbiotic. Web Services can help software agents by proving further encapsulation and broader integration capabilities [18] standards based description and execution of methods, web based architecture and ease of deployment. On the other hand, the dynamic creation of software agents, their mediation and reasoning capabilities, their flexibility and robustness [19] allow for a cleaner management of web service sets. Moreover, reinforcement learning [20] is another important feature for enabling an appropriate collaborative-based integration among business partners and systems during a virtual enterprise life-cycle [21], which can be enabled by using Web Services combined with agent technology.

AVESP Architecture

Figure 2 illustrates the general architecture of the proposed platform for A/VE synthesis in the context of an Ubiquitous Manufacturing System network [1]. The platform's main components are the Web Service Layer, that handles incoming requests from customers; Order Agents, that process orders received from customers; Production Agents, that identify outsourcing/ supplier candidates and perform negotiation with them; Local Agents, that implement a communication interface between local business partner systems and production agents and Data Brokers, that control how data import and export is managed, promoting system encapsulation.

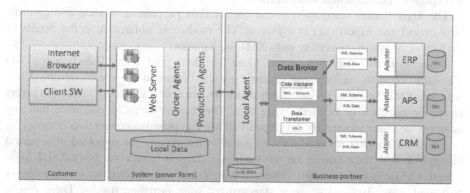

Fig. 2. General architecture of the proposed platform for A/VE synthesis

In order to maximize platform's reusability customers will interact with the platform using HTTP for data transfer. A set of Web Services is available for servicing customer applications. These applications can range from locally installed software packages (that post order information by calling web service methods) to server pages that are viewed using standard browser clients. Messages will be formatted using SOAP and they will be written in XML. Proxies will be used to support the integration of mobile equipment.

Integration with local systems from constituent Business Partners is a key component of a dynamic and distributed platform. The proposed architecture includes integration modules that support the integration of heterogeneous production management systems in the distributed management process. These modules provide a consistent abstraction of the actual data structure and functional details of each local system. As long as each business unit system can accept the input data, process it and return output data, it can be integrated in the proposed architecture. By allowing each business unit to integrate their existing systems, the proposed architecture supports maintaining each factory's autonomy. The abstraction also allows for the sharing of limited amounts of information, using controlled software components. Business units can join or leave the network without changing their internal systems.

The architecture includes local agents that interact with the production agents. They are the only visible communication endpoints, encapsulating the details from local internal systems. Production agents will not have to deal with system heterogeneity and will implement a unique and standardized communication protocol to communicate with all local agents.

Integration with local systems will be built using connection modules called adapters. Several adapters will be available for reading and writing information from/ into external systems (ERP, SCM, APS, among others). These modules feature Read and Write connectors. Each read connector is responsible for reading the information available in a backend system and transform this information into XML. Write connectors receive XML data and convert it to a format that is adequate for the associated system. XML Schemas (XSD) will be used to help validate the information and check its completeness and integrity.

The Data Broker component is the central data processing module and controls how import and export data is managed. The module is isolated from the details of each external system, accepting only XML information.

It includes two sub-components: Data Validator and Data Transformer. Data Validator maps the information received by the broker to the corresponding XML Schema. XML Schemas define which structures are acceptable. Any validation errors cause the rejection of the underlying data. This feature helps to guarantee that any adapters that were incorrectly developed will not compromise system data integrity.

The Data Transformer module is responsible for making the imported information compatible with the structure the service broker expects to receive, using XSLT Style Sheets (XSL Transformation). These Style Sheets are applied to the previously validated XML data and generate standardized transformation results. These results are delivered to the local agent.

3.3   Proposed AVESP Main Functionalities

Figure 3 illustrates the main expected functionalities of the proposed platform for A/VE synthesis.

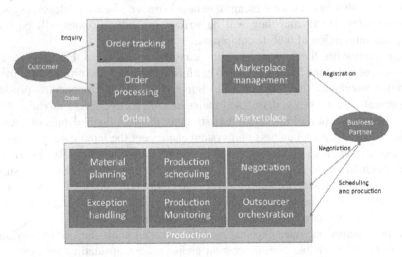

Fig. 3. Main functionalities of the proposed platform for A/VE synthesis

Customers will publish orders to the platform by submitting using available Web Services or server web pages. This paper assumes that order format and product description follow a base XML schema definition, mapped to a shared catalog of valid product references.

Whenever an order is received by the system a new order agent is associated to it. The agent starts by analyzing the order and available data to identify the list of ordered products. Each product may have different production requirements. Once the products have been defined, the order agent performs material planning in order to identify how many finished goods or components have to be produced. It then builds an activity sequence made of (Component/ Service, Start Date, Due Date, Qty) nodes, mapped to order delivery dates. The agent also identifies production dependencies and parallelism opportunities then it instantiates one production agent for each component that must be produced. The order agent next enters a monitoring cycle, analyzing feedback from production agents, checking for completion and handling exceptions. When production completes, the agent performs the closing steps associated with shipping and invoicing procedures.

The production agents receive production assignments from the order agents. The agents perform a second phase of material planning, if needed, further decomposing components in production units. For each activity the agents define free slack (amount of time it may be delayed without affecting the next task) and total slack values (the amount of time the activity can be delayed without affecting the production deadline). Next they build a list of potential suppliers for each of the components or materials. For each of the components the agents initiate a bidding session, inviting registered business partners to place a bid in the system. The bid is made through local agents that are available on each of the registered business partners. These local agents are assigned to the business partners/ suppliers when they register in the system. After receiving bid proposals from invited local agents, the production agents first evaluate production capacities. Each business partner that has enough production capacity is included in a list of qualified outsourcers for the associated component. If none of the business partners has enough capacity during the request period, the agent tries to coordinate the production order, checking dependencies and trying to change production schedule, trying to create compatibility with available capacities. If the coordination process is possible, the agent notifies business partners about proposed changes. If coordination is not possible, the agent tries to split production of the associated components between multiple producers, according to reported capacity availability from compatible partners. It then asks for updated bids according to proposed schedule and capacity allocation. If splitting is not successful, the agent triggers the reject order process. This process involves the order agent and, optionally, asks from further human approval to perform order rejection.

If there was enough capacity among bidders or production coordination was successful or even if production splitting occurred, the agent ends the process with a list of qualified outsourcers. For each entry on the list the agent evaluates and updates first level bidding factors (like cost, delivery, quality ratios and previous information). Next it evaluates transportation costs between suppliers that need to perform cumulative and sequential production. After that, the agent builds an ordered outsourcer short list based on first priority selection criteria. Next, it applies second and third level priority selection criteria, to decide between outsourcers with similar ratings. Finally, the agent selects one (or more in case of splitting or coordinated work) outsourcers, and notifies them of the final production schedule. Global production is saved locally along with associated data.

As soon as production scheduling is completed, the production agent enters a production monitoring cycle. The agent continuously checks information sent by local agents and sends them enquiries. Whenever a problem occurs, local agents may trigger an exception that is captured and handled by the production agents.

Whenever an exception signal is received, the production agent analyses it and evaluates the impact of the exception on the production plan. If there are no rescheduling requirements that may impact other outsourcers, the agent adjusts scheduling and notifies the local agent accordingly. If the changes affect other partners the agent starts a negotiation process with them. If the negotiation process is successful local data is updated and the monitoring cycle is resumed. If the negotiation was not successful and may compromise a final production deadline, the production agent interacts with the order agent, which will validate if the delay is acceptable. If it is not, the production may be cancelled. In this case, the production agent waits for formal production cancel approval, and informs local agents accordingly. During regular production monitoring cycle the production agent sends enquiries to local agents. In reply they send status reports and time estimates. If the production agent detects production delays it evaluates if they compromise production schedule, analyzing dependencies and total/ free slack values. If scheduling is compromised, the agent checks with the order agent to see if the delay is acceptable, when matched with order delivery dates. If the delay is not acceptable, the agent starts the replace outsourcer process. After notifying the local agent from the outsourcer, the production agent starts a new bidding session for the work that was previously assigned to it.

4   Conclusion

Agile/Virtual Enterprise (A/VE) integration is still a major concern of current manufacturing organizations that are worried about overcoming concurrency and surviving difficulties. Therefore, in this paper we make a contribution in terms of technological and organizational perspectives regarding these concerns, by putting forward a framework for A/VE synthesis, considering important requirements and trying to show how technology can serve the needs of an expanding and increasingly competitive A/VE organizational model. A/VE is seen as a new and most advanced organizational paradigm, and is expected to serve as a vehicle towards a seamless perfect alignment of the enterprise within the market. Agile/ Virtual Enterprises are addressed as a highly dynamic, reconfigurable agile network of independent enterprises sharing all resources, including knowledge, market, and customers; using specific organizational architectures that introduce the enterprises' true virtual environments. The new organizational models are required for enabling a truly

Ubiquitous Manufacturing System network, with high adaptability and reconfigurability dynamics and permanently aligned with businesses. Agility, distributivity, virtuality, integrability, scalability and evolutionary capability are the requirements for competitiveness that the new organizational models must address.

The proposed platform architecture will support A/VE operations assuming that participating business partners may have heterogeneous information systems and legacy systems. Future work includes the implementation of a mechanism to incorporate demand forecast in the order scheduling and negotiation processes. The adoption of a peer-to-peer architecture, without any central server mediation, will also be evaluated.

Acknowledgements. The authors wish to acknowledge the support of: 1) The Foundation for Science and Technology – FCT, under the scope of the financed Project on 'Ubiquitous oriented embedded systems for globally distributed factories of manufacturing enterprises' PTDC/EME-GIN/102143/2008, and 2) EUREKA, by the Project E!4177-Pro-Factory UES.

References

1. Cruz-Cunha, M.M., Putnik, G.D.: Environments for Virtual Enterprise Integration. International Journal of Enterprise Information Systems (IJEIS) 5(4), 71–87 (2009)
2. Cruz-Cunha, M.M., Putnik, G.D.: Agile Virtual Enterprises: Implementation and Management Support, pp. 1–402. Idea Group Publishing, IGP (2006)
3. Ghiassi, M., Spera, C.: Defining the Internet-based supply chain system for mass customized markets. Computers & Industrial Engineering 45, 17–41 (2003)
4. Lu, L., Wang, G.: A study on multi-agent supply chain framework based on network economy. Computers & Industrial Engineering 54, 288–300 (2008)
5. Chen, W.-L., Huang, C.-Y., Lai, Y.-C.: Multi-tier and multi-site collaborative production: Illustrated by a case example of TFT-LCD manufacturing. Computers & Industrial Engineering 57, 61–72 (2009)
6. Rabelo, R., Camarinha-Matos, L.M.: Towards Agile Scheduling in Extended Enterprise. In: Balanced Automation Systems II: Implementation Challenges for Anthropocentric Manufacturing. Chapman and Hall, London (1996)
7. Afsarmanesh, H., Garita, C., Ugur, Y., Frenkel, A., Hertzberger, L.O.: Design of the DIMS Architecture in PRODNET (1999)
8. Malucelli, A., Rocha, A.P., Oliveira, E.: B2B Transactions enhanced with ontology-based services (2004)
9. Nwana, H.S.: Software Agents: An Overview. Knowledge Engineering Review 11(3), 1–40 (1996)
10. Genesereth, M.R., Ketchpel, S.P.: Software Agents. Communication of the ACM 37(7) (July 2004)
11. Rocha, A.P.: Metodologias de Negociação em Sistemas Multi-Agentes para Empresas Virtuais. Tese de Doutoramento, Faculdade de Engenharia, Universidade do Porto (2001)
12. Jennings, N.R.: On Agent-Based Software Engineering. Artificial Intelligence 117(2), 277–296 (2000)

13. Huhns, M.N.: Software Agents: The Future of Web Services. In: Kowalczyk, R., Müller, J.P., Tianfield, H., Unland, R. (eds.) NODe-WS 2002. LNCS (LNAI), vol. 2592, pp. 1–18. Springer, Heidelberg (2003)
14. Gates, B.: Why We're Building NET Technology, Microsoft. NET Today (June 18, 2001), http://www.microsoft.com/presspass/misc/06-18BillGNet.mspx
15. Gibbins, N., Haris, S., Shadbolt, N.: Agent-based Semantic Web Services. In: Proceedings of the 12th Int. WWW Conf. WWW 2003, Budapest, Hungary, pp. 710–717. ACM Press (2003)
16. Ardissono, L., Goy, A., Petrone, G.: Enabling conversations with web services. In: Proc. of the 2nd Int. Conf. on Autonomous Agents and Multi-agent Systems, Melbourne, pp. 819–826 (2003)
17. Ermolayev, V., Keberle, N., Kononenko, O., Plaksin, S., Terziyan, V.: Towards a Framework for Agent-Enabled Semantic Web Service Composition. Int. J. of Web Services Research 1(3), 63–87 (2004)
18. Jung, J.-Y., Him, H., Kang, S.-H.: Standards-based approaches to B2B workflow integration. Computers & Industrial Engineering 51, 321–334 (2006)
19. Fernandes, O.: Construção e Exploração de Ontologias para a Negociação Automática em Empresas Virtuais. FEUP (2007)
20. Sutton, R.S., Barto, A.G.: Reinforcement Learning: An Introduction. MIT Press (1998)
21. Rocha, A.P., Cardoso, H.L., Oliveira, E.: Contributions to an Electronic Institution supporting Virtual Enterprises life cycle. In: Putnik, G.D., Cunha, M.M. (eds.) Virtual Enterprise Integration: Technological and Organizational Perspectives, ch. XI, pp. 229–246. Idea Group Inc. (2005); ISBN 1-59140-406-1

Supplier Selection Using Multiobjective Evolutionary Algorithm

Vladimir Rankovic[1], Zora Arsovski[1], Slavko Arsovski[2], Zoran Kalinic[1], Igor Milanovic[1], and Dragana Rejman-Petrovic[1]

[1] Faculty of Economics, University of Kragujevac, Djure Pucara, 3, 34000 Kragujevac, Serbia
[2] Faculty for Mechanical Engineering, University of Kragujevac, Sestre Janjic, 6, 34000 Kragujevac, Serbia

Abstract. Supplier selection is one of the most critical activities of purchasing management. Nowadays, supplier selection includes a number of different and usually conflicting objectives. Because of that, modern supplier selection techniques imply solving of multiobjective optimization problems. In this paper supplier selection using evolutionary algorithm (SPEA method) is presented. As criteria for selection optimization we used variance of quality and total costs. Results show that described methodology can be applicable for the practical purposes.

Keywords: Supplier selection, multiobjective optimization, evolutionary algorithms, strength Pareto evolutionary algorithm.

1   Introduction

An effective supplier selection process is very important for the success of any manufacturing organization [9]. As an example, in most industries the main product cost consists of the cost of raw materials and component parts. In some cases cost of raw materials and component parts constitutes up to 70% of total product costs [5]. It shows that the appropriate supplier selection is one of the most important activities for final cost of product.

Supplier selection is very complex process consisting of identifying, evaluating and contracting with suppliers. Supplier evaluation and selection is the most sensitive activity because the identified suppliers have different weaknesses and strengths. This requires precise assessment of suppliers' characteristics that are relevant for following selection.

After suppliers' performance assessment is made, the next step is making selection decision. This process would be simple if only one criterion was used. However, there are, usually, a number of relevant criteria that must be satisfied for final vendor acceptance. In that case it is necessary to determine importance of each criterion for decision making process, i.e. to determine weight parameter that have to be assigned to each criterion before final vendors evaluation [17].

G.D. Putnik and M.M. Cruz-Cunha (Eds.): ViNOrg 2011, CCIS 248, pp. 327–336, 2012.
© Springer-Verlag Berlin Heidelberg 2012

Defining of criteria for supplier evaluation and selection is the major aspect of the purchasing function [4]. There are a number of studies addressed to this research field. One of the first studies was made by Dickson [3] who performed an extensive identification and analysis of criteria that were used in the selection of a firm as a supplier. His study was based on a questionnaire sent to 273 purchasing agents and managers selected from the membership list of the National Association of Purchasing Managers. Respondents had to assess the importance of each criterion on a five point scale from extreme to no importance value. Based on respondents' reply "quality" was selected as the most important criterion. Classification presented by Weber e al [15] based on analysis of all the articles published since 1966 showed that price, delivery, quality and production capacity and location were the most often treated criteria. On the other hand, study by Tullous and Munson [13] discovered that quality, price, technical service, delivery, reliability, and lead time were among the most important selection factors. This study was performed by analysis of eighty manufacturing firms,

More recently, Zhang et al [18] presented study based on 49 articles published between 1991 and 2003 which confirmed that net price quality and delivery were the most important supplier selection criteria. Finally, the review performed by Bross and Zhao [2] study concluded that the most valuable supplier selection criteria were cost, quality, service, relationship, and organization.

2   Supplier Selection

Existing methods for solving supplier selection problems can be classified into three major categories.

First category contains methods based on elimination of suppliers which do not satisfy defined selection rule. For each chosen criterion must be defined minimal mark. Applying "conjunctive" rule [16], suppliers whose mark is lower than minimal mark are eliminated. Suppliers whose marks satisfy minimal marks of all chosen criteria go in next phase. Next phase is usually application of "lexicographic" rule [16] which implies selection of the most significant criterion for suppliers' assessment. Supplier who satisfies chosen criterion much better than other supplier is selected.

Second category of supplier selection methods are probabilistic methods. One of the most famous methods is "Payoff Matrix" [10] which implies defining several scenarios of the suppliers' future behavior. Then, for each scenario and each criterion we associate mark to supplier. Finally, for each supplier the total mark is computed. Supplier with stable total mark according to various scenarios is selected.

Third category refers optimization methods. In the optimization method we optimize an objective function by varying potential suppliers. Objective function can include only one criterion or a set of criteria. Also, each criterion can involve a set of constraints on its value. This kind of optimization methods are known as single objective optimization problems. The problem can be much complex if several different objective functions are involved. This kind of optimization problems are known as multi objective optimization problems.

If the objective function consists of only one criterion, supplier selection is very simple. Supplier with best performance with regard to chosen criterion will be selected. The much complex challenge is the selection of the most important criterion. A considerable number of companies in this case use total cost (direct costs, purchase costs, transport costs etc.) as criterion. So, after computing the total cost for each supplier purchase management selects the supplier which is the least expensive one [12]. On the other hand, a number of companies as the selection criterion use supplier quality. In any case, single criterion optimization is rarely in use today.

In this paper we present supplier selection using multiobjective optimization genetic algorithm. In the next section we present general concepts of multi objective optimization based on Pareto dominance. In the Section 4 we present the fundamentals of genetic algorithm. In the Section 5 strength Pareto evolutionary algorithm is presented. Key relations of our model for supplier selection and results of research are presented in the Section 6.

Finally, in the concluding remarks we emphasize that the described method is generally applicable in this area of supply management.

3   Multiobjective Optimization

In single-objective optimization the optimal solution is clearly defined. This is because there is usually only one optimal solution. Unlike single-objective optimization in multiobjective optimization there is a set of alternative solutions (trade-offs). These "optimal" solutions are usually called Pareto-optimal solutions. We can say that these solutions are optimal solutions because there is no other solution in the search space which is superior to them considering all objectives [19].

In the following text we present the basic definitions of multiobjective optimization theory based on Pareto dominance which are necessary for further discussion.

A general MOP (Multiobjective Optimization Problem) includes a set of n parameters (decision variables), a set of k objective functions, and a set of m constraints. Objective functions and constraints are functions of the decision variables. Generally we can say that the optimization goal is to:

maximize $y = f(x) = (f_1(x), f_2(x), \ldots, f_k(x))$
subject to $c(x) = (c_1(x), c_2(x), \ldots, c_m(x)) \leq 0$
where $x = (x_1, x_2, \ldots, x_n) \in X$ and $y = (y_1, y_2, \ldots, y_k) \in Y$

X denotes the decision space, Y denotes the objective space, x is the decision vector, and y is the objective vector. The constraints are defined as $c(x) \leq 0$ and determine the set of feasible solutions.

The second definition regards to the term of Pareto dominance and can be presented as follows. Here we consider that optimization problem implies maximization of objective functions

For any two decision vectors **a** and **b**, we can differ three cases:

1. $\mathbf{a} \succ \mathbf{b}$ (**a** dominates **b**)   if $\mathbf{f}(\mathbf{a}) > \mathbf{f}(\mathbf{b})$
2. $\mathbf{a} \succeq \mathbf{b}$ (**a** weakly dominates **b**) if $\mathbf{f}(\mathbf{a}) \geq \mathbf{f}(\mathbf{b})$
3. $\mathbf{a} \approx \mathbf{b}$ (a is indifferent to b)   if $\mathbf{f}(\mathbf{a}) \not\succeq \mathbf{f}(\mathbf{b})$ and $\mathbf{f}(\mathbf{b}) \not\succeq \mathbf{f}(\mathbf{a})$

If the optimization problem implies minimization of objective functions the relations are the same but with adequate symbols ($\prec, \preceq, \approx$), respectively.

In solving an MOP, we can identify two distinct phases. The first is search for optimal solutions regarding to considering objectives, and the second is decision making, i.e. choosing the appropriate one among the number of solutions within the set of Pareto optimal solutions, obtained during the search [7]. Comparing to single-objective optimization, search space is very often even larger and more complex what induces inability of use of some exact optimization methods such is linear programming [11]. The second phase is related to the problem of selecting a suitable compromise solution from the Pareto-optimal set. With regard to the fact that Pareto optimal set consists of solutions that are non dominated to each other it is obviously that a human decision maker (DM) have to make trade-offs between conflicting objectives.

4   Genetic Algorithm

The term evolutionary algorithms (EA) or evolutionary strategies address a class of stochastic optimization methods which emulate the natural evolution. The origins of EAs can be found in the late 1950s, and since the 1970s several evolutionary methodologies have been proposed. This class of optimization methods addresses genetic algorithms, evolutionary programming, and evolution strategies [1]. Very important characteristic of these methods is ability for relatively simple implementation of parallel processing. Because of their ability to solve high dimensional and highly complex optimization problems that are impossible to be solved with conventional, deterministic methods, this class of methods became important part of modern intelligent systems.

In this section we briefly present fundamentals of the one type of the evolutionary methods called genetic algorithms.

Genetic algorithm is a stochastic optimization technique invented by Holland [6] based on the Darwin principle that in the nature only "the fittest survive". In order to realize this principle Holland introduced the basic phenomena of the biological evolution such as inheritance, crossover and mutation. So, in GA there is a set of individuals often called population. Each individual from population presents candidate solution of optimization problem. The individuals are usually referred to as chromosomes. Each chromosome, i.e. candidate solution, represents decision vector made of decision variables and has fitness values that correspond to defined objective functions. In the vocabulary of genetic algorithms each decision variable in the chromosome is called gene.

Generally, genetic algorithm consists of following steps:

1. Initialization of population with random individuals,
2. Fitness evaluation of the individuals in the population,
3. Generation of new population, using crossover and mutation,
4. Selection of individuals according to their fitness using some strategy (e.g. a Roulette wheel selection),
5. Stop if terminating condition is satisfied (e.g., a fixed number of iterations), otherwise go to step 2

First step of genetic algorithm is initialization of population. In this step we generate individuals using random approach. So, each gene (decision variable) within the individual is generated randomly and independently. Due to specificity of optimization problem presented in this work we introduce here constraint that must be handled in algorithm execution. Sum of the genes (decision variables) within each individual must be equal to 1. Hence, generation of individuals have to be realized with the respect to this constraint.

In our research we have implemented crossover operator denoted basic crossover. This crossover operator involves two parents and produce two offspring (two new individuals) swapping their genes. Idea is to divide both parents' chromosomes in two segments at dividing point (gene), and then to swap obtained segments. Operator is stochastic one because the dividing point is chosen randomly each time operator is applied. In our case, additional normalization of offspring's is required. The schematic presentation of basic crossover operator is shown in Figure 1a [14].

The mutation of individuals (chromosomes) has the same effect as the mutation of living beings. So, in nature unpredictable changes of genes occur. These changes induce that characteristics of offspring differ from characteristics of parents. In genetic algorithm mutation operator simulate the mutation process found in the nature. In this work we realized the mutation operator as follows. For randomly chosen individual from previous population we randomly chose two genes. Then, we increase the first gene with user defined value (e.g. 0.1) and second gene decrease with the same value. Again, in order to satisfy constraints of problem, normalization of chromosome must be applied. The schematic presentation of basic crossover operator is shown in Figure 1b [14].

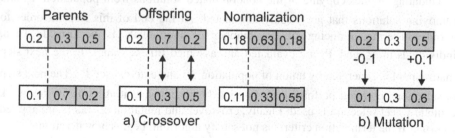

Fig. 1. a) Basic crossover; b) Mutation [14]

During the execution of the one iteration of genetic algorithm there is a risk that the best solution (individual which best fits the objective functions) can be lost. In order to avoid that scenario we implemented elitism strategy. Elitism strategy assures that the best individual from previous population will be transmitted to the next generation without changes.

5   Strength Pareto Evolutionary Algorithm (SPEA)

In this work we used Strength Pareto Evolutionary Algorithm (SPEA) for solving multiobjective optimization problem [19]. In this section we present the fundamentals of this optimization strategy. The following text refers [19].

The first step in strength Pareto evolutionary algorithm is initialization of the population. Within this step empty external set $\overline{P}$ is generated.

After initialization the main loop executes until termination criteria is satisfied. The main loop of the algorithm is presented in Figure 2. At the beginning of each loop iteration, the external set $\overline{P}_i$ is updated.

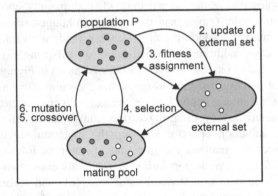

Fig. 2. Schematic presentation of SPEA procedure [19]

Updating implies copying of the nondominated solutions from population P_i and removing solutions that are weakly dominated. At the end of this step, in order to avoid clustering, reducing of the number of individuals is performed. Then, individuals in $\overline{P}_i$ and P_i are evaluated and assigned fitness values. In the next step mating pool is generated by union of population P_i and external set $\overline{P}_i$. The next step is selection operation performed on previously generated mating pool. In this work roulette wheel selection is used. Finally, crossover and mutation operators are applied as usual. If the termination criteria is not satisfy algorithm begins new iteration.

6   Supplier Selection Using SPEA

As we found in literature listed in the Section 2, the most frequently used criteria for supplier selection are the maximization of quality and minimization of total costs. In our research we analyzed variance of suppliers' total quality and total cost for the chosen number of deliveries of single raw material, realized in the previous period. We observed 40 deliveries of six suppliers. For each delivery quality rating is performed. Also, during observed deliveries total costs per unit of raw material and per supplier are assumed to be constant.

So, we can say that total amount of raw material delivered in single delivery of all suppliers can be calculated as:

$$A_{total} = \sum_{i=1}^{n} a_i \tag{1}$$

where a_i denotes amount of raw material delivered by i-th supplier and A_{total} denotes total amount delivered by all suppliers.

Using Eq. 1 we can introduce weight parameter w_i which denotes participation of i-th supplier's amount in total amount of delivered raw material.

$$w_i = \frac{a_i}{A_{total}} \tag{2}$$

By introducing weight parameter we can define the total cost per unit of raw material as follows:

$$C_{total} = \sum_{i=1}^{n} w_i C_i \tag{3}$$

where C_i denotes cost per unit of raw material and C_{total} denotes total cost per unit of raw material.

Also, by introducing weight parameter we can define quality of each delivery made by all suppliers.

$$Q_k = \sum_{i=1}^{n} w_i Q_{k,i} \tag{4}$$

where Q_k denotes quality of k-th delivery and $Q_{k,i}$ denotes quality rating of i-th supplier his k-th delivery.

It is obviously that variance of quality depends on variance of quality of each delivery of each supplier. Variance of total quality can be defined using standard deviation in the following manner.

$$Var = \sqrt{\frac{\sum_{k=1}^{m} (Q_k - \bar{Q})^2}{m}}, \qquad for \ k = 1,...,m \tag{5}$$

where m denotes number of deliveries and $\bar{Q}$ denotes average of quality considering all deliveries.

The main goal of this work was to determine weights (participation of each supplier) which would lead to minimization of quality variance and minimization of total costs.

Formal definition of described optimization problem would be as follows:

$$\text{Minimize } C_{total} = \sum_{i=1}^{n} w_i C_i$$

$$\text{Minimize } Var = \sqrt{\frac{\sum_{k=1}^{m} (Q_k - \bar{Q})^2}{m}}$$

$$\text{Subject to } \sum_{i=1}^{n} w_i = 1, \quad 0 \le w_i \le 1$$

where m denotes number of deliveries and n denotes number of suppliers.

For this purpose we used SPEA method described in the Section 5. Historical data, we used for optimization, consist of quality ratings for 40 deliveries performed by 6 suppliers. Quality ratings are in the range from 0 to 100 and total costs per unit of raw material are expressed in euros.

In the table below standard deviation and mean value of total quality rating, and total costs of each supplier are presented. Table 1. Quality mean value and standard deviation and total costs per unit of raw material

	Supplier 1	Supplier 2	Supplier 3	Supplier 4	Supplier 5	Supplier 6
Quality. Mean Val.	78.9	82.2	86.7	84.3	80.0	87.0
Quality St. Dev.	9.5	10.0	9.3	7.2	5.8	3.5
Costs (€)	0.0113	0.0105	0.0125	0.0131	0.0152	0.0180

SPEA method was executed with following input parameters: initial population size was 200 and number of iterations 2000.

As the result of optimization Pareto optimal solutions are obtained and presented in the Figure 3. Also, in order to demonstrate improvement made by performed optimization no optimized solutions are included.

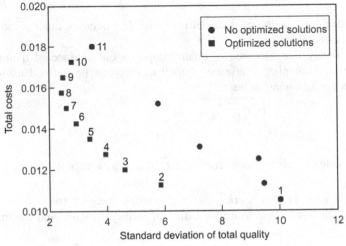

Fig. 3. Pareto optimal solutions for supplier selection problem

We can see that Pareto optimal solutions (squared dots) give significantly better trade-off between variance of quality and total costs. Each solution in Pareto optimal set implies different delivery portions of observed suppliers.

In the Table 2 are presented weight parameters obtained by optimization. Each set of weights corresponds to each point in the Figure 3.

Table 2. Weight parameters obtained by optimization

Points/weights	w1	w2	w3	w4	w5	w6
Point 1	0.00	1.00	0.00	0.00	0.00	0.00
Point 2	0.31	0.44	0.22	0.02	0.00	0.00
Point 3	0.22	0.29	0.21	0.21	0.08	0.00
Point 4	0.17	0.22	0.19	0.19	0.18	0.05
Point 5	0.14	0.18	0.16	0.17	0.18	0.17
Point 6	0.11	0.14	0.13	0.15	0.18	0.29
Point 7	0.09	0.09	0.11	0.13	0.18	0.40
Point 8	0.06	0.05	0.08	0.11	0.18	0.52
Point 9	0.03	0.01	0.05	0.09	0.18	0.64
Point 10	0.00	0.00	0.01	0.05	0.16	0.78
Point 11	0.00	0.00	0.00	0.00	0.00	1.00

7   Conclusions

Conventional methods for solving the supplier selection multiobjective problems are dominantly based on aggregation of objectives (criteria) into single objective using weighted sum with weights defined by decision maker. This multiobjective optimization approach is known as *decision making before search* [8], [7]. This approach implicitly includes preference information given by the DM and has the advantage that the classical single-objective optimization strategies can be applied without modifications. However, it requires profound domain knowledge which is usually not available.

In this paper we presented different approach in multiobjective optimization based on evolutionary algorithm and Pareto dominance theory. In the literature this approach is known as *search before decision making*. Optimization is performed considering each objective separately and the result of the search process is a set of Pareto-optimal solutions. So, decision maker can choose the most suitable solution. In our research we used SPEA. As criteria for selection optimization we used variance of quality and total costs. Presented results show that this methodology can be applicable for the practical purposes.

Acknowledgement. Research presented in this paper was supported by Ministry of Science and Technological Development of Republic of Serbia, Grant III-44010, Title: Intelligent Systems for Software Product Development and Business Support based on Models.

References

1. Bäck, T., Hammel, U., Schwefel, H.P.: Evolutionary computation: Comments on the history and current state. IEEE Trans. on Evolutionary Computation 1(1), 3–17 (1997)
2. Bross, M.E., Zhao, G.: Supplier selection process in emerging markets – The case study of Volvo Bus Corporation in China. Master Thesis. School of Economics and Commercial Law. Göteborg University (2004)
3. Dickson, G.W.: An analysis of vendor selection systems and decisions. Journal of Purchasing 2(1), 5–17 (1966)
4. Farzad, T., Osman, M.R., Ali, A., Yusuff, R.M., Esfandiary, A.: AHP approach for supplier evaluation and selection in a steel manufacturing company. JIEM 01(02), 54–76 (2008)
5. Ghodsypour, S.H., O'Brien, C.: A decision support system for supplier selection using an integrated analytical hierarchy process and linear programming. International Journal of Production Economics 56-67, 199–212 (1998)
6. Holland, J.H.: Adaptation in natural and artificial systems: An introductory analysis with applications to biology, control, and artificial intelligence. Univ. of Michigan Press (1975)
7. Horn, J.: F1.9 multicriteria decision making. In: Bäck, T., Fogel, D.B., Michalewicz, Z. (eds.) Handbook of Evolutionary Computation. Inst. of Physics Publ., Bristol (1997)
8. Hwang, C.-L., Masud, A.S.M.: Multiple Objectives Decision Making—Methods and Applications. Springer, Berlin (1979)
9. Liu, F.H.F., Hai, L.: The voting analytic hierarchy process method for selecting supplier. International Journal of Production Economics 97(3), 308–317 (2005)
10. Soukup.: Supplier selection strategies. Journal of Purchasing and Materials Management 26(1), 7–12 (1987)
11. Steuer, R.E.: Multiple Criteria Optimization: Theory, Computation, and Application. Wiley, New York (1986)
12. Timmerman.: An approach to supplier performance evaluation. Journal of Purchasing and Materials Management 22(4), 2–8 (1986)
13. Tullous, R., Munson, J.M.: Trade-Offs Under Uncertainty: Implications for Industrial Purchasers. Int. Journal of Purchasing and Materials Management 27(3), 24–31 (1991)
14. Dallagnol, V.A.F., Van den Berg, J., Mous, L.: Portfolio Management Using Value at Risk: A Comparison between Genetic Algorithms and Particle Swarm Optimization. International Journal of Intelligent Systems 24, 766–792 (2009)
15. Weber, C.A., Current, J.R., Benton, W.C.: Vendor selection criteria and methods. European Journal of Operational Research 50, 2–18 (1991)
16. Wright: Consumer choice strategies/simplifying vs. optimizing. Journal of Marketing Research 12, 60–67 (1975)
17. Yahya, S., Kingsman, B.: Vendor rating for an entrepreneur development program: a case study using the analytic hierarchy process method. Journal of the Operational Research Society 50, 916–930 (1999)
18. Zhang, Z., Lei, J., Cao, N., To, K., Ng, K.: Evolution of Supplier Selection Criteria and Methods. European Journal of Operational Research 4(1), 335–342 (2003)
19. Zitzler, E., Thiele, L.: Multiobjective evolutionary algorithms: A comparative case study and the strength Pareto approach. IEEE Trans. on Evol. Computation 3(4), 257–271 (1999)

Technologies Integration for Distributed Manufacturing Scheduling in a Virtual Enterprise

Gaspar Vieira, Maria Leonilde R. Varela, and Goran D. Putnik

Department of Production and Systems, School of Engineering, University of Minho,
Azurém Campus, 4800-058 Guimarães, Portugal
gaspar_vieira@hotmail.com, {leonilde,putnikgd}@dps.uminho.pt

Abstract. Distributed scheduling problems are challenging tasks to researchers and practitioners that have been gaining increasing popularity over the years. This is partly attributed to the fact that multi-site production and networked manufacturing environments are increasing as a consequence of globalisation. In this paper a system for technologies integration for supporting distributed scheduling in a Virtual Enterprise, by combining a simulation-based approach, with the Hungarian algorithm, for solving job-shop scheduling problems is presented, in order to show how we can benefit from this combination of procedures for distributed manufacturing scheduling.

Keywords: Distributed scheduling, technologies integration, virtual enterprise.

1 Introduction

The manufacturing environment has changed from traditional single-site manufacturing to decentralized multi-site manufacturing network in the last decades. Companies have established new manufacturing sites in different locations or formed strategic relationships with business partners, in order to increase their responsiveness to market changes and to share resources more effectively and efficiently, through integrated manufacturing systems environments. In this context, collaboration among different sites becomes more critical. Thus, development of appropriated approaches, integrated for enabling accurate distributed and concurrent planning and scheduling, in order to maximize the overall benefits of business partners within such a networked scenario, subject to a set of settings, have become even more challenging and the integration of scheduling approaches for distributed scheduling suite well for this purpose.

In this paper we propose a scheduling system for supporting decision-making under the scope of distributed manufacturing scheduling. The proposed system is applied to a job-shop scheduling problem where a set of jobs' components have to be processed on a set of machines and next subject to an assembly line for obtaining final articles.

Manufacturing scheduling is an activity that affects all branches of organizations (industrial, trade and services). Its dynamics occurs through the operationalization of

G.D. Putnik and M.M. Cruz-Cunha (Eds.): ViNOrg 2011, CCIS 248, pp. 337–347, 2012.

the basic functions of scheduling (orders release, allocation of jobs to production resources or vice versa, jobs sequencing on each resource of machine, and detailed jobs programming, defining its starting and finishing times on each resource/ machine), in order to successfully promote activities related to each enterprise. Scheduling is particularly important in creating wealth and satisfying the needs of society and is particularly challenging, given that organizations are continually exposed to markets generally very dynamic and competitive.

Seeking to obtain an optimized manufacturing schedule, we integrate the Hungarian algorithm through an application developed in Visual Basic and another mathematical model developed through the Excel's Solver, on which the model was implemented for resources allocation and sequencing of jobs. Moreover, this implementation is combined with a simulation-based approach, by using the ARENA 13.5. Software.

The Hungarian algorithm was proposed by Harold Kuhn, in 1950 [1] to solve problems of maximum matching in bipartite graphs. Since that time it has been widely implemented and used, having achieved significant results in several areas [2].

The ARENA was released in 1993, by Systems Modeling and consists of a set of modules used to illustrate a real situation, through various graphical user interfaces [3]. Through ARENA, we will simulate a manufacturing facility consisting of six machines and an assembly line, where components of articles are produced, being next assembled to produce three final articles.

The objective of combining and integrating the Hungarian algorithm, the Excel Solver model and ARENA simulation is to reduce the time needed to produce the articles, determining the optimal sequence of first shipment of raw materials for the machines that produce the components and then the optimal sequence of delivery and production components for assembly lines, for producing the respective final articles.

The problem is to find the value of decision variables that ensures the maximization of income, which in this article is to reduce the production time of both components and articles assembly, subject to some restrictions, treated through linear expressions, which depend on certain problem dependent parameters.

Therefore, the main purpose of this paper consists on proposing an integrated approach of the Hungarian algorithm and Arena simulation for distributed scheduling problems solving. According to this integrated approach, a data representation model is used for data processing as well as for communication on the Internet. In this situation, a distributed scheduling system is proposed for collaboratively making a schedule, by talking to other systems. In contrast to the traditional EDI-based communication, which depends on closed and strict relationships, web-based communication sometimes meets a case where the business partners cannot be identified in advance. Therefore, in order to make dynamic collaboration of virtual enterprises on the Internet, the proposed data representation model has to have a fundamental data structure and a basic framework of representation and processing of distributed scheduling problems, which was implemented through VB.Net.

The remainder of this paper is organized as follows. Next, on section 2 a brief contextualization about a virtual enterprise context and real-time collaborative management is provided. After, section 3 briefly refers to distributed manufacturing scheduling. Next, on section 4, distributed scheduling technologies integration is described, as well as the underlying data model for production scheduling problems solving and web-based communication data exchange. Moreover, the web-based interface for distributed scheduling problems solving is illustrated, through an example of use. Finally, on section 5 presents some additional discussion and concluding remarks.

2   Real-Time Collaborative Management in a Virtual Enterprise

Real-time Collaborative Virtual Enterprise Management (RTCVEM), at its higher level, can be viewed as a framework to connect people, processes, data (information), knowledge and decision-making processes. In this context, it is our conviction that innovation, through an Ubiquitous Manufacturing System (UMS), for Virtual Enterprise (VE) integration plays a fundamental role. This UMS environment is characterized by the possibility of enabling a widly spread, distributed and intesive existence of multiple manufacturing systems or cells, integrating corresponding management support technoligies (UMS Cells), which work all interconekted in a collaborative way, under the supervision of a market-of-resources (MR) manager, which controls the whole UMS, including connections with clients, bellonging or not to this Meta-Organization (MO) environment, where brokering services also play a fundamental role, for accomplishing a trully integrated real-time collaborative management of the whole networked manufacturing environment, where distributed manufacturing scheduling consists on an important function (Figure 1).

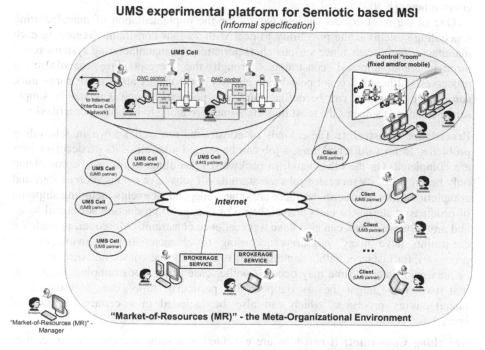

Fig. 1. Meta-Organizationational Environment of a Virtual Enterprise [4, 5]

Moreover, this UMS environment promotes innovation, which although being a term difficult to describe or define, due to its general understanding as being more an art than science and to a certain extend inherently intangible perception, its behaviour measurment turns out to be quit important, while difficult to evaluate. In this sense, it becomes important to enable corporate innovation instead of focusing on individual innovation, and technology integration can enable this kind of innovation, which can be seen as a commodity, thus finally giving some concrete shape to the abstract UMS concept and with this work we intend to make a contribution on that direction, by enabling tecnologies integration for distributed scheduling within a Virtual Enterprise.

3   Distributed Manufacturing Scheduling

Distributed scheduling problems are strategic in manufacturing enterprises, which are expected to provide products under an unexpectedly varying market. Considering a networked manufacturing environment, enterprises have to make some alliances with their suppliers, business partners and customers, and then, one enterprise takes only a part of the whole production processes [6]. Due to this situation, scheduling problems should be concerned as decentralized decision processes. In other words, an information infrastructure for the distributed scheduling is necessary for coordination, collaboration and communication among different enterprises [7]. Distributed Manufacturing Scheduling is a topic widely investigated along the past decades and nowadays, in the context of Virtual Enterprises it plays even a more important role as it enables to better fulfill the requisites of this kind of networked manufacturing environments [8, 9].

One of the most critical success factors for the implementation of manufacturing scheduling systems is the possibility to deal with various constraints, regarding each manufacturing process, since various characteristics of a manufacturing systems result through some imposed constraints, through the corresponding manufacturing processes. Although it is not possible to classify and consider all of these constraints, some main categories can be defined and incorporated through a relatively simple schema and next some of the most important ones are going to be briefly described.

Precedence Constraint: These kinds of constraints are well known in scheduling problems. In forward scheduling, a job can be started after all of its predecessor jobs are completed. On the other hand, in backward scheduling, a job can be completed only before all of its successor jobs are started. All jobs have events such as start and completion times. Furthermore, there are other independent events including shipping of products, materials or parts arrival, begin or change of production shifts and so on and any of these events can also have a precedence constraint. Moreover, precedence constraints have many variations according to characteristics of manufacturing processes, for instance, within some scenarios a precedence constraint with minimum or maximum interval time may occur. Another case arises, for example, considering that two jobs might be overlapped for particular time, due to continuous manufacturing processes, which can also be included in a certain category of precedence constraints types.

Switching Constraint: If two jobs are executed in a same occupied resource, they have an exclusive relation, which means that one job should be started after another job is completed or vice versa. Therefore, the two jobs cannot be executed at a same time. The proposed model includes this constraint, grouped to a category of switching constraints, which are constraints that also may have many variations. Generally, practical scheduling problems deal with switching constraints in a context where constraints are predefined due to some engineering reasons. An example occurs when one job can be started after some time interval, after the completion time of another one, or a case in which one job should be started just after the other job is completed. Another practical situation of use of this constraint occurs due to variable interval setup time, depending on the combination of two jobs' characteristics.

Stock Constraint: Stock level of each item or component can vary during the scheduling horizon. Every kind of items, such as final products, work-in-progress inventory, parts or components and raw materials can have some stock, so that we can define stock constraints in which the level of stock should be greater than a minimum level value and less than a maximum level value. Typically safety stock levels are defined as well as maximum stock levels, which may correspond to space constraints of buffers and/ or to manufacturing politics used, like just-in-time (JIT).

Loading Constraint: The loading constraints deal with items' levels. This kind of constraint concerns about a usage level of charged resource, during the planning horizon. So, an amount level of resource usage for jobs, which are allocated to that resource at a same time, should be within a predefined range between a minimum and a maximum level. In this type of constraint, a maximum level is described as availability of the resource performance. If the target resource is occupied allowable range of the constraint may vary from zero to one, and the level of usage may take whether zero or one. The minimum and the maximum level of each loading constraint are sometimes static, but usually they are variable, during the planning period, for instance, due to a varying number of workers regarding part-time work.

State Constraint: The state constraints restrict the jobs or events execution in a general form. These constraints are represented using pre-conditions and post-conditions for execution of particular jobs or events. Post-conditions perform as actions of jobs or events. These conditions are defined through attributes of primitives and some mathematical expressions. These attributes of primitives are changed during the planning horizon, by the execution of the jobs or events arising from a schedule.

4   Scheduling Technologies Integration

Manufacturing scheduling, in terms of optimal schedules, means to find absolutely the best solution for a problem, but practical scheduling problems, found in real world, usually does not reach such optimal solution, as most of them deal with various constraints, which only enables to reach some feasible solutions. Moreover, generally, it is hard to find an explicit relationship between a required solution and its appropriate solving method. Therefore, several optimization methods may be applied, in order to obtain the required solution.

In this paper we propose an integrated distributed scheduling approach, by combining excel-based technology with simulation-based one. Moreover, the underlying problem data representation schema allows users to add their own domain specific constraints. These constraints are then used through dispatching rules, where a resource of the manufacturing system is available to start, and there is more than one job ready to start on a given resource. The dispatching rules are part of a specific scheduling method. They are used partially in a step of a total scheduling approach. Therefore, there are two different approaches, i.e., one that is an excel solver based model, through the Hungarian algorithm, or some other approach, namely based on genetic algorithms, simulated annealing or tabu search and so on, and another is an approach based on simulation through ARENA Software. The latter does not directly focus on optimization, but it is very practical for real world problems solving. Therefore, the proposed approach enables different types of scheduling procedures for supporting distributed manufacturing scheduling.

4.1   Excel Solver

The Excel Solver can be used to solve optimization problems, namely of linear and integer types, where decision variables and constraints can be added, enabling to solve problems with up to 200 decision variables, 100 constraints and implicit 400 simple constraints (lower and upper limits and/ or integrality constraints on the decision variables) [10]. The Excel interface is illustrated through Figure 2.

The case proposed is a classical problem of allocating resources, namely m machines, which may be used for performing n tasks, including production of parts or components and considering knowledge and time allocation of each machine i, to each task j (i, j = 1, 2, ..., n).

In this Excel Solver interface, the problem parameters are added by using a button, enabling to specify the constraints necessary to implement our mathematical model.

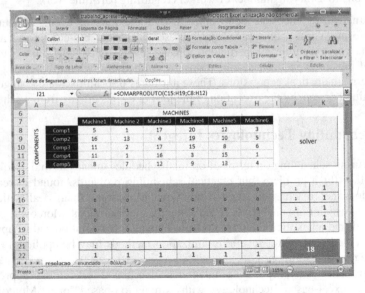

Fig. 2. Use of Excel Solver Illustration

Table 1. Processing time of each component on each machine

		MACHINES					
		Machine1	Machine 2	Machine3	Machine4	Machine5	Machine6
COMPONENTS	Comp1	5	1	17	20	12	3
	Comp2	16	13	4	19	10	5
	Comp3	11	2	17	15	8	6
	Comp4	11	1	16	3	15	1
	Comp5	8	7	12	9	13	4

Table 1 shows an example of the processing times required for producing each of five components on each of six machines available.

4.2 Interfaces Implementation on Visual Basic

The visualization of distributed schedules, which are managed in different places, is much valuable especially in a global manufacturing. If these distributed sites have their own scheduler developed by different IT vendors, their schedules cannot be visualized by a common viewer without particular adapting programs. This actually causes a huge effort on a system's implementation, and both the cost and the risk of the system, which will be increased. Using interfaces developed through Visual Basic (http://visualbasic.ittoolbox.com) enables end user to have a personalized scheduling viewer. This provides flexibility for visualizing distributed schedules everywhere through the Internet. This section discusses a general model for scheduling problems data representation. In order to better present the model an illustration of the web system that is provided, in order to more clearly show how the proposed model, implemented through Visual Basic, enables to accurately provide the syntax for problem data description, on one hand and, in a broader sense, how it can be seen as a general modeling schema, for problem data specification. Figures 3 and 4 show the system's interface for the execution of the Hungarian algorithm, for performing the assignment of each component to each machine.

In order to contribute to a specification standard for scheduling problems, the data is described through XML, based on a data structure that can be easily visualized through

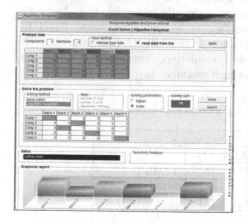

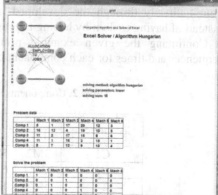

Fig. 3. Interface Illustration   **Fig. 4.** Report with optimal sequence

the Internet. Figure 3 shows a chart about the schedule plan obtained, which consists on a powerful visualization tool, implemented through Visual Basic language. Moreover, by using XML based problem specifications, different kind of charts, namely Gantt charts, can be easily presented through the integrated application and visualized through the web.

4.3   Arena-Based Simulation

To perform the manufacturing processes of three given articles, for our example, through Software ARENA [3], the system requires that three entities are defined. We choose the entities A1, A2 and A3, which correspond to those three articles. Therefore, three "Creates" were used to define the name and the weekly demand of each article, following a normal distribution. These "Creates" are directly connected to the Visual Basic implementation, as shown in Figure 5, thereby automatic insertion of corresponding demand values, without having to access "Creates" in ARENA, is also possible, whenever we want to change the demand for each item.

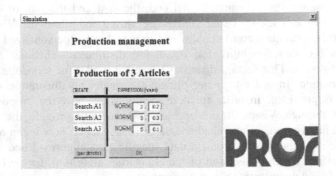

Fig. 5. VB interface for automatic articles information searching

This integration application developed through VB consists on an important contribution of this work, by enabling the users to directly insert data (e.g. demand of items) directly through the developed interface or by uploading some Excel file instead of having to do it by having to program it, on the ARENA Software.

Continuing the given example problem resolution, consider the processing sequences and times for each component on each machine, as given in Table 2.

Table 2. Components integration on each article

Components	Operations				
	O1	O2	O3	O4	O5
C1	3M2	5M1	4M5	12M6	
C2	12M1	6M3	4M2	3M4	6M6
C3	5M3	1M1	2M4	8M5	7M6
C4	5M2	6M3	3M4	5M5	10M6
C5	5M1	7M2	2M3	4M5	

Figure 6 illustrates the machines disposal within the Job-shop environment.

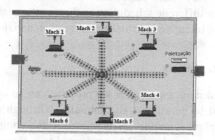

Fig. 6. Job-shop manufacturing model illustration

Once the components production is finished its ordering is performed in pairs, in order to be organized to follow later to the assembly line, thus avoiding any unnecessary waste of time, and this will take about 2 minutes for loading and unloading. Still considering our example, Table 3 shows the components and respective amounts for obtaining the three final articles (A1, A2, and A3).

Table 3. Components integration on each article

Articles	Components				
	C1	C2	C3	C4	C5
A1	2		1		1
A2	3	2	1	1	
A3	2		2		3

The final manufacturing stage of the three articles is performed on an assembly line, which integrates three processing machines (PM1, PM2 and PM3), associated with several operators, following, for instance, a normal distribution, which varies according to each article. Figure 7 illustrates this final assembly line environment.

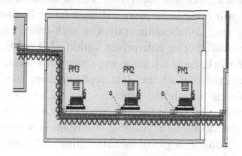

Fig. 7. Assembly Line Illustration

Regarding the networked manufacturing processes management, distributed scheduling problems play an important role. Therefore, collaboration and communication between different scheduling technologies enables to enrich business models, in the context of integrated Virtual Enterprises in an UMS context.

4.4   Approaches Integration

The integration of scheduling approaches we propose can be applied when more than two plants are required to coordinate dynamically. Through the example given we may consider that one plant schedule exists related to the components processing and then the final assembly process has to be outsourced to a company's business partner, being the corresponding new schedule performed at a different site.

As a final remark we may be able to state that the proposed integration of approaches put forward with this work, may appear appropriate for solving large problem instances, arising in the context or distributed scheduling, within networked manufacturing environments, by combining the implemented VB-based interface for integrating approaches, namely the here presented Hungarian algorithm and the Excel Solver, by enabling an user-friendly way for problems solving and results providing.

5   Conclusion

This paper described a proposed distributed production scheduling approach, by combining an Excel-based one with ARENA simulation, through an implemented VB interface. In this context a standard format to exchange data among different manufacturing enterprises were used. In manufacturing enterprises, there are many ICT applications including distinct scheduling software. In order to make a flexible communication between different applications, XML based data modeling was useful.

The effectiveness of the integrated approaches was briefly described an illustrated through an application example about a practical job-shop scheduling problem. An important aspect is that data can be generated and visualized by computers in appropriate and distinct ways. It is important that the data representation schema is general for distinct kind of manufacturing enterprises requisites.

Moreover, we can state that this underlying standardization, through a general data representation model will bring us to more valuable future business models, by using the Internet. Besides that, collaboration provides web-based application integration infrastructure for all manufacturing enterprises, within a Virtual Enterprise context.

In terms of future work, there are some important improvements to be performed, namely regarding an extension of the data representation model. Therefore, more vocabulary for distributed scheduling problems has to be added. As we selected a XML based specification, extending the data model will be relatively easy. So, we are hopeful that we are able to make a valuable contribution with this work in order to enhance distributed scheduling in global manufacturing UMS environments.

Acknowledgements. The authors wish to acknowledge the support of: 1) The Foundation for Science and Technology – FCT, under the scope of the financed Project PTDC/EME-GIN/102143/2008, and 2) EUREKA, by the Project E!4177-Pro-Factory UES.

References

1. Kuhn, H.W.: Contributions to the Theory of Games, I (AM-24). Princeton University Press (1950); ISBN 978-0-691-07934-9
2. http://en.wikipedia.org/wiki/Hungarian_algorithm
3. http://www.actsolutions.it/File/Arena/Arena%AESoftware_Tutorial.pdf
4. Putnik, G.D.: BM_Virtual Enterprise Architecture Reference Model. Technical Report RT-CESP-GIS-2000-<GP-01>. Universidade do Minho, Portugal (2000b)
5. Putnik, G.D.: BM_Virtual Enterprise Architecture Reference Model. In: Gunasekaran, A. (ed.) Agile Manufacturing: 21st Century Manufacturing Strategy, pp. 73–93. Elsevier Science Publ., UK (2001)
6. Shen, W., Wang, L., Hao, Q.: Agent-Based Distributed Manufacturing Process Planning and Scheduling: A State-of-the-Art Survey. IEEE Transactions on Systems, Man and Cybernetics – Part C: Applications and Reviews 36(4) (July 2006)
7. Herbsleb, J.D., Grinter, R.E.: Splitting the organization and integrating the code: Conway's law revisited. In: 21st International Conference on Software Engineering (ICSE 1999), p. 85 (1999)
8. Wu, S.H., Fuh, J.Y.H., Nee, A.Y.C.: Concurrent process planning and scheduling in distributed virtual manufacturing. IIE Transactions 34(1), 77–89 (2002)
9. Hong, D., Li, C., Chentao, W., Qianni, D.: A grid-based scheduling system of manufacturing resources for a virtual enterprise. The International Journal of Advanced Manufacturing Technology 28(1-2), 137–141
10. http://peltiertech.com/Excel/SolverVBA.html

Linked Architects and Urban Planners: Using Social Network Analysis to Capture Connections

Madalena Cunha Matos and Tânia Beisl Ramos

Faculty of Architecture – TU Lisbon / CIAUD
Rua Sá Nogueira, Pólo Universitário - Alto da Ajuda, 1349 – 055 Lisbon, Portugal
{mcunhamatos,taniaramos}@fa.utl.pt

Abstract. The methodology of *Social Network Analysis* has received little attention in the fields of architecture and urban planning. This paper sets out to show through two case studies the use it might have in the establishment of new perspectives on the knowledge of the profession. Architects and urban planners' careers, professional opportunities and life trajectories are dependent on the personal and job-related networks in which they live and work. Architects travelling and establishing themselves in colonial territories, and architects grouped in the oppositionist circles in the Portuguese dictatorship's period of the 20th century, are the focus of the case studies presented.

Keywords: Social Network Analysis, architecture, urbanism, Modern Movement.

1 Introduction

Professions are rooted in epistemological demarcations as well as in social *habitus*. While the process of creativity and procedures of work of architects has been minimally investigated, the conditions for exercising the profession have remained a ground of many gaps. Clientage, the market, opportunities for living and working do not correspond to presuppositions and differ from other professions. Issues of size and organization of architectural practice, of geographical distribution of practices, of prospects of commissions, all encroach the continuity and mere possibility of survival in the profession.

Whereas the history of the profession has been drafted in the pioneering work organized by Spiro Kostof (2000) [1], and the profession's social functioning scrutinized in 1987 by Judith R. Blau [2], and further investigated by Dana Cuff in 1992 [3], the corresponding perspective in Portugal has not been drawn. Advances have been made in 2000 by Sandra Gomes [4], and in 2002 by Ana Isabel Ribeiro concerning the first 90 years of the professional body of architects, ranging from 1863 to 1953 [5]; a large canvas has been drawn by Manuel Vilaverde Cabral and Vera Borges concerning a moment in time, the year 2006 [6]. No overall study however has been made so far; knowledge of the 20th century in particular is particularly fragmented.

The supposedly distinctiveness of architects as a social group and even as an elite social class is an assumption rapidly flouted by close inspection of reality. They being

G.D. Putnik and M.M. Cruz-Cunha (Eds.): ViNOrg 2011, CCIS 248, pp. 348–356, 2012.

a group disconnected, distanced and isolated from the society that they are held to serve is defied by evidence brought from personal testimonials, from life accounts and from objective data, such as life trajectories.

The set of postulations and techniques known as *Social Network Analysis* offers an interesting course for the investigation into these less evident but nonetheless crucial conditions of exercising the profession.

Social Network Analysis (SNA) is a mathematical and informatics models supported methodology of the Social Sciences that deals with the structure of social relations and allows the dynamics of the group under analysis to be grasped and studied[7] [8] [9]. It identifies the interaction patterns and behaviors between individuals - whom it designates as agents. It differs from the metaphoric current use of the expression 'social networks' in the Worldwide Web.

Already well established in the realms of History and Social Studies – being born out of Sociology - the methodology of *Social Network Analysis* has received little attention in the fields of architecture and urban planning. This paper sets out to show through two case studies the use it might have in the establishment of new perspectives on the knowledge of the profession. Architects and urban planners' careers, professional opportunities and life trajectories are dependent on the personal networks in which they live and in job-related networks in which they create and transform buildings and urban environments. Both networks are partly superimposed, adding a further degree of interdependence between professional and personal realms and creating a layer of ambiguity in life patterns.

Architects travelling and establishing themselves in colonial territories, and architects grouped in the oppositionist circles in the Portuguese dictatorship's period of the 20th century, are the focus of the case studies presented.

2 Architects in the Colonies

The study[1] involved making a register of all architects working in the Portuguese colonies in the 20th century[2]. This was done irrespective of the duration of their stay and the specific purpose of their journey, as long as it signified a professional activity. It also involved an open-end register, due to the ever-growing data being collected and knowledge of hitherto unheard of architects. The data collected was organized in various steps, differentiated mainly by the growing numbers of individuals. It was obtained thorough a patient retrieval of discrete elements of information from archives and mainly from published materials – books, thesis, articles in journals and other media. The study includes a number of variables, of which a very significant

---

[1] Research was initated in 2005 and a first paper was presented in September 2006 at the IXthInternational DocoMomo conference in Ankara by M. C. Matos and T. B.Ramos: 'A Two-Way Street: Migrants of the Modern across Portuguese-speaking countries' [10]; from there many subsequent publications and have developed, such as the June 2010 position paper and presentation at the first EAHN International Meeting held in Guimarães [11].

[2] This includes architects designing buildings as well as architects designing urban plans. Note that in Portugal, urban planning was traditionally done by both architects and civil engineers, with an emphasis during the 20th century on urban-scale planning being dealt with by architects while regional planning being coped with by engineers and other professionals, such as geographers; certainly, many exceptions occur in this broad pattern.

one is co-authorship: it indicates the combined work effort and responsibility for a design project, and denotes a minimally stable relationship between two or more people, necessarily based on trust and/or mutual interest. It might indicate a deeper sort of relationship, i.e. friendship. On the long run, co-authorship is a reliable sign for the detection of important links in the professional and personal life of architects.

As said, ARS identifies the interaction patterns between agents: it therefore deals with connections. From then on, it allocates the relative position of the architects in the social net and permits an evaluation of their role in the net. This analysis is done by means of statistical bases that sort the actors into numerical values according to various socio-centric measures of the direct relationships that were identified. For the study, the measures that were selected were Centrality, betweeness and proximity; the identification of the 'cliques' between architects was also pursued. In Table 1, the degree of centrality[3] is shown for the topmost positioned architects in the first stage of 131 individuals considered

Table 1. Degree of Centrality of topmost positioned architects - first stage, 131 individuals

FREEMAN'S DEGREE CENTRALITY MEASURES.

```
Diagonal valid?        NO
Model              SYMMETRIC
Input dataset        tabela arq_colaboracoes
   1      2        3
Degree  NrmDegree   Share

12   AntMatosVeloso    18.000   11.180   0.059
56   FernaoSimoesCarvalho  13.000   8.075   0.043
23   CarlosChaveAlmeida   12.000   7.453   0.039
59   FranciscoFigueira    12.000   7.453   0.039
31   CarlosWorm       12.000   7.453   0.039
8    AntBarataFeyo     11.000   6.832   0.036
76   JoãoJoseTinoco    9.000   5.590   0.030
14   AntSilvaCampino    8.000   4.969   0.026
52   FernandoMesquita    7.000   4.348   0.023
48   FernandoAlfPereira   7.000   4.348   0.023
88   JoséBruschy      6.000   3.727   0.020
100  JoséPintoCunha     6.000   3.727   0.020
20   BernardRamalhete    6.000   3.727   0.020
109  LuisAmaral       6.000   3.727   0.020
83   JorgeSilva       6.000   3.727   0.020
42   DomingosSilva     6.000   3.727   0.020
115  LuisVasconcelos    5.000   3.106   0.016
70   JanuarioGodinhoAlmeida 5.000  3.106   0.016
118  ManuelSepúlveda    5.000   3.106   0.016
1    AdalbertoDias     5.000   3.106   0.016
```

```
DESCRIPTIVE STATISTICS

   1      2        3
Degree  NrmDegree   Share

1 Mean       1.877    1.166   0.008
2 Std Dev     2.916    1.811   0.010
3 Sum      304.000  188.820   1.000
4 Variance    8.503    3.280   0.000
5 SSQ      1948.000  751.514   0.021
6 MCSSQ    1377.531  531.434   0.015
7 Euc Norm    44.136   27.414   0.145
8 Minimum    0.000    0.000   0.000
9 Maximum    18.000   11.180   0.059

Network Centralization = 10.14%
Heterogeneity = 2.11%. Normalized = 1.50%

Actor-by-centrality matrix saved as dataset
FreemanDegree

Running time. 00:00:01
Output generated:  16 Jun 10 15:47:03
Copyright (c) 2002-8 Analytic Technologies
```

An architect better positioned in the net has a greater number of alternatives of contact with other architects. He receives more information and in a faster way.

---

[3] "Actors who have more ties to other actors may be advantaged positions. Because they have many ties, they may have alternative ways to satisfy needs, and hence are less dependent on other individuals. They may have access to, and be able to call on more of the resources of the network as a whole. (…) So, a very simple, but often very effective measure of an actor's centrality and power potential is their degree". Hanneman, 2005[12].

António Matos Veloso, Fernão Simões de Carvalho, Carlos Chaves Almeida, Francisco Figueira and Carlos Worm stand out as the most central of this set of individuals. According to SNA, they have a larger number of links and therefore have a higher degree of exposure to information and ultimately to power.

Figure 1 transcribes the data, as it was available in the 131 individuals phase into a visual recognizable pattern. It was expanded to aggregate institutions – the three main planning public bodies that promoted planning work in the colonies, namely the Gabinete de Urbanização Colonial, later called 'do Ultramar', the Gabinete de Urbanização de Luanda and Gabinete de Urbanização de Lourenço Marques.

These institutions act as linking bodies; equivalence to persons in this context is justified by the fact that in these collective and public institutions co-authorship is almost unavoidable. In these government establishments, relationships were established and maintained in time, as they had permanence and means.

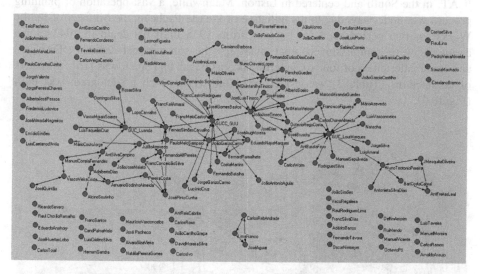

Fig. 1. 1st phase of SNA performed with 131 architects

Links between architects were recorded, leaving out those either that had no links or whose interconnections have not been testified so far. Seemingly low-profile architects substitute in centrality rank the more notable architects such as they are known in the Metropolis, measured by celebrity and status. Alongside this apparent reversal, the provisional conclusion is the emergence of a vast 'community' of interlocked individuals, crossing geography and institutional work situations.

3   The 1948 Congress

In 1948 took place the '1° CongressoNacional de Arquitectura', the first congress of the professionals graduated in architecture in Portugal [13].

Fig. 2. Bookcover of the 1948 Congress Proceedings

In the same year were operating in social and political activism two groups of architects, the ODAM [14] in the North of the country, centered in Porto, and the ICAT, in the South and centered in Lisbon. Meanwhile, a vast operation of planning process was underway, due to the initiative of Duarte Pacheco, the Minister of Public Works for two periods and the last one from 1938 until his death in 1943. Some architects were commissioned urban plans for the sub-regional capitals ('Distrito') and for smaller cities of touristic interest such as beach and spa towns [15] . A matrix of connections (Table 2) was established, following which a sociogram was built (Figure 3).

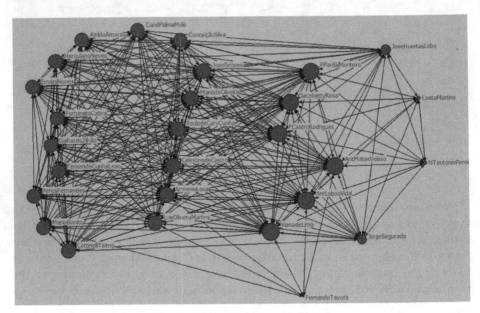

Fig. 3. 1948: Sociogram indicating the degree of centrality (dimensioned: 4)

Table 2. 1948: Table of Afilliations

AFFILIATIONS

```
                              1  2  3  4  5  5  7  8  9 10 11 12 13 14 15 16 17 18 19 20 21 22 23 24 25 26 27 28 29
                             CI OD K  Te 2T Te Te FC Ce Co Jo He Jo Fl Br Av Po V  Se Fa Be Co Li Po Sa Vi Gu V  Le

   1      CIAM               3  3  0  2  0  1  0  0  0  0  0  0  0  C  2  1  1  1  0  0  0  0  0  0  0  0  0  0  0
   2      ODAM               3  7  0  6  1  3  0  0  0  0  0  0  0  C  3  1  1  1  0  0  0  0  0  0  0  0  0  0  0
   3      ICAT               C  0 12  1  0  3  7  2  1  1  1  1  2  5  1  1  0  1  2  3  1  1  2  2  2  1  1  0  0
   4      TeseCong1948Arq    2  6 11 23  3  6  6  1  1  1  1  1  2 10  2  2  1  2  2  3  1  1  2  2  4  1  2  0  1
   5      2TesesCong1948Arq  0  1  0  3  3  1  0  0  0  0  0  0  C  1  0  0  0  0  0  0  0  0  1  0  0  0  0
   6      TeseCong1948Hab    1  3  3  6  1  13 2  1  0  0  1  0  1  3  1  0  0  0  1  1  0  0  1  1  0  1  1  0
   7  TeseCong1948co-autoria 0  0  7  6  0  2  7  2  1  1  1  1  2  1  0  0  0  0  0  0  0  1  1  1  0  0
   8   FCastroRodrigues      0  0  2  1  0  1  2  2  0  0  0  C  1  0  0  0  0  0  0  0  0  1  0  0  0
   9   CelestinodeCastro     0  0  1  1  0  0  1  0  0  0  0  C  0  0  0  0  0  0  0  0  0  0  0  0  0  0
  10    ConceicaoSilva       0  0  1  1  0  0  1  0  0  1  0  0  1  0  0  0  0  0  0  0  0  0  0  0  0  0  0
  11    JoseHuertasLobo      0  0  1  1  0  1  1  0  0  0  1  0  1  0  1  0  0  0  0  0  0  0  0  0  0  0  0
  12    HerculanoNeves       0  0  1  1  0  0  1  0  0  0  0  1  C  1  1  0  0  0  0  0  0  0  0  0  1  1  0  0
  13      JoaoSimoes         0  0  2  2  0  1  2  0  0  1  1  0  2  0  0  0  0  0  0  0  0  0  0  0  0  0  0
  14    PlanosUrb1948        2  3  5 10  1  3  2  1  0  0  0  1  0 11  2  2  1  2  2  3  1  1  2  2  4  1  3  1  1
  15       Braga             1  1  1  2  0  1  1  0  0  0  1  C  2  2  0  0  0  0  0  0  0  0  1  1  0
  16       Aveiro            1  1  1  2  0  0  0  0  0  0  0  C  2  0  2  1  0  1  1  0  0  0  0  0  0
  17       Porto             1  1  0  1  0  1  0  0  0  0  0  C  1  0  1  1  0  0  0  0  0  0  0  0  0
  18      VilaReal           0  1  1  2  0  0  0  0  0  0  0  C  2  0  0  2  0  1  1  1  1  1  1  0  0  0
  19      Setubal            0  0  2  2  0  1  0  0  0  0  0  C  2  0  1  0  0  2  2  0  1  1  0  0  0  0
  20       Faro              0  0  3  3  0  1  0  0  0  0  0  C  3  0  1  0  1  2  3  1  2  2  1  0  0  0
  21       Beja              0  0  1  1  0  0  0  0  0  0  0  C  1  0  0  1  0  1  1  1  1  1  1  0  0  0
  22      Coimbra            0  0  1  1  0  0  0  0  0  0  0  C  1  0  0  1  0  1  1  1  1  1  1  0  0  0
  23       Lisboa            0  0  2  2  0  1  0  0  0  0  0  C  2  0  0  1  1  2  1  2  1  2  1  0  0  0
  24     Portalegre          0  0  2  2  0  1  0  0  0  0  0  C  2  0  0  1  1  2  1  2  1  2  1  0  0  0
  25     Santarem            0  0  2  4  1  0  1  1  0  0  0  C  4  0  0  1  0  1  1  1  1  1  4  0  1  0  1
  26       Viseu             0  0  1  1  0  0  1  0  0  0  1  C  1  1  0  0  0  0  0  0  0  0  1  1  0
  27       Guarda            0  0  1  2  0  1  1  0  0  0  1  C  3  1  0  0  0  0  0  0  0  1  1  3  1  1
  28   VianadoCastelo        0  0  0  0  0  1  0  0  0  0  0  C  1  0  0  0  0  0  0  0  0  0  0  1  1  0
  29       Leiria            0  0  0  1  0  0  0  0  0  0  0  C  1  0  0  0  0  0  0  0  0  1  0  1  0  1
```

1-mode matrix

Correspondences between five situations were searched therefore: Congress, ICAT, ODAM, CIAM and government sponsored urban plans. As regards the Congress, it distinguished the authors of theses presented at the meeting under the two main themes; of these authors, it inquired into their belonging to either one of the ODAM/ICAT groups; it then inquired into their affiliation into the CIAM (CongrèsInternationalesd'ArchitectureModerne'); and finally, as regards the *Distritos*, it selected those architects who shared the same sub-regional territories.

Miguel Jacobetty Rosa, JoãoSimões, Celestino de Castro, Mário de Oliveira[4] and Alfredo Viana de Lima were found to be the most central to the network.

---

[4] Although being an engineer, Mário de Azevedo was included in the set of professionals in the study due to his essential role in the planning process both in Portugal and in the colonies.

This preliminary enquiry allowed probing into the social and professional relations between individual in a historical period in which the *Estado Novo* (Salazar's regime as an institutional and ideological organization) was yet at its peak and repressed expressions of modernity. Nevertheless, it was found that an intense sharing of professional interests and political affinities counteracted the authoritarian attitude of the State apparatus. An active presence at the Congress, participation in either the ICAT or the ODAM and affiliation in the CIAM's was closely associated with commissions of urban plans from the government. Benefits for working opportunities are enhanced by sharing two or more of these bonds.

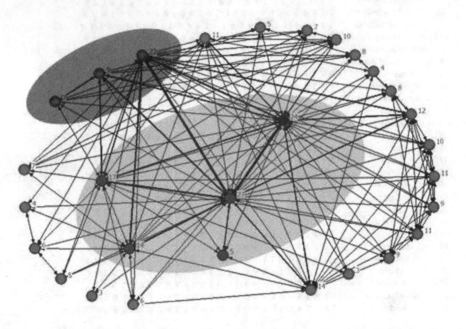

Fig. 4. 1948: Affiliations' sociogram (dimensioned links). In the darker oval, the formal groupings of ICAT, ODAM and CIAM; in the ligher oval, the distinct modes of relation to the Congress and the planning commissions; and in white, the individual professionals.

Figure 4 shows the affiliations sociogram discriminating by background tone between formal groupings of ICAT,ODAM and CIAM, presentations at the Congress in their distinct modes (different Sessions and co-authorships) and on-going planning commissions and the set of individual professionals. It allows one to visually distinguish the most important links, as the edges in the graph have widths that are proportional to their relative weights. A main route links the presenters of theses in the Session Architecture to the Planos de Urbanização' underway in that year. A further incorporation of the whole set of *districtos* into the graph would supplement the picture of the work opportunities at this first post-war period.

4   Conclusion

Architecture theory and criticism have for too long been keeping aloof of the infrastructural state of affairs in which creative production takes place. Material conditions for work include work opportunities. These are often presented as *deus ex machina* advents, suspended in thin air. A more thorough enquiry into the opaque mesh of work opportunities is necessary and the methodology of *Social Network Analysis* provides a valuable tool to systematically investigate this blind spot in research. Travel, expatriation, patterns of commission, institutional and informal organizations, beliefs, ideologies, the role of the State apparatus, all fall into the field to be viewed and examined.

The exploratory use of SNA considered the architects and urban planners' activities in a colonial setting – colonization has been for centuries, and up to the last quarter of the 20th century, an essential part of the nation's *hubris* - and in a single year in the metropole.

SNA acknowledges the essential role of social relations in the establishment of work opportunities at home and in life-supporting networks over vast territories in the colonies. As announcements of up to now unheard of individuals emerge, and as a meticulous and painstaking analysis with SNA is carried out, a more global and reliable picture of the colonial networks is made possible. In the metropole, a complete integration of data from active professionals during the 20th century, particularly in the long Estado Novo period, is key to the development of a more mature historiography of the Modern Movement and its brother movement, the Athens Charter, in sustaining on objective infra-structure, to be found in this instance in social relations, the lighter side of artistic production.

Acknowledgments. This paper is based on research entitled 'Networks and Mobility' conducted at the Faculty of Architecture, Technical University of Lisbon and at the CIAUD / FCT - Foundation for Science and Technology.

References

1. Kostof, S.: The Architect: Chapters in the History of the Profession, 3rd edn. University of California Press, Berkeley (2000)
2. Blau, J.R.: Architects and Firms A Sociological Perspective on Architectural Practices. The MIT Press, Mass. (1987)
3. Cuff, D.: Architecture: The Story of a Practice. The MIT Press, Mass. (1992)
4. Gomes, S.V.: A construção da profissionalização dos arquitectos em Portugal: um estudo sociológico. Ms thesis in Sociology of Organizations, ISCTE, Lisboa (2000)
5. Ribeiro, A.I.M.: Arquitectos portugueses: 90 anos de vida associativa 1863-1953. FAUP Publicações, Porto (2002)
6. Villaverde Cabral, M., Borges, V. (eds.): Relatório Profissão: Arquitecto/a, Instituto de Ciências Sociais / Ordem dos Arquitectos, Lisboa (2006)
7. Scott, J.: Social Network Analysis. Sage, London (2000)

8. Wasserman, S., Faust, K.: Social Network Analysis: Methods and Applications, 14th printing. Cambridge University Press, Cambridge (1994)
9. Quiroga, Á., et al.: Talleres de autoformación con programas informáticos de análisis de redes sociales Borrador (2005)
10. Matos, M.C., Ramos, T.B.: A Two-Way Street: Migrants of the Modern across Portuguese-speaking countries. In: Salman, Y., Prudon, T., Malishewsky, K. (eds.) Proceedings of the IX International DOCOMOMO Conference 2006, pp. 169–176. Istanbul Technical University, Middle East Technical University, Yildiz Technical University, Ankara (2006)
11. Matos, M.C., Ramos, T.B.: Recapturing the network: a position paper. In: 1st International Meeting EAHN – European Architectural History Network, Guimarães (2010) CD ISBN 978 98995563-9-3/978-989-96163-2-5
12. Hanneman, R.: Spatial Dynamics of Human Populations: Some Basic Models (2005), http://faculty.ucr.edu/~hanneman/spatial/index.html
13. dos Arquitectos, S. N.: 1º Congresso Nacional de Arquitectura. Relatório da Comissão Executiva, Teses, Conclusões e Votos do Congresso. Promovido pelo Sindicato Nacional dos Arquitectos com o patrocínio do Governo, Lisboa (1948)
14. Barbosa, C.: ODAM - Organização dos Arquitectos Modernos Porto 1947-1952. Compilação, Edições ASA, Porto (1972)
15. Lôbo, M.S.: Planos de Urbanização à Época de Duarte Pacheco, DGOTDU, FAUP, Porto (1995)

Social Networks as Vital Resources for Adults' Learning

Kathleen P. King

University of South Florida, Tampa
4202 E Fowler Ave EDU 105, Tampa, FL 33620
kathleenking@usf.edu

Abstract. It is clear that, when researched and analyzed critically, social networks provide a ubiquitous and powerful tool to provide insight into current and past societal trends and perspectives. This paper provides a model for thinking about and implementing social networks for organizations which function in and serve across virtual spaces. From distance learning to e-commerce, b-learning and corporate training to informal learning, sports and entertainment industries, social media is a powerful context for dialogue, expression and lived experience. How well prepared are our organizations to understand current trends and perspectives in virtual spaces? Where do we begin? What skills do employees and students need to analyze critically the data gathered from social media and other virtual spaces? This paper presents specific strategies, valuable recommendations, and further direction for social networks' use in these areas.

Keywords: social networks, social media, distance learning, e-learning, b-learning, corporate training, cybercommunities, cyberculture, professional development, virtual communities.

1 Introduction to Social Networks Today

Even though wide varieties of definitions for social networks exist, there are three essential elements evident among complete descriptions: using *technology resources* to build *communities* around *common topics of interest or need*. Since 2005, social network use has exploded among people of all ages. Examples of popular social media tools and platforms include Flickr, Tumblr, Facebook, LinkedIn, Twitter, YouTube, Scribd, Digg, etc.

Who uses social networks? Simply stated, people across all age groups use them. Unlike in the 1990s, it is now the norm to see adults and children of every age connected by handheld devices to the entire globe no matter where they are. From the gym to the grocery store, classroom to boardroom, airport to ball field, we are globally connected. The popularity of these virtual communities and communication tools scaffold upon critical characteristics: they (1) are usually free, (2) provide online (or digital handheld device) virtual environments for conversations, content sharing,

G.D. Putnik and M.M. Cruz-Cunha (Eds.): ViNOrg 2011, CCIS 248, pp. 357–366, 2012.

and community building in real time, (3) function both asynchronously and simultaneously, and (4) are ubiquitously accessible (accessed through several routes).

A recent search for lists of "Social Media Networks" yielded hundreds of different sites, some listed with no identifying information, others including numbers of subscribers and year of origin, Alexa ranking, some divided by categories of network purpose or focus. The most comprehensive list had 40 categories and yielded the greatest number of social networks. Table 1 presents the top 22 social network categories ranked by the number of different networks.

Table 1. Rank and number of social network sites per category. Analyzed from data available at Traffikd.com [1].

Rank	Category	Sites	Rank	Category	Sites
1	Bookmarking	57	12	Cooking/Food	14
2	Miscellaneous	56	13	Fashion	14
3	General networking	44	14	Travel	12
4	Professional	28	15	Photo sharing	11
5	News	25	16	Music	10
6	Family	18	17	Shopping	10
7	Cultures/Foreign language	17	18	Video sharing	10
8	Microblogging/IM/Mobile	16	19	Dating	9
9	Education/Books	15	20	Health/Medical	9
10	Sports	15	21	Pets	9
11	Technology	15	22	Connecting with friends	8

This vast array of topics and number of sites reveals that social media as a network and communication resource far exceeds the few sites familiar to the general adult public. It also exposes an expansive resource which most teaching and training efforts still do not use. Furthermore, the scope of resources, contacts and possibilities increases exponentially when one considers the availability of this enormous body of resources and number of people globally connected any minute of the day and night.

From the 1990s through the 2000's, the study of cyberculture emerged as sociology and information technology specialists studied and discussed its emergence and development [2], [3], [4], [5]. This literature documents the development and shaping of cyberculture from the early days of inter-computer communication (ICC) and online communication, to web-based platforms and virtual worlds. Another interesting development is that, since 2005, web-based cell phones (also identified as Smartphones, iPhones and Androids) and less expensive broadband Internet connections extended cyberspace participation beyond technical experts (geeks) to mainstream citizens in developed countries.

The critical point for our discussion is that today adults already use social network tools for daily functions in more global ways than many trainers and educators comprehend [6], [7], [8], [9]. For greatest benefit, we need to include learning how to leverage social media networks and vital data/resources within our training efforts, to transform learning fully and for greater global connectivity [10]. In order to do so, trainers must shift pedagogical perspectives and strategies. Refusing to include social network resources and communication in education and training will (1) convince people that education and training is irrelevant to their world, (2) ill-prepare our learners to use these tools for business and academic purposes, (3) lose opportunities to construct new knowledge, and (4) widen the gap of relevance between experts and the 'real-world.'

1.1   Social Networks and Virtual Spaces Meet Higher Education

The specific context of distance learning is the dominant virtual space in which higher education operates. There are many benefits beyond those listed above to incorporate social media in distance classes. A more egalitarian and peer-learning experience emerges as active learning, greater student voice, and empowerment replace traditional classroom power structures [11]. Using social media in learning activities means transforming traditional teaching practices to active learning, including problem solving, and critical thinking, both strategies which require students to identify needs and questions, discover necessary resources, gather and evaluate data. Effectively constructed social media activities challenge collaborative understandings. As Lave and Wenger [12] describe, these experiences are opportunities for situated learning. The difference is that it occurs in a virtual space within public and/or private forums. In addition, social media is precisely *social* and *media;* this medium pushes the learning process into a community space thereby providing limitless opportunist for dialogue, articulation of understanding, debating, negotiation, persuasion and compromise [11], [13]. These changes in learning experiences enable students to be active participants in their learning, building habits which support lifelong learning, greater motivation, and self-directedness.

Using social networks in our distance classrooms builds instant and powerful connections to real-world business and research, case studies, problem solving opportunities, primary sources, and more [10]. Asking learners to evaluate public opinion about a critical course topic evidenced in social networks makes the discussion more urgent and relevant to their world. In essence, these simple actions access the pulse of the current state of the field and public perspectives. Beyond theory, discovering how businesses swiftly execute damage control regarding client complaints and rants in social media, learners see real-life examples of public relations, customer service, and marketing disasters. Facilitating dialogue about benefits of public forums as opportunities for innovation, product development, and services breathes new life into ethics, communication skills, and business courses.

1.2   Social Networks as Professional Learning Contexts

How do people in the business world learn the best strategies, opportunities, and responsible practices for using and participating in social networks? We do not currently receive training in handling the details and pitfalls of social media. Yet technology outstrips all other areas of our work in the urgent need for upgrading and training. Social media is a prime example of this continued need for relevant training.

Recent headlines emphasize the difficulty people have understanding their corporate identity and responsibility when they post in Facebook and Twitter for the company [14]. Consider the volume and breadth of legal battles over defamation and information leaks via email; with how much more spontaneous social media site updates are, problems may quickly outstrip benefits unless people learn professional actions and behaviors.

The solution is to include professional learning in order to scaffold your organizational potential. How? First, begin by establishing safe, responsible, and innovative strategies and approaches. Second, focus on how social networks assist in gathering valuable consumer, rival, and product data and trends, and strategic distribution of company-approved information provides direction and boundaries [15]. Effective methods of delivering this professional learning includes using social media in active, problem-based, collaborative, and situated learning [15] [16].

2   Social Networks as Innovative 21st Century Learning

The 21st Century Learning Skills framework is valuable for understanding how to use social networks for learning in virtual spaces. Developed over 10 years, the model emerged from the gap between the technologically advanced and changing worlds of work, business and academics [17]. The 21st Century Learning Skills framework addresses both the content and skills that people need for success today. Figure 1 portrays the critical sectors of content: (1) Core subjects and 21st century themes; (2) Learning and innovations skills; (3) Information, media and technology skills; and (4) Life and career skills. This model reflects the complexities of our global society, the changing nature of our political and economic worlds, and the reliance on information and technology literacy, all standing upon a foundation of basic and advanced literacies.

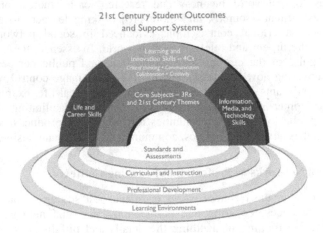

Fig. 1. 21st Century Student Outcomes and Support Systems [18]. (Reprinted with permission from Partnership for 21st Century Skills (www.p21.org).

According to Senge [19], a learning organization needs support by continuous learning, generation of new knowledge, and continuous improvement based on needs of the field, discipline, and outside world. Considering social networks, Figure 1 demonstrates that a systems view of outcomes provides a comprehensive and essential frame for real world access to professional development and learning.

The specific content needed for workplace and higher education professional learning depends upon the field. However, one achieves the vital elements of 21st century learning in formal and informal contexts by using social networks as an immediate context for interaction. This medium enables professionals to examine current and/or past trends thereby developing skills, which differ greatly from the more theoretical vein often yielded in contemporary colleges, universities, and corporate training settings [20], [21], [22].

This issue of higher education not matching work needs is why so many people believe we face academic, economic and career crises [23], [24], [25], [26]. Formally, learners cultivate critical thinking and problem solving through studying past and current trends from social networks using search engines and analytical strategies. Informally, professionals join social networks to build professional relationships, exchange ideas, collaborate to solve real problems and widen their circle of professional networks for understanding, opportunity, and creativity [15]. The next two sections illustrate two strategies used to accomplish these goals. In both cases, appropriating popular social networks for professional learning is a pivotal transformation in instructional planning, design, and delivery.

2.1   Critical Thinking and Problem Solving

As stated previously, situated learning is a powerful and inherently relevant vehicle to cultivate adept critical thinkers and problem solvers, and situated learning [12]. Examples abound in the media and literature of how entrepreneurs and corporations use social media every day as a tool to gather potential solutions [27]. Similarly, trainers and educators can use social networks to provide real-time data for analysis on an infinite number of dimensions and descriptors. The example provided illustrates building critical thinking skills specifically by recognizing data trends' accuracy and appropriateness to specific situations. It not only parallels the opportunities for using social networks in business settings, but also formally prepares professionals to build and apply critical thinking skills.

Social Media Learning Activity: A camera manufacturer's market research reveals that technology-using individuals have greater interests in new models and features of digital cameras. From prior experience, they also know that this group is very savvy and responsive to accurate phrasing of ads and social network posts. In other words, if marketing campaigns appear irrelevant to their daily community dialogue, biased, or too "corporate" they are deleted or tuned out immediately. Therefore, this activity introduces a strategy for determining which diversity phrases best reflect current language use, practices, sentiments and perspectives of the key market group in order that the campaign fits accurately.

Learners divide into market research teams to work collaboratively; throughout the project, they gain consensus with their team on courses of action, interpretation of data, etc. Using the online small group discussion among Group 1 as an example of the details of this activity, we discover that they decided to analyze the use of diversity terms among major social networks during the prior 24 months. They list their search terms including lesbian, gay, LGBTQ, GLBT, and "trans" with the understanding that these basic terms will lead to more "conversations." These longer exchanges can reveal trends in opinions and perspectives and other terms which the target population employs. Based on the extensive number of social networks available, Group 1 chooses Facebook, Technorati, Twitter, and Digg and Flickr as viable communities of public discussion on technology related topics. They use Google to extract samples of data from three month segments across the two years and then analyze the data in three ways. The group (1) documents the frequency of diversity terms used, (2) identifies common and recurrent themes of conversation on this topic using qualitative thematic coding [28], and (3) analyzes the postings using discourse analysis [29].

Rather than theory, hypothetical example or token data, the participants conduct meaningful research and explore current events and real opinions [3], [5]: the essence and power of situated learning. Specifically, they develop and practice skills they will continue to use in future research, the world of business, and their daily lives- critical research, analysis, discussion and collaboration skills [15], [18]. The convenience of this learning space complements the vibrant experience of discovering the power of social networks in revealing information with appropriate understanding and skills. Developing similar research activities for any content area or business application provides participants fresh insights on topics, products and services.

2.2   Creativity and Innovation

A dramatic revelation in 2006, Tapscott and Williams' [27] book "Wikinomics" revealed that in many business settings, corporations monitor the postings within social communities or host contests to discover and inspire creative ideas for new or improved products, marketing and customer service. Building on this widely understood trend, trainers and educators can use social networks as a valuable tool and strategy for developing virtual creative collaborative initiatives. Next, there is an example of how trainers, educators, and learners may scaffold traditional classroom activities into virtual innovative "think tanks."

Learners use R&D Brainstorming through Virtual Think Tanks to "fish" for ideas such as new product needs, product improvements, new products, marketing approaches, service needs and improvements, production means, efficiencies, etc. via virtual social networks. In addition, the learners submit their emergent ideas back to the social network to vet it and determine its viability and potential additional development/modification/improvement possibilities. Learners, whether alone or in groups, locally or dispersed throughout the world, can benefit from these activities.

This activity engages learners in evaluating different social networks and their strengths, merits and fit for the task. When peers share their information, the group gains valuable information in these dimensions for immediate and distant use. Logistically, once selecting their social networks, learners post a potential product problem and swiftly receive answers.

Next steps in the learning activity include monitoring responses, determining if interaction is needed, desired or permitted, tracking postings and results, determining the timeframe for the engagement and then closing the discussion to commence analysis of the data. Designing the activity with several open-ended learner choices increases learner freedom, ownership and responsibility. In addition, it provides experience and insight into the multitude of dimensions which affect a collection of responses.

Once data is collected, learners must choose what approach to use for analysis: whether they use qualitative and/or quantitative methods, and which specific analysis tools. For most learners, it takes working through the process several times to gain confidence in the decisions and steps involved. In just a few sessions, using short activities such as these, learners build confidence and transfer of learning quickly.

Returning to the 21st century lifelong learning skills, this activity develops and cultivates critical thinking, collaboration and communication. Consider the following detailed examples which flow from the described activity. Learners engage in developing the ability to

- Facilitate discussions virtually to maximize new developments;
- Collaborate in goal setting, decision making, and problem solving;
- Confirm and extend findings through iterative social network interaction;
- Analyze data for accuracy, feasibility and best fit;
- Synthesize and determine a best solution using global collaboration; and
- Create a formal proposal of findings / solutions.

2.3   A Model: The Social Media Web of 21st Century Learning

Figure 2 illustrates the approach to leveraging social networks as a situated learning context for 21st Century Learning. This model demonstrates that different learning settings apply to this means of situated learning: individual and group, professional learning and higher education. It is a model for considering the use of social networks in instructional settings to cultivate 21st century learning skills through active learning, relevant learning, socially constructed meaning and constructivist discovery.

The very essence of cyberculture in social networks builds upon the power of socially constructed meaning [31]. In no other time have we had the opportunity to tap into globally constructed dialogue and opinions as we may now through social networks. As we examine Figure 2, consider the flow of constructed meaning and see the individual at the center of the activity with social media network spokes/arms extending in many directions (the inner circle is the individual, the outer is community). These activities engage the individual with collaborative problem solving to reach solutions. Social media provides access, but it also brings the interaction back to the individual's need for solution. Each of the learning activities described above could be new spokes in the web.

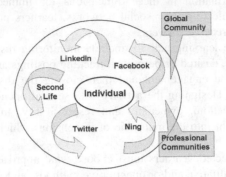

Fig. 2. A Social Media Web of 21st Century Learning © Kathleen P. King, [30]

3   Recommendations

There are boundless opportunities for using social networks in adult learning settings across content areas and disciplines, business sectors and forums; but the greater challenge is transforming our paradigm of virtual learning to include our traditional venues and allow virtual networks as part of our learning experiences. Such transformation requires rethinking our learning outcomes and determining how data gathering activities through the burgeoning primary source data of virtual networks can be immediate data sources and learning labs. Based on the history and literature of cybercultures as well as the rapid rate of change today, these media provide new opportunities for relevant and valuable intersections of learning.

Recommendations for practice include instructional design, philosophy and curriculum. Regarding instructional design, educators and trainers need to develop innovative learning activities which leverage the social discourse nature of social networks across content areas and disciplines. This action requires reconceptualizing learners' roles to be more active. Rather than just learning about issues, trends, and "flat" perspectives of concepts in a static format, social networks provide a multi-dimensional, divergent community in which opinions are transparent and open. This context incorporates an immediate view into real-world perspectives, compelling critical thinking and problem solving opportunities. In addition, social networks are infinite, constantly changing case studies, available on scores of topics (See Table 1). These characteristics and opportunities require us to shift our thinking and practice of designing learning experiences.

Using social networks, the curriculum aspect of this equation transforms the traditional models of research activities customarily only available to experts into research skills development activities for all learners. Simply increasing or decreasing the steps in an activity and the decision making variables scales it for different learner expertise and readiness, while still providing analysis of real data and the relevance of empowered learning.

4   Future Research

Currently, social media is one of the easiest, most convenient and widely used vehicles for reaching specific communities across the globe and sectors/fields. However, there is a parallel set of risks which continually need to be evaluated and mitigated. Unlike educators' and trainers' prior practices, isolated from real-world interactions, the risks are a significant, necessary change of practice.

While any of us who have used social networks conscientiously and professionally can enumerate several recommendations for safe and prudent participation, we need additional research regarding best strategies for teaching adults how to evaluate the risks and potentials of social media action for individual success and collective advancement. Moreover, our fields need more generative and innovative models of problem solving, including strategies for mastering, questioning and leveraging unknown technologies and collaborations, closed and open-ended. Just as technology is advancing rapidly, so are technology's business applications: but our formal instruction using even the most basic skills in this area lags because educators often use closed models of problem solving and research.

Increased knowledge construction provides a vital trend which can be addressed [20], [9] with the concurrent growth demand for collaborative teams. How can the literature and research on learning communities [13] illuminate the means of knowledge generation through collaboration via continuing virtual networks? Can we build new understanding and opportunities not yet materialized with them? Based on historical trends, the answer is yes. Exploring how to understand, facilitate and promote these relationships, with the current and future social network and technology tools best suited for community is fertile ground for future possibilities.

5   Conclusion

Educators and trainers have the opportunity to lead the development and adoption of current virtual social networks as modalities of instruction and to cultivate new forms and applications. Business knows that international and interdisciplinary dialogue is the essential ingredient for knowledge construction today. Similarly, adults use vast social networks for every aspect of their life... except, for the most part, learning and training efforts. Connecting these two elements provides a powerful and generative platform for relevant learning. Moreover, such learning activities as those described can cultivate lifelong learning habits of self-directed learning and continued professional development.

References

1.   Traffiked (2011), http://traffikd.com/social-media-websites/
2.   Barrett, E. (ed.): Sociomedia. MIT Press, Cambridge (1992)
3.   Bell, D.: Cybercultures. Routledge, New York (2006)
4.   Levy, P.: Cyberculture. R. Bononno (Trans). University of Minnesota Press, Minneapolis (2001)
5.   Levy, P.: Collective Intelligence. Basic Books, New York (1999)
6.   Prensky, M.: Digital Natives, Digital Immigrants. On The Horizon 9(5), 1–6 (2001)

7. Prensky, M.: Young Minds, Fast Times: The 21st Century Digital Learner. Edutopia (2008),
    `http://www.edutopia.org/ikid-digital-learner-technology-2008`
8. King, K.P., Sanquist, S.: 21st Century Learning and Human Performance. In: Wang, V., King, K.P. (eds.) Fundamentals of Human Performance and Training, pp. 61–88. Information Age Publishing, Charlotte (2009)
9. Wankel, C. (ed.): Cutting-edge Social Media Approaches to Business Education. Information Age Publishing, Charlotte (2010)
10. Veletsianos, G.: Designing Opportunities for Transformation with Emerging Technologies. Educational Technology 51(2), 41–46 (2011)
11. King, K.P.: Empowerment and Voice: Digital Media. In: Miller, M., King, K.P. (eds.) Empowering Women through Literacy, pp. 271–280. Information Age Publishing, Charlotte (2009)
12. Lave, J., Wenger, E.: Situated Learning. Cambridge University, Cambridge (1991)
13. Palloff, R., Pratt, K.: Collaborating Online. Jossey Bass, San Francisco (2005)
14. Popkin, H.A.S.: Twitter Gets You Fired in 140 Characters or Less. Technotica (March 23, 2009), `http://www.msnbc.msn.com/id/29796962/ns/technology_and_science-tech_and_gadgets/`
15. King, K.P.: Transformative Professional Development in Unlikely Places. In: Proceedings of the AERC Annual Conference, OISE Toronto (2011)
16. Fink, L.D.: Creating Significant Learning Experiences. Jossey-Bass, San Francisco (2003)
17. The Partnership for 21st Century Skills: Framework for 21st Century learning,Tucson (2004),
    `http://www.21stcenturyskills.org/documents/frameworkflyer_072307.pdf`
18. The Partnership for 21st Century Skills: 21st Century Skills Education and Competitiveness, Tucson (2008),
    `http://www.p21.org/documents/21st_century_skills_education_and_competitiveness_guide.pdf`
19. Senge, P.: The Fifth Discipline. Doubleday, New York (1994)
20. Altbach, P.G., Berdahl, R.O., Gumport, P.J. (eds.): American Higher Education in the Twenty-First Century. John Hopkins University Press, Baltimore (2005)
21. Bozarth, J.: Social Media for Trainers. John Wiley, New York (2010)
22. Schuster, J.H., Finkelstein, M.J.: The American Faculty: Restructuring of Academic Work and Careers. The John Hopkins University Press, Baltimore (2006)
23. Christensen, C.M., Johnson, C.S., Horn, M.B.: Disrupting Class: How Disruptive Innovation Will Change the Way We Learn. McGraw Hill, New York (2008)
24. Hirsh, R.H., Morrow, J., Wolfe, T.: Declining by Degrees. Palgrave, New York (2006)
25. Morrow, J.: Below C Level: How American Education Encourages Mediocrity. CreateSpace, Los Angeles (2010)
26. Zemsky, R.: Making Reform Work. Rutgers University Press, New Brunswick (2009)
27. Tapscott, D., Williams, A.D.: Wikinomics. Portfolio, New York (2006)
28. Creswell, J.: Research Design, 2nd edn. Sage, Thousand Oaks (2003)
29. Wodak, R., Meyer, M. (eds.): Methods for Critical Discourse Analysis. Sage, Thousand Oaks (2009)
30. King, K.P.: Social Media as Positive Disruption in Higher Education, e-Learning and b-Learning. In: Manuela Cruz-Cunha, M., Putnik, G.D., Lopes, N., Gonçalves, P., Miranda, E. (eds.) Handbook of Research on Business Social Networking: Organizational, Managerial, and Technological Dimensions, IGI Publications, New York (in Press)
31. Vygotsky, L.S.: Mind in Society. Harvard University Press, Cambridge (1978)

Author Index